T0305668

China's Economic Development

Cai Fang is one of China's most distinguished economists. This book elucidates the worldwide significance of China's economic development over the past 70 years from the perspectives of economic history and growth theory.

The Chinese economy has undergone an unprecedented period of growth and development since the reform and opening-up in the late 1970s; a process which the hallmarks of neoclassic economic theory have often proved inadequate to explain. Examining the Chinese economy in the light of Chinese history and the development of the world economy as a whole, the book charts the milestones and critical reforms of China's economic development, providing insights into unique attributes as well as more generic patterns. The discussion covers multiple hot topics in the field, including the so-called great divergence, dual-sector economic development, real-world experience of the reform and opening-up, rural reform, urbanization, economic reform, poverty reduction, the latter-day slowdown of China's economic growth, and China's role in and response to globalization, global supply domination, and other headwinds.

The book will be a must-read for students, scholars, and general readers interested in the Chinese economy, economic development, political economy, and development economics.

Cai Fang is Academician of Chinese Academy of Social Sciences and Member of the Monetary Committee of the People's Bank of China. His main research areas include labor economics, population economics, economic growth, income distribution, China's economic reform, etc. His recent publications include *China's New Normal, Supply-side, and Structural Reform, Economics of the Pandemic: Weathering the Storm and Restoring Growth* (editor), *Demographic Perspective of China's Economic Development, Perceiving Truth and Ceasing Doubts: What Can We Learn from 40 Years of China's Reform and Opening-Up?*, and *Routledge Handbook of the Belt and Road* (editor-in-chief), among others.

China's Economic Development
Implications for the World

Cai Fang

The book is published with financial support of the Innovation Program of the Chinese Academy of Social Sciences.

First published in English 2023
by Routledge
4 Park Square, Milton Park, Abingdon, Oxon OX14 4RN

and by Routledge
605 Third Avenue, New York, NY 10158

Routledge is an imprint of the Taylor & Francis Group, an informa business

© 2023 Cai Fang

Translated by Wu Yisheng, Jing Fang

English Version by permission of China Social Sciences Press.

British Library Cataloguing-in-Publication Data
A catalogue record for this book is available from the British Library

Library of Congress Cataloging-in-Publication Data
Names: Cai, Fang, author.
Title: China's economic development : implications for the world / Fang Cai.
Description: New York, NY : Routledge, 2023. |
Series: China perspectives | Includes bibliographical references and index. |
Identifiers: LCCN 2022020061 (print) | LCCN 2022020062 (ebook) |
ISBN 9781032359083 (hardback) | ISBN 9781032359588 (paperback) |
ISBN 9781003329305 (ebook)
Subjects: LCSH: Economic development–China. |
China–Economic conditions–1949– | China–Economic policy–1949–
Classification: LCC HC427.9 .C345 2023 (print) |
LCC HC427.9 (ebook) | DDC 330.951/05–dc23/eng/20220714
LC record available at https://lccn.loc.gov/2022020061
LC ebook record available at https://lccn.loc.gov/2022020062

ISBN: 978-1-032-35908-3 (hbk)
ISBN: 978-1-032-35958-8 (pbk)
ISBN: 978-1-003-32930-5 (ebk)

DOI: 10.4324/9781003329305

Typeset in Times New Roman
by Newgen Publishing UK

Contents

Figures

Tables

Preface

Since the People's Republic of China was founded in 1949, and especially since the reform and opening-up policy was implemented in 1978, China has made outstanding achievements in its economic development. As is the case with the economic development history of any country, China has also suffered setbacks and paid a painful price in the course of economic development. However, in these 70 years, especially in the 40 years of reform and opening-up, China has eventually achieved successful development unprecedented in human history. During the period from 1978 to 2018, China's economy maintained an average annual real growth rate of 9.4%, far higher than that of any other country in the same period, and became a classic example of what Maynard Keynes had called the "wonder of compound interest."[1]

The achievements of China's economic development are miraculous and highly praised by the international community. Chinese and foreign economists have been trying to make a theoretical summary of these achievements, with some of them trying to reveal the world significance of this miracle. The study of a country's economic development should be based on whether it conforms to the actual course of the country's development, whether it can reveal the essential characteristics of the course, and whether it can extract the regularity with general significance, but not on whether it conforms to the teachings of some deceased economists.

On this basis, we have considered some literature on interpreting the sharing of China's experiences in implementing the reform and opening-up policy. Foreign scholars have lost touch with Chinese history and reality, while Chinese scholars have generally been lacking in global vision and historical depth. Therefore, there have been few works that can combine the general laws with Chinese characteristics. These defects have inevitably led to underestimating the significance of China's economic development to the world. Let us first look at the perspectives that cannot be ignored in studying China's economic development from the following four aspects, and understand why economics can't work without these perspectives.

First, in 1950, a year after the People's Republic of China was founded, China had a total population of 554 million, accounting for 21.9% of the world population; in 1978 when the reform and opening-up policy was enacted, China's population reached 966 million, accounting for 22.4% of the world population; and by 2017, China's total population was 1.39 billion, occupying 18.41% of the world population. The exploration and practice of economic development carried out by Chinese people, who accounted for a fifth to a quarter of the global population, remained identical with the wishes and efforts of people in other countries. It is thus clear that Chinese remarkable achievements naturally have outstanding significance to the world.

Second, just as any country's economic development took place at its own unique historical starting point and in a specific environment for a period of time; China's economic development also had its own historical origin and realistic environment. However, the world economic history and the history of economic theories have also shown that some economic development laws that need to be respected by all countries were refined and abstracted from the economic development experience of each unique country. The unity of generality and particularity and the unity of diversity and individuality are not only the source of development laws, but also a scientific knowledge governing and benefiting the people. It is also of world significance to compare China's experience of economic development with general laws and draw beneficial enlightenment.

Third, successful economic development, structural change and achievement sharing are all goals pursued by economists, especially by those proficient in development economics and growth theory. The way and path of reform and opening-up are also the process of institutional change to which other branches of economics, such as institutional economics and transition economics, have paid close attention. China's practice in all these fields has its own characteristics, although it is also more or less, directly or indirectly linked by means of verification or falsification with many economic theories, theorems, and hypotheses, providing beneficial nutrients for revising, testing, enriching, and innovating economics. Moreover, China's experience can be described as a rare rich mine in economic research, thanks to its huge economy, varied contents of institutional changes, and remarkable achievements.

Finally, after China became the second largest economy in the world in 2010, its total economic scale continued to expand. In 2018, its gross domestic product (GDP) reached US$13.61 trillion, equivalent to 66.4% of that of the United States, and accounting for 42.9% of the total of low-income countries and middle-income countries, and 15.9% of the total world economy. It is predicted that China's per capita GDP will reach the threshold standard of high-income countries in the early 2020s, and its total economic output will surpass that of the United States in the early 2030s. In other words, China will soon become an unprecedented big country that has witnessed the stages of low income, lower middle income and upper middle income in such a short time and entered the ranks of high-income countries. If we agree that this economic development is of great world significance, the future path, trend, and direction of China's economy will inevitably affect the development of the world economy, especially of emerging economies and other developing countries, to a very significant extent.

This book attempts to look into the 70-year economic development of the People's Republic of China, especially the past 40-year economic development since implementation of the reform and opening-up policy. In a vertical dimension of Chinese history and in a horizontal dimension of the world economy, the focus will be on describing key moments in this process, revealing key links in the development of reform and opening-up, and analyzing various key issues that may mislead people's understanding of China's experience and wisdom. At the same time, this book will reveal the characteristics and general significance of China's economic development. The book consists of 14 chapters, and its logical context, structural arrangement, and main contents are briefly described as follows.

Chapter 1, as the beginning of the book, focuses on the significance of China's economic development to the world. After the founding of the People's Republic of China, China's economy embarked on an independent development path, made arduous explorations at different stages, accumulated successful experiences and useful lessons, and eventually achieved remarkable achievements under the conditions of reform and opening-up. On the basis of economic construction in the first 30 years, the reform and opening-up in the past 40 years gradually eliminated the institutional drawbacks of the planned economy to form an effective incentive mechanism under the market economy and promoted reallocation of resources. China's all-round participation in the division of labor in the world economy has created an unprecedented miracle of development and made remarkable contributions to the development of the world economy.

First, with the fastest growth rate and expanding total scale in the world in the same period, China's economy has become the second largest economy that made the largest incremental contribution, playing the role of the engine and stabilizer of the world economy.

Second, the successful practice of the Chinese people, who account for one fifth of the world's population, has established the cosmopolitanism and significance of China's experience in a quantitative sense, and provided precious experience and wisdom for the vast number of developing countries.

Finally, the common development laws embodied in China's economic development exploration and the methodology of combining the general laws with special national conditions have provided useful materials for revising, enriching, and innovating economic theories, especially facilitating the revival of development economics. To fulfill the "two centennial goals,"[2] China's economy is moving from the middle-upper-income stage to the high-income stage. A higher level of reform and opening-up is not only the key to maintaining sustainable development, but also will make greater contributions to the world.

Chapter 2 tries to establish a historical coordinate for China's economic development from the perspective of growth theory and economic history. Based on the development experience of Western countries, the neoclassical growth theory regards economic growth as a single and homogeneous process. Understanding and explaining the actual economic development of many developing countries, including China, exposes the theory's theoretical and methodological limitations.

This chapter attempts to penetrate various economic development theories, form a unified analytical framework, and explain the success or failure of economic growth from the perspective of material capital and human capital accumulation incentives. From the perspective of economic history, economic growth can be divided into several types or stages, such as the Malthusian poverty trap, the Lewis dual-sector model, the Lewis turning point, and neoclassical growth. At the same time, the problem of China's economic development is embedded into the corresponding growth types and stages, and major Chinese propositions related to each stage—such as the "Needham Puzzle," "Lewis turning point," and "middle-income trap"—are empirically analyzed to make policy suggestions.

Chapter 3, based on the theoretical framework of economic growth, analyzes the Chinese "Needham Puzzle" of the "mystery of great divergence" in economic history research, trying to enhance the historical depth of China's economic development. In a poverty trap cycle, we must have the conditions to form a critical minimum material capital accumulation, and form a human capital incentive mechanism to realize the combination of innovation and production activities; otherwise we cannot break the poverty equilibrium trap. Therefore, the "Needham Puzzle" can be redefined as: why did China fail to form the accumulation of material capital and human capital necessary to break the Malthusian poverty trap in history and transform it into scientific and technological innovation, so that China failed to become the birthplace of the industrial revolution and missed the historical opportunity to embrace modernization?

This chapter reveals the great differences between the typical feudal system in Europe and the imperial system in China in the premodern period, creating quite different incentive mechanisms for the accumulation of material capital and human capital, and trying to provide an economic growth perspective for understanding the "Needham Puzzle."

Chapter 4 paves the way for the theoretical and economic history of the dual-sector economic development stage experienced by China, and tries to give it general significance. Traditionally, the mainstream growth theory recognized only one type of economic growth, i.e., neoclassical growth, and lost sight of the dual-sector economic development type and stage prevalent in developing countries. This not only underestimated the contribution of Lewis's economic development theory to the academic history, but also weakened the explanatory and predictive power of neoclassical growth theory for a large number of development phenomena.

This chapter attempts to remedy this logical defect of the neoclassical growth theory. By combing economic growth theory and economic history literature, and by integrating some experiences and findings of economic history research, it is demonstrated that all countries have experienced the process of accumulating large-scale agricultural surplus labor in economic history, thus forming a dual-sector economic structure, known as the "Geertz involution" economic development stage. In this way, the economic development of Eastern and Western countries may be typically summarized as "Malthusian poverty trap," "Geertz involution," "Lewis dual-sector mode," "Lewis turning point," and "Solow neoclassical growth." Therefore, based on Chapter 2, the division of economic growth types and stages is more complete in logic and richer and more inclusive in experience.

Chapter 5 uncovers the sharing experience of China's reform and opening-up as a whole. Summarizing the 40-year experience of China's reform and opening-up can significantly enhance the understanding of the law of human social development, and also provide rich material for reviewing and summarizing economics, analyzing experiences, and refining theories. Although the success of China's experience is affirmed by economists both at home and abroad, the dominant paradigm in the theoretical explanation and evaluation of China's reform and development has complied with standards of the neoclassic economic theory and discourse.

Based on China's reality and in combination with the discussion of relevant literature in economic circles at home and abroad, this chapter reveals the uniqueness of China's experience and its consistency with the general law of economic development, and summarizes China's wisdom and solutions. With the thinking method of united historical logic and theoretical logic, this chapter briefly describes the course of China's reform and opening-up; explains their mutual relations and promotion logic; summarizes the effects of economic growth, structural adjustment, and productivity improvement through the reform of the incentive mechanism, factor accumulation, and resource allocation system, market development, macro-policy conditions, etc.; looks forward to the reform in combination with the changes in development stages; and proposes policy suggestions.

Chapter 6 summarizes the contribution of China's rural reform to economic development from the perspective of economic development law. Under the background of agricultural involution, this chapter explains several alternative paths from agricultural involution to modern agricultural production methods and their applicability in different countries, so as to explain the logic of agricultural people's communalization and the reasons for the failure of people's communes. The implementation of the household contract responsibility system in rural areas has thoroughly solved the lack of incentives for agricultural production. During more than 40 years of reform and opening-up, the rural reform and even the overall economic reform have always revolved around giving farmers the right to allocate factors of production, enabling the rural labor force to continuously withdraw from low-productivity production activities, increasingly fully flow between regions, between urban and rural areas, and between industries, and successively enter higher-productivity production activities.

With the change of economic development stage, the scale of agricultural operations has once again risen in importance. On the one hand, due to the scale restrictions of land management, agriculture has a diminishing return on capital, showing that it lacks self-reliance and competitiveness as an industry. On the other hand, the traditional concept represented by the special theory of agricultural industry has imprisoned the policy thinking of agricultural development, making China's agriculture begin to rely too much on subsidies and protection, and postponing the new stage of agricultural development. This chapter attempts to clarify the traditional concepts that are not conducive to the construction of modern agricultural production methods in theory, reveal the difficulties faced by China's agriculture due to the small scale of land management, and propose policies to remove such institutional obstacles as the land system and household registration system, which hinder the expansion of land management.

Chapter 7 selects the most representative historical moments or events to describe the path of urbanization with Chinese characteristics as a process of reform and development from three aspects: the "withdrawal" of labor force from low-productivity agriculture and rural industries; the "flow" of labor force between agriculture and non-agricultural industries, between urban and rural areas, and between regions; and its "entry" into cities, sectors and society in terms of residence, employment, and social identity.

China's reform and development experience represented by urbanization can answer the following important questions and provide solutions to general development problems. First, through the reform, we can solve the incentive problem of accumulation of production factors and the mechanism problem of reallocation of production factors, transforming essential conditions into actual economic growth. Second, based on the redistribution of labor force, we can promote fuller employment, and integrate reform, opening-up, development, and sharing to reach a consensus of the whole society on the reform and enable it to continue to advance. Finally, with the change of development stage, we can constantly adjust the reform priorities to maintain and create essential conditions for economic growth. Following the same logic, further reform and development need to be motivated by improving agricultural labor productivity and promoting withdrawal of the labor force so as to eliminate deep institutional obstacles, promote its fuller mobility, and build a social vertical mobility ladder to promote its higher entry.

Chapter 8 focuses on an important perspective on the effect of China's economic reform on promoting economic growth, i.e., observing how the reform can promote the reallocation of production factors, especially of labor, by improving incentive mechanisms, correcting price signals, and dismantling institutional barriers, and how it can improve the efficiency of resource allocation from two aspects of increment and stock. This chapter introduces domestic and foreign studies on China's economic reform and its growth effect, and tries to make its own supplement to the shortcomings of the existing research literature from the aspects of sufficient conditions, mechanism, and structural perspective and stage changes of China's economic development miracle. This chapter briefly describes the process and logic of a series of structural reforms from the perspective of labor reallocation, estimates the contribution of the three industries as a whole and the change of industrial structure to the improvement of labor productivity, reveals the resource reallocation effect of rapid economic growth, and explains its meaning to the further reform and development of China's economy.

On the basis of the analysis and with the help of three classical models of development economics and key tasks of labor transfer, this chapter puts forward policy suggestions for further realizing labor transfer from the logical relationship and time progression of the Lewis transition stage, Todaro transition stage, and Ranis-Fei transition stage.

Chapter 9 analyzes China's most effective and successful practice—large-scale poverty reduction. A series of economic reforms implemented in China have removed the institutional obstacles hindering the flow and allocation of production factors, promoting the continuous withdrawal of the labor force from the field of low-productivity employment, realizing the increasingly full flow between urban and rural areas, regions, and industries, and then obtaining more efficient reallocation. This has not only created the necessary conditions for rapid economic growth, but has also increased farmers' income through labor transition and employment expansion, realizing development and sharing at the same time.

Parallel to the overall shared development, a special rural poverty alleviation and development strategy was carried out by the Chinese government. With the changes in the development stage and the nature of poverty, the strategy has adjusted its focus on people living below the poverty line, breaking the puzzle of diminishing marginal poverty alleviation effect, and fulfilling remarkable poverty reduction achievements.

This chapter briefly describes the 40-year reform and development process from the perspective of poverty reduction, reveals the source of economic growth in this period, and shows the shared nature of development. It also reviews the implementation process of the national rural poverty alleviation strategy, reveals its people-centered development thought, and summarizes the practice, main experience and significance of the reform to promote development and poverty reduction. In addition, this chapter looks forward to new tasks faced by the rural poor after achieving the goal of getting rid of poverty according to the current standards in 2020, and puts forward corresponding policy suggestions.

Chapter 10 discusses the slowdown of China's economy when it enters a new stage of development. This chapter summarizes three popular paradigms used by Chinese and foreign economists to analyze the phenomenon of growth slowdown, and analyzes their suspicion of cutting the foot to fit the shoes in understanding China's economy. This chapter explains the slowdown of China's economic growth from the perspective of the supply-side reason; that is, the disappearance of demographic dividend and the decline of potential growth rate negates the rationality of explaining the slowdown from demand side or cyclical factors, distinguishes the difference between the slowdown in the new stage of China's economic development and the cyclical slowdown in previous years, and the difference between the new normal of China's economic development and the new mediocrity of the world economy, and explains the potential risks of excessive adoption of demand-side macroeconomic stimulus policies based on international experience and lessons.

In view of the special stage of China's economic development, Chapter 10 puts forward the threshold trap, a more focused version of the middle-income trap, so as to reveal China's new challenges in economic growth, structural reform, and improvement of people's livelihood when China is about to enter the rank of high-income countries. Drawing lessons from international experience and based on China's problem orientation, this chapter points out the factors of further decline in potential growth rate from the aspects of labor supply, human capital accumulation, return on investment, and total factor productivity. On the basis of revealing the institutional obstacles hindering the supply of production factors and improvement of productivity, this chapter proposes the necessity of improving the potential growth rate through structural reform, and logically points out the key areas to win the reform dividend.

Chapter 11 examines China's economic development from the perspective of globalization and world economic convergence. The climax of globalization formed on the basis of previous industrial revolutions can be expected theoretically to provide a powerful driving force for the world economy and economic growth of various countries, but the first and second industrial revolutions as well as Globalization 1.0 and Globalization 2.0 have excluded the vast number of developing countries from their beneficiaries. Since the 1990s, developing countries and those in transition have extensively participated in the division of labor in the global value chain, and also carried out domestic economic system reform, which promoted Globalization 3.0 and benefited from it, and allowed late-developing countries to catch up with advanced economics, resulting in the obvious convergence of the world economy.

Parallel to this round of globalization, China has carried out the reform and opening-up policy, created the "Chenery conditions" necessary for development, realized the unity of incentive improvement and resource allocation efficiency improvement, and reached the forefront of a new round of industrial revolution while sharing the dividends of globalization. With changes in the international situation and China's development stage, China's economic development has also encountered severe challenges in face of the headwind from globalization and the decline of traditional growth momentum. China's economy will achieve long-term sustainable development by deepening economic reform and opening wider to the outside world, staying open and inclusive in the process of globalization, and improving the "Chenery conditions" necessary for its own development.

Chapter 12 expounds the trend of globalization and the strategies China should take. The upsurge of globalization since the 1990s has gone beyond its past in both breadth and depth, so that the domestic economic and social policies of many industrialized countries could not keep up with its pace, resulting in job loss and income stagnation. The middle class and low-income people became "losers" and expressed their dissatisfaction increasingly strongly, and politicians were blaming the development of emerging economies, including China. The policy represented by the credit expansion of the United States served as a fruitless approach that failed to solve the problem of productivity stagnation from the supply side and share the benefits of globalization through redistribution; instead, it added fuel to the flames of the real estate bubble, eventually leading to the bursting of the bubble and to the international financial crisis and the European debt crisis, plunging the world economy into a sluggish state.

With the populism of the West's political structure and the prevalence of protectionist policies in the fields of trade, investment, and immigration, the trend of globalization has been in danger of being reversed or blocked. During the period of reform, opening-up, and dual economic development, China made full use of the opportunity of the last round of globalization, and achieved rapid economic growth and employment expansion, thus enabling the fruits of globalization to be shared on a broader basis. In face of the declining globalization, China should take the initiative in international affairs and become the driving factor of the new round of globalization by taking advantage of its economic volume and potential consumption power in the world economy.

Chapter 13 discusses the global supply of public goods and China's solution. The traditional global governance model, which takes the United Kingdom and the United States as single hegemonic powers and dominates the supply of international public goods, cannot provide real public goods after all because it fails to widely represent the common will and equal interests of all countries. With the multi-polarization of the world economy and its contributors, the traditional governance methods and patterns are no longer indispensable, and the formation of a new model of global co-governance is inevitable.

Therefore, there is no "Kindleberger trap" about the vacuum of public goods supply or the transfer of governance dominance in today's world. With the continuous improvement of its position in the world economy, China will actively participate in global governance and strive for a greater voice on behalf of emerging economies and developing countries. However, this does not mean seeking the position of a hegemonic power and its implied dominant position as a global public goods supplier. With the desire to make greater contributions to the cause of peace and the development of mankind,

China is willing to share its successful experience of reform and opening-up with other countries in the world, and has the responsibility and ability to put forward China's solution to global poverty reduction, and work with people of other countries to contribute wisdom and efforts to solve the anti-poverty problem called the Easterly tragedy.

Chapter 14 explains the economic revolution needed to meet the new industrial revolution. Both China's economy and the world economy are facing the new challenges of Industry 4.0 and Globalization 4.0. Previous industrial revolutions and different versions of globalization have undoubtedly played the role of engines of economic growth. However, looking back at the history of economic development, we can find that industrial revolutions and globalization have also brought chronic diseases such as world economic divergence, unbalanced domestic development, income inequality, and even poverty.

From the perspective of the history of economic thought, two traditional economic concepts, trickle-down economics and infiltrative economics—assuming the existence of "trickle-down effect"—have long generated misleading and endless consequences. Combining a review of economic history with reflections on economics, we have concluded that technological change will not infiltrate into all fields to the same extent, which will naturally lead to balanced development, so we should not expect to enjoy the benefits and wait for equal sharing of the fruits of economic growth.

Since economic theory is the basis of methodology and the source of ideas for making economic policies, we should correctly cope with the ongoing new industrial revolution and higher version of globalization, eliminate the empirical economic methodology that misled policy-making, the doctrine-only theory in policy-making, and the invariable theory in dealing with the relationship between market and government, and formulate and implement people-centered economic development strategies and industrial policies.

Notes

1 Keynes proposed the "wonder of compound interest" to express his optimistic judgment on the prospect of human economic development. However, the economic growth experience on which his theory was based is far from comparable to the miracle achieved by China in the past 40 years, and the facts of productivity progress on which his theory was based cannot be compared with today's new technological revolution. See John Maynard Keynes, Economic Possibilities for Our Grandchildren (1930), in Lorenzo Pecchi and Gustavo Piga (eds.), *Revisiting Keynes: Economic Possibilities for Our Grandchildren*, Cambridge, MA: MIT Press, 2008, pp. 17–26.
2 Translators' note: The first goal calls for completing the building of a moderately prosperous society and doubling China's 2010 GDP and per capita income by the time the Communist Party of China (CPC) celebrates its centenary in 2021; the second goal calls for building China into a modern socialist country that is prosperous, strong, democratic, culturally advanced, harmonious, and beautiful by the time the People's Republic celebrates its centenary in 2049, reaching the level of moderately developed countries.

Part I

Perspectives of economic history and growth theory

1 Contributions made by one fifth of the world's population

Introduction

At the end of the second decade of the 21st century, China's achievements in economic development have attracted worldwide attention. Today, China's important position in the global economy comes from both the reform and opening-up in the past 40 years and the exploration in the 30 years before the reform and opening-up. The founding of the People's Republic of China in 1949 changed the colonial and semi-colonial nature of China's economy, and made China embark on the road of independent development. Before the reform and opening-up in late the 1970s, China's economic construction recovered from years of war, and its people were able to live and work in peace and contentment. With dramatic decline in the death rate, the population transformed from the first stage of high birth rate, high death rate, and low natural growth rate to the second stage of high birth rate, low death rate, and high natural growth rate. This has also been a necessary stage for economic growth to reap demographic dividends in the process of transitioning to a low birth rate, low death rate, and low natural growth rate after the reform and opening-up.

The complete industrial system established in the first 30 years has laid a solid foundation for industrial restructuring and resource reallocation efficiency during the reform and opening-up period. Since the founding of the People's Republic of China in 1949, China's industrialization strategy has been to give priority to the development of heavy industry. At that time, the implementation of this strategy had its rationality under specific historical conditions. The West's blockade led to many bottlenecks in China's development, which must be broken by giving priority to the development of heavy industry.

Take the petroleum industry as an example. Petroleum was an indispensable strategic industry that had been in the hands of foreign companies, so China's petroleum self-sufficiency was both a last resort and an inevitability at that time. Similar industries include chemicals, electronics, nuclear, and aerospace, in which breakthrough development has been achieved thanks to the priority given to them.

DOI: 10.4324/9781003329305-2

Nevertheless, China's economy has missed an opportunity for global economic convergence in the first 30 years since the founding of new China in 1949,[1] and has failed to catch up with developed economies. If we simply observe from the figures, China's economic growth rate in the planned economy period seemed to be unsatisfactory. According to Maddison's data, constructed according to the international purchasing power parity dollar in 1990, the average annual real growth rate of China's GDP was 4.4% from 1952 to 1978. However, since the 1950s, many late-developing countries and regions have overtaken developed economies at a relatively fast growth rate. During the same period, the overall growth rate of "rich countries (as defined)" reached 4.3%, while that of "other countries" (mainly low-income and middle-income countries) not belonging to this group reached 4.9%, and the world average growth rate was 4.6%.[2]

During this period, the gap between China and the world widened because the per capita income of some low-income and middle-income countries (regions) was close to that of "rich countries," but China failed to keep up with this trend. According to the above data, China's per capita GDP in 1952 was only US$538, 8.7% of the average income level of "rich countries," 46.5% of the average income level of "other countries," and 23.8% of the world average income. Since the growth rate of China's per capita GDP was lower than that of the above groups, by 1978 the percentage of China's per capita GDP (US$978) relative to the average level of these three groups saw a decline, 6.8%, 42.1%, and 22.1% respectively.

In fact, due to the Cold War and the resulting separation of the world economic system, the so-called global convergence mentioned by Spence is actually very limited in scope. Only some less-developed European countries as well as Japan, the Four Asian Tigers, and other economies have truly caught up with the leading countries, not including a wider range of developing countries. Since 1990, emerging economies and many countries in transition from planned economies have implemented open-door policies and deeply participated in the new round of economic globalization, which has led to global convergence and fundamental changes in the world economic structure.[3] China was an active participant and beneficiary of this round of economic globalization, and has miraculously caught up with developed countries in the past 40 years.

Every country or economy, as a component of the world economy, theoretically has an impact on the whole economy by its own improvement or deterioration. However, in order to have a real impact, the economy as a component needs to possess a sufficiently large total size and proportion. Entering the 21st century, China's economy, with its rapid growth and the resulting scale expansion and proportion increase, has exerted increasing influence on the world economy.

If this output contribution is a contribution to the world economy in the form of a private product, the development experience and concept to achieve such a performance, as well as the right to speak on rule-making, the beneficial insight on development concept, and the constructive challenge to routine, will belong to the contribution made by public goods to the world economy.

China has never sought world economic hegemony, nor has it exported its own development model. However, as the world's second largest economy, the largest industrial country, the largest trader of goods, and the largest foreign exchange reserve country, China is duty-bound to express its demands on international economic and trade rules on behalf of the vast number of developing countries and emerging economies, and even leads the transformation of global governance patterns. Moreover, due to following prominent characteristics, China and its development are of particular importance to the world.

First, China has the largest population in the world, accounting for approximately 18.5% of the world's total population in 2017. The achievements created by the Chinese people, who account for one fifth of mankind, are incomparable to other countries.

Second, intellectuals are born with academic curiosity to explore the mystery of ups and downs, and the "Needham Puzzle" about why China's science and technology (development) went from prosperity to decline, which has attracted many scholars' answers, is the same as the well-known Chinese version of the "great divergence" in the world economic history since the 16th century.

Finally, in regard to satisfying the same academic curiosity, China is the only developing country that has witnessed economic development from prosperity to decline and then to prosperity again, and that has completely experienced every necessary stage of economic development.

As early as 1742, David Hume, pioneer of British classical economics, made a famous prophecy. He believed that "when the arts and sciences come to perfection in any state, from that moment they naturally, or rather necessarily decline, and seldom or never revive in that nation, where they formerly flourished."[4] The Chinese miracle observed by the whole world so far, if not completed, is also breaking this prophecy. At least in terms of economic development levels, China has experienced a turbulent history from prosperity to decline and then to prosperity again.

By the use and upgrading of long-term historical data constructed by economic historian Angus Maddison according to the same or similar aperture, we have shown in Figure 1.1 that in the past 2,000 years, Chinese economy's position in the world, as expressed by the share of GDP in the global economy and the percentage of GDP per capita relative to the world average, has experienced an obvious V-shaped trajectory of change. It is particularly noted that the second half of China's economic transition from decline to prosperity shown in the figure is rare worldwide, no matter how short the time is or how large the scale is.

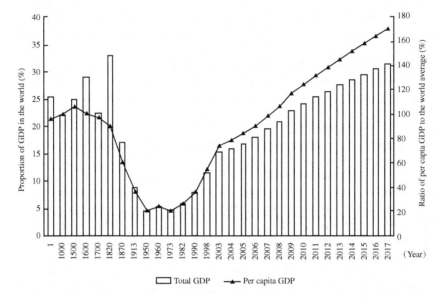

Figure 1.1 China's economic development from prosperity to decline and back to prosperity again

World economy's engine and stabilizer

A country can be identified as large or small by its economic scale, as robust or sluggish by its economic growth. In the past 70 years of economic development, China has experienced ups and downs and learnt more lessons from success than failure. Since the implementation of the reform and opening-up policy over 40 years ago, China has steadily become a unique country in the world with a large enough economy and a fast enough growth rate, which have not only changed its own aspects but also changed the world economic structure. It can be said that China's role as the engine and stabilizer of the world economy has brought about unprecedented change in the world.

First, China's economy has contributed much to the world economy with its total economic size, rank in the world and its proportion in the world economy. According to World Bank data, in 1978, China's total GDP in 2010 constant US dollars was US$294.3 billion, ranking 14th in the world, merely equivalent to 1.1% of the global economy and 4.6% of the US economy. By 1990, China's GDP had increased to US $829.6 billion, and its proportion of the world economy had increased to 2.2%, accounting for 9.2% of that of the United States, surpassing Mexico, Australia, the Netherlands and Saudi Arabia respectively, ranking tenth in the world. In the following ten years, China's economy surpassed Spain, Canada, Brazil, Italy and Britain successively, ranking fifth in the world economy in 2000, with a total amount of

US$2.24 trillion, accounting for 4.5% of the world economy and 17.6% of the US economy. In 2010, China became the world's second largest economy, with a total amount of US$6.1 trillion, accounting for 92% of the world economy and 40.8% of the US economy. By 2017, China's GDP reached US$10.2 trillion, accounting for 12.7% of the world economy and equivalent to 58.7% of that of the United States.

Second, with the increase in economic volume and the longest-lasting high-speed growth in the world, the significance of China's economic growth has increased year by year, making substantial incremental contributions to world economic growth. For example, the annual increase of China's GDP has exceeded the total GDP of countries such as Vietnam, Luxembourg, and Kenya in 1990, Israel, Nigeria, and Ireland in 2000, Switzerland, Saudi Arabia, and Argentina in 2010, and the Netherlands, Poland, and even all low-income countries in 2017. China's contribution to world economic growth was negligible before the 1990s, and even "dragged down" the world economic growth before the reform and opening-up. After the 1990s, however, the incremental contribution of China's economy to the world economy exceeded 10% and has remained at approximately 30% since the international financial crisis in 2008.

Third, due to the gradual expansion of China's annual GDP increment, its contribution to world economic growth has increased significantly since the 1990s, especially thanks to the high stability of China's economic increment as compared with other parts of the world. Therefore, the role of China's economy as a stabilizer of the world economy has become increasingly prominent. From the annual growth rate in comparison with the world economic growth, China's economic growth fluctuated greatly in the early days; however, its impact on the world economy as a whole was not significant due to its small total amount and increment. However, this feature has gradually changed.

In Figure 1.2, the annual increment of China's economy is compared with the economic increment of other parts of the world excluding China's data and the total increment of the world economy including China. It is clear that the stability of world economic growth varies greatly with or without the factor of China's economic growth.

From the comparison of the variance of the annual growth rate of world GDPs including and excluding China's data, this effect has appeared since 1990; afterward, the role of China's economic growth in stabilizing world economic growth has become more prominent due to gradual expansion of China's annual economic increment and the increasing stability of China's economy. Especially in the years of abnormal fluctuations in the world economy in the 21st century, China's economy has provided a stabilizing effect that has significantly reduced global volatility.

Finally, the economic catch-up of more developing countries and emerging economies represented by China has made possible the economic convergence, which has long been discussed only in theory and eventually has

(in hundred million dollar)

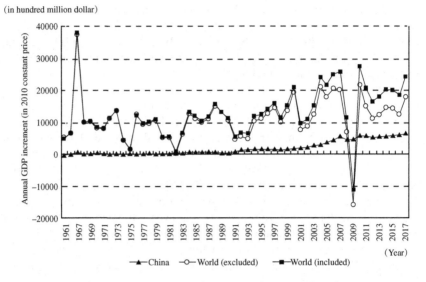

Figure 1.2 Annual increment of China's economy and its contribution to world economic stability

become a reality of the global economy. At the same time, as a result of economic convergence, the per capita income level of developing countries has greatly increased, and the scale of absolute poverty-stricken population and the poverty incidence in the world have dropped unprecedentedly. Apparently, the development and sharing brought about by China's reform and opening-up have produced the overall effect of increasing the income of urban and rural residents, thus greatly reducing poverty and making great contributions to global poverty reduction. In addition, the reduction of China's absolute poverty-stricken population has made a quantitative contribution to the reduction of the global poverty population.

According to World Bank data, in 1981 there were 1.89 billion people around the globe living below the World Bank's absolute poverty standard (less than US$191 per day according to purchasing power parity in 2011); 880 million of those people were in China, accounting for 46.4% of the global poverty-stricken population. In 2015, the number of global poor people in the world decreased to 750 million, while that in China was 9.6 million, accounting for only 1.3% of the global poverty-stricken population. During this period, China contributed 76.2% to poverty reduction in the world. In fact, after 2015, China implemented a rural poverty alleviation strategy higher than the World Bank standard, and reduced the rural poor population by 12.4 million, 12.89 million, and 13.86 million in 2016, 2017, and 2018 respectively. It is thus clear that China has eliminated absolute poverty under the World Bank standard as a whole.

Seeking basic conditions for economic development

After the Second World War, many countries embarked on the road of independent development, trying various explorations to reduce poverty. Economics, as a science governing and benefiting the people, had also formed the development economics targeting the vast number of developing countries in the 1950s; since then, various theoretical hypotheses and strategic propositions concerning development have emerged. Although some economically less-developed European countries as well as Japan and the Four Asian Tigers have achieved rapid catch-up with developed countries; however, it was not until the 1980s that the convergence emerged in the world economy as expected by economists. In other words, what could be observed from that period was at best the "club convergence" between economies with similar conditions or the catch-up phenomenon of a few small economies.

When looking at the reasons why developing countries failed to catch up with advanced economies, and thus the worldwide poverty problem failed to be effectively solved, economists also conducted reflections on the popular development theory. Some pioneers of development economics conducted their own defense,[5] while others aimed to deny the pioneers' theoretical foothold and try to reveal the "poverty" of development economics itself.[6] The final result is that development economics as a whole was left out in the cold.

Accordingly, neoclassical economics has gradually become the mainstream, among which neoliberalism prevailed and exerted an impact on the development strategies of developing countries, on the reform strategies of countries in transition and on the aid concepts of international and regional development institutions and developed countries. However, these theories and concepts have neither guided countries to find their own development path with correct epistemology, nor helped countries seeking development to gain the necessary conditions for their own development.

In the era of the Cold War between East and West and the separation between North and South, China did not have close ties with Western countries and international aid organizations; instead, it explored a road of development in an independent environment. After the reform and opening-up in 1978, China developed trade relations with other countries, introduced foreign capital and established cooperative relations with international institutions such as the World Bank. However, since the beginning of the reform, China has not accepted any transcendental dogma; that is, it has not copied any existing model, road, or so-called consensus, but rather has taken an approach of gradual reformation and followed the concepts of reform, development, and sharing for the purpose of developing its productive forces and improving national strength and people's livelihoods.

By an overview of the process of China's reform, opening-up, development, and sharing, we can see the logic embodied in it, and then we can extract the wisdom of how to discover and follow the necessary steps and create the necessary development conditions for a country seeking to catch up with and surpass advanced economies. These steps to create necessary conditions are closely related to economic system reform, so the reform is also a sufficient condition for economic growth.

The first step is activating the incentive mechanism of "turning stone into gold." A famous saying by Theodore Schultz goes that farmers could turn stone into gold once given investment opportunities and effective incentives.[7] In fact, "getting incentives right" has become a textbook creed and suggestion on economic transformation. However, this general statement, or simply blaming the problem on the existence of a private property rights system, does not help to identify the key points of the drawbacks of the planned economic system in China.

Under the condition of implementing the strategy of giving priority to the development of heavy industry, the system of unified purchase and marketing of agricultural products is required in order to restrain the price of agricultural products and take the price scissors between industrial and agricultural products as a means of industrial accumulation. The people's commune system and the household registration system came into being in order to ensure no loss of production factor in agriculture and strictly limit production factors, especially the labor force, to agricultural activities. These three systems gave rise to distorted allocation of resources, inefficient agricultural production, and insufficient labor incentives. On the eve of the reform, the drawbacks of these systems reached its peak. In 1977, the per capita output of agricultural products in China was less than 300kg of grain, only 2kg of cotton, 4kg of oil, and 21kg of sugar. In 1978, the annual income of 250 million rural people was less than RMB100.

Under such circumstances, any reformation that could improve the current situation of agricultural production would be recognized by the people of the whole country, including farmers. After the Third Plenary Session of the Eleventh Central Committee of the Communist Party of China created a political environment for reform, the rapid popularization of the household contract responsibility system was not only an institutional change that met this demand, but also a "Pareto improvement." The direct link between labor effort and output and income as well as the increase in the purchase price of agricultural products have activated the incentive mechanism, significantly increasing the output of agricultural products in a very short period of time, reducing the poverty incidence of the rural population, and satisfying farmers' basic living needs.

The second step is the "Kuznets process" of resource reallocation. The incentive mechanism improved in agriculture has mobilized the enthusiasm of production and labor, raised the productivity of agricultural labor, reduced the labor time used per unit land area, and explicated the long-term accumulated agricultural surplus labor force. At this time, there emerged another effect of the household contract responsibility system, i.e., farmers acquired the right for free allocation of production factors, especially of the labor force. According to the signal of income increase, the rural labor force has migrated into different economic activities and regions according to the increasing signal of their income.

For example, the rural labor force has experienced the reallocation from single grain production to diversified farming and further to all-round involvement in agriculture, forestry, animal husbandry and fishery. Moreover, a vast number of rural workers found jobs in rural non-agricultural industries such as township enterprises, or migrated into small towns and cities of various sizes, or moved from the central and western regions to coastal regions. According to National Bureau of Statistics, the proportion of agricultural labor force decreased from 70.5% in 1978 to 27.0% in 2017. According to the author's research results, the proportion of agricultural labor force is likely to be approximately 10 percentage points lower than this official figure.

As a series of institutional obstacles hindering labor mobility have been gradually eliminated, the individual motivation of laborers to increase their income and the efficiency driving force of reallocation have been closely linked, jointly promoting large-scale labor transition and forming a process of resource reallocation in a macro sense, which has promoted the upgrading of industrial structure. Since it was Simon Kuznets that first revealed the essence of continuous improvement of labor productivity behind the change of industrial structure, Masahiko Aoki called the change of industrial structure represented by the transition of agricultural labor force and the decline of relative share the "Kuznets process."[8] During the period from 1978 to 2015, China's overall labor productivity (GDP per laborer) increased nearly 17 times, in which the labor force was reallocated among the primary, secondary, and tertiary industries; that is, the labor force migrated from agriculture to non-agricultural industries, and its contribution rate to the overall situation was as high as 44.9%.[9]

The third step is full participation in the world economic division of labor system. China's economic reform coincided with its opening up to the outside world. Since the establishment of special economic zones in 1979, China has experienced the opening and all-round opening of coastal cities and provinces. In 1986, China reapplied its status as a contracting party to the General Agreement on Tariffs and Trade (GATT) and joined the World Trade Organization (WTO) in 2001. The expansion of trade, the introduction of foreign capital, and the development of an export-oriented economy in coastal areas have provided a large number of employment opportunities for a migrated labor force, guided the industrial structure to conform to the comparative advantages of resources, and enhanced manufactured products' international competitiveness. In 2017, the net inflow of foreign direct investment into China accounted for 8.6% of the world; the total export of goods and services accounted for 10.5% of the world, 70% of which were exported to high-income countries as defined by the World Bank, reflecting China's comparative advantage in the middle-income stage in international trade.

As a result of the abovementioned three steps of reform and opening-up, China's economy has achieved an average annual growth rate of 9.4% in

40 years. On the one hand, China's achievement has made great contributions to developing countries catching up with developed countries and to the convergence of the world economy. On the other hand, it is precisely because a vast number of developing countries participated in this round of globalization that emerging economies have made remarkable development achievements, and the world economy has shown a trend of convergence for the first time in history. From 1978 to 2017, the proportion of GDP of low-income and middle-income countries in the world economy increased from 21.3% to 35.3%, while the proportion of China's GDP in the total economic output of low-income and middle-income countries increased from 5.3% to 36.0%. During this period, calculated at constant prices, the total GDP of low-income and middle-income countries quadrupled, of which China contributed as much as 43.6%.

Reviving development economics

Goethe once said that the theory is gray while the tree of life is evergreen. This statement does not necessarily mean that the theory is not important. To understand this statement from a more positive perspective, we can conclude that refining characteristic facts from successful practical experience to constantly enrich and even revise the existing theoretical system and create new theoretical paradigms and systems can make the theory itself evergreen.

To date, Chinese and foreign economists have not wasted the rich experience resources of China's reform and opening-up, but formed the following three research paradigms in their research activities. First of all, Chinese economists have formed a series of unique understandings of China's reform and opening-up development by using the principles of Marxist political economy, by drawing lessons from economic discussions on countries in transition, and by absorbing theories of Western economics on market economy, and tried to guide practice with them. Second, foreign economists have tried to explain China's experience and influence policy-making with Western mainstream theories. Finally, many economists also utilized the uniqueness of China's experience to challenge, revise, and even deny mainstream economics.

According to new experience formed by the practice of economic development, it is the logic and source of the evolution of economic theory, especially of development economics, to re-recognize, reposition, and integrate various theoretical schools, thus proposing an alternative cognitive system. The reform and development achievements created by the Chinese people, who account for one fifth of the world's population, are duty-bound to make rich contributions to development economics. Therefore, it is necessary to generalize the unique path of China's development in response to its challenges to mainstream economic theories or their implicit assumptions, and provide theoretical answers that can not only explain the whole process but also provide reference for more general development problems. Some of these issues will be briefly described below.

First, is there a dual economy development stage? Neoclassical growth theory holds that there is only one way to Rome. Alwyn Young, Paul Krugman et al. tirelessly criticized the East Asian model and slandered China's economic growth because they did not recognize the existence of such a stage of dual economic development, nor did they see the demographic dividend could become the source of economic growth at a specific stage. They subjectively believed that the labor force was in short supply and the phenomenon of diminishing capital returns was unconditional. Therefore, they denied that factor input could maintain sustainable growth. Thus, they argued that the good growth performance of East Asian economies and China's economy is not sustainable.

It was not wrong for them to take total factor productivity as the only sustainable growth factor. However, without recognizing the development of dual economy, how can resource reallocation become a huge source of total factor productivity at this stage, and even be greatly improved by Pareto improvement? Constrained by the hypothesis of neoclassical theory, these economists subjectively denied the development of dual economy and disgracefully used various statistical techniques to deny the fact that total factor productivity has been improved in an economy characterized by an unlimited supply of labor.[10]

Nevertheless, some economists discovered that economic development was not Solow-style neoclassical growth from beginning to end. In fact, Edward C. Prescott et al. tried to incorporate the Malthusian stage into the economic growth model,[11] and implied that there was still a transitional stage of agricultural labor reallocation between Malthus and Solow.[12] Cai Fang believes, by reviewing the economic history, that the formation process and the development stage of dual economy are common in the economic development process of all countries, and that human economic development can thus be divided into five types or five stages, such as the Malthusian poverty trap, Geertz involution, Lewis dual economy, Lewis turning point, and Solow neoclassical growth.[13]

Before the founding of the People's Republic of China in 1949, the country's industrialization process lagged far behind the rest of the world, and its agriculture had been in the process of "involution"—as Clifford Geertz labeled it—for a long time,[14] accumulating a large amount of surplus labor. After the founding of the People's Republic of China and under the condition of implementing the strategy of giving priority to the development of heavy industry, the institutional arrangements for the people's commune system, householder registration system and coupon-based supply system hindered the transition of agricultural surplus labor force, and formed a low-level industrial structure while rapidly promoting industrialization. Not until the reform and opening-up did the Kuznets process truly begin, which greatly improved the labor productivity while adjusting the industrial structure. In this process, the potential demographic dividend formed by a favorable population age structure has been realized and become the source of high-speed economic growth.

Second, what was the source of economic growth in the stage of dual economic development? Mainstream economics argued, based on the neoclassical growth hypothesis that labor shortage is normal, that capital accumulation is crucial to growth but susceptible to constraints of diminishing capital returns. Therefore, this theory insisted that total factor productivity is the only source of economic growth. However, if we admit that not all economic growth is of the neoclassical type, we can absolutely believe in the existence of other growth sources than the neoclassical type.

Under the condition that the age structure of the population has productive characteristics (the working-age population grows rapidly and has a high proportion, so the population dependency ratio is low and remains declining) and that there is a general surplus labor force: (1) the supply of labor force is sufficient as long as there is effective incentive and mobilization mechanism; (2) the human capital of the overall labor force can be significantly improved as long as education is developed and the newly growing labor force continues to enter the labor market; (3) the low and declining population dependency ratio is conducive to maintaining a high savings rate; (4) an unlimited supply of labor force can delay the occurrence of diminishing returns on capital; (5) the transition of labor force from low-productivity sectors (agriculture) to high-productivity sectors (non-agricultural industries) can improve the efficiency of resource reallocation and total factor productivity. These sources of growth do not exist in the expectations of neoclassical growth theory.[15]

The existence of this unique source of growth has been proven by the rapid growth of China in the stage of dual economic development, by the slowdown of growth after the Lewis turning point, and by the disappearance of the demographic dividend. Many measurement results have also justified the existence of a unique growth source of dual economic development.

For example, the period 1978–2010 witnessed the rapid increase in the working-age population and the decline in the population dependency ratio; meanwhile, it was estimated that the average annual GDP grew 9.9%, to which the labor force contributed 9%, human capital 6%, capital accumulation 61%, resource reallocation efficiency 8%, and other unexplained residuals (total factor productivity other than resource reallocation efficiency) contributed 16%.[16]

According to the supply and allocation of such production factors, it can be estimated that the potential growth rate of China's economy was between 9.7% and 10.4% during this period. With the negative growth of the working-age population and the rise in the dependency ratio of the population after 2010, the abovementioned sources of growth have weakened significantly. Correspondingly, the potential growth rate also decreased to an average of 7.6% during the 12th Five-Year Plan period (2011–2015) and an average of 6.2% during the 13th Five-Year Plan period (2016–2020).[17]

Finally, what is the difference between the path for getting out of the poverty trap and the path for getting through the middle-income stage? For a long time, economists interested in development have mainly focused on summarizing the basic conditions for breaking the poverty trap, such as the level of capital accumulation that reaches the critical minimum requirement, the system that plays the role of market and the policy of opening up to the outside world. As more and more countries have got out of the poverty trap and become emerging middle-income countries, development economists discovered that it is as difficult to enter the ranks of high-income countries from the middle-upper income countries and then continue to improve the per capita income ranking in the latter group as it was to get out of the poverty trap. Many studies have also revealed from the perspective of experience that there are indeed many countries that remain in the middle-income stage for a long time, so there is the proposition of "middle-income trap" that has aroused extensive discussion.[18]

China has nearly completed the transformation process from a low-income country via a middle-income stage to a high-income country. According to the constant price in 2010, China's per capita GDP in 1978 was US$308, belonging to a typical low-income country; in 1993, it reached US$1,001, marking China's entry into the ranks of lower-middle-income countries; and in 2009, the figure was US$4,142, enabling China to become one of upper-middle-income countries. According to the current price, China's per capita GDP reached US$9,771 in 2018, which means that China is approaching the threshold of entering the ranks of high-income countries. China's successful experience and practical challenges help answer the similarities and differences between the two stages of development.

The so-called "trap" in economics refers to a superstable equilibrium state; that is, for any deviation caused by disturbance, the growth rate will still return to the initial state. Therefore, in order to get out of the poverty trap, early development economists proposed a critical minimum effort, the most important condition of which is that the savings rate reaches the critical minimum level. After the Second World War, a vast number of developing countries began to develop their own economies independently. The strong desire to eliminate colonialism, the urgency to catch up with developed countries, and the successful performance of the planned economy of the Soviet Union at that time played an important role in promoting many countries to make choices; that is, using the power of the government to accelerate accumulation and promote the industrialization process.

As this catch-up strategy ignored the role of market mechanisms, there formed a closed economic system featuring a lack of entrepreneurial vitality and labor enthusiasm in micro-links, the inefficiency of resource allocation, and the deviation of industrial structure and technology choice from comparative advantages, which made most countries fail to achieve catch-up development. As a result, various economic development theories have been criticized, and development economics itself has fallen into a development dilemma.[19]

In the planned economy period, China had a strong ability to mobilize resources and has achieved a high rate of capital accumulation. During

1953–1978, China's accumulation rate averaged 29.5%, higher than the world average. The conditions for China's human capital accumulation were also better than those of countries with the same level of development. However, the planned economy could not solve the other two necessary institutional conditions of economic growth, namely resource allocation and incentive mechanisms, so the favorable population factors had not been transformed into the source of economic growth. It was not until 1978 that the traditional economic system was profoundly reformed and the opening to the outside world was expanded, creating the basic conditions for growth and realizing the leap from the low-income stage and the transition to the high-income stage.

The process of moving from the middle-upper-income stage to the high-income stage was often accompanied by the severe challenge of weakening the traditional growth momentum. In China, the process of demographic transition and the process of economic development, as well as the development stages formed by the two processes, have influenced each other in cause–effect relations and thus coincide completely in time. Therefore, after the demographic dividend helped China achieve rapid growth for more than 30 years, the rapid disappearance of the demographic dividend after 2010 inevitably led to a natural slowdown in economic growth.

In the new stage of development, when economic growth increasingly needs to be supported by the improvement of total factor productivity,[20] the transition of labor and other factors from agriculture to non-agricultural industries has slowed down, narrowing the space for improving the efficiency of resource reallocation. The improvement of total factor productivity needs to rely more on technological innovation and institutional innovation under the creative destruction mechanism.[21] Constructing the conditions for realizing this innovation is a higher requirement of reform and opening-up, and it is also necessary to redefine the government functions and their relationship with the market. It is also at this time that the reform opportunities that could bring about "Pareto improvement" have become increasingly scarce. Further reform and opening-up will inevitably affect vested interests and bring growing pains while encountering obstacles.

Therefore, at this critical moment when it is close to entering the ranks of high-income countries, a country is bound to encounter more difficulties and face greater risks, and there is no room for hesitation or retreat. Only in this way can we avoid forming a superstable equilibrium state at the middle-income level. Any methods effective in the past can no longer guarantee crossing the new gap, in which reform, development, and stability must be combined in a more coordinated and organic way. Judging from successful experience and failed lessons in economic history, from this stage on, dealing with the severe challenges faced by further development will prove as difficult as was getting out of the poverty trap, and the required conceptual innovation is enough to constitute a special branch of development economics.

Conclusions

The People's Republic of China has developed for 70 years, during which the economic development includes the exploration and lessons from the first 30 years, as well as the innovation and experience from the past 40 years. Both detours and successes are precious wealth in the sense of knowledge, worth cherishing by Chinese people. This wealth should also be offered to other developing countries in the same pursuit and added into the latest version of development economics. According to the refined wisdom, the established direction and goal, and the same logic and path of reform and opening-up, China will continue to carry out practical exploration and make new and greater contributions to the world.

First, we will continue and upgrade the momentum of economic growth in time. With China's economy crossing the Lewis turning point, the demographic dividend has disappeared, and the stage of dual economic development is drawing to an end. From the perspective of growth momentum, the sources of economic growth have the nature of "low-hanging fruits," i.e., the effect of large-scale labor transition on factor supply and productivity improvement gradually disappears, while economic growth increasingly relies on those sources expected by neoclassical growth theory, such as improving total factor productivity through the survival of the fittest under market mechanisms, promotion of human capital, and technological innovation.

However, as proven by the lessons of many middle-income countries, it is not at this stage that the dogma of neoclassical economics can naturally lead China's economic growth. The so-called "middle-income trap" is intended to reveal the truth that the transformation of growth kinetic energy is not natural, but requires creating conditions for developing new growth sources according to the actual conditions of each country. For China, this requires comprehensively deepening the system reform in many fields.

The substantial advancement of reform has the effect of increasing the potential growth rate. By making reasonable assumptions about the reform effect, we can predict China's potential growth rate in the future. Generally speaking, although China's economic growth is gradually slowing down, for a long time China's economic growth rate will still be higher than the world average, especially higher than the growth level of high-income countries such as the United States.[22]

Therefore, assuming that the US economy continues to grow at the trend rate of the past 20 years (excluding the two-year negative growth during the subprime mortgage crisis), China is expected to surpass the US and become the world's largest economy by approximately 2035. Also, at constant prices in 2010, China's per capita GDP will exceed US$18,000 by 2035. This means that once the middle-income stage is over, China will become the first economy to completely experience all forms of economic development and complete the transformation from low-income to middle-income and high-income stages.

Second, the logic of reform, opening-up, development, and sharing should be extended in space. China's reform and opening-up development in the past 40 years has a certain gradient; that is, coastal areas took the lead in reform and opening-up, and achieved economic development results earlier, realizing the idea of "letting some regions get richer first." With the interregional development level gap widening, the two mechanisms began to play a role in narrowing regional differences. The first mechanism is mainly market-oriented; that is, the development of manufacturing industry in coastal areas has generated large-scale labor demand, attracting the inflow of rural labor in the central and western regions, increasing the participation rate of workers in non-agricultural industries, increasing the income of farmers, and improving the overall labor productivity. The second mechanism relies more on the role of government policies, i.e., enforcing various regional balance strategies, including the western development strategy, to promote the improvement of infrastructure and investment environment in the central and western regions.

As the Lewis turning point appeared in China's economy, labor shortages became more prominent in coastal areas where manufacturing was the first to lose its comparative advantage. Meanwhile, the central and western regions just had the conditions to meet industrial transfer, thus forming a domestic version of the flying-geese model.[23] At the same time, China began to make regional development patterns such as Guangdong-Hong Kong-Macau Greater Bay Area construction and integration of the Yangtze River Delta in order to maintain manufacturing advantages by gathering economies of scale.

However, labor-intensive industries will eventually lose their comparative advantage in China, and it is still necessary to build a new international version of the flying-geese model, which means that some manufacturing industries will be transferred to neighboring countries with abundant labor and countries or regions such as Africa. The "Belt and Road" initiative begins with infrastructure construction and then drives industrial transfer, which not only conforms to the general development law of the flying-geese model, but also proves effective for China's own gradient development practice.

Finally, deepening reform and opening wider to the outside world from the dimension of sharing. Economic development is pursued not for the sake of development itself but for the purpose of improving people's well-being. Therefore, the reform and opening-up aiming to promote economic development can only be affirmed and applauded by people from this purpose. The core of China's great achievements in the process of reform and opening-up over past 40 years lies in the unification of the following three processes. First, reallocation of labor resources, which has ensured the full supply of production factors, improved the overall labor productivity, and provided demographic dividends for economic growth; second, transformation of the resource endowment with abundant labor force into the comparative advantage of manufacturing industry so as to help Chinese products gain competitive advantages on international market, enjoying the dividend of globalization; and third, creation of a large number of jobs to enable fuller employment of the urban and rural labor force to such extent that ordinary workers have obtained higher labor market returns as the labor force is gradually becoming a scarce factor.

As China's economy enters a new stage of development, the effect of improved income distribution from the market mechanism itself will be weakened. With the economic growth model changing from an input-driven model to an innovation-driven mode, the source of productivity improvement has also changed from resource reallocation among industries to survival of the fittest among business entities, and the role of the creative destruction mechanism will be enhanced. Participating in the division of labor in the global value chain at a higher stage of development will have a greater competitive effect than a complementary effect with developed countries. The deeper the reform and opening-up, the smaller the room for Pareto improvement, and the more obstacles it may encounter from vested interests. All these require that under the guidance of the people-centered development thought, sharing should be instantiated in the whole process of further reform and opening-up; meanwhile, the government should make more efforts on redistribution and give full play to the supporting function of social policies.

Notes

1 American scholar Michael Spence once concluded that the global economy started an era of great convergence around 1950. See Michael Spence, *The Next Convergence: The Future of Economic Growth in a Multispeed World*, New York: Farrar Straus and Giroux, 2011.
2 Angus Maddison, *Long-term Performance of China's Economy: AD 960–2030*, Shanghai: People's Publishing House, 2008, pp. 108–109.
3 Cai Fang, Globalization, Convergence and China's Economic Development, *World Economics and Politics*, Vol. 3, 2019.
4 David Hume, On the Rise and Progress of the Arts and Sciences, in *Essays: Moral, Political and Literary*, edited by E.F. Miller, Indianapolis, Liberty Fund, p. 135.
5 Gerald M. Meier, *Leading Issues in Economic Development* (revised edition), Oxford: Oxford University Press, 1995.
6 Deepak Lal, *The Poverty of "Development Economics,"* London: Institute of Economic Affairs, 1983.
7 Theodore Schultz, *Transforming Traditional Agriculture*, translated by Liang Xiaomin, Commercial Press, 1987, p. 5.
8 Masahiko Aoki, The Five Phases of Economic Development and Institutional Evolution in China, Japan and Korea, in Masahiko Aoki, Timur Kuran, and Gérard Roland (eds.), *Institutions and Comparative Economic Development*, Basingstoke: Palgrave Macmillan, 2012, pp. 13–47
9 Cai Fang, Analysis of the Effect of China's Economic Reform from the Perspective of Labor Reallocation, *Economic Research Journal*, Vol. 7, 2017.
10 See Alwyn Young, The Tyranny of Numbers: Confronting the Statistical Realities of the East Asian Growth Experience, *The Quarterly Journal of Economics*, Vol. 110, No. 3, 1995, pp. 641–680; Alwyn Young, Gold into the Base Metals: Productivity Growth in the People's Republic of China during the Reform Period, *Journal of*

Political Economy, Vol. 111, No. 6, 2003, pp 1220–1261; Paul Krugman, Hitting China's Wall, *New York Times*, July 18, 2013.

11 Gary D. Hansen and Edward C. Prescott, Malthus to Solow, *American Economic Review*, Vol. 92, No. 4, 2002, pp. 1205–1217.

12 F. Hayashi and E. Prescott, The Depressing Effect of Agricultural Institutions on the Prewar Japanese Economy, *Journal of Political Economy*, Vol. 116, No. 4, 2008, pp. 573–632.

13 Cai Fang, Understanding the Past, Present and Future of China's Economic Development: Based on a Connected Growth Theoretical Framework, *Economic Research Journal*, Vol. 11, 2013; Cai Fang, The Formation Process of Dual Economy as a Development Phase, *Economic Research Journal*, Vol. 7, 2015.

14 See Clifford Geertz, *Agricultural Involution: The Process of Ecological Change in Indonesia*, Berkeley: University of California Press, 1963; Huang Zhongzhi, Development or Involution? Great Britain and China in the 18th Century: A Comment on Kenneth Pomeranz's *Great Divergence: Europe, China and Development of Modern World Economy*, *Historical Research*, Vol. 4, 2002.

15 When the neoclassical growth theory deduces the convergence hypothesis from the phenomenon of diminishing returns to capital, it can actually recognize the source of growth in the development phase of dual economy with the same theoretical hypothesis. However, when facing the reality of developing countries, an overwhelming majority of economists voluntarily gave up the consistency of this theory.

16 Cai Fang and Zhao Wen, When Demographic Dividend Disappears: Growth Sustainability of China, in Masahiko Aoki and Jinglian Wu (eds.), *The Chinese Economy: A New Transition*, Basingstoke: Palgrave Macmillan, 2012.

17 Cai Fang and Lu Yang, The End of China's Demographic Dividend: the Perspective of Potential GDP Growth, in Ross Garnaut, Cai Fang, and Song Ligang (eds.), *China: A New Model for Growth and Development*, Canberra: ANU Press, 2013, pp. 55–74.

18 This concept was first proposed by World Bank economists. See Indermit Gill and Homi Kharas, *an East Asian Renaissance: Ideas for Economic Growth*, Washington, DC: World Bank, 2007.

19 See Deepak Lal, *The Poverty of "Development Economics*, London: Institute of Economic Affairs, 1983.

20 Eichengreen et al. discovered that the decline in total factor productivity could explain 85% of the slowdown in growth at a specific phase of development. See Barry Eichengreen, Donghyun Park, and Kwanho Shin, *When Fast Growing Economies Slow Down: International Evidence and Implications for China*, NBER Working Paper, No. 16919, 2011.

21 Cai Fang, Get Rid of the Old to Leave Room for the New: Promote Transformation of Growth Power by Clearing Ineffective Production Capacity, *Comparative Studies*, Vol. 1, 2018.

22 See Cai Fang and Lu Yang, The End of China's Demographic Dividend: the Perspective of Potential GDP Growth, in Ross Garnaut, Cai Fang, and Song Ligang (eds.), *China: A New Model for Growth and Development*, Canberra: ANU Press, 2013, pp. 55–74.

23 Qu Yue, Cai Fang, and Zhang Xiaobo, Has the "Flying Geese" Phenomenon in Industrial Transformation Occurred in China?, in Huw McKay and Ligang Song (eds.), *Rebalancing and Sustaining Growth in China*, Canberra: ANU Press, 2012, pp. 93–109

2 The development track of Chinese economic history

Introduction

Since reform and opening-up, China's economic development has aroused widespread praise and attention in the world with miracles it has created. However, what is more special is that from a historical perspective, this growth miracle shows that China may become the only case of economic growth that has experienced the process from prosperity to decline and to rise again, which poses intellectual challenges to economists keen to explore the puzzle of economic development and will undoubtedly greatly satisfy the academic curiosity of economic historians and growth economists. At the same time, the impact of China's economic growth on the world economy also calls for the birth of a theory with explanatory power. Although there are many different evolution paths and successful cases in the history of the world economy, it will be meaningful once these experiences are interpreted in general growth theories.

Traditional growth theory starts with doctrines of neoclassical economics that are much inconsistent with the reality of China, but it cannot very well interpret the Chinese miracle. Although institutional economics aims to explain the major institutional change shown in China's experience, it always dogmatically uses "consensuses" on some minds to shape a specific track of institutional changes in advance, so it ultimately fails to satisfy Friedman's "predictive" function set by empirical economics, thus encountering the embarrassment of missing the point.

To date, there have been numerous divergent opinions to interpret China's economic miracle from different realistic observation points and theoretical perspectives. However, there are currently no unified theories among economists to interpret the Chinese miracle. It is no wonder that theories to interpret economic development were originally divided into different schools, each based in one place and restricted to one concept. These theoretical interpretations are not yet satisfactory to judge from the following criteria.

First, the interpretation of economic growth should be consistent in theoretical logic and historical logic. The theoretical framework to interpret today's phenomenon should also be able to interpret the past and predict the future.

DOI: 10.4324/9781003329305-3

Only in this way can economic theory have the function of guiding reality and looking forward to the future.

Second, the theoretical framework to interpret a country's economic development should also be able to interpret that in other countries so that it can work as a reference for the later-moving countries through interpreting the experience of the first-mover countries.

Third, the largest and fastest economic growth in human history should make contributions to economics and economic history to enhance people's understanding of the overall development of the world economy.

To respond to this challenging task, this chapter attempts to examine the following three propositions together from a larger historical level, i.e., to use a unified theoretical analysis framework to answer consistently: (1) The "great divergence puzzle," a more general sense of the Needham Puzzle; that is why Chinese science and technology were once far ahead of other civilizations in premodern society, but it does not have such a leading position anymore; (2) "Puzzle of China's miracle"; that is, why and how the Chinese economy achieved rapid growth during the reform period; (3) "Worries about the middle-income trap"; that is, whether China can continue its past high-speed growth process and thus enter the ranks of high-income countries as expected.

Ultimately, the author attempts to combine growth theory with economic history and answers the grand proposition of how China's economic development has gone from prosperity to decline and whether it can go from decline to prosperity. For this purpose, the consistent theoretical framework proposed here is based on economic growth at all times. After all, it relies on a specific incentive mechanism to promote the accumulation of material capital and human capital and with it as a carrier to turn all kinds of inspired ideas into productivity improvement to realize increasing returns.

To simultaneously or separately express the increasing returns, decreasing returns, decreasing marginal substitution rate of factors, increasing factors in the same proportion, and the connection between them, to distinguish the growth brought by factor accumulation and the growth brought by productivity improvement and to simultaneously express the stagnant state of economy, the growth state, and its reasons, we give up the expression form of the production function and use the analytical tool of the isoquant curve to describe different types of economic growth processes.

Only the two factors of production, capital and labor, are considered; because of their relative scarcity, they form a different combination of factors with relative prices, which determines the specific output level. Due to the increase in production factors or productivity, the output can be increased, and the isoquant curve moves outward (upper right), forming economic growth.

At different stages of economic development, there are huge differences in the endowment and accumulation method of production factors, as well as the possibility and approach of productivity improvement and, correspondingly, the types of economic growth are also different. We have identified and included three types or states of economic growth that have existed in human history so far, namely the poverty trap state represented by the Malthusian model, or M-type of growth for short, and the dual economy development represented by the Lewis model, abbreviated as L-type of growth (including Lewis turning stage, or T-type of growth), and the neoclassical growth represented by the Solowian model, referred to as S-type of growth. From a historical perspective, the above three types of economic growth can also be seen as different stages of economic development with successive relationships.

In the eyes of contemporary mainstream economists, there is not a stage of dual economy development characterized by the unlimited supply of labor. They may either regard the neoclassical growth represented by developed countries as a given case such as Solow or see a change from traditional economic growth to modern economic growth in connection with history such as Kuznets. A more recent study by Gary Hansen and Edward Prescott unified Malthusian economic growth and Solowian economic growth into a theoretical framework.[1] However, in a collaborative paper, Prescott admitted that there is a transitional stage between Malthus and Solow, and its key task is to remove barriers that restrict labor movement.[2] Masahiko Aoki admitted the existence of such a transitional stage, although he did not call it the Lewis stage but took the Kuznets-like structural change as the characteristic of this stage.[3]

The entire economy is divided into agricultural and non-agricultural industries. The surplus labor in agriculture has been continuously transferred with the process of industrialization and urbanization. Such a process is not just a phenomenon unique in later-moving but also in catching-up countries; Western countries that were first industrialized did not leap from the Malthusian trap into the neoclassical growth stage through the industrial revolution. Nevertheless, in Western economic history, the transition from the Malthusian era to the Solow era, lasting for thousands of years, was as slow as a crawling snail, and the demographic transition process could not show significant stage change so that it is difficult for people to clearly see the Lewis era that existed between the two eras.

Therefore, when we observe the history of human economic development, it does not reduce the explanatory power about the history of early industrialized countries at all to add a stage of dual economy development named after Lewis, but it greatly enhances the understanding of problems faced by the later-moving industrialized regions (typical countries such as Japan and the Four Asian Tigers), as well as the developing countries that have not yet completed this transition. In particular, the purpose of growth research is to provide as consistent an explanation as possible for as many types of economic growth as possible, while development economics should aim more at the phenomenon of contemporary economic development.

We will see that when the dual economy development works as an organic logical chain of economic growth, it can help us eliminate the longstanding "high-level equilibrium trap" theory in explaining the Needham Puzzle, and it can also provide an observation dimension and an explanatory framework about the "middle-income trap."

M-type of growth and the "great divergence puzzle"

For much of history, mankind was stuck in the Malthusian poverty trap. The term "trap" means a state of high equilibrium in economics. Any disturbance change will not continue, and it will eventually return to the original equilibrium. The Malthusian trap, as a stage of economic development, has ruled human history for the longest time.

From the history of the world's overall economy, per capita income was always at the lowest subsistence level at any time in any part of the world until the industrial revolution took place in the second half of the 18th century and the beginning of the 19th century, and there was no essential difference; that is, all were in a state of Malthusian poverty. As a result, some people thought that there was almost no such thing as economic growth in the Malthusian era. However, economic growth is based on accumulation, and the later vigorous industrial revolution did not happen from nowhere. Therefore, there is ultimately a Malthusian economic change, that is, M-type economic growth.

As shown in Figure 2.1, in such a poverty trap, the combination of capital and labor investment, such as the capital investment of Ok_0 and the labor investment of Ol_0, forms an investment that can only maintain the subsistence level on the isoquant curve represented by Q_0. Meanwhile, such a growth model can also generate an economic surplus, thereby forming new capital, while population growth can increase the labor supply, and inventions and creations can often emerge as well.[4] Therefore, because of the factor accumulation, capital investment is increased to the Ok_1 level and labor investment is increased to the Ol_1 level or because of improved productivity out

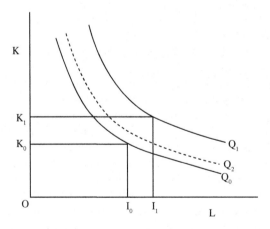

Figure 2.1 Malthusian poverty trap

of innovation (in most cases, the two occur simultaneously), the production level expands to the isoquant curve represented by Q_1. That's how economic growth happens.

However, the essence of the Malthusian equilibrium trap is that any increase in output will reduce the death rate and increase the birth rate by improving the means of living (mainly food) owned by each person, thereby stimulating population growth and diluting the per capita means of production (capital). For example, such an effect can reduce the output to the level of the isoquant curve Q_2. In this way, the level of per capita means of living will decrease, which will lead to an increased death rate, decreased birth rate, and thus a declining population. When the population decline affects the supply of labor, labor investment is reduced from Ol_1 to the level of Ol_0, and the output returns to the poverty equilibrium level of Q_0. Under such Malthusian conditions, so-called "economic growth" repeats fruitlessly in this way.

The M-type of growth is not necessarily just a stage of past history, and it can also be regarded as a type of growth that breaks through the historical time coordinate. That is, this type of growth is aimed at several economic development situations at the same time, namely, the general situation before the industrial revolution, the laggards in the great diversion after the industrial revolution, and the poor countries and areas in the contemporary world.

Before the industrial revolution, the whole human history was actually always in the long night of the Malthusian trap. As Keynes pointed out, since there was no major technological innovation and capital accumulation, the living standards of mankind did not substantially improve over a long period of at least 4,000 years, and human beings were unable to eliminate plagues, famines, wars, and disasters.[5] However, in the era characterized by the Malthusian trap, especially in its late period, some countries began to slowly but irreversibly accumulate the factors necessary to break this trap, especially the relevant institutional conditions behind the appearance that "there was no very great change in the standard of life of the average man living in the civilized centers of the earth," as described by Keynes.

On this basis, the industrial revolution took place in Great Britain, and it quickly spread to other European countries and further to many European colonial countries. As a result, for the first time in human history, positive economic growth was achieved, and at the same time, a "great divergence" came into being in the world economy. In other words, after the industrial revolution, many countries continued to be in the Malthusian trap or M-type growth state for a long time. For quite a long period of time, very few countries could catch up with the early industrialized countries.

The phenomenon of "great convergence," truly in contrast with the great divergence, did not appear until after the 1950s. Moreover, such a so-called convergence phenomenon was actually just that some countries homogeneous with the early industrialized countries caught up with the latter, so at best it was just a kind of "club convergence." The following chapters reveal that the phenomenon of broader global economic convergence did not appear until after the 1990s.

It is worth noting that currently, many countries in the world are still in the ranks of "low income" in the World Bank grouping. Some of these countries may have entered the stage of dual economy development, but there are also some countries that are still in the Malthusian trap or M-type of growth stage. For example, calculated in constant 2010 prices, the share of low-income countries with a per capita GDP below US$1,000 among countries in the statistical range was as high as 22.2% in 1990 and 13.6% in 2017.

It should be pointed out that if low-income countries in the current world economy are still in the M-type of growth stage, they actually have many characteristics different from the era before the industrial revolution. In particular, since these poor countries are surrounded by the vast ocean of a great number of middle-income and high-income countries, they can obtain assistance in terms of finance, investment projects, medical and health services from those countries and international institutions, such as the World Bank, the United Nations Development Programme, and the World Health Organization. As a result, the "backwardness" of these low-income countries has some new manifestations corresponding to the times.

Different from the lack of material capital in the era before the industrial revolution, today's low-income countries can obtain external capital inflows through bailouts and loans to fill the gap in domestic investment funds. Therefore, for these economies, the problem of low returns on capital is more prominent than the problem of insufficient capital factor endowment.

There have been extensive discussions among growth economists on the proposition of "why capital doesn't flow from rich to poor countries." The growth theory represented by Solow came to the hypothesis that if return on capital is diminishing, the growth of poor and rich countries will converge. The resulting conclusion was that the returns on capital in poor countries should be higher than those in rich countries. However, based on assumptions such as differences in human capital, the spillover of human capital, and capital market imperfection, Robert E. Lucas Jr. believed that the returns on capital in poor countries were not as high as expected in traditional theories, trying to answer the question of why capital doesn't flow from rich to poor countries.[6]

In addition, there are other factors related to the era that make today's low-income countries have different characteristics from the era before the industrial revolution. For example, first, similar to the principle of material capital, the shortage of human capital faced by poor countries in the final analysis is also due to the low level of returns, thus lacking accumulation incentives. Second, the demographic transition in low-income countries in the present is no longer fully endogenous but is affected by exogenous birth rate concepts, government policies, birth control methods, and medical and health conditions. Finally, even in developing countries that have eliminated the Malthusian trap, there are also some poor areas in their countries that are still in a state of M-type growth.

China is no exception, and had been struggling in the Malthusian poverty trap for thousands of years before entering the modern historical period. However, in terms of total GDP and per capita GDP, China was once ahead of the world average. According to economic historians such as Mark Elvin, China was in a "high-level equilibrium trap" for a long time.[7]

According to historical data from Angus Maddison, China's per capita income was roughly at the world average between 1000 and 1600 CE. Regarding the scale of the economy (total GDP), China unexpectedly accounted for one-third of the world's total in 1820. It was at that moment that China fell into the ranks of stagnant countries in the "great divergence" of the world economy. Its share in the world's aggregate economy fell all the way with the level of per capita income compared with the world average.

The hypothesis of a "high-level equilibrium trap" was popular for a long time. It claimed that agricultural practice in Chinese history combined traditional technology and production factors to the level of excellence so that it maintained a higher level of subsistence compared with early European history, and thus there was a rapid growth of population, correspondingly resulting in too much and too cheap labor, leading to an underdevelopment of labor-saving technologies.[8] However, obviously, this interpretation failed to answer why China formed such agricultural practices.

We would rather say from the previous explanation of the Malthusian poverty trap that generally speaking, if a country with M-type of economic growth stays on the extended equal output line (such as Q_1 in Figure 2.1) for a long time, it will be slow to return to the equilibrium isoquant curve of Q_0, and it will be easier for it to initiate the next movement to Q_1, and this country will have the nature of high-level equilibrium trap. Research by scholars such as Mark Elvin proved that the Chinese economy in the premodern period was often stuck in such a special equilibrium trap, but it could not exclude China from the M-type of economic growth.[9]

Although there are numerous theoretical hypotheses that intentionally or unintentionally explain the causes of the great divergence, economic growth theory and economic history are increasingly focusing on two mainstream directions. They attribute the reasons for the success of economic growth to the fact that a society can encourage the creation of enough inventions, creations, and innovations, and the formation of an institutional arrangement to effectively protect property rights to reward creators and inventors. Therefore, the key to solving the great divergence puzzle is whether society can form an institutional system that enables the accumulation of material capital and human capital to meet the critical minimum requirement for breaking the low-level equilibrium trap.

Furthermore, whether the "great divergence puzzle" takes world economic history as the object or the Needham Puzzle as a special Chinese version, it should be explained from two poles of divergence, such as the incentive mechanism of material capital and human capital in China and Western countries and the actual effect of accumulation. Therefore, these two puzzles can actually be expressed generally or especially as follows: Why are necessary institutions missing in underdeveloped countries (such as ancient China) to form the accumulation of material capital and human capital for breaking the Malthusian equilibrium trap and for turning it into scientific and technological innovation and economic development?

In fact, if the research starts for the purpose of providing guidance and reference for the world's low-income countries to break the equilibrium trap and meanwhile it is realized that the gap between rich and poor and the difference between the North and South in the current world are more or less a continuation of the great divergence, we should at least pay the same attention to the economic growth in the contemporary world as to economic history. That is, studying the Malthus poverty trap is meaningful not only for explaining economic history but also for understanding poverty in contemporary developing countries.

Regarding the stock and increment of a country's material capital and human capital, endowment factors are not unchangeable. The driving force for this change and its stimulating mechanism are affected by many factors. It can be proven from the history of economic theories that "determinism" built on a single influencing factor cannot fully reveal why there are differences in material capital and human capital accumulation among countries after all, and therefore it is difficult to have general theoretical explanatory power.

However, geographical location and environment, natural resource endowment, political system heritage, economic system choice, occasional historical events, culture, and religion all have different influences on capital accumulation. When all these factors are combined in different ways, a certain force will be formed to promote the accumulation of material capital and human capital to change in one direction or another. At this time, a specific path of economic development will be formed, and a country will depend on a certain path. When the country is too dependent on the development model determined by a certain combination of factors, it will correspondingly fall into a highly stable equilibrium state—the Malthusian trap.

It can be seen that understanding M-type growth requires not only a general analysis framework but also finding out this unique combination of influencing factors of relevant specific countries or regions. Because this task puts forward such strict knowledge and practical requirements, the mystery of big diversion and the mystery of Needham have become the academic goals pursued by researchers in related fields, which makes people not only enjoy it but also find it difficult to make a widely recognized breakthrough.

In the premodern period, China had a different institutional pattern from the feudal society in Western Europe, which derived a series of factors that were not conducive to material capital and human capital accumulation. First, due to the lack of an independent and large-scale economic entity between the huge central empire and scattered small farmers, it could not form a critical minimum size of material capital accumulation, making it difficult to break the low-level equilibrium trap. Second, such a society lacked the necessary innovation-driven factors; correspondingly, talents could not be trained and selected according to the innovation orientation, and human capital accumulation also failed to meet the critical requirement of breaking the low-level equilibrium trap. In the next chapter, we will attempt to answer the Needham Puzzle from these two aspects.

L-type of growth and China's miracle

The stage of dual economy development, which is inseparable from the theory of Arthur Lewis, means that in a country, the entire economy is clearly divided into agriculture with a large amount of surplus labor and non-agricultural sectors with unlimited supply of labor. The process of releasing surplus labor force from agriculture and absorbing labor force from non-agricultural industries constitutes an economic growth process.[10] China and many developing countries are at this stage of development. The later-moving industrialized economies represented by Japan and the Four Asian Tigers have experienced such a stage of development as well.

The reason why this type of growth is more vivid outside the early industrialized countries in Europe and America is that the later countries and regions have a faster process of population transformation. When the population changes rapidly and enters the stage of a high birth rate, low death rate, and high growth rate, a labor surplus will be formed. On the other hand, some institutional factors hinder the full flow of the labor force, which cannot change the imbalance of labor supply exceeding demand at once. Therefore, gradually digesting the surplus labor force constitutes the basic feature of economic growth. This is what we have defined as the L-type of economic growth.

As shown in Figure 2.2, capital investment Ok_0 and labor investment Ol_0 form an initial output level at the isoquant curve of Q_0. This type of growth is

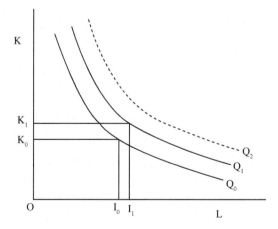

Figure 2.2 Lewisian dual economy development

characterized by an unlimited supply of labor, and any possible economic surplus will form new capital investment once accumulated, and the proportional labor investment can be obtained to form economic growth. For example, in Figure 2.2, the expanded capital investment Ok_1 and labor investment Ol_1 form a new output level at the isoquant curve of Q_1. As long as the supply of labor is still sufficient, the aforementioned process of output expansion or economic growth will continue.

Moreover, in this cyclical process of expanded capital and labor investment, the labor force changes from a surplus state to be used in production. It also means shifting from agriculture with very low productivity of marginal labor to non-agricultural industries with much higher productivity of marginal labor. This forms a process of resource reallocation, thereby obtaining a source of total factor productivity unique to the stage of dual economy development—resource reallocation efficiency.

Moreover, developing countries after the industrial revolution also had a unique late-mover advantage owing to the technological gap with the developed countries, and they increased the total factor productivity by introducing technology and machinery and equipment. As shown in Figure 2.2, while the increase in capital and labor causes the output level to move from Q_0 to Q_1, it moves further to Q_2 due to the increase in total factor productivity. The experiences of many countries have shown that in the stage of dual economy development, total factor productivity can not only be improved but also can improve at a fast rate and to a great extent. Therefore, the period of dual economic development is usually accompanied by extraordinarily high-speed growth.

As shown in this model, there are already modern economic growth sectors and modern education systems in the process of dual economy development, so there is no natural bottleneck in material capital and human capital accumulation. The problem lies in the incentive mechanism to achieve necessary accumulation and its efficient allocation.

For example, during the planned economy period, China was far ahead of countries with equivalent income in terms of material capital and human capital accumulation, but it was not effectively allocated, and its economic growth did not perform well. Therefore, if the period of reform and opening-up is taken as the typical L-type economic growth stage in China, what is worth exploring is how the institutional reform in this period can create an incentive mechanism to effectively allocate material capital and human capital and release abundant resources of the labor force to achieve unprecedented high-speed economic growth with the help of the demographic dividend.

China started reform in the late 1970s. It first utilized the principle of material benefits to mobilize laborers' enthusiasm and increase corporate motives for profits. With changes in the pricing mechanism and increased corporate competition, the reform further touched the resource allocation system. The planned economic system was gradually abandoned by adopting reforms such as the dual-track pricing system. In this process, two incentive mechanisms were formed conducive to material capital and human capital accumulation.

The first was the incentive mechanism for direct microeconomic activities. The agricultural household contract system, the reform of the labor compensation system, the development of the labor market, the reform of state-owned enterprises, and the development of the non-public economy enabled the accumulation and reasonable allocation of capital and labor to maximally benefit parties involved in economic activities.

The second was the incentive mechanism for local governments to be involved in economic development. Reforms in fiscal decentralization, government assessment systems, and promotion systems for officials stimulated the enthusiasm of governments at all levels (especially those with the power of fiscal budgets) to promote the development of the local economy and form intergovernmental competition for economic growth speed.[11] Local governments not only directly attracted investment and helped enterprises go for projects and strive for resources from higher-level governments but also encouraged the contribution of various human capitals and implemented talent introduction policies. They formulated and released policies to attract rural migrant laborers in the case of labor shortages.

With the gradual improvement of incentive mechanisms, the feature of unlimited supply of labor was utilized to promote high-speed growth, and the potential demographic dividend was presented as economic growth performance. From 1979 to 2010, China's GDP grew at an average rate of 9.9% per annum. Such a typical and perfect miracle of dual economy development comes from many "disequilibrium" phenomena related to the feature of the unlimited supply of labor, so that resources can be reallocated.

Next, according to our own growth decomposition (Figure 2.3), we observe a series of special growth opportunities related to the development of the dual economy, study how to become the source of high-speed growth, and compare our decomposition results with other scholars' relevant conclusions. Economists usually add the population dependency ratio (the ratio of the dependent population to the working-age population) as a variable to the growth decomposition to distinguish the contribution of the demographic dividend to economic growth.[12] However, we find from China's experience that the role of the demographic dividend cannot be covered by the dependency ratio variable. In fact, it is reflected in almost all growth sources (or explanatory variables).

During the whole period of China's reform, there was a rapid demographic transition; that is, the birth rate dropped rapidly, which led to the continuous growth of the working-age population, and the proportion of the working-age population in the total population increased continuously, ensuring the full supply of the labor force. Another indicator of this demographic transition, the dependency ratio of the population, has also been greatly reduced, expanding the surplus created by economic growth and achieving a high savings rate, thus creating favorable conditions for capital accumulation. The

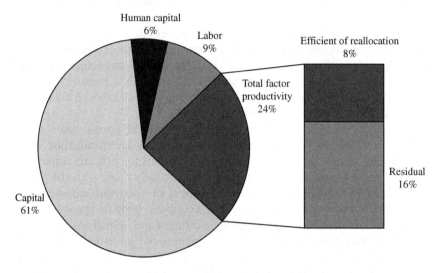

Figure 2.3 Source of economic growth during the reform period (1979–2010)

characteristics of unlimited supply of labor force prevent the phenomenon of diminishing returns on capital, break the restrictive conditions of neoclassical growth, and make capital an important engine of high-speed economic growth over a long period of time. This is shown as the contribution of capital. The education level of the new entrants to the labor force continues to increase substantially, and human capital accumulates at an unprecedented speed; thus, it is shown as the contribution of human capital. A large amount of decomposition of China's economic growth during the reform has drawn similar empirical results and conclusions. In summary, it can be generally summarized that the biggest factors contributing to China's rapid economic growth are capital formation and labor force growth, and the improvement of workers' education levels has also made notable contributions.

The increase in total factor productivity and its contribution to economic growth are key to distinguishing the period of reform and opening-up from the period of planned economy. The narrowing of the technological gap and the effect of institutional changes are largely reflected in the improvement of total factor productivity, which is the source of growth other than the accumulation of the production factor.

However, it is particularly worth noting that the productivity source related to this type of economic growth—that is, the shift of labor from agriculture to nonagricultural industries—created unique resource reallocation efficiency and constituted an important part of the increase in total factor productivity. Total factor productivity changed from a negative contribution before the reform to a positive contribution during the reform,[13] among which an important part was the resource reallocation efficiency brought by the transfer of the labor sector.[14] Given the significant contribution share of factor accumulation to growth, economists generally attributed China's economic growth during this period to factor investment-driven growth. However, it was just because of the nature of the unlimited supply of labor with the L-type of economic growth that such a growth model worked.[15]

T-type of growth and "the middle-income trap"

If we first assume that the surplus agricultural labor force only needs to maintain the survival level without increasing wages, then we can obtain a steady supply of labor force. If we further define that marginal labor productivity is significantly lower than that of non-agricultural industries, the development of the dual economy will eventually encounter the end of the surplus labor force.

Although this is a gradual process, the most characteristic change, such as the emergence of labor shortages and the rise in wages of ordinary laborers, will be obviously shown at a certain point of time. We call this point of time the Lewis turning point.

At this turning point, a growth type with its own characteristics is formed accordingly, namely the T-type of economic growth. This is a special stage of dual economy development or a special pattern of transition from L-type economic growth to S-type economic growth.

As shown in Figure 2.4, the combination of capital and labor investment corresponding to k_0 and l_0, k_1 and l_1, and k_2 and l_2 respectively forms specific output levels at the isoquant curves of Q_0, Q_1, and Q_2, constituting the growth process of the aforementioned period of dual economy development. However, when labor investment reaches the level of l_2, economic development

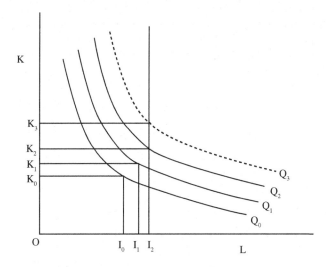

Figure 2.4 Lewis turning points

meets the Lewis turning point; that is, if labor investment further increases, the wages of laborers must be increased. In theory, this can also be seen as the depletion of surplus labor and the beginning of labor force becoming a scarce factor of production. Therefore, in the case of further increasing capital investment to k_3, when there is no longer a proportional investment of labor to go with it, the phenomenon of diminishing returns to capital will occur. After that, economic growth will enter the Solowian neoclassical stage.

Nevertheless, just as in the dual economic theory, the Lewis turning point is only the beginning of labor shortage and rising wages of ordinary laborers. The turning point to truly end the stage of dual economy development is when the marginal labor productivities of agriculture and non-agricultural industries are equal, and it reaches the so-called commercialization point.[16] In other words, reaching the Lewis turning point does not mean that economic growth will immediately enter the Solowian neoclassical world. In fact, the T-type of economic growth is still a stage of the L-type of economic growth, and it has the dual characteristics of dual economic development and neoclassical growth.

In 2004, "a lack of migrant laborers" appeared in China's coastal areas, and this quickly spread to other urban areas, becoming a nationwide phenomenon of labor shortage, and wages of ordinary laborers continued to rise accordingly. According to surveys conducted by the National Bureau of Statistics over the years, the annual growth rate of the actual wages of nationwide rural migrant laborers was 12% during the period from 2003 to 2012. The wages of urban employees and wages of agricultural employees also increased rapidly over the same period.

According to the definition of dual economic theory, 2004 was the year of the Lewis turning point. At the same time, reaching the Lewis turning point was closely related to the disappearance of the demographic dividend.[17] According to data from the sixth census, the working-age population aged 15–59 reached its peak in 2010, and then negative growth began. Therefore, if we conservatively take 2004 (the Lewis turning point was reached) as the beginning and 2010 (the working-age population to stop growing and the demographic dividend disappeared) as the end, the so-called Lewis turning interval has already been completed, and China's dual economy development has entered the final stage.

Although China's economy, which has surpassed the Lewis turning point, cannot be said to have become a neoclassical growth type yet, it has been on the fast track to change to the latter. Countries at this stage of transition, on the one hand, are faced with declining traditional growth factors and thus slower growth, and on the other hand, many previously effective incentive mechanisms for material capital and human capital accumulation may no longer work, so economic growth is facing the possibility of slowdown.[18]

The Chinese economy, which has completed the Lewis turning interval, is at this stage of economic development. According to the trends of the potential employment growth rate, investment growth rate, and total factor

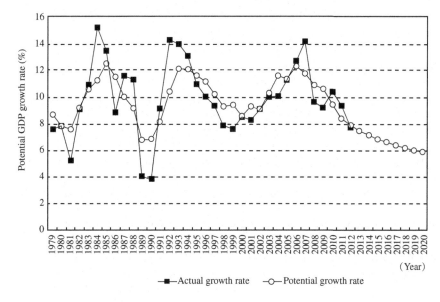

Figure 2.5 Declining trend of the potential growth rate

productivity, earlier estimates show that if there are no changes in other growth factors, China's potential economic growth rate will significantly fall during the 12th Five-Year Plan, and it will continue to fall during the 13th Five-Year Plan (Figure 2.5). The study of past economic development experiences and lessons shows that if a country cannot address such a slowdown properly, there is a risk of falling into the "middle-income trap."[19]

The potential economic growth capacity reduces due to changes in the development stage, but this does not necessarily mean that it will lead to a middle-income trap. However, if the reasons for slowdown are misjudged— that is, focusing on stimulating economic growth from demand factors, rather than focusing on increasing the potential growth rate from supply factors—then inappropriate policy tendencies will be formed. The key to increasing the potential growth rate and maintaining a reasonable economic growth rate is to increase the total factor productivity, and the way to achieve it lies in institutional innovation and technological innovation.

Generally, the means to be used for innovation is a kind of "creative destruction." However, the government, with a high degree of intervention to stimulate demand, is keen on picking winners but cannot accept failure. Therefore, the result is bound to maintain monopoly and protect backwardness and create "zombie enterprises," ultimately damaging the incentive of material capital and human capital accumulation.

Once the natural slowdown in economic growth is transformed into long-term stagnation due to policy failures, rent-seeking behaviors will be rampant in the absence of a good incentive mechanism, and resource and income distribution will change in the direction of the widening unreasonable gap, thus inevitably forming an unfair and unequal pattern of interests.

The experiences of some countries in Latin America indicate that when there is no cake increment and the existing cake distribution pattern is inseparable from vested interest groups, politicians' commitment to redistribution can never be fulfilled, and social policies fall into the mud of populism. As the vested interests become increasingly significant in the unequal distribution pattern, the resistance to reforms by beneficiaries becomes stronger, leading to the ossified system and the rigidified vested interests, which is hard to eliminate.[20] There is a popular proverb in the West, which reads: For the want of a nail the shoe was lost, for want of a shoe the horse was lost, for want of a horse the knight was lost, for want of a knight the battle was lost, for want of a battle the kingdom was lost. So a kingdom was lost—all for want of a nail. The middle-income trap and all kinds of hard-to-get-rid-of problems usually originate from improper policies and measures after economic growth slows down. Therefore, in the face of the slowdown of economic growth, we should have a correct understanding and policy response to prevent this slowdown.

To date, many economists and policy researchers have not yet understood the principle that the disappearance of the demographic dividend will reduce the potential growth rate. They mistakenly believe that the slowdown in China's economic growth is caused by a lack of demand. Therefore, they actively seek the central government to implement the investment-oriented regional development strategy and stimulate macroeconomic policies to achieve the purpose of boosting investment demands. The local government borrowing phenomenon caused by such policy tendencies and overcapacity is getting worse. In fact, from the perspective of historical lessons, local debts and overcapacity cannot be considered the greatest risks. The painful lessons of Japan show that excess liquidity will eventually flow to non-productive or speculative investment places, such as wealth management, real estate business, and overseas real estate investment, forming a more dangerous bubble economy.

The decline in the potential growth rate means that the comparative advantage and competitive advantage in the manufacturing sector are declining, and it is difficult for production enterprises with existing productivity to continue. When the general real economy is not strong, the enthusiasm for infrastructure and other project construction is not high either. When the Japanese government tried to stimulate the economy with large-scale public investment, it encountered the dilemma that it was difficult to finalize investment funds. Miyazaki, the former head of Japan's Economic Planning Agency, found that when fiscal stimulus policies were implemented, public investment first encountered that "there is a budget but not allocated," and then "the allocation is not in place," until "the funds are in place but the project has not started," which has been watered down step by step.[21]

After all, Miyazaki did not figure out where the funds finally went; in this regard, the critics of Keynes were prescient as far back as 1933. In response to Keynes's recommendation on stimulus policy, his colleague Hubert Henderson, an economist at the Economic Information Committee, wrote to him: "If you announce to launch an ambitious plan of GBP200 million, you won't get an order in at least one year, meanwhile, it will have a rapid impact on markets such as Phnom Penh stocks. In this way, you may have been surrounded by a vicious circle before the virtuous circle starts and cannot pull out of it."[22] After the bubble burst in Japan, it fell into the "lost 20 years."

While the incomes of urban and rural residents increase with China's rapid economic growth, there is a tendency to widen the income gap. Some studies show that if the property income caused by the unequal possession of resources is taken into account—especially the off-the-books income, which might be legitimate or not—there may be a higher degree of income inequality.[23] Behind such an income distribution pattern is the non-standard and non-transparent distribution mechanism of resources caused by a series of institutional factors. Therefore, to solve the problem of income distribution, one must start with deep reforms and break the pattern of vested interests in institutions and mechanisms.

While efforts are made to solve the problem of unfair income distribution and eliminate the pattern of vested interests that hinder reform, it is more important to correctly address the slowdown in economic growth and ensure that the cake continues to grow. In the following text, we will see where we should start to avoid an unmanageable economic collapse and stagnation at the stage of China's economic development. The key for dual economic development to avoid diminishing marginal returns to capital is that there is the unique phenomenon of unlimited supply of labor, which can break the neoclassical conditions of labor shortage. Therefore, before reaching the Lewis turning point, there will be no diminishing returns to capital, and the returns on investment will not decrease in the process of continuously releasing and absorbing surplus labor.

As shown in Figure 2.6, before the economic development stage reaches the L point (the Lewis turning point), the return on capital and the return on investment both remain at the constant level of R. After point L, with the occurrence of diminishing returns to capital, it will be a natural trend that the marginal return on capital and the return on investment decline along the trajectory of R_0R_1.

However, when abstractly examining the return on capital and the return on investment separately, we can see from Figure 2.6 that there are two approaches to prevent or delay their declines. The first approach is that any practice that can increase the supply of labor and alleviate labor shortages can slow down the process of diminishing marginal returns to capital, as shown by the change trajectory of R_0R_2 in Figure 2.6.

Singapore is an example that introduced a large foreign labor force to postpone the reaching of the Lewis turning point and further prolong the harvest period of the demographic dividend. Since the decline in the birth rate led to a slowdown in the growth of the working-age population and rapid economic

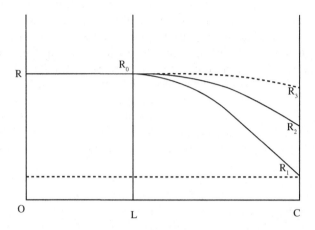

Figure 2.6 After the Lewis turning point

growth resulted in labor shortages, Singapore began to relax its immigration policy in the mid-1970s and gradually began to welcome foreign workers. In 2010, foreigners accounted for 34.7% of Singapore's national labor force.[24] It is precisely because there has been a relatively sufficient supply of labor force for a long time in Singapore that the phenomenon of diminishing returns to capital is delayed, so it has maintained high-speed growth for quite a long time and gained time to shift to total factor productivity-driven development.

In China, without considering the introduction of foreign immigrants, there is a huge potential to increase the supply of labor through reform. Since rural migrant laborers lack stable employment and living expectations in cities and cannot enjoy equal basic public services, their labor participation rate has been depressed. Therefore, substantively promoting the household registration system reform with urbanization of rural migrant laborers as the core can directly play the roles of prolonging the demographic dividend and delaying the diminishing returns to capital.

However, the period of dual economy development will eventually come to an end, and the neoclassical growth stage is exactly the destination that any late-mover country will reach. Therefore, the declining return on capital is inevitable after all, and the key to maintaining the return on investment lies in the improved labor productivity. This is the second approach; that is, to fill the gap caused by diminishing returns to capital to hinder the decline in the return on investment. In other words, the increase in labor productivity does not prevent the decrease in capital marginal return but counteracts the decrease in return on investment caused by the latter and maintains economic growth. This effect is shown in the diagram as the change trajectory of R_0R_3 until economic development reaches the commercialization point (represented by C in the diagram); thus, economic growth is completely transformed into a neoclassical type, and the only factor to support the return on investment is increased productivity.

S-type of growth and its sustainable source

Once any economy crosses the Lewis turning point and further reaches the commercialization point where the marginal labor productivities of agriculture and non-agricultural industries are equal, its economic growth belongs to the neoclassical type defined by Solow. In the S-type of economic growth, which mainstream economists have devoted their full attention to, and even come to the state of "knowing nothing about new theories," the labor force is assumed to be in short supply. Although the capital–labor ratio can still be reasonably improved due to the continuous improvement of the quality of the labor force, the continuously increasing investment due to capital accumulation will eventually encounter the phenomenon of diminishing returns at some point.

In Figure 2.7, the initial combination of capital and labor investment is that Ok_0 corresponds to Ol_0, forming an output level at the isoquant curve of Q_0. When capital investment expands to Ok_1, labor investment remains at the constant level of Ol_0. Although the output level can be raised to the isoquant curve represented by Q_1, the phenomenon of diminishing returns to capital still occurs. Therefore, sustainable economic growth depends entirely on the increase in total factor productivity; that is, at the constant investment level of production factors, the output level will reach the isoquant curve represented by Q_2 due to the increased productivity.

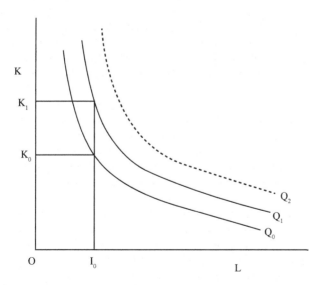

Figure 2.7 Solowian neoclassical growth

It is just because developed countries belonging to this type of growth are alone on the technological front that their economy cannot grow as fast as L-types could. Therefore, when an economy is in the process of being close to the neoclassical state, it will necessarily experience a significant slowdown in growth.

The economic development experiences in various countries show that the Solowian neoclassical economic state is not a "promised land" away from risks. The things that may cause economic growth risks in the neoclassical state generally include the following: competitiveness will increase or decrease among countries and regions, economic cycles are inevitable after all, and social insurance projects, especially public pension insurance projects, have encountered sustainability crises in many countries.

Specific experiences and lessons include the Japanese-styled "high-income trap" that led to the "lost 20 years," the low growth, high unemployment, and fiscal unsustainability in various countries caused by the sovereign debt crisis in Europe, as well as the financial risks and jobless recovery that occur quite often in the United States.

In addition, there have been long-lasting arguments in almost all mature institutional forms with no decisions reached. For example, should we pay more attention to economic laissez-faire or emphasize government intervention? And is it necessary to have social protection and labor market system, or has it caused a loss of efficiency? Should it strengthen regulation over the financial market? And so on. Nevertheless, some consensus has been formed on the S-type of economic growth out of economic research results, which can provide a reference about economic growth sources and institutional construction for an economy such as China, which is transforming into a neoclassical growth stage.

First, neoclassical growth is not a stable equilibrium, but there are many disequilibrium states. The process of approaching equilibrium from disequilibrium is full of creative destruction. Only in this way can it form a window of opportunity to enhance productivity. Therefore, neoclassical growth is also a Schumpeterian innovation process.

For example, studies by economists show that in a country with a mature market economy such as the United States, the entry and exit, growth and extinction of corporate departments form a process of creative destruction, generating resource reallocation efficiency. The resulting increase in total factor productivity accounted for 30–50% of the total productivity improvement.[25] It is just because of this that there is the phenomenon of so-called increasing returns.

Second, it is just because of such a process of creative destruction that enterprises compete for survival in new birth, growth, subsistence, and death. Accordingly, laborers will suffer periodic, structural and frictional unemployment trouble from time to time. In particular, when there is a rapid technological change and it is just the time when Schumpeterian innovation occurs, laborers whose skills cannot meet the requirements of the labor market need to be protected by a social safety net. Therefore, no matter how much economists care about efficiency and how indifferent they are to uncompetitive laborers, social protection mechanisms, including labor market systems and social insurance systems, are ultimately indispensable. Facts have proven that with the transition from the low-income stage to the middle-income stage and the high-income stage, almost all countries have carried out institutional construction related to this without exception.[26]

Finally, although there is no rule to determine the relations between the government and the market, the theoretical debate related to this is protracted and almost an eternal topic. Generally, it has become the mainstream practice to divide the boundary between the government and the market according to the nature of public goods and private products to handle their relations and define their respective functions. Lewis once perplexedly pointed out the fact: "The failure of the government may be that it has done too little or it has done too much."[27] The meaning implied in the "Lewis paradox" is that there is already no way out to talk about doing too much or too little.

Based on theoretical progress and economic development practices in various countries, there has been an increasing consensus to abandon the Lewis paradox, which is entangled in the fact that the government has "too much" or "too little," and rather to focus on how to better define what the government should "do" or "not do." As soon as this fundamental question is relatively clear, we can further explore the secondary question of "how to do"; that is, the function to be performed by the government is to prevent various monopolistic behaviors, protect the equality and adequacy in market competition, and establish a social security system and a labor market system. For direct economic activities, the government also needs to adopt fiscal policies and monetary policies and instruments to regulate the macroeconomic operation. During industrial policy implementation, the government should minimize direct participation in the economic process, stop distorting the prices of production factors, and prevent discriminatory treatment of different business entities. The government plays an indispensable role in promoting necessary system reforms.

China's economy will eventually enter a stage of neoclassical growth. On the one hand, it will face the same problems as other developed economies. For example, it must explore ways to increase total factor productivity to maintain the sustainability of economic growth; on the other hand, it will still face many unique challenges, such as the characteristic of "getting old before getting rich" that has been formed during the period of dual economy development. It will not only bring China a special middle-income trap risk but also be brought to a higher development stage in different forms, putting a special mark to the economic growth and social development of the neoclassical stage.

In addition, as revealed by the "lost 20 years" in Japan's economic development, in the high-income growth stage, economic growth will not naturally go ahead smoothly and triumphantly, but it will have to overcome more challenging problems. In fact, many future challenges have been incubated during the transition from the stage of dual economy development to the neo-classical growth stage, so it is necessary to plan ahead.

Conclusion

From the perspective of a fairly long span of world economic history, the types or stages of economic growth that mankind has experienced and each country is experiencing can be summarized, respectively as the Malthusian poverty trap (M-type of growth) and Lewisian dual economy development (L-type of growth), Lewis turning point (T-type of growth) and Solowian neoclassical growth (S-type of growth).[28] These types of growth have different characteristics in essence; economic incentives and growth sources are not the same, and the resulting demands for systems and policies are also very different, but because of their mutual historical and logical connections, it is fully possible and should be possible to use a unified economic theoretical framework to explain it.

Similar to the efforts made in this chapter, it can provide a useful analytical tool to establish such a unified theoretical framework so that it provides an interpretation of economic history with consistency in theory, continuity in observation, and comparability in practice in terms of various phenomena at the economic development stage and various dimensions of economic development dynamics.

For example, the framework can incorporate such economic and growth dynamics as the economic states of poverty, catch-up, and prosperity experienced by human beings, the growth states of stagnation, take-off, high speed and low speed under a high steady state, material capital and human capital accumulation, technological and institutional innovation, and productivity improvement. In this way, we can endow all kinds of theoretical schools of economic development that have been fragmented and formalized for a long time with brand-new explanatory power.

More importantly, the purpose of this chapter is also to use a consistent theoretical framework to interpret the history and reality of China's economic development and look forward to the future. From a fairly long historical perspective, China has experienced the first three processes of the four types of growth. Moreover, China has experienced changes in these development stages when it caught significant attention in the world economy. It not only has rich materials about experiences, lessons, references and inspiration but also provides convenience for observation with its rapid changes.

In this way, we are able to utilize more available theoretical weapons and unique development courses to sublimate China's experience, turn our "self-action" to "conscious" action, enhance our confidence in China's economic development path, and increase our understanding of future challenges. Meanwhile, it will make due contributions from Chinese economists to the rejuvenation of development economics.

Notes

1 Gary D. Hansen and Edward C. Prescott, Malthus to Solow, *American Economic Review*, Vol. 92, No. 4, 2002, pp. 1205–1217.
2 F. Hayashi and E. Prescott, The Depressing Effect of Agricultural Institutions on the Prewar Japanese Economy, *Journal of Political Economy*, Vol. 116, No. 4, 2008, pp. 573–632.
3 Masahiko Aoki, The Five Phases of Economic Development and Institutional Evolution in China and Japan, in Masahiko Aoki and Jinglian Wu (eds.), *The Chinese Economy: A New Transition*, Basingstoke: Palgrave Macmillan, 2012.
4 Both Michael Kremer and Justin Yifu Lin pointed out that a large population size was conducive to generating more creations and innovations and solving population pressure. See Michael Kremer, Population Growth and Technological Change: One Million BC to 1990, *The Quarterly Journal of Economics*, Vol. 108, No. 3, 1993, pp. 681–716; Justin Yifu Lin, *The Needham Puzzle, the Weber Question and China's Miracle: Long Term Performance since the Sung Dynasty*, CCER Working Paper Series, No. E2006017, November 22, 2006.
5 John Maynard Keynes, Economic Possibilities for Our Grandchildren (1930), in Lorenzo Pecchi and Gustavo Piga (eds.), *Revisiting Keynes: Economic Possibilities for Our Grandchildren*, Cambridge, MA: MIT Press, 2008, pp. 17–26.
6 For example, see Robert E. Lucas, Jr., Why Doesn't Capital Flow from Rich to Poor Countries? *The American Economic Review*, Vol. 80, No. 2, 1990, pp. 92–96.
7 Mark Elvin, *The Pattern of the Chinese Past: A Social and Economic Interpretation*, Stanford: Stanford University Press, 1973
8 See Daniel Little, *Micro Foundations, Method and Causation: On the Philosophy of the Social Sciences*, New Jersey: Transaction Publishers, 1998, pp. 151–169 for the simplest and refined summary about this theory.
9 We will comment on this popular hypothesis of "high-level equilibrium trap" in the next chapter.
10 Arthur Lewis, Economic Development with Unlimited Supplies of Labor, *The Manchester School*, Vol. 22, No. 2, 1954, pp. 139–191.
11 Steven Zhang attributed China's "almost spectacular economic growth" to an institution that could induce fierce competition among local governments (he specifically referred to county-level governments). However, we disagree with his unconditional advocation of such institutional effect. See Steven Zhang, *The Economic System of China*, China CITIC Press, 2009.
12 For example, Jeffrey Williamson, *Growth, Distribution and Demography: Some Lessons from History*, NBER Working Paper Series, No. 6244, 1997.
13 For example, Jianbai Yang, Speed, Structure, Efficiency, *Economic Research Journal*, Vol. 9, 1991; Zhu Xiaodong, Understanding China's Growth: Past, Present, and Future, *Journal of Economic Perspectives*, Vol. 26, No. 4, 2012, pp. 103–124; Dwight H. Perkins, China's Economic Growth in Historical and International Perspective, *China Economic Quarterly*, Vol. 4, No. 4, 2005.
14 See Lauren Brandt and Zhu Xiaodong, *Accounting for China's Growth*, Working Paper No. 395, Department of Economics, University of Toronto, 2010.
15 Fang Cai and Zhao Wen, When Demographic Dividend Disappears: Growth Sustainability of China, in Masahiko Aoki and Jinglian Wu (eds.), *The Chinese Economy: A New Transition*, Basingstoke: Palgrave Macmillan, 2012. Zhu Xiaodong, used a unique method to breakdown the sources of China's economic

growth, and drew a different research conclusion, i.e., he discovered that during the reform period, the main source of China's economic growth was not capital investment, but increased total factor productivity. See Zhu Xiaodong, Understanding China's Growth: Past, Present, and Future, *The Journal of Economic Perspectives*, Vol. 26, No. 4, 2012, pp. 103–124. Actually, as displayed from the discussion about the Singaporean experiences, factors for technical advances can be represented as capital contribution and productivity contribution as well, which depends on the theoretical assumption and model selection (for example see Jesus Felipe, *Total Factor Productivity Growth in East Asia: A Critical Survey*, EDRC Report Series, No. 65, Asian Development Bank, Manila, Philippines, 1997). Zhu Xiaodong, method and conclusion aimed to build a consistency with the neoclassical growth theory to avoid the embarrassment that the traditional theory did not understand the particularity of L-type of economic growth.

16 Gustav Ranis and John C.H. Fei, A Theory of Economic Development, *The American Economic Review*, Vol. 51, No. 4, 1961, pp. 533–565.

17 Cai Fang, Demographic Transition, Demographic Dividend, and Lewis Turning Point in China, *China Economic Journal*, Vol. 3, No. 2, 2010, pp. 107–119.

18 Barry Eichengreen, Donghyun Park, and Kwanho Shin, *When Fast Growing Economies Slow Down: International Evidence and Implications for China*, NBER Working Paper, No. 16919, 2011.

19 Indermit Gill and Homi Kharas, *An East Asian Renaissance: Ideas for Economic Growth*, Washington, DC: World Bank, 2007.

20 Rudiger Dornbusch and Sebastian Edwards, *Macroeconomic Populism in Latin America*, NBER Working Paper, No. 2986, 1989.

21 Isamu Miyazaki, *A Record of Japan's Economic Policy*, Beijing: China CITIC Press, 2009, pp. 188–189.

22 Robert Skidelsky, *John Maynard Keynes*, Hong Kong: SDX Joint Publishing Company, 2006, p. 550.

23 Xiaolu Wang, *Off-the-Books Income and Distribution of National Income, Income Distribution in China: Exploration and Controversy*, edited by Xiaowu Song, Shi Li, Xiaomin Shi, and Desheng Lai, Beijing: Economic Press China, 2011.

24 Siow Yue Chia, Foreign Labor in Singapore: Rationale, Policies, Impacts, and Issues, *Philippine Journal of Development*, Vol. 38, No. 1–2, 2011, pp. 105–133.

25 Lucia Foster, John Haltiwanger, and Chad Syverson, Reallocation, Firm Turnover, and Efficiency: Selection on Productivity or Profitability? *American Economic Review*, Vol. 98, No. 1, 2008, pp. 394–425.

26 See Richard Freeman, Labor Markets and Institutions in Economic Development, *AEA Papers and Proceedings*, Vol. 83, No. 2, 1993, pp. 403–408.

27 Arthur Lewis, *The Theory of Economic Growth*, translated by Xiaomin Liang, Shanghai: Sanlian Publishing House/People's Publishing House, 1994.

28 In fact, the author will add an economic development pattern or phase in Chapter 4, which is called the "Geertz involution" as a preparatory phase for Lewisian dual economy development. The reason to put it in Chapter 4 is that it needs enough space for special illustration. Nevertheless, such arrangement does not affect the completeness of this chapter.

3 Re-understanding the Needham Puzzle from the growth perspective

Introduction

Economic growth theory usually explores the growth issue from two perspectives. One is to focus on diminishing returns, that is, to seek the convergence of poor countries to rich countries; the other is to focus on increasing returns to explore the source of sustained growth in developed countries. The theoretical starting points of these two research traditions seem to be opposite, but they together constitute a focus on all types of economic development in history and their stage transitions, which is particularly helpful in explaining the economic development phenomena in the current developed countries, middle-income countries, and poor countries.

The developed and underdeveloped division is the result of a long historical process. In general, the so-called the "great divergence" that occurred approximately 400 years ago can be taken as a landmark starting point. If not limited to the strict time dimension but considered from the unified dimension of history and logic, the great divergence represents the most important watershed for human economic development, and the latter distinguishes different countries at a specific point of time. Countries that have achieved the industrial revolution at different paces have since eliminated the Malthusian trap and entered a new stage of economic development.

Countries that have neither become the initiators of the industrial revolution nor caught the last train of the industrial revolution have long remained in the Malthusian trap. Since the science and technology needed for industrialization became public knowledge in the 19th and 20th centuries, it also gave poor countries the opportunity to catch up with the early industrialized countries. Some countries, washed away by the great divergence to the other side, have certain modern economic sectors, but many are still stagnant at the middle-income development stage.

It can be seen that the issue of economic development constitutes the research field of economic history from the vertical perspective and the research field of growth theory from the horizontal perspective. Both research fields have left many development puzzles that have led researchers to diligently explore, which are related to such fundamental issues as explaining why

DOI: 10.4324/9781003329305-4

there is a "great divergence" of economic development among countries or why rich countries and poor countries keep their own development states. It can be imagined that once the two dimensions are combined and integrated, it will enhance our understanding of long-term economic development and help answer those fascinating research puzzles in the two academic fields.

"The Needham mystery" is such an important academic puzzle, although it is the Chinese version of the broader proposition the "great divergence mystery." Needham, who has long been engaged in research of China's science and technology history, tried to use a large amount of historical data to prove that from the 3rd century BCE to the 15th century CE, China's scientific inventions and discoveries far exceeded those in Europe in the same period and were in the world's leading level, but after that, China was overtaken by Western countries. Therefore, it is undoubtedly necessary to answer the Needham riddle in two steps. The first step is to answer why China's early technological and economic development was far ahead of others, and the second step is to answer why China's technological and economic development fell far behind Europe after the 15th century.

For this puzzle, there is a direct footnote and more extensive background information. First, based on Needham's research conclusions, many researchers summarized China's scientific and technological inventions in various periods, revealed its status in the world's scientific and technological invention history, and then elaborated on many important discoveries.

For example, Robert Temple concluded that almost more than half of the basic inventions and creations on which the modern world is built originated in China.[1] However, China's share of the world's inventions and creations dropped sharply from 1500, and it became insignificant once the industrial revolution began. For example, data from science and technology history show that during the period from 401 to 1000, 32 of the world's 45 major scientific and technological inventions originated in China, while during the period from 1501 to 1840, only 19 of the world's 472 major scientific and technological inventions belonged to China.

Second, economic historians generally acknowledge that the current world economic structure—that is, the absolute leading position of Europe and its overseas immigration regions in terms of science and technology and economy and per capita income—has not always been the case. Scholars' research shows that around the world in approximately 1500, wealth was mainly concentrated in the East, while China played a decisive position in this "Eastern" concept. It was only after that that Europe began to gradually rise, and the "great divergence" between the East and the West did not appear until late in the 18th century.[2] Approximately in the same timeframe, there was a bigger and bigger gap between China and the West in economy, technology, and living standards, when it eventually became a poor and weak country. Therefore, while economic historians and growth theorists spent plenty of time trying to answer why there is the "great divergence" between the East and the West, the Needham Puzzle is actually just a special Chinese version of the "great divergence puzzle."

Economic historians have devoted plenty of academic enthusiasm to try to answer the "great divergence puzzle" and the Needham Puzzle, forming various hypotheses that are both complementary and contradictory. The relevant literature is numerous but inconsistent. In a nutshell, a so-called hypothesis of a "high-level equilibrium trap" either occupies the mainstream position or becomes the starting point of most relevant studies,[3] aiming to explain why China cannot embark on the evolution path to the industrial revolution. Such major challenging historical propositions naturally attracted the economists to participate. The most frequent one is undoubtedly derived from the explanation of traditional institutional economics by Douglass C. North, who focused on explaining why China failed to form the institutional change conducive to the industrial revolution.[4]

Existing research results have undoubtedly enhanced our understanding from different angles. However, most of these theoretical explanations have the disadvantage of attributing one proposition to another. To date, we are still looking forward to an answer to the "great divergence puzzle" and the Needham Puzzle, which is more comprehensive in framework, more thorough in theory, and tenable empirically.

As an attempt to pursue this goal, this chapter uses a growth theory that runs through the economic development history as a framework and redefines the "great divergence puzzle" as why the Eastern countries failed to form a mechanism of material capital and human capital accumulation necessary to break the Malthusian equilibrium trap and transform it into scientific and technological innovation so that they not only missed the opportunity of the industrial revolution but also failed to catch up with the last bus. However, the author of this book only focuses on the special Chinese case of this important proposition—the Needham Puzzle. Although the latter statement can be completely consistent with that of the aforementioned "great divergence puzzle," we still need to build a further theoretical base in the following text.

From the discussion in Chapter 2, we can identify four stages of economic development with a time-successive relation from the long-term process of economic history: the Malthusian poverty trap, the Lewisian dual economy development, the Lewis turning point, and the Solowian neoclassical growth. It is easier to master the most important characteristics of each development stage by naming these stages of economic development after economists.

It is a general topic in the study of economic growth theory of how to transform from the previous development stage to the next development stage; it is a topic raised by the "great divergence puzzle" when to specifically answer why the Eastern countries did not take the lead or at least keep pace with the Western countries to get rid of the Malthusian poverty trap to enter the modern economic growth stage; the special purpose of solving the Needham Puzzle is to answer why China did not become the hometown of the industrial revolution and maintain its leading position in science, technology, and economy in history.

Among various growth theories, the theoretical trends in two directions are gradually becoming mainstream. One is to attribute economic growth to whether a society can produce sufficient and good enough inventions, creations, innovations, or, in short, ideas. The other is institutional determinism; that is, economic growth performance depends on whether it can form an institutional arrangement to effectively protect property rights so that inventors and creators can be rewarded. Generally, it determines what kind of economic growth performance can be achieved and even determines the rise and fall of the country when there is an institutional arrangement that is able to protect property rights so that people with ideas can be rewarded. In special cases, it determines whether a country can become the birthplace or the main battlefield of the industrial revolution.[5]

To solve the special obstacles for China to get rid of the Malthusian trap in a targeted manner, it is necessary to make certain corrections or supplements to the abovementioned two growth theory trends. First, ideas must be combined with material capital and human capital before they can be transformed into an engine and fuel conducive to economic growth. Second, human capital is the source of production ideas, while material capital is the carrier of creations and inventions. Moreover, the factors affecting material capital and human capital accumulation are the same. In reality, the two are indispensable and must cooperate with each other. Finally, it is theoretically more sufficient to attribute the source to the unsound incentive mechanism than to the unsound property rights system, which hinders the formation of material capital and human capital because the concept of incentives is more comprehensive. For example, factors to encourage human capital accumulation also include the promotion system and do not exclusively come from the property rights system.

Now, we can redefine the "great divergence puzzle" or its Chinese version, the Needham Puzzle, with a more empirical meaning and try to answer it. The differences in Malthusian-type economic growth between China and the West are shown in different incentive mechanisms of material capital and human capital, i.e., the typical feudal system in Europe and the dynasty and imperial system in China created very different incentive mechanisms.

In other words, in a recurrent poverty trap, there must be conditions available to form a critical minimum capital accumulation and to form a human capital incentive mechanism to combine innovation and production activities; otherwise, the poverty equilibrium trap cannot be broken. Therefore, the "great divergence puzzle" (Needham Puzzle) can be rephrased as follows: Why did the Eastern countries (China) not form the necessary accumulation mechanism of material capital and human capital to break the Malthusian equilibrium trap in ancient times and transform it into scientific and technological innovations so that they missed the opportunity of the industrial revolution?

China's economy in the Malthusian trap

The economic development of mankind has gone through a long history, and it was struggling in the Malthusian poverty trap most of the time. Growth economist Charles Jones once made the following analogy: Imagine that human history of one million years proceeded from the beginning to the end along the length of a football field. On this timeline, humans were hunters and gatherers until the agricultural revolution, perhaps 10,000 years ago—that is, for the first 99 yards of the field. The height of the Roman Empire occurs only 7 inches from the rightmost goal line, and the industrial revolution begins less than one inch from the field's end, known by us to divide the Malthusian era and the industrialized era.[6]

Many economic historians have tried to restore remote data of economic history to reflect the world's economic aggregates and human living standards since the savage days. Although it is difficult for such estimates to make an accurate evaluation, it can finally give us an overall concept; that is, the world's per capita GDP level was stagnant for a long time until 1500, after which it slowly increased, while it was not possible to see the per capita income had been substantially improved until 1800, the representative year of the industrial revolution (Figure 3.1), and the great divergence occurred just after that.

In this long historical process of world economic development, China is not only an extremely important component but also has a special significance. China's population has always accounted for a huge share of the world's total population. For example, Jianxiong Ge estimated that at least since the first year CE, the proportion of China's population has been approximately 20–30% of the world's population.[7] China's high proportion in the world's population has remained unchanged until now. Correspondingly, China's economic aggregates have naturally accounted for a huge share of the world's economy.

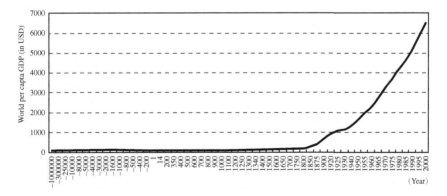

Figure 3.1 The stagnation of the world's per capita GDP and its growth

First, according to Maddison's estimate, China's GDP accounted for 32.9% of the world's total in 1820, while it remained at approximately a quarter in more than a thousand years before that.[8] Therefore, in a certain sense, China's economic development represents the general trend of world economic development. Second, the most important event in the world economy, the great divergence, also takes it as its representative event that China lagged behind the economic development of Western Europe. From these two perspectives, this chapter explains China's long-term economic development—the struggle in the Malthusian trap, the stagnation after the great divergence, and the revival trend and prominent position in the new round of convergence—and explains and understands the world economic development and a number of puzzles reflected in academia.

China's economic development in the premodern period not only had the same characteristics as those in the rest of the world before the industrial revolution—that is, it had always been in the Malthusian poverty trap—but also had a unique feature; that is, it was alternately in a high-level equilibrium trap and a low-level equilibrium trap. As revealed from the observation about the "great divergence" of the world economy, China's economic aggregate was still greater than the sum of Western European countries until the first half of the 19th century (Figure 3.2).

However, this was not enough to draw the conclusion that China's economic development performed better and the per capita income level was higher because throughout the whole Malthusian era, China's total population was significantly higher than that of Western Europe, and the closer it was to the

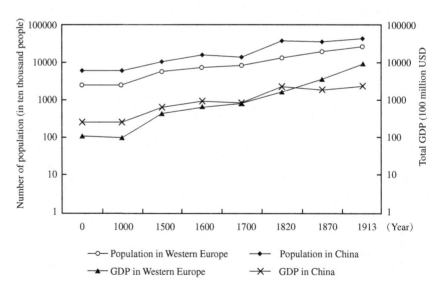

Figure 3.2 Comparison between Chinese history and Western European history: total size of population and economy

industrial revolution or the turning point of the "great divergence," the more China's population growth rate was ahead of Western Europe. Therefore, in terms of per capita GDP, China's early economic development featured a high degree of stability and long-term stagnation, but later, it quickly lagged behind Western Europe.

The living standard of the Chinese people was highly stable and stagnant over a long period of time in history. The per capita GDP was not always lower than the world average, but it started to lag behind the average level of Western European countries at least after 1500. According to the per capita GDP data compiled by Maddison, from 1500 to 1820, China's per capita GDP remained unchanged at US$600, while the average level of Western European countries increased from US$774 to US$1232. After that, the gap widened more rapidly. When it came to the eve of the industrial revolution, China's stagnation became a typical backward end in the "great divergence," in contrast with the rapidly improved living quality in Western Europe.

The grand proposition thus put forward is undoubtedly why the Chinese economy was often in a state of high-level equilibrium but always stood still and was even quickly behind the trend, that is, the Chinese version of the "great divergence puzzle"—the Needham Puzzle. A smaller but indispensable proposition in the logical process to answer the abovementioned larger proposition is how the "high-level equilibrium trap" characteristic of the Chinese economy could coexist with its high degree of stability and stagnation.

If only from the perspective that before the industrial revolution China's economic aggregate was huge and continuously grew and could stimulate population growth and feed a huge population, we may say the history of China's economic development featured a high-level equilibrium trap. However, the subsequent argument shows that this feature does not necessarily mean that China was ahead of the world in terms of technological development, economic growth, and living standards in history, nor can it be used to indicate why there was a widened development gap between China and Western countries in the watershed of the industrial revolution.

For thousands of years, China maintained a high level of equilibrium trap, but it eventually lagged behind the economic development of Western Europe, which must mean that China's economic development has a special performance of stepping forward without moving forward, thus repeating itself. Therefore, we need to examine the nature of fluctuations in China's economic development throughout history to determine the logic behind it, to explain the fluctuations and stagnation when it was eventually washed away by the world history trend to the other end of the "great divergence."

Since the per capita income level remained long unchanged in China's history, we cannot see the fluctuation of economic development by observing this statistical indicator and thus cannot describe the dynamics of economic growth based on this. However, as seen in Figure 3.2, the long-term stability of per capita GDP is actually because the change effect in economic aggregate is just offset by the population change, which happened to be the way

Malthusian mechanism works; that is, population growth is the result of increased income level. However, population growth will subsequently reduce per capita capital and output levels, thereby diluting per capita income and pulling the economic development level and living quality back to the original point. Therefore, it is methodologically well grounded and beneficial to use the dynamics of population change in history as a proxy indicator of long-term fluctuations in economic development.

Historians summarized the time series data of the total population in Chinese history based on historical records, where there are many problems, but no consensus has ever been reached in academic circles. The factors affecting the data accuracy and identification, just to name a few, mainly include statistical caliber issues, such as the number of men used to replace that of women and the number of family households used to replace that of people in the official statistics in some historical periods; statistical scope issues, such as changes in territories leading to inconsistency in demographic statistics; and routine issues such as missing data and unclear records.

Therefore, the estimates provided by various studies vary greatly. Since the purpose of this chapter is not to discuss the historical changes in population size but to reflect the recurrent stagnant state of economic development with its volatility, we refer to the research of John Durand and compile to list time series data for as many years as possible.[9] From the perspectives of the population fluctuation trend shown in Figure 3.3 and the economic fluctuations and stagnation behind the assumption, the data series is far from satisfactory. The trend is consistent with the general belief of Chinese and foreign historians that the rise and fall of the population in Chinese history is a regular phenomenon, reflecting the ups and downs of economic development.

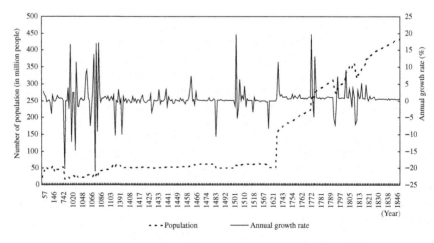

Figure 3.3 China's population change over its long history

It must be noted that this study, the source of China's historical population data shown in Figure 3.3 is rather old. Compared with more recent studies, the data series from Durand showed a significant difference in that the estimated total population of China before the 17th century was much lower than that in other studies.

First, from the starting point, Durand's estimate was 21 million in 57 CE; Jianxiong Ge's estimate showed 60 million in the first year CE;[10] and Maddison's estimate was 40 million in 50 CE.[11]

Second, for the years when the Chinese population exceeded 100 million, Durand estimated a period between 1626 and 1741; Jianxiong Ge estimated a period between 700 and 1100 CE, and after that, there were also times when it fell below 100 million, such as 75 million in 1400; Maddison estimated it was the year of 1280, but then it fell below 100 million again, and it did not exceed 100 million until 1470, when it generally maintained a level of more than 100 million and gradually increased in fluctuations.

Nevertheless, all estimates of China's historical population have one thing in common; that is, the trend of population change is shown as slow growth in large fluctuations. Therefore, when we take Durand's observations about long-term population change data, the advantage more lies in that we do not focus on the absolute size of the population but mainly observe its fluctuation characteristics so that we can still obtain very useful information behind the stagnant nature of economic growth.

Although there is a large span of missing data and lost information that may cover the possible fluctuation characteristics, the macro characteristics of population change can still be revealed; that is, over the period of 1,793 years covered by the data series, there was a fierce fluctuation of the population growth rate per annum, i.e., from the highest positive growth of 19.7% to the lowest zero growth and even a negative growth of 21.0%. The variance of the growth rate was as high as 16.4%.

Combining the violent fluctuation of population with the high stability of GDP per capita, we can undoubtedly draw a conclusion: the expansion of the total economic scale has not made China eliminate the Malthusian trap, and whether China is in a high-level equilibrium trap or a low-level equilibrium trap in history, it is a typical interpretation of the Malthusian equilibrium trap and provides empirical evidence for this general theory. In fact, in the era when economic historians can provide the modern statistical index of GDP per capita for our reference, the highest per capita income enjoyed by China before the industrial revolution (1000–1600) was only the world average level.[12]

Hypothesis of "high-level equilibrium trap"

While observing China's long-term stagnant state in the alternating high-level equilibrium trap and low-level equilibrium trap, one cannot help but wonder whether there is truly a Needham Puzzle in the way that Needham meant. In other words, it needs to be re-examined whether China was truly ahead of the rest of the world in terms of technological invention and economic development in the premodern period. Obviously, this is much bigger and more difficult task, and it is not possible to overthrow the conclusion that Needham drew throughout his lifelong efforts with the author's knowledge structure.

Nevertheless, we can see that the relevant literature has opened a small window in Needham's conclusion, which is worth further investigation. To make best use of the advantages and bypass the disadvantages (or someone might think that it is to avoid the important and dwell on the trivial), this chapter raises and discusses this issue from the perspective of economic growth research, but not from the perspective of the technological development history, or even from the perspective of economic history.

To some extent, the hypothesis of a "high-level equilibrium trap" put forward by economic historians such as Mark Elvin is also a deviation from the original meaning of the Needham Puzzle. This school believed that agricultural practice combined traditional technology and production factors to a perfect degree in Chinese history, so it maintained a higher level of subsistence income compared with that of early European history. Therefore, there was rapid population growth, and furthermore, it aroused a highly strained man–land relationship. Accordingly, it led to too much and too cheap labor, so labor-saving technology was not required.[13]

It can be seen that this hypothesis itself negated the claim that China was ahead of Western Europe in science and technology and economic development in the premodern period when it took the period represented in its research (generally the Ming and Qing dynasties). Assuming that the per capita income level can comprehensively reflect science and technology development and system maturity and that the per capita GDP data provided by economic historians are not in the wrong direction, the conclusion is self-evident. It can be said at least that even though ancient China was ahead of the rest of the world with numerous inventions and creations, these inventions and creations were not transformed into science and technology to be applied to economic activities, so China did not occupy a world leading position in terms of economic development level.

In addition, from the perspective of economic growth theory and historical experience, such resource endowments of large populations and high man–land ratios do not constitute fundamental obstacles to innovations, inventions, and technological progress.

First, a large population does not inhibit technological progress. In a growth model that combined population growth with technological change, Michael Kremer assumed that the opportunity for each person to create and invent had nothing to do with the total population. Therefore, countries with large populations will have a larger number of innovations, although population growth caused by technological progress will in turn dilute the per capita income in the Malthusian development stage. His quantitative studies of history verify the conclusion from the empirical perspective.[14]

Second, the man–land ratio will not constitute an obstacle to technological progress. The theory of induced technological change points out that technological change is induced by the relative scarcity of production factors and thus by relative prices.[15] Under the condition of an imbalanced man–land ratio, even though the resource endowments of surplus labor and scarce land do not induce labor-saving technological changes, land-saving technological changes can still improve production efficiency, and this does not mean technological stagnation.

In another study, although Justin Yifu Lin did not challenge the conclusions of Needham, he admitted that in the premodern period, China's leading technology, active market economy, and prosperous cities made it hard for Western European countries to match. However, when answering "Needham's Mystery," he explained why China's technological innovation was at the leading level in the world in the premodern period, especially in the 8th–12th centuries, because of the large amount of "trial and error" and the high probability of success, as well as the greater technological demand generated by higher productivity. However, China failed to change the invention and innovation from the "probability trial and error" mode to the "active experiment" mode in the 18th century, which explains why the scientific and technological revolution did not happen in China.[16]

Although Justin Yifu Lin was critical of the hypothesis of the "high-level equilibrium trap" for solving the Needham Puzzle, he actually used the "high-level equilibrium trap" as previously defined by the author to answer the first half of the Needham Puzzle. Nevertheless, the significance of this explanation is that it proves that both China and Western Europe had the opportunity to realize technological inventions in the premodern period.

When analyzing modern economic growth, economists do not regard the availability of technology as a constraint factor to analyze whether economic growth is successful. For example, Stephen Parente and Edward Prescott pointed out that the existing stocks of experiences, ideas, and scientific knowledge in the world are available to every country and every company. Therefore, this is not the cause of differences in total factor productivity.[17]

For a long time, all countries in the world have had mutual economic exchanges, so this conclusion is more or less applicable to economic growth in the premodern period as well. If we take a specific regional scope as the object of investigation, whether it is a unified regional power, a loose or tight empire or a region composed of several city states, principalities or princes, as long as there is population migration, trade or even war between them, it is bound to form exchanges of ideas, technologies and even institutional forms so that countries can accumulate their own knowledge stock by learning from each other and imitating each other. Such exchanges of politics, commerce, technology, and even thoughts develop with the overall progress of human society and complement each other. Policies at the national level can be open or closed, while in reality, political, cultural, and technological communications caused by population movement have never been banned.

The history of thousands of years clearly recorded by human beings provides sufficient evidence for such knowledge to flow within specific regions and even across regions. For example, the early Romans knew to introduce Etruscan craftsmen to improve their skills, rape the Sabine women to balance the sex ratio, and send the Senate to study Greek law; during the Spring and Autumn Period and Warring States Period, there were business transactions among different kingdoms and the vertical and horizontal alliance of states with the state of Qin as a pivot. The "all roads" built during the expansion of ancient Rome and the "vehicles on the same track" in the Qin Dynasty of China not only carried soldiers and merchants but also naturally included the exchanges of ideas and skills from various countries.

The Silk Road, which started more than 2,000 years ago, opened the business, cultural, technological, religious, and diplomatic links between China and West Asia, Central Asia, the Arab world, and even Europe through land and sea. The Arabs played a crucial role in recording, preserving, and disseminating European civilization and further in communicating science and technology between China and the West. For example, although the Chinese empire formed during the Qin and Han dynasties did not directly converge with the two empires of Greece and Rome in Europe, it already had direct contacts with the two empires of India and Persia in the East and had some communications with the West through them and the affiliated areas of the two empires in the West.[18]

After the Han Dynasty, especially when it came to the Tang and Song dynasties, there were more frequent exchanges on politics, business and trade, culture, and religion between China and the outside world. Some capital cities, such as political and cultural centers and thriving commercial cities, were crowded with people and even attracted a large number of foreigners. If it is said that the Eastern Expeditions of the Christian Crusades had indirect communications with China through the Arab world, Genghis Khan's Western Expeditions expanded direct communications with the Western world.

The more direct and large-scale exchanges between China and Europe started in 1517 at the latest when the Portuguese merchant ships arrived in Guangzhou. After the Yuan Dynasty and even in the Ming and Qing dynasties, when China was generally believed to have begun to close the door, there were still many foreigners, such as Marco Polo and Matteo Ricci in China. Some foreigners came to China to travel as missionaries. When they lived in China for a long time, some later acted as consultants for the central government and upper-class intellectuals to provide policy advice in fields such as scientific principles, calendars, agriculture, water conservancy engineering, military industry, economics, and commerce.[19]

When a country with a large population (such as China) and the sum of several small countries (such as Western Europe or the whole of Europe or even the whole of the West) are compared (in fact, the Needham Puzzle focuses on the differences between these two regions), the differences between Chinese and Western technological invention modes in the premodern period mentioned by Justin Yifu Lin will be greatly reduced or even no longer exist. The assertion in Needham Puzzle that China's science and technology were ahead of the world in the premodern period mostly used enumeration methods, giving examples that a certain technology was first invented in China, and it did not appear in Western European countries until years and years later.[20]

Conversely, similar examples with the opposite order of invention can also be cited. For example, although Euclid's *Elements* was published more than 2,000 years ago, it was in 1607, more than 400 years ago, when Matteo Ricci and Xu Guangqi translated it into Chinese together. Therefore, when the world becomes more or less "flat," the priority of the listed inventions can disappear in academic discussions.

In other words, once the application, its scope, depth, and subsequent effects of creations and inventions are taken into account (for example, it results in a series of other creations and inventions and even socioeconomic consequences), the issue of invention rights is almost meaningless. The more significant problem is that under the condition that the opportunities for invention creation are roughly the same, the institutional environment for innovation will appear in places where the demand is stronger, thus forming path dependence, and technological progress will develop rapidly. If there is not enough incentive to apply the corresponding inventions and creations to economic activities, various inventions produced under high-level equilibrium conditions will not help to break the Malthusian equilibrium trap.

For example, the steam technology and lever equipment invented by the Romans, the wheels invented by the Mayans and the Aztecs, the high-quality steel made by the Hyderabad people in India, the gunpowder, papermaking technology, printing technology, and compass invented by the Chinese people, and the three-masted sailing ship[21] are all well-known examples of creations and inventions that were not transformed into necessary innovations in their birthplaces, so they were unable to promote economic development.

A particularly typical example is that of China's "four great inventions," namely, the inventions of gunpowder, the compass, printing technology, and papermaking technology, praised by Bacon as having the power and influence to change the entire world. However, they were spread through direct and indirect channels, and were first applied in Europe, which led to a substantial expansion of its commercial activities at the right time, accelerated gestation and occurrence of the industrial revolution, and rapid transformation of the economic system.

Incentives for human capital and material capital accumulation

Under the conditions that there are roughly the same chances for potential inventions and creations and the probability of success, if the incentive for human capital and material capital accumulation is missing in any society, it is not possible for it to produce enough innovations and inventions to promote technological progress and economic growth. The incentive mechanism of such capital accumulation fundamentally lies in the institutional arrangement; that is, only under a certain appropriate institutional environment will the main body for economic activities have a strong motivation for human capital and material capital accumulation. Regardless of the reason for the initial institutional arrangement and how it works under specific historical conditions, it will eventually produce corresponding path-dependent results.

We find that the early history of every corner of the world has to go through the process from tribes to tribal alliances and then realize annexation, union, and the establishment of kingdoms through war. Naturally, the next step was to unify separate and scattered small kingdoms to a large empire or nation. In fact, all major civilized areas were full of repetitions and changes of unity and alternating of divided kingdoms and unified empires in thousands of years of development history.

As proven by historians, China's history cannot be simply summarized as a long and highly unified one,[22] but after Qin Shi Huang unified China, the more frequent, mainstream, and normal form of governance was top-down management by the central government (imperial dynasty) through the management system of departments at different levels and regions, such as the state government, prefectures, counties, provinces, and ministries, as well as unified national defense, tax, and household registration systems. The centralized state has always existed, so it is opposite to the feudal system in Western Europe, in which rights and obligations were divided between kingdoms and enfeoffment lords.

In the process of forming and developing the Western feudal system, the relation between the monarch and the local lords was a typical enfeoffment relation, that is, the former enfeoffed the land to family members, war heroes, and nobles, which was the so-called feudal system of "enfeoffing the land to rule." In return, the monarch demanded that the lords and nobles serve in wars that could break out at any time, especially when a permanent national army was not yet set up. This kind of military service provided by the feudal lord with the identity as a knight or armed leader, as well as the quick action, was a contractual relationship between the monarch and the lord, and the legitimacy of the monarch's ruling was established.

In contrast to the West, China's feudal society is atypical. Since a unified central empire was set up at an earlier time, the relation between the imperial dynasty and local officials and gentry was not a typical contractual relationship but an authoritarian hierarchical structure, i.e., the so-called Chinese feudal system of "centralized system to rule," and the legitimacy of imperial ruling was not built on reciprocity with local officials and nobles. Therefore, it was the fundamental and only guarantee of legitimacy to establish feudal ideology and ritual rules supplemented by the authority conferred by the monarchy and the central military power. The difference in the legitimacy of feudal regimes between China and the West in ancient times produced huge differences in material capital and human capital accumulation under the Malthusian poverty trap.

In Western Europe, once the reciprocity between land-centric property and military services was implicitly or explicitly determined in the form of a contract, the lords who obtained such resources as fief enjoyed the same legitimacy of property rights. Economic growth and resource appreciation achieved accordingly were also guaranteed by property rights. Therefore, the lord was a class that is close to economic activities and benefits directly from them and obtained stable incentives to promote the economic prosperity of the territory.

In addition, even the unstable factors of property rights became an incentive for economic development. In many cases, foreign invasion and looting by neighboring lords might cause property damage or even loss. Therefore, it was the only effective way to protect private property to build as strong a castle as possible with one's utmost economic strength and technical ability. Whether it was to protect homes and defend the land or to attack cities and seize territories, it was undoubtedly closely related to the economic development level of the manor or territory.

Under such an institutional framework, the elite class could obtain enfeoffment by fighting for the king, expand their wealth by becoming organizers for the local economy or even high-ranking monks, or rob or erode the wealth of other manors until they entered the ruling class. This objectively formed a strong incentive to develop the local economy.

Historian Niall Ferguson argued that in European history, the competitions among hundreds of political units (such as countries) or autonomous bodies (such as autonomous cities) and the greater number of companies with them, trade unions and hierarchies provided the competitive impetus for economic development.[23] Many economic historians have also found evidence to support this hypothesis from European history. Although many documents were completed independently and might not directly correspond to each other, the argumentation process of economic historians can still be sorted out according to the following logic.

D.S.L. Cardwell pointed out that most societies can only maintain technological creativity in a relatively short period of time.[24] This conclusion is called the Cardwell Law. However, other scholars believe that it might be true for a single European society, but it might not be true for the entire European continent composed of divided societies. For example, Nathan Rosenberg and L.E. Birdzell, Jr. believed that in Western history, if a political body failed to gain industrial and commercial advantages through technological changes, it would lose to a rival with a competitive relationship. Therefore, such competition among political bodies can restrain the political resistance of interest groups to technological progress.[25] Joel Mokyr used the method of econometric history to test this, proving that the Cardwell Law was not applicable to such situations, as there was competition among diversified independent economies in European history.[26]

It can be seen from history that due to the competitive pressure among economic autonomous bodies, it is necessary to break the barriers of vested interest groups to innovation and form incentives to allow and encourage technological innovation. In this process, it was more important to understand the requisites to make such incentives effective, i.e., that these autonomous bodies should have the natures of economies of scale, clear property rights, and internalization of revenues.

In ancient China, because the emperor was in a high position and far away from people, the central government was not directly involved in general production activities, except for the necessary infrastructure constructions, such as building the defensive Great Wall and constructing large-scale water conservancy facilities, which needed to mobilize the national forces and organize economic activities. The local government, as an agency of the central government, was accountable only to the central government and had no direct interest relationship with the local economy. Therefore, economic development was only the superposition of the decentralized economic activities of every household. As Marx described, such decentralized small-holding peasants "are formed by the simple addition of homologous magnitudes, much as potatoes in a sack form a sack of potatoes."[27]

Such a typical peasant economy (the landlord economy was usually shown as an individual tenant economy) had greater flexibility and vitality, and many institutional forms—such as the free sale and purchase of land—were also conducive to promoting economic activities, but there was a lack of competition among economies to generate pressure for technological innovation, and there was also a lack of an intermediate level with direct interests and large-scale economies to organize and motivate technological innovation. It impeded material capital accumulation and made it difficult for wealth growth and capital accumulation to reach a critical minimum scale, thus preventing technological advances from achieving revolutionary breakthroughs.

At this point, an extremely important factor related to the accumulation of human capital has become clear. That is, since the relation between the monarch and the lord in Western Europe was more similar to a reciprocal and contractual relationship, in which the legitimacy of the monarchy was rooted, there was no need to form a mechanism that tirelessly required the lord to express his loyalty to the monarchy. This is why there was no system formed in early Western society that hindered human capital accumulation, such as the civil-service examination system. Moreover, the fierce competition among various local autonomous economic units and the desire for revenues made the lords, nobles, and city rulers willing to fund and encourage all kinds of talents to exert their creativity.

It is well known that almost all great classical musicians and painters, without exception, were protected and nurtured by royal families and nobles; in fact, scientists and inventors, more often various craftsmen and artisans, were also funded and protected by rulers of autonomous bodies. Furthermore, economic development and artistic creation are also relevant to and interlinked with technological invention.[28] For example, a classic example is that Leonardo da Vinci, adept in arts, inventions, and manufacturing, was directly employed by the nobles of the commercial autonomous city of Florence and rulers of other regions, and his creations and inventions were protected and funded.

The thirst for talent will inevitably intensify the competition for talent, generating demands to nurture talent, and then the development of education. What is not well known is that the wool processing industry in Great Britain, which played an important role in promoting capitalism development and the industrial revolution, benefited from the British King Henry VII, who personally planned to openly study the development experience in the "low countries" and secretly competed for skilled workers.[29] As early as the end of the 9th century, the first university in the modern sense appeared in Europe. Later, universities sprang up in various places, and what was taught expanded from theology to the literature, law, medicine, and natural sciences.

Since Joseph Needham himself, most scholars have listed the imperial examination system as stifling the creativity of talent, failing to realize the transformation to the experiment-based scientific and technological innovation mode, and finally becoming the institutional shackles that hinder the development of Chinese science and technology. However, there are few satisfactory research conclusions on how this talent idea and system that inhibits innovative thinking and rejects invention creation is induced.

In fact, the institutional basis for the formation of the imperial civil examination system also lies in the differences between Chinese and Western feudal systems. In ancient China, when the legitimacy of imperial power was more dependent on the demonstrative identification and loyalty of elites at all classes to the central authority, the Confucianism of self-discipline and rites was inevitably chosen as the main ideology. Following Dong Zhongshu's "ousting a hundred schools of thought and respecting Confucianism alone" in the Western Han Dynasty, the imperial examination system was formed in the Sui and Tang dynasties with the sole intent of explaining the ideology of the ruling class and loyalty and lasted for more than a thousand years, which was a logical result.

Such an imperial civil examination system was regarded as an open system for the selection of officials, and it only played a role in guiding all elites (and potential troublemakers) to enter the ruling class through the only selection method. After the imperial civil examination system was established, in the Tang Dynasty, it was clearly stipulated that merchants and craftsmen were not allowed to take the examination, completely cutting off the genetic link between the social elite and the main body of capital accumulation. Under this elite selection system, expressing the recognition of the mainstream ideology, demonstrating the legitimacy of imperial rule, and being loyal to the system became the promotion path of elite talents.

If Wang Anshi's reform of the imperial examination system in the Northern Song Dynasty still focused on reciting Confucian classics and righteousness and highlighted morality (loyalty) as the ultimate criterion for selecting candidates and obtaining talent loyal to the imperial dynasty, then in the

Ming and Qing dynasties, the implementation of the imperial examination system became a big stage for stereotyped writing, cronyism, and exclusion of dissidents.

However, in the institutional environment where the imperial examination system guides intellectuals' orientation, science and technology and technological skills all became wicked tricks, which were shameful to mention, and education had no connection with science and technology, finance, and even people's livelihood. Therefore, the imperial examination system firmly blocked the road of human capital accumulation that was beneficial to scientific and technological innovation.

After a macro comparison for the material capital and human capital accumulation models in China and Europe in the pre-industrial revolution period, it is easy to make another answer to the Needham Puzzle from the perspective of economic growth. Although the whole world is in the Malthusian poverty trap, China fell in the high-level equilibrium trap early or may often be in the high-level equilibrium trap. However, such a phenomenon of alternating low-level equilibrium traps and high-level equilibrium traps is nothing more than just a mapping of a political cycle (sometimes a natural cycle) in economic rise and fall.

It was widely observed by historians that the feudal society of China was featured with the political cycle that "rise abruptly and perish rapidly," and even the general public was familiar with it. In fact, such a political cycle and economic rise and fall are mutually cause and effect. Regardless of China and the West, the rulers in feudal society were often in a state of legitimacy crisis. In other words, the feudal regime was in an alternating cycle of "legitimacy window of opportunity—anxiety about legitimacy—legitimacy crisis."

Robert Dahl pointed out that people's recognition of the government's effectiveness will increase, weaken, or change people's trust in the authority or legitimacy of the government. Because of the periodicity of the government's performance and the resulting trust, a reservoir of legitimacy is formed, which is in a state of being full, scarce, or even dry in different periods.[30]

According to this principle, Figure 3.4 is used to explain the above mentioned recurring political cycle. In the figure, D represents the "water line" of legitimacy meant by Dahl. Once it falls below this critical point, the legitimacy of the regime will be severely threatened and challenged. Starting from origin O, the area shown in OO_w represents a legitimacy window of opportunity, which can be the beginning of a new dynasty, or the effect of various efforts to enhance legitimacy. In the area represented by O_wO_a, anxiety about legitimacy appears with the diminishing marginal effects of the aforementioned efforts conducive to enhancing legitimacy. This situation often leads to the extremity in the efforts to enhance legitimacy, which is so distorted that it goes too far, ultimately leading to the legitimacy crisis period represented by O_aO_c. Once the regime falls into this stage, the ruling will inevitably end either by being replaced with a new regime or by being self-adjusted after violent turbulence and reforms, when a new cycle of ruling will start.

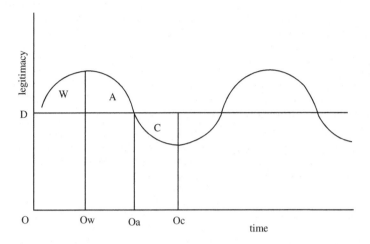

Figure 3.4 Legitimacy cycle of a feudal dynasty

Under the enfeoffment system of Western Europe, whenever such a legitimacy crisis arose, influential parties such as monarchs and nobles would usually renegotiate contracts based on the relative changes in power, without eliminating and harming the existing economic incentives or further hindering the normal accumulation of material capital and human capital. When China was ruled by the central imperial system, there were practices to help the people recuperate, reduce the burden of tax, and expand territories in efforts to repair and enhance the foundation of legitimacy, but in most cases, it was ultimately reflected in advocating divination, strengthening the power centralization, reducing the power of vassals and suppressing the powerful, and controlling capital.[31]

When the effect of such efforts is beneficial to the economy and people's livelihood, it will form a legitimacy window of opportunity. When the effect of such practices diminishes or when such types of ruling measures go too far, which may further harm the economy and people's livelihood, it will form a new round of legitimacy crisis. However, no matter which situation occurs, none of them can fundamentally change the accumulation mechanism of material capital and human capital.

The more feudal society came to its end in China, the more serious and frequent legitimacy crises it encountered, the less often the legitimacy window of opportunity appeared and the shorter the time it lasted. Because of the intense anxiety of legitimacy and its frequent and repeated attacks, the ruling means become increasingly extreme; instead, it pushes it into a deeper crisis of legitimacy, and it is difficult to return to a new window of opportunity.

For example, Qin Shi Huang's burning books and burying Confucian scholars is not an isolated case in history. During the Qing Empire, when the territory reached the widest and the commodity economy became more developed, in the process of compiling the *Imperial Collection of Four* under the official auspices, thousands of ancient books that did not conform to the mainstream consciousness or violated the taboo of rulers were banned and tampered with. The prevalence of literary inquisition fully reflects that "preventing people's mouths is better than preventing floods." Ultimately, the advantages of China's feudal social and political system were maximally suppressed, while its disadvantages were maximally exposed, making it unsustainable. When Europe gradually accumulated the necessary material capital and human capital for the industrial revolution by upgrading from a low-level trap to a high-level trap, China did not enter this stage of development and missed the opportunity to realize the industrial revolution.

Conclusion

The history of scientific advance indicates that when previous scholars put forward academic puzzles out of limited knowledge and curiosity, it inspired the latecomers to dedicate themselves and make unremitting explorations. Therefore, these puzzles have played a unique and important role in academic development. The rich research results about the "great divergence" and its Chinese version, the Needham Puzzle, have thus far greatly enhanced people's understanding of the issue and enriched and developed the study of economic history. However, in contrast to natural science, social science has a shortcoming that is difficult to overcome; that is, related hypotheses cannot be tested under fully controlled conditions. Economic history takes past events as the research object, which makes this shortcoming even more prominent.

Therefore, there is actually no ultimate answer to such questions about economic history as the "great divergence" and the Needham Puzzle. As such, these questions are more fascinating and have obsessed researchers in related fields throughout time. As the economist Mankiw said, once one starts thinking about the mysteries in economic growth, it is difficult to think about other things.[32]

As far as the "great divergence" and the Needham Puzzle mentioned in this chapter are concerned, all the efforts of scholars ultimately only serve such a purpose (in fact, this is the only purpose); that is, by answering such puzzles, to put forward respective hypotheses from different perspectives and compete with each other, open up scholars' visions, expand the dimensions of thinking, and extend the reach of each independent discipline; at the same time, in the process of trying to conduct empirical tests, to discover and accumulate more experiences and materials, enrich the human academic library to finally enhance people's understanding of economic history, economic reality and the laws of future economic development.

By properly positioning the discipline, this chapter examines the Needham Puzzle from the dimension of economic growth, and its purpose is also limited to proposing an alternative new angle and a new framework to organize historical materials and documents. In this chapter, the author attempts to answer the Needham Puzzle as a key link in the four types or development stages of human economic growth. Any research must seek deep roots from past thoughts and experiences and should not expect to reinvent all analytical tools.[33]

This chapter tries to absorb and digest achievements in related fields as much as possible and, on this basis, proposes a hypothesis that expects to arouse attention; that is, the differences in the framework of feudal systems between China and the West induced different material capital and human capital accumulation (and its incentive) mechanisms, which ultimately resulted in major differences in technological development and economic growth performance and prevented China in the premodern era from forming the critical minimum size of capital accumulation required to break the Malthusian equilibrium trap, resulting in a "great divergence" with Europe at a specific point in time.

History can be a mirror for the present, and it also helps to learn about history to understand reality. In terms of its framework, the theory of interpreting history should also be applicable to analyzing real problems. However, it is not possible to simply compare history with reality. People are accustomed to thinking or hoping that history and reality can be mirrors of each other, and it makes people smart to learn from the past and use the past to allude the present. Nevertheless, the long distance of the times has inevitably caused profound optical mutations in this mirror. It is a subject that far exceeds personal ability and imagination and is even more complicated and bigger than the "great divergence puzzle" and the Needham Puzzle to clear the dust of history and unify the analytical framework of history and reality, so that is why it is so fascinating. It is hoped that this chapter will be a useful beginning for such an academic pursuit, and it is also hoped that the retrospect of China's past economic development will be helpful to understand its present and future.

Notes

1 K.G. Robert Temple, *The Genius of China: 3000 Years of Science, Discovery, and Invention*, London: Carlton Publishing Group, 2007, p. 11.
2 See Kenneth Pomeranz, *The Great Divergence: Europe, China and the Making of the Modern World Economy*, Nanjing: Jiangsu People's Publishing Ltd., 2003, for representative and influential literature which resulted in the formation of a famous school (known as the "California School" because most of the main scholars taught at the University of California).
3 Mark Elvin, *The Pattern of the Chinese Past: A Social and Economic Interpretation*, Stanford: Stanford University Press, 1973.
4 Douglass C. North and Robert Paul Thomas, *The Rise of The Western World: A New Economic History*, Beijing: Huaxia Publishing House, 1999.
5 In addition to the literature from Douglass C. North et al., see also Charles Jones, *Was an Industrial Revolution Inevitable? Economic Growth Over the Very Long Run*, NBER Working Paper, No. 7375, 1999.

6 Charles Jones, *Was An Industrial Revolution Inevitable? Economic Growth Over the Very Long Run*, NBER Working Paper, No. 7375, 1999.

7 Jianxiong Ge: *The History of Chinese Population, Volume I*, Shanghai: Fudan University Press, 2005, p. 147.

8 Angus Maddison, *The World Economy: A Millennial Perspective*, Beijing: Peking University Press, 2003, pp. 259, 238.

9 John D. Durand, The Population Statistics of China, AD 2–1953, *Population Studies*, Vol. 13, No. 3, 1960, pp. 209–256.

10 Jianxiong Ge: *The History of Chinese Population, Volume I*, Shanghai: Fudan University Press, 2005, p. 147.

11 Angus Maddison, *Chinese Economic Performance in the Long Run*, Beijing: Xinhua Publishing House, 1999, pp. 280–281.

12 Angus Maddison, *Contours of the World Economy, 1–2030 AD: Essays in Macro-Economic History*, Oxford: Oxford University Press, 2007, Table A.4 (p. 379), Table A.7 (p. 382).

13 For example, see Daniel Little, *Micro Foundations, Method and Causation: On the Philosophy of the Social Sciences*, New Jersey: Transaction Publishers, 1998, Chapter 8: The High-level Equilibrium Trap, pp. 151–169.

14 Michael Kremer, Population Growth and Technological Change: One Million BC to 1990, *The Quarterly Journal of Economics*, Vol. 108, No. 3, 1993, pp. 681–716.

15 Gustav Ranis and John C.H. Fei, A Theory of Economic Development, *American Economic Review*, Vol. 51, No. 4, 1961, pp. 533–565.

16 Justin Yifu Lin, *The Needham Puzzle, the Weber Question and China's Miracle: Long Term Performance since the Sung Dynasty*, CCER Working Paper Series, No. E2006017, November 22, 2006.

17 See Stephen L. Parente and Edward C. Prescott, *Barriers to Riches*, Beijing: China Renmin University Press, 2010, Chapter 6.

18 Da Xiang, *The History of Communication between China and the West*, Changsha: Yuelu Press, 2011.

19 Da Xiang, *The History of Communication between China and the West*, Changsha: Yuelu Press, 2011.

20 For example, K.G. Robert Temple, *The Genius of China: 3000 Years of Science, Discovery, and Invention*, London: Carlton Publishing Group, 2007, pp. 278–282.

21 William Easterly, *The Elusive Quest for Growth: Economists' Adventures and Misadventures in the Tropics*, Beijing: CITIC Publishing House, 2005, pp. 160–161.

22 Jianxiong Ge, *Reunification and Split: A Lesson from Chinese History*, Beijing: The Commercial Press, 2003, p. 65.

23 Niall Ferguson, *Civilization*, Beijing: China CITIC Press, 2012.

24 D.S.L. Cardwell, *Turning Points in Western Technology*, New York: Neale Watson, 1972, p. 210.

25 Nathan Rosenberg and L.E. Birdzell Jr., *How the West Grew Rich: The Economic Transformation of the Industrial World*, New York: Basic Books, 1986, pp. 136–139.

26 This is mainly summarized based on an article by the economic historian Joel Mokyr that combines the nature of literature review and fact checking. See Joel Mokyr, Cardwell's Law and the Political Economy of Technological Progress, *Research Policy*, Vol. 23, 1994, pp. 561–574.

27 Karl Marx, The Eighteenth Brumaire of Louis Bonaparte, in *Marx Engels Werke*, compiled by the CPC Central Committee Compilation & Translation Bureau

of the Works of Marx, Engels, Lenin and Stalin, Volume 2, Shanghai: People's Publishing House, 2009, pp. 566–567.

28 Economist John R. Hicks pointed out that "Perspective once caused a revolution in the paintings of Florence and Venice in the 15th century. If one wants to explore how perspective was first introduced, he'd better to seek explanations from commerce." John R. Hicks, *A Theory of Economic History*, London: The Commercial Press, 1987, p. 54.

29 Ha-Joon Chang, *Kicking Away the Ladder: Development Strategy in Historic Perspective*, Beijing: Social Sciences Academic Press, 2009, pp. 20, 21, 64.

30 Robert A. Dahl, *Polyarchy: Participation and Opposition*, New Haven and London: Yale University Press, 1971, pp. 124–188.

31 Mu Qian, *The Political Gains and Losses of Chinese Dynasties*, Hong Kong: SDX Joint Publishing Company, 2001, pp. 170–173.

32 Quoted from Robert J. Barro and Xavier Sala-i-Martin, Foreword, in *Economic Growth*, Beijing: China Social Sciences Press, 2000.

33 Karl August Wittfogel, *Oriental Despotism: A Comparative Study of Total Power*, Beijing: China Social Sciences Press, 1989, p. 26.

4 Dual economy as a general development stage

Introduction

As the Western saying goes, Rome was not built in a day. However, in the eyes of Western scholars for economic growth, not only was Rome built in just a day, they even think that Rome has always existed. The neoclassical growth theory represented by Robert Solow has long recognized only one type of economic growth and never distinguished the development stages. This unique type or stage of economic growth is the so-called neoclassical growth, or Solowian growth. The growth theory that defines the type of economic growth takes Solow as a representative and has been formed under the framework of neoclassical economics.[1]

Such growth theory usually focuses on three sources of growth: capital accumulation related to the savings rate, supply of labor restricted by population growth, and productivity brought about by technological advances, institutional change, and other efficiency improvements, especially total factor productivity.

A priori assumption of such theory is that the supply of labor is restricted by population growth, so the phenomenon of diminishing returns to capital will inevitably occur. This assumption has two extended meanings: First, backward economies can achieve faster growth rates than developed economies, thereby forming a convergence of economic development levels; second, a country's long-term and sustainable economic growth can only come from an exogenous source other than production factor contribution, i.e., the so-called Solow residual or total factor productivity.

As an alternative to the post-Keynesian growth theory—Harrod–Domar Model—the neoclassical growth theory and a series of economic growth theories derived from this theoretical model, such as the Cass–Koopmans–Ramsey Model, endogenous growth theory, conditional convergence hypothesis and testing, have more or less explanatory power for the growth source and growth mechanism of contemporary developed economies. However, these theories can be applied neither to interpret the traditional economy of the typical poverty trap type nor to interpret contemporary developing countries with dual economic characteristics. Therefore, it is beyond the

DOI: 10.4324/9781003329305-5

power of these theories to answer the rise and fall puzzle of countries in the sense of economic history or to try to provide policy advice for developing countries to catch up.

Mankind has a long historical memory of being in the Malthusian poverty trap, and contemporary poor countries are still in the underdeveloped non-neoclassical stage, which requires economists to stop turning a blind eye in the research perspective and furthermore to abandon the prejudice of impractical solutions in theoretical analysis.

It is worth mentioning in economics history that it was not until the 21st century that important economists admitted that there was indeed a Malthusian growth stage before Solowian growth, and they tried to put two stages or types into a unified analytical framework.[2] One of the authors, Edward C. Prescott, also felt that there should be a transitional growth stage between the Malthusian stage and the Solow stage.

Masahiko Aoki proposed a transitional Kuznets stage (K stage) based on the experience of East Asian economic development to emphasize the characteristics of its industrial structure change.[3] Aoki reluctantly used the Lewis model to interpret this development stage and claimed that the Lewis model mechanically integrated two different models: the classical model with unlimited supply of labor and the neoclassical model with a fully competitive labor market. Nevertheless, the author guessed that because Lewis's analytical methods and theoretical assumptions were far from the neoclassical criteria, he insisted on naming this development stage after Kuznets but refused to take Lewis. Therefore, accepting Lewisian dual economic development as a mainstream development type or stage is bound to be more difficult to control from the perspective of methodology and concrete analysis, so that the consistency of theory cannot be maintained.

To present a full description of the human experience and the history of economic growth that is being experienced, the previous parts of this book divide economic growth into four types or stages that ensue in time and coexist in space, namely, the Malthusian poverty trap (M-type of growth), Lewisian dual economy development (L-type of growth), Lewis turning point (T-type of growth), and Solowian neoclassical growth (S-type of growth). This division aims to explain the catch-up process of late-mover countries and the evolution process of early industrialized countries in a logic that is interconnected and even causal. It not only grants the dual economic theory greater explanatory power but also enhances the tolerance of economic growth theory.

The key part of Lewisian dual economic theory is that there is a surplus of labor in traditional sectors so that a country can achieve economic development on the condition of unlimited supply of labor by transferring between two sectors.[4] Lewis seemed to discover the relation between demographic transition and dual economic structure, and such a relation can be verified by the reality of many contemporary developing countries. However, he himself and his followers tended to exclude the early industrialized countries from the dual economic model.

Previous studies generally believed that the demographic transition in developing countries had an exogenous nature. For example, industries introduced from developed countries and enterprises helped to form modern economic growth sectors, and foreign medical and health technologies could quickly and significantly reduce the death rate; in contrast, these processes were endogenous in the early industrialized countries, which occurred slowly in the long development process.

However, if we can determine that this difference between the late-developing countries and the early industrialized countries is not the fundamental difference between existence and non-existence but only the degree of difference between fast and slow or between obvious and hidden in statistical sense,[5] then the development process of the dual economy can become the general stage of economic development, and Lewis's theory should be given more attention. Accordingly, the theory of economic growth is facing a great challenge of remodeling or even rebuilding.

To interpret the differences between China and the West into modern economic growth, economic historians put forward a concept of economic involution and launched a heated debate on it, providing a large amount of historical evidence and its extended and respective, very different interpretations. Of course, many of such different materials and their interpretations aimed at answering why the "great divergence" of the world economy began in 1800, or for China, it aimed at answering the Needham Puzzle.[6]

The purpose of this chapter is not this, but to try to avoid this kind of argument, to jump out of the fragmented historical materials, integrate the recognized historical facts that have been excavated from the perspective of economic growth, and demonstrate that there is a process of involution of traditional economy in history, whether in the West or the East. Different from the Malthusian poverty cycle, the process was the starting point of demographic transition in the modern sense, so it was the early process of forming a dual economic structure. Once the modern economic growth department has the condition to expand along with absorbing surplus labor force, the Lewisian development process of the dual economy will begin.

In terms of methodology, in this chapter, the discussion will continue from three dimensions and serve the three purposes accordingly.

First, as far as economic growth theory is concerned, a complete analytical framework is missing for the moment that integrates theoretical logic with historical logic. To contribute to the formation of this analytical framework, we attempt to fill in an important logical fault zone in neoclassical growth theory with Lewisian dual economic theory. Therefore, this chapter intends to reveal that regardless of the historical stage in China and the West, there will be a period when a large amount of surplus labor will be accumulated in agriculture, resulting in subsequent dual economic development.

Second, as far as the history of economics is concerned, when Lewis's development theory is integrated with neoclassical growth theory into a complete framework, it will not only help the former to regenerate and become the mainstream but also significantly enhance the theoretical explanatory power of the latter.

Third, as far as economic history is concerned, in view that a consensus is missing among researchers on the theoretical framework and methodology, drawing lessons from the unified framework and hypothesis of growth theory may help economic historians understand and elaborate historical logic and reverse the fragmented tendency in analyzing historical data to borrow from the unified framework and hypotheses of growth theory.

Back to classical economy

Lewis pointed out at the beginning of his most important essay that the paper was written in the tradition of classical economics to make assumptions and ask questions.[7] He claimed that the core of going back to classic economics lay in that Smith and Marx both observed that an unlimited supply of labor could be obtained by living wages in the early days of capitalism. However, Lewis also claimed to focus on the reality in contemporary (observed around the 1950s) developing countries and humbly admitted that the assumption of an unlimited supply of labor was not applicable to the United Kingdom and the developed countries in Northwest Europe.

Lewis divided a typical developing economy that fit his model into two sectors. He himself and later discussants often used different expressions to define the two. Here, we call them the traditional sector and the modern growth sector. The former is represented by agriculture. In traditional departments, because the labor force is surplus relative to land and capital, it is characterized by large-scale accumulation of surplus labor force. The latter is represented by industry. In the modern growth sector, the speed of industrial expansion and the speed of capital accumulation determine how fast the surplus labor force of traditional departments can be absorbed.

Lewis tried to demonstrate the existence of this dual economic feature, which was neglected by mainstream neoclassical economics in developing countries but did not truly return to the research object of classical economics that year, so he also laid the groundwork for himself to be forgotten again by mainstream economics later. For example, the development economist Gustav Ranis found that Lewis's theory is not accepted by the mainstream economics of Anglo-Saxon tradition, and the key point lies in his view that wages are not determined endogenously by the relationship between supply and demand but are determined exogenously by the characteristics of high population density according to specific institutional arrangements.[8]

After in-depth observations of contemporary developing countries, many researchers have gradually tended to admit that the theoretical summary of the dual economic theory for these developing economies is valid.[9] However, since the Lewisian hypothesis is not yet believed to have explanatory power for the experience in the early development of developed countries, this theory is still marginalized. Therefore, if theories and facts can prove that the early industrialized countries also experienced the development process of dual economy, the explanatory power of Lewisian dual economic theory can be enhanced in depth and breadth so that this theory can be saved in the sense of economics history.

Smith actually solved a contradiction in the driving force of capital accumulation in the Lewis way. He observed that manufacturers engaged in capital accumulation needed more laborers, and such greater demand for employment tended to increase workers' wages above the "natural" price, thus leading to a decline in capitalists' profits and placing the accumulation process in danger of suspension.[10]

Nevertheless, Smith discovered a law in the meanwhile: "just as the demand for other commodities inevitably dominates the production of other commodities, the demand for population will inevitably dominate the production of population";[11] that is, the increasing demand for laborers tends to increase wages above the survival level to stimulate population growth, while population growth expands the supply of labor, thereby inhibiting the continued increase in wages. When wages are lowered below the survival level again, the profits of capital accumulators can be maintained.

We can also explain this mechanism in a neoclassical way and with counterfactual analysis. Under the assumption of labor shortage, neoclassical growth theory draws the conclusion that too much capital investment relative to a limited labor force will lead to diminishing returns to capital. With the counterfactual analysis law, we can see that once the assumption of labor shortage is broken, the phenomenon of diminishing returns to capital will be curbed, and economic growth can be achieved under the condition of increased input. This type of growth is, by nature, Lewisian dual economy development.

It is worth noting that Smith started to write *An Inquiry into the Nature and Causes of the Wealth of Nations* in 1764, and it was not published until 12 years later. Even though the book is regarded as the pioneering work of modern economics, the industrial revolution had not yet been completed at the time of Smith's writing, and the economic growth on which modern economics is based had not yet taken shape.

Even more paradoxically, Smith's research was claimed to be evidence-based, but he led a secluded life during his writing. He had neither personal experience nor direct observation of economic reality, nor sufficient and constantly updated books and materials.[12] Therefore, in fact, his observation object was the same as Malthus's to a considerable extent. In other words, the research object of Smith was actually a transitional growth period at the end of the Malthusian growth type and before the formation of the modern economic growth type. Different from Lewis 200 years later, Smith was confined to the observation of a specific period and did not know how to accurately define the nature of this period by dividing the development stages and could not accurately summarize the unique economic growth types of this period, thus forming a theory of economic development.

On the surface, the "law of population demand" observed by Smith was very similar to the vicious cycle of poverty described by Malthus, but in fact, the former discovered "a clever mechanism" during the specific period of British economic development that population growth could suppress wage increases. Obviously, that was not what the Malthusian development stage could have. In fact, this is precisely the mechanism of Lewisian dual economy development.

This chapter intends to prove that the phenomenon observed by Smith and expressed as a stylized fact to a certain extent is no longer a Malthusian poverty trap but is closer to a Lewisian growth type; in other words, he discovered the prerequisites to lead to the Lewisian dual economy development. It is just because of such an inheritance relation between Smith and Lewis, rather than a certain inherent connection with Malthus, that he deserves to continue to hold the throne as the founder of modern economics.

It is inappropriate to say that Smith discovered the core connotation of the Lewis model. This expression certainly does not conform to the order of elders and juniors, nor does it conform to the order of historical development and the logic of theoretical formation. The correct statement should naturally be that Lewis followed Smith's tradition and promoted Smith's vague observation of the theoretical model of economic development. Unfortunately, Lewis did not bravely take the next step, that is, applying the dual economic theory to understand and explain the early economic growth of European countries. Neoclassical economic theory or the neoclassical explanation of the history of economic development in the classical period is so powerful that the latecomers with the most innovative ability will inevitably hesitate, eventually being unable to get rid of the fate of being restricted to the concept, and fail to completely part way with the former.

Population growth as take-off condition

Economic growth in the Malthusian era was not completely stagnant but evolved at an extremely slow speed. Therefore, the Malthusian growth type was not always the same at all times and places. Generally, the Malthusian equilibrium means that any disturbance conducive to income increase is short-lived. Income higher than the subsistence level will lead to an increase in the birth rate and a decrease in the death rate, thereby increasing the natural growth rate of the population and further causing the deteriorating population–land relationship; as a result, the severity of land pressure will eventually pull per capita income back to the equilibrium level that is just enough for survival.

However, economic historians found that Western Europe was still in the Malthusian trap long before the industrial revolution, for example, in 1700, and the per capita income was significantly higher than that of the rest of the world.[13] Other economic historians discovered a unique phenomenon in China, i.e., the so-called "high-level equilibrium trap."[14] Are these two phenomena a deviation from the Malthusian trap, are neither of them, or do they represent different and even exactly opposite situations? Such questions must be answered in order to solve the "great divergence puzzle."

Before answering the above questions with confidence, we can put aside the reasons for higher per capita income in Europe and the formation of a high-level equilibrium trap in China. Let us first look at the result caused by this unexpectedly higher income level in the subsequent era—long-term population growth that occurred but may continue or may be interrupted.

According to the data provided by Yujiro Hayami,[15] during the period from 1000 to 1750, most regions in the world experienced extremely slow long-term population growth, and the average population growth rates per annum in that period were 0.13%, 0.14%, and 0.09%, respectively, in Europe and regions its descendants lived, Asia, and Africa without large differences. However, subsequently, there was a rapid increase in the population growth rate in the regions where Europeans lived, the population growth rate in Asia was steadily stagnant, and Africa once experienced large fluctuations. For example, from 1750 to 1850, the average population growth rates per annum were 0.73%, 0.45%, and 0.00%, respectively, in the three regions. The population of European descent reached its growth peak at the end of the 19th century. Asia and Africa achieved rapid population growth around the 1930s, when the population growth of European descent slowed down. For example, during the period from 1900 to 1990, the average population growth rates per annum were 0.91%, 1.48%, and 1.69%, respectively, in the three regions.[16]

It can be observed according to the economic development order that the industrial revolution first originated and spread in Europe and then expanded to the European residential areas on other continents. Except for Latin America, which once achieved a high level of development and then became stagnant in the middle-income stage for a long time, and Eastern Europe, which fell behind, Western Europe, Northern Europe, North America, Australia, and New Zealand have all become high-income developed countries (regions); Asia has also developed rapidly after Japan, the Republic of Korea, Singapore, Hong Kong, and Taiwan took the lead in development; Africa's development started late and is currently accelerating to catch up.

Therefore, it can be seen that the industrial revolution was first realized in the regions where the population grew fast. A much-debated question among economic historians is why Europe, rather than Asia (especially China), became the hometown and growth place for the industrial revolution. In addition, there is another question that must be answered: How can it be distinguished whether a specific population growth is a permanent breakthrough in the Malthusian trap or a temporary deviation from the Malthusian equilibrium? This can be said to be the same proposition as the aforementioned distinction between early European high-income phenomena and China's "high-level equilibrium trap."

According to the data provided by Maddison, Asia produced 61.8% of the world's total GDP until 1700.[17] As the largest Asian country, China contributed 22.3% to the world's total GDP. Since Asia, Japan, and China each had a larger share of the population, the per capita GDPs of this region and these two countries were lower than the world average, but the difference was not large. From 1500 to 1820, the population growth rate in Asia was slightly faster than the average levels of the world and Western Europe, the population growth rate in Japan was slightly lower and that of China was significantly higher than the average levels of the world and Western Europe.

China's GDP growth rate in this period was faster than the world average and maintained roughly the same level as Western Europe. Although its total GDP accounted for 32.9% of the world's GDP, China's per capita GDP was not only significantly lower than that of Western Europe but also lower than the world average by 1820 due to its fast-growing population. Although Japan and other Asian countries were different from China in many aspects, Asian countries showed roughly the same trajectory in terms of their per capita incomes lagging behind the average levels of Western Europe and even the world.

It is worth noting that during the subsequent period from 1820 to 1870, both China's GDP and population fell into negative growth. Since then, as a representative country on the disadvantageous side in the global "great divergence," the development gap has greatly widened between China and Western countries.

If the so-called "great diversion" period of economic historians is defined as the period from 1600 to 1950,[18] it could be seen that the picture presented at one end of this divergence was that the industrial revolution originated in the United Kingdom and quickly spread to Northwestern Europe and North America and even the whole West, while the picture at the other end was that countries in Asia and Africa continued to be deeply stuck in the Malthusian poverty trap. The "great divergence" was shown as the increasing gap in per capita GDP. However, for the purpose of this chapter, we do not intend to examine the divergence of per capita income but to return to the differences in population growth.

When understanding historical population growth and making international comparisons, we are often confused by the unstable and even fractured changes shown by the data. For example, China's population grew rapidly from 1700 to 1820, which was much higher than the average of the 12 countries in Western Europe and that of Japan in Asia. However, it fell sharply for the following long period, and it even experienced negative growth during the period from 1850 to 1870 (Figure 4.1).

To remove the disturbance factors from the long-term trend, here is the criterion to judge whether the population change in a country conforms to the staged trend summarized by the demographic transition theory. The demographic transition theory points out that after experiencing the Malthusian "high birth rate—high death rate—low (natural) growth rate," the demographic transition will enter the new stage of "high birth rate—low death rate—high (natural) growth rate" with the substantial increase in per

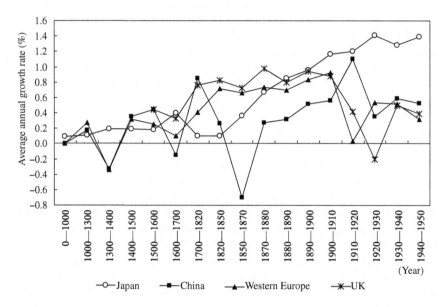

Figure 4.1 Comparison of population growth rates across countries in the long run

capita income, so that it will subsequently form a stage of "low birth rate—low death rate—low (natural) growth rate" at a higher level of economic development.[19]

This demographic transition is of essential significance and has been confirmed by historical data. Therefore, it is particularly worth emphasizing that it begins with the steady reduction in the death rate.[20] Economic historians have sufficient evidence to indicate that from the second half of the 18th century, the traditional Malthusian population suppression mechanism changed in Western Europe. "The phenomena of population crises caused by long-term poor harvests in agriculture and infectious diseases have gradually decreased. By the 19th century, it has almost completely disappeared."[21]

In other words, only when the death rate drops substantially and the high birth rate still continues can the natural growth rate of the population increase greatly. We can thus establish the following criteria: The demographic transition associated with economic development is a long-term regular trend and is the initial representation bypassing the Malthusian trap. Otherwise, it is a disturbance change caused by special or cyclical factors, indicating that a country has not yet eliminated the Malthusian trap.

According to this criterion, Figure 4.1 shows that among the economies being compared, the order of population growth acceleration is exactly the same as that of economic take-off. Whether in terms of the time to enter the post-Malthusian demographic transition trajectory or in terms of the time to have the conditions for economic take-off, the non-Western world lagged significantly behind European countries, which happened to constitute the so-called "great divergence" era.

The population in Western Europe (the most representative country is the United Kingdom) was long in an upward trend from 1700, and due to its endogenous nature—that is, affected by economic and social development—it gradually entered the normal trajectory of demographic transition with the death rate decline as the main mechanism, permanently getting rid of the Malthusian trap.[22]

Therefore, such a population growth trend continued until Western European countries became developed economies and entered the third stage of demographic transition, when population growth began to slow down significantly in the 20th century. For example, the population numbers in England and Wales provided by Kuznets fully demonstrated the change process and mechanism.[23] After the mid-18th century, the death rate continued to decline, but the birth rate remained relatively stable until the mid-19th century and did not decrease significantly until the beginning of the 20th century. Therefore, the natural growth rate of the population showed an inverted U-shaped trajectory.

As the first country in Asia to undertake the industrial revolution, Japan did not see fast population growth until 1870. It was not until after World War II that Japan became an advanced economy when its demographic transition entered a higher stage and its population growth slowed down significantly.

The population growth in China underwent a far more complicated and tortuous process of change. As shown in Figure 4.1, in more than a century from 1700 to 1820, the average growth rate of the population in China per annum was as high as 0.85%, which was not only significantly higher than that of Japan (0.10%) and the average of 12 Western European countries (0.41%), it was even higher than that of the United Kingdom (0.76%). However, the following reasons can make us refuse to make the judgment that China had started to get rid of the Malthusian trap.[24]

First, grain tax based on population was decoupled during this period, eliminating local officials' worries about increasing taxes with increased people. Therefore, much historical data revealed that China's population grew rapidly in the 18th century. This may be due to the incentives for the actual reported population, leading to the exposure of the previously hidden population but not entirely new increments.

Second, starting in the mid-17th century, American crops such as corns, sweet potatoes, and peanuts were introduced and popularized, and they helped China make fuller use of marginal land, increase agricultural production, and improve its ability against famines, which undoubtedly played a significant role in stimulating population growth. On the other hand, although this effect was gradually shown, it was ultimately a one-off effect.

Finally, the trend of rapid population growth in the 18th century did not continue after all, indicating that the Malthusian trap, as a mechanism to maintain a highly stable equilibrium state, was still working. The population growth rate began to decline from the beginning of the 19th century and once even fell to a negative number. It was not until the end of the 19th century that it started rapid population growth again; however, it reached the highest growth rate in the second decade of the 20th century (the average growth rate was 1.1% per annum from 1910 to 1920) and fell again after that.

After the founding of the People's Republic of China, the well-known population growth type in China was as follows: it completely followed the demographic transition law and finished the complete cycle of demographic transition in a relatively short period of time at a rate much faster than that experienced by developed countries. Meanwhile, since the reform and opening-up in 1978, China has created a miracle of rapid economic development, entered into the ranks of upper-middle-income countries from the ranks of low-income countries, and it is transforming to a high-income country.

Agricultural involution and the formation of dual economy

People think that the concept of dual economy originated from Lewis. In fact, to be more accurate, Lewis first created the dual economy development theory. However, just as any theory has its academic origins and any great theory must stand on the shoulders of giants, the connotation of Lewis's dual economic concept should undoubtedly come from far-reaching observation and generalization of Clifford Geertz.[25] According to the interpretation of Geertz's works by later generations,[26] we can determine where his contribution lies and its connection with other theories and observations.

Let us first look at what causes the so-called agricultural involution. Whenever and wherever, the increase in agricultural labor productivity will usually produce surplus labor. At this time, if the conditions are ripe—i.e., factors for modern economic growth already exist, other industries representing these new factors can expand normally and have the ability to absorb the transferred surplus labor, and there are no institutional or policy obstacles for labor transfer—then expected changes in industrial structure, the economic development process, or evolution will take place. If colonial policies and government deprivation policies, urban preference policies, or any other distortive policies prevent agricultural employment from turning to non-agricultural employment, surplus labor will accumulate in agriculture, leading to agricultural involution.

From the interpretation of Geertz's text, it can be seen that involution is actually the antonym of evolution. Therefore, if the latter is understood as outward evolution, the former can be understood as inward evolution. Since farmers are rational and determined by the close nature of the community in traditional society, they obviously do not truly distinguish which labor force is surplus and let it do nothing, but they have to make at least two adjustments to cope with it. Observing these two adjustments, we can also reveal the two internal meanings of involution.

First, under the condition of traditional farming practice, excessive refinement farming is implemented with non-modern factors and means, thus maintaining the rigid and unchanging agricultural production approach. In essence, this is still traditional agriculture as defined by Schultz. That is, when agriculture has the possibility of differentiation, specific institutional arrangements will neither destroy nor reform the traditional smallholding economy but keep it at the previous living level by inhibiting labor transfer, forming a solidified dual economic structure.

Second, since surplus labor cannot be transferred, it means that the labor force must share labor opportunities. Correspondingly, in the sense of Lewis's theory, each labor can only obtain a shared wage lower than the marginal labor productivity level; when Geertz emphasized the concept of involution itself, it included the meaning that peasants would not be divided, so he called it shared poverty. Later, researchers believed that this was exactly the reason why the conditions for economic take-off were not formed in those involution societies (such as the hypothesis of the "high-level equilibrium trap" discussed in Chapter 3).

Is there a way to get a country out of such an involution state? If so, are there different types? What do the differences between them mean and what do they not mean? It is of great significance to our discussion to answer these questions. As a matter of fact, all the patterns we have seen from the traditional agricultural society to modern economic growth are based on this involution state.[27] The difference only lies in the duration of staying in the involution state, and the path taken in the transformation process may be radical or gradual, thus resulting in different consequences. From a historical perspective, we can see several different paths and results.

The first situation is to use certain compulsory means. The British Enclosure Movement and related legislation were among the most famous methods, which were to squeeze the surplus labor out of traditional agriculture to gather a huge reserve team for industry and form an opposition between a large production system and a smallholding economy. As the former destroyed the latter, the capitalist economy developed. In fact, the evolution process of this path is also in multiple models, with the British Road, the Prussian Road, and the French Road being among the ones often mentioned. However, the general and common feature of these "roads" is often forgotten, that is, the agricultural involution stage before changes.

The second situation is that through the development of the dual economy, modern economic growth continuously expanded, and the traditional agricultural economy gradually modernized with the declining share. This change continued until the Lewis turning point was reached, and the characteristics of the dual economy eventually disappeared. In this path, it is easy to see that agricultural involution as a starting point did once exist.

The third situation is long-term stagnation in agricultural involution, forming a rigid dual economic structure. Generally, people do not describe this situation as stagnation in involution but only stagnation in traditional agriculture under the dual economic structure. For example, in fact, Schultz's research on "transforming traditional agriculture" is aimed at involution agriculture.

The evolution process of economic history is not like a continuous function, which can be defined as the slight and continuous change in the dependent variable caused by the change in the independent variable approaching zero. Because as far as the development events of human society are concerned, we simply cannot think exactly what degree of adaptability should exist between independent variables and dependent variables to distinguish continuity from discontinuity. Although Lewis revealed a special type of dual economy from the observation of the late-developing countries, both the agricultural involution and the economic duality of these countries existed in the development process of the early industrialized countries, but the process was too slow to be clearly observed.

Traditional economic involution before take-off

The traditional concept regards the continuous growth of the population over a long period of time as a sign of economic take-off. Economists believe that it was the industrial revolution that broke the Malthusian poverty trap, and per capita income was no longer pulled back to the subsistence level due to the hard restriction of the population–land ratio, so that population growth could overtake the Malthusian equilibrium that dominated human production over a long period of time and realize the real economic take-off.

For example, Kuznets summarized the stylized facts of (early) modern economic growth, and the first was "the high rates of growth of per capita output and the high growth rate of population achieved by developed countries."[28] Observations by demographers and the demographic transition theory abstracted from this supplemented the views of economists that rapid population growth could initially serve as a condition for economic take-off, and the subsequent period was the result of economic development entering the modern stage. Further economic development will lead to a slowdown in population growth. Regarding how population became the condition and starting point for the industrial revolution or economic take-off and what the mechanism was, there are abundant clues in economic growth theories and the literature of economic history, but there is no clear or systematic theoretical summary.

However, it is very important to answer such questions. It is not only helpful to judge whether and when an economy has achieved breakthroughs in the Malthusian trap so as not to be confused by the appearance of history but also a very important logical link to construct an analytical framework for understanding the history of economic development.

The author constructed a framework of four stages (types) for long-term economic development. At first, the initial acceleration of population growth, which is the first turning point in the stage of population transformation, plays an important role in economic take-off by helping a country form a traditional economic sector in the dual economy defined by Lewis, and then there will be a subsequent development stage of the dual economy. According to the generally accepted understanding of the dual economy, its essential characteristics and working conditions lie in the fact that a large amount of surplus labor accumulates in the agricultural economy so that the marginal productivity of labor is very low, and the remuneration of laborers cannot be determined by this. Rural families can only share the average labor productivity of agriculture through institutional arrangements.[29]

In the typical Malthusian poverty trap, the surplus of agricultural labor is not normal. It is true that there is such a stage in the Malthusian vicious cycle; that is, the income increase driven by some accidental factors leads to excessive population growth, thereby increasing the population–land ratio and thus generating a population force that once again pulls the real per capita income back to the survival level.

However, the demographic pressure formed at this time more often refers to newborn babies and minors in other age groups. In most cases, before they grow into the labor force, the Malthusian vicious circle once again enters a stage where only the minimum survival level can be maintained, regenerating the force to suppress population growth. In rare cases, such a cycle may last for more than a generation and then return to the traditional equilibrium in more painful suppressing ways (such as large-scale disasters and wars).

In contrast, the dual economy with surplus labor will be created only when there is a trend of rapid population growth that follows the laws of demographic transition, and this trend continues to a new stage that affects the age structure of the population, while it steadily generates economic and social forces sufficient to curb periodic natural and man-made disasters. The key to understanding the making of a dual economy lies in revealing how large-scale surplus labor is accumulated in agriculture. To distinguish whether a phenomenon of population growth is the result of entering a new trajectory of demographic transition, or still a representation in the Malthusian trap, the most direct way is to see whether the observed population growth can continue for a long time until a country enters the dual economic development and even the neoclassical growth period.

For many economic historians, the process of forming a large-scale and serious surplus labor force in agriculture is characterized by the involution of agriculture. Regarding the comparison between China and Europe before or at the beginning of the "great divergence," most studies focused on the Jiangnan region of China and the United Kingdom. Based on almost identical observation objects and different interpretations of the observed results, economic historians reached different conclusions.

For example, Philip Huang compared agriculture in the Yangtze Delta with that in the United Kingdom in the 18th century and found that the former was obviously involuted, so there was no demand for labor-saving technologies and agricultural capitalization as in the UK.[30] In his view, only the labor productivity improvement caused by the increase in material capital can produce "development" in the modern sense. Since China experienced agricultural involution, there has been no agricultural revolution at all, not to mention any hint of industrial revolution.

According to economic theory, technological change in agriculture is not simply the improvement of labor productivity, but the improvement of land productivity can also be the means of agricultural revolution in the case of a high population–land ratio, but this is not the core of the dispute. The focus of the dispute in our concern is whether the United Kingdom experienced the same "involution" of agriculture sooner or later, and when a comparison was made for agriculture in the 18th century, were the two sides arguing about the same thing?

The opposite side of Philip Huang's argument was represented by Kenneth Pomeranz, who believed that there were numerous surprising similarities for what happened in agriculture in both China and Western Europe at that time. Pomeranz cited plenty of historical data to point out that from 1500 to 1800 it was also common in Europe that agricultural output expanded because more labor input was used, rather than any breakthrough in productivity.[31] He not only disagreed to take England and Jiangnan of China as "the two ends of the continuum with opposite nature from development to involution" but also opposed to take the labor-intensive trend as the opposite side of early modern development.[32]

With regard to this, Peter Kriedte's statement was more straightforward. In his works describing the primitive industrialization in the United Kingdom, it was found that the involution of English agriculture was no difference from the "economic development under unlimited supply of labor" summarized by Lewis, and he further concluded that the applicability of Lewisian dual economic theory to Europe's primitive industrialization even exceeds that of contemporary underdeveloped countries.[33]

The observations and analysis of Pomeranz and others have much in common with economic theories and the views of economists, so they can be interpreted by economic theories. For example, according to the research of Yujiro Hayami and Vernon Ruttan, under different conditions of production factor endowment, the path of agricultural technology change can be different. According to the relative scarcity of land, agricultural technology change may be of the fully labor-using (capital-saving) type or the labor-saving (capital-using) type.[34]

On the other hand, the highly (or even excessively) intensive labor input may also occur in the typical traditional agriculture that has not yet got rid of the Malthusian trap. For example, Theodore Schultz pointed out that even in traditional agriculture, poor peasants can make the most effective allocation of their limited resource endowment.[35] In other words, if the population–land ratio is too high and the laborers do not have any opportunity cost (income from non-agricultural work), they will be highly intensively involved in

agriculture, and the marginal productivity of labor will not be zero or negative. It can be imagined that such labor input will inevitably reduce the marginal productivity of labor, but still increase output more or less, forming a
shared but varying level of subsistence income.

Both parties to this famous argument in the study of economic history
shared valuable historical data with us and put forward meaningful and
insightful conclusions. However, only when the relevant research results
are integrated under a unified theoretical framework and based on seeking
common ground while reserving differences is it possible to form a conclusion
with theoretical explanatory power for economic history.

The debaters unanimously regarded the United Kingdom as the epitome
of Western Europe and even the West on the one hand and the Jiangnan (the
Yangtze Delta) region as the epitome of China on the other hand. It can be
said that in view of the representativeness of the United Kingdom to Western
European countries and Jiangnan to China, the comparative study about the
two regions is not a comprehensive or adequate study in terms of explaining
the significant historical puzzle of the "great divergence," but regional study
with typical significance similar to this, after all, provides us with vivid information that is easy to explain with obvious contrast, thereby helping us find
answers to related questions.

As shown in Figure 4.1, regarding the long-term population growth trend,
Western European countries were always in a state of being behind but closely
following the United Kingdom. Combined with the similar status of Western
European countries in the industrial revolution, it can be said that there is no
doubt about the representativeness of the United Kingdom to the Western
world in terms of economic development trends. It is true that Jiangnan has
been a relatively developed region in China all along, but China is a unified
country with population migration and economic activity transfer, and
Jiangnan's population and economic development will not and actually have
not become an outlier at the national level.

For example, according to the population data compiled by Cao Shuji,[36] we
calculated the population growth rate from the middle of the Qing Dynasty
to the beginning of the 20th century and found that the average growth rate
of the Chinese population per annum dropped from 0.47% in 1776–1820 to
0.42% in 1820–1851 and further decreased to 0.00% in 1850–1910. During
the same period, the Yangtze Delta region was a representative place. In
1776, after the population of Jiangsu, Anhui, and Zhejiang provinces were
examined, which accounted for 25.9% of the national population, the trajectory of population change was roughly the same as that of the whole country
(Figure 4.2).

On the surface, the involution tendency of agriculture in the Jiangnan
region around the 18th century was even more obvious than that of the United
Kingdom. For example, according to Robert Allen's calculations, in 1600 and
1800 the labor productivity of agriculture was both high and stable in Jiangnan
region, not inferior to the levels of the United Kingdom, the Netherlands,

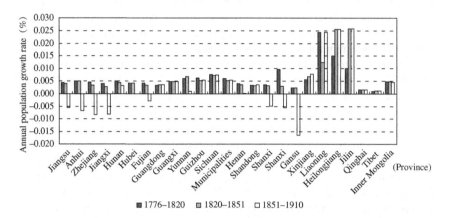

Figure 4.2 Population growth rate by province from the middle of the Qing Dynasty

and Belgium in approximately 1750 at all. Yangtze farms produced almost seven times as much as English grain farms.[37] If the achievement of Jiangnan region was linked with the rapid growth of the Chinese population during the period of 1700–1820, it seemed that we could agree with Allen's conclusion, i.e., it was regarded as a dual effect of agricultural involution and agricultural revolution.

However, the subsequent population growth and the destiny of economic development denied the judgment that China got rid of the Malthusian trap from then. China as a whole did not keep up with the population growth rate of the United Kingdom and Western Europe in the following nearly 200 years, including the Jiangnan region in China. During the same period, population growth in the United Kingdom and Western Europe continued to accelerate. In other words, Europe, represented by the United Kingdom, saw agricultural involution along with population growth, which created conditions to subsequently realize the dual economic development driven by the industrial revolution. For China, the same conditions did not form in a stable manner until the 1950s.

Since what happened in the 18th century was very different in the United Kingdom and Jiangnan region of China, then the development path of Western Europe and China was very different, the widespread use of the concept of "involution" regardless of the occasion would further weaken the usefulness of this concept, which was originally lacking theoretical bases.

After carefully thinking over how Philip Huang, Pomeranz and other debaters used this concept, we find that the phenomenon referred to as involution is actually variable. In an explicit sense, this concept is used to describe the equilibrium state of traditional agriculture under the condition of an excessively high population–land ratio, including the formation of system-determined survival level income and low marginal labor productivity. In an implicit sense, this concept is also used to describe the formation mechanism equivalent to the traditional sector in dual economy development. Only at this starting point will there be a subsequent dynamic development process to release surplus labor.

Therefore, thinking back to the original meaning of involution, it may be said that the concept first used by Philip Huang to describe Chinese agriculture in the 18th century deviated from the real intention of the originator. For example, Geertz, who first used the concept of involution to analyze agriculture in Indonesia, actually reflected a dual economic structure between the island of Java and the outer islands. In fact, in an earlier time, the Dutch scholar Julius Herman Boeke made the concept of dual structure come into being based on observations and arguments of the Indonesian economy,[38] which gave birth to Lewis's theory.

As mentioned earlier, if people discuss the phenomenon that the input of the agricultural labor force is too intensive so that marginal labor productivity is extremely low, either in the typical Malthusian era or in the typical dual economic development, as mentioned earlier, there have been highly conceptualized theoretical models for economic growth theories that are both ready-made and easy to use. The concept of involution is redundant here. If the involution stage is placed at a certain transitional development stage between the Malthusian growth type and the Lewis growth type, it is very appropriate to use this concept to express the formation history of agricultural labor surplus in the dual economy.

In this way, such involution is not what we are concerned about as the cyclical population growth that fails to finally get rid of the Malthusian trap, such as the agriculture in the Yangtze Delta under Philip Huang's focus or the "high-level equilibrium trap" discovered by Mark Elvin. However, the real involution is the population growth and the accumulation of surplus labor force in agriculture, which is shown in the initial stage of permanent population transition.

Overall, involution is a stage to form a dual economic structure and a prelude to subsequent dual economic development, and, of course, it is also the end stage of Malthusian growth. The author takes the liberty of imagining that in the long history of human economic development, perhaps a place should be given to this stage of economic growth. For example, it can be called Geertz involution (or G-type of growth), as a subtype or a substage for M-type of growth to change to L-type of growth.

The author ventures to assume that in the long history of human economic development, perhaps a place should be given to this stage of economic growth.

Conclusion

This chapter sorts out the thoughts and theoretical models of economic growth from Smith and Malthus to Lewis and Solow and tries to reveal the internal logical relationship between different theories and viewpoints on the process and stages of economic growth. Under this analytical framework, while referring to the (although scattered) historical evidence discovered by economic historians, the author finds that if all the economic development that human beings have experienced thus far is divided into M-type growth, L-type growth, T-type growth, and S-type growth, and these types are regarded as a type or stage of Lewis's dual economic development (thus corresponding Lewis turning point or T-type growth), then these unique development stages can be seen not only in contemporary developing countries but also in early industrialized countries.

This discovery fills a gap in the theoretical generalization and modeling of the economic growth history, enabling us to apply a more consistent analytical framework to describe the overall structure of human economic development history and derive more general theories and empirical conclusions.

To judge if the development stage of the dual economy existed in the economic history of China and the West, the key lies in proving if there has been a process of forming a dual economic structure with surplus labor as a typical feature. Here, by distinguishing two different population growth situations, namely, population growth determined by the Malthusian mechanism on the one hand and population growth caused by the demographic transition law on the other hand, it is found that there are actually two completely different types in terms of the over-intensive labor in agriculture. The over-intensive labor caused by the Malthusian population mechanism has nothing to do with the making of a dual economic structure. Only over-intensive labor will become a necessary process to create conditions for subsequent dual economic development, which appears after entering the demographic transition trajectory. For the sake of argument, we only regard the latter situation as the involution process of the traditional economy.

So far, we can use Figure 4.3 to illustrate the main points to form the development stage of the dual economy. First, if a disturbance to population

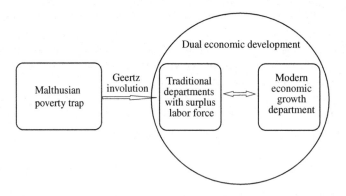

Figure 4.3 Transition from the Malthusian trap to dual economic development

growth is generated only in the Malthusian trap, it will certainly lead to an over-intensive labor input in the traditional economy. However, this situation is not an involution in the sense of this book because the population growth model will eventually return to the Malthusian equilibrium state.

Second, only when population growth breaks through the Malthusian trap in accordance with the demographic transition law can modern economic growth appear at the same time, thus forming the coexistence and interaction of the traditional sector with the labor surplus and the modern economic growth sector to absorb surplus labor, which constitutes economic development or dual economic development under the condition of unlimited supply of labor defined by Lewis.

Third, the successful development of the dual economy will eventually lead to the arrival of the Solowian neoclassical growth stage beyond the scope described in Figure 4.3, so that a country's economic development experiences a complete process from poverty to prosperity, and it is the same whether for the early industrialized countries, emerging industrialized economies, or for contemporary developing countries, whether it is typical or atypical.

In this way, from the perspective of economic growth theory, we can summarize the growth types or development stages to date according to the chronological order in history as follows: M-type of growth characterized by the Malthusian trap, G-type of growth characterized by the Geertz involution, L-type of growth characterized by Lewisian dual economic development, T-type of growth characterized by the Lewis turning point, and S-type of growth characterized by Solowian neoclassical growth.

The modeling ability of economic growth theory is very powerful. Once growth theorists admit based on facts that there are the abovementioned growth types or stages in economic history and that there are inherent logical connections in time (and space) among them, we can expect that an analytical framework or theoretical model with consistency will eventually appear and gradually improve. Although the research work done by the author is preliminary, he still hopes to make a breakthrough in the initially defined goal; that is, to make contributions from the following four aspects.

First, we put forward the subtype of economic development of Geertz involution (or G-type growth) and summarize the historical origin, stages, and mechanism of the formation of the dual economy, making the division of economic growth types and stages logically more complete and laying a necessary cornerstone for constructing a more self-consistent and inclusive growth theory.

Second, since the Lewisian or L-type of growth is prevalent and has been tested significantly in theory and historical logic, the theory of dual economy should occupy a more important position in academic history. Of course, there is still a long way to go for subsequent research in this direction.

Third, the analytical framework proposed here can be used as a basis to integrate data about economic history that have long been used in a fragmented way, increasing the complementarity of research on the same subject, promoting more academic consensus, and eliminating as much as possible the zero-sum nature of the dispute in this field caused by long-term adherence to their respective opinions.

Fourth, the proposal of the analytical framework, all in all, serves to analyze China's economic development in this book. To place the achievements from economic development since the reform and opening-up in a grander historical perspective, we need to look back to a longer history, and we also need to have an internationally comparative perspective.

Notes

1 Robert M. Solow, A Contribution to the Theory of Economic Growth, *The Quarterly Journal of Economics*, Vol. 70, No. 1, 1956, pp. 65–94.
2 Gary D. Hansen and Edward C. Prescott, Malthus to Solow, *American Economic Review*, Vol. 92, 2002, pp. 1205–1217.
3 Masahiko Aoki, The Five Phases of Economic Development and Institutional Evolution in China, Japan and Korea, in Masahiko Aoki, Timur Kuran, and Gérard Roland (eds.), *Institutions and Comparative Economic Development*, Basingstoke: Palgrave Macmillan, 2012.
4 Arthur Lewis, Economic Development with Unlimited Supplies of Labor, *The Manchester School*, Vol. 22, No. 2, 1954, pp. 139–191.
5 For example, it took 84 years for France to reduce agricultural employment share from 52% in 1866 to 33% in 1950 (see Masahiko Aoki, The Five Phases of Economic Development and Institutional Evolution in China, Japan and Korea, in Masahiko Aoki, Timur Kuran, and Gérard Roland (eds.), *Institutions and Comparative Economic Development*, Basingstoke: Palgrave Macmillan, 2012), while it only took 13 years for the ROK in the period from 1968 to 1981 to see a decline of the same percentage with agricultural labor (Cai Fang, *Avoid the Middle-Income Trap*, Beijing: Social Sciences Academic Press, 2012, p. 98).
6 For the most recent representative literature, please refer to Philip Huang, Development or Involution? The United Kingdom and China in the 18th Century: A Review of Kenneth Pomeranz's *The Great Divergence: Europe, China and the Making of the Modern World Economy*, *Historical Research*, Vol. 4, 2002; Kenneth Pomeranz, *The Great Divergence: Europe, China and the Making of the Modern World Economy*, Nanjing: Jiangsu People's Publishing Ltd., 2003.
7 Arthur Lewis, Economic Development with Unlimited Supplies of Labor, *The Manchester School*, Vol. 22, No. 2, 1954, pp. 139–191.
8 Gustav Ranis, *Arthur Lewis' Contribution to Development Thinking and Policy*, Yale University Economic Growth Center Discussion Paper, No. 891, 2004.
9 For example, D. Gale Johnson, an economist of the Chicago School, once held a severely critical attitude toward the discussion and estimate of rural surplus labor. He believed that the concept of surplus labor was wrong and could not be proved in reality. However, after in-depth investigation and reflection on China, he went against the neoclassical tradition and admitted that there were a large number of rural surplus laborers in China, whose productivity was much lower than that of the urban labor force. See D. Gail Johnson, Can Agricultural Labor Adjustment Occur Primarily through Creation of Rural Nonfarm Jobs in China?, in *The Issues*

    of Agriculture, Rural Areas and Farmers in Economic Development, Beijing: The Commercial Press, 2004, p. 65.

10 See Yang Jingnian, Preface by the Translator, in Adam Smith, *An Inquiry into the Nature and Causes of the Wealth of Nations*, Beijing: Shaanxi People's Publishing House, 2011.

11 Adam Smith, *An Inquiry into the Nature and Causes of the Wealth of Nations, Volume I*, translated by Guo Dali and Yanan Wang, Beijing, The Commercial Press, 1996, p73.

12 Gavin Kennedy, *Adam Smith*, Beijing: Huaxia Publishing House, 2009, p. 194.

13 Nico Voigtlander and Hans-Joachim Voth, Malthusian Dynamism and the Rise of Europe: Make War, Not Love, *American Economic Review: Papers and Proceedings*, Vol. 99, No. 2, 2009, pp. 248–254.

14 Mark Elvin, *The Pattern of the Chinese Past: A Social and Economic Interpretation*, Stanford: Stanford University Press, 1973.

15 Yujiro Hayami, *Development Economics from the Poverty to the Wealth of Nations*, Beijing: Social Sciences Academic Press, 2003, p. 56.

16 It is worth pointing out that there are many different estimates and summaries about the historical population data in the world, countries, and China with varying results. The relevant data are quoted here only in the sense that the opinions of each school are consistent with judgments on the trend.

17 Angus Maddison, *The World Economy: Historical Statistics*, Beijing: Peking University Press, 2004, pp. 262–269.

18 Both scholars' analysis and the facts of economic history indicate that with consensus reached, the approximate starting year of the great divergence is undoubtedly the time when the industrial revolution substantially rose in the early 19th century (Kenneth Pomeranz, *The Great Divergence: Europe, China and the Making of the Modern World Economy*, Nanjing: Jiangsu People's Publishing Ltd., 2003). As for the ending year of the great divergence, we can accept Spence's statement that it is 1950, because he believed that just at this time the global economy began a new era of great convergence (Michael Spence, *The Next Convergence: The Future of Economic Growth in a Multispeed World*, New York: Farrar Straus and Giroux, 2011).

19 See John C. Caldwell, Toward a Restatement of Demographic Transition Theory, *Population and Development Review*, Vol. 2, 1976, pp. 321–366, for a brief introduction of the theory.

20 See Massimo Livi-Bacci, *A Concise History of World Population* (fifth edition), , Chichester: Wiley-Blackwell, 2012, Chapter 4.

21 Walt Whitman Rostow, *How It All Began: Origins of the Modern Economy*, Beijing: The Commercial Press, 2014, p. 71.

22 Many researchers in the field of international history believe that the main cause of the population growth in the UK in the 18th century was the increase in fertility (for example, see Jinyao Yu, Review of the Academic History of British Population and Development in the 18th Century, *Historiography Bimonthly*, Vol. 3, 1995). However, the increase in fertility is also related to the increase in economic and social development level, so it does not negate the conclusions drawn in this chapter and the subsequent analytical logic based on this.

23 Simon Kuznets, *Modern Economic Growth*, Beijing: School of Economics Press, 1989, p. 34.

24 If it is said that China's population growth has since then started to have characteristics different from the earlier history, it just reinforced the pertinence to the proposition of Geertz's involution to be discussed later.

25 Clifford Geertz, *Agricultural Involution: The Process of Ecological Change in Indonesia*, Berkeley: University of California Press, 1963.

26 The author here refers to a relatively comprehensive and systematic summary and interpretation. See Benjamin White, *Agricultural Involution and Its Critics: Twenty Years after Clifford Geertz*, Working Papers Series, No. 6, Institute of Social Studies, The Hague, February, 1983.

27 Of course, we do not rule out that in some countries, regions, or communities, there might be such situations as the labor force could not be transferred, and there was no agricultural model of refinement farming. However, the key point is that there is surplus labor. Whether they work in agriculture with extremely low labor productivity or do nothing, they all have the motivation to transfer outward once the conditions are met. Any state of surplus labor can become the starting point of dual economy development.

28 Simon Kuznets, Modern Economic Growth: Findings and Reflections, *American Economic Review*, Vol. 63, 1973, pp. 247–258.

29 Arthur Lewis, Economic Development with Unlimited Supplies of Labor, *The Manchester School*, Vol. 22, No. 2, 1954, pp. 139–191.

30 Philip Huang, Development or Involution? The United Kingdom and China in the 18th Century: A Review of Kenneth Pomeranz's *The Great Divergence: Europe, China and the Making of the Modern World Economy*, *Historical Research*, Vol. 4, 2002.

31 Kenneth Pomeranz, *The Great Divergence: Europe, China and the Making of the Modern World Economy*, Nanjing: Jiangsu People's Publishing Ltd., 2003, p. 86.

32 Kenneth Pomeranz, Late Imperial Jiangnan in World Economic History: Comparative and Integrative: A Discussion with Professor Philip Huang, *Historical Studies*, Vol. 4, 2003.

33 Peter Kriedte, The Origins, the Agrarian Context, and the Conditions in the World Market, in Peter Kriedte, Hans Medick, and Jurgen Schlumbohm (eds.), *Industrialization before Industrialization*, Cambridge: Cambridge University Press, 1981, p.28.

34 Yujiro Hayami and Vernon Ruttan, *Agricultural Development: An International Perspective*, Baltimore and London: Johns Hopkins University Press, 1980.

35 See Theodore W. Schultz, *Transforming Traditional Agriculture*, translated by Liang Xiaomin, Beijing: The Commercial Press, 1987.

36 Cao Shuji, *The History of Chinese Population, Volume V Part 3*, Shanghai: Fudan University Press, 2005, pp. 703–704.

37 Robert Allen, Involution, *Revolution, or What? Agricultural Productivity, Income, and Chinese Economic Development*, Paper delivered at meeting of All-UC Group in Economic History on "Convergence and Divergence in Historical Perspective," Irvine, CA, November, 2002, pp. 8–10.

38 Julius Herman Boeke, *Economics and Economic Policy of Dual Societies*, New York: Institute of Pacific Relations, 1953.

Part II

Narrative of reform, opening-up, development, and sharing

5 What can be learned from China's experiences?

Introduction

The 19th National Congress of the Communist Party of China established Xi Jinping's Thought on Socialism with Chinese Characteristics for a New Era as the guiding ideology that the Party must adhere to and further develop on a long-term basis. In the report of the 19th National Congress of the Communist Party of China, President Xi Jinping pointed out that the Party "has adopted an entirely new perspective to deepen its understanding of the laws that underline governance by a Communist party, the development of socialism, and the evolution of human society. It has worked hard to undertake theoretical explorations and has achieved major theoretical innovations, ultimately giving shape to the Thought on Socialism with Chinese Characteristics for a New Era."[1] The practices of China's reform and opening-up and the promotion of development and sharing are an important source of forming this thought.

Based on the time points of two landmark events, it is believed that China's economic reform and opening-up to the outside world began in 1978.

First, the Third Plenary Session of the Eleventh Communist Party of China Central Committee was held from December 18–22, 1978, which re-established the Party's ideological line of freeing minds and seeking truth from facts, and it was decided to shift the emphasis in the work of the Party to economic construction, laying a theoretical foundation for reform and opening-up.

Second, at almost the same time, 18 households of peasants in Xiaogang Village, Fengyang County, Anhui Province, decided to abandon the labor pattern of the production team and implement agricultural output quotas fixed by households. This pattern was called the rural household contract responsibility system, which was subsequently implemented throughout the country and led to the abolition of the people's commune system. This was the initial breakthrough to the traditional planned economic system. The disruptive institutional innovation by Xiaogang Village is naturally considered to be the first practice of China's economic reform.

DOI: 10.4324/9781003329305-7

China's economic reform and opening-up also occurred at the same time. In April 1979, Deng Xiaoping first proposed establishing "special export zones." In July of the same year, the Central Committee of the Communist Party of China and the State Council decided to establish special export zones (later called special economic zones) in Shenzhen, Zhuhai, and Shantou in Guangdong Province, and Xiamen in Fujian Province, marking the beginning of opening-up. The initial opening to the outside world was experimental and regional, starting with the establishment of special economic zones and opened up coastal cities and coastal provinces; when it came to the 1990s, China made efforts to join the World Trade Organization (WTO) and began to embrace economic globalization in all directions.

China's economic reform is a reform under the conditions of opening-up, and opening to the outside world has also been promoted in the reform process. Domestic economic development and integration into the global economy are intertwined.

In 2018, it was exactly 40 years since the reform and opening-up. Let us use famous words of Confucius here that "at 40, I no longer suffered from doubt." First, 40 years of successful practice has undoubtedly proved the correctness of the path of reform and opening-up with Chinese characteristics; to go further, it can be said that 40 years is a point of time worthy of serious summarizing so that our understanding of reform and opening-up will rise to a higher theoretical level to better guide future reform practice.

In contrast to entering adulthood at the age of 20 and standing firm at the age of 30, having no doubts at 40 means that we have accumulated a wealth of historical materials, cases, and documents and have the conditions to reflect and look forward to China's economic reform more profoundly. Generally, on the basis of mastering more complete and rich materials, the reform process can be recorded more accurately, or theoretical hypotheses can be verified in an econometric way. Meanwhile, it is also necessary to take a comparative angle to put the Chinese story in the perspective of the general development and institutional change laws to make China's contributions to development economics.

Many economists have described and summarized China's economic reform process. Some were limited to specific professional fields,[2] some tried to describe the whole process,[3] and others focused on studying certain key issues, for example, such as whether productivity was improved during the reform period.[4] In general, the research of foreign and overseas economists has a dominant influence on mainstream economic circles. However, these studies generally have some obvious shortcomings. The main shortcomings are directly applying mainstream Western theories to China, comparing Chinese practices with certain existing criteria, and explaining the Chinese experience with neoclassical dogma in addition to misinterpreting the facts due to being away from the locale of the event and insufficient information, which led to misjudging the trends.

In this way, one would either deny the successful experience of China's reform and repeatedly make pessimistic judgments on the prospects of China's economic development,[5] treat the Chinese experience as a special case and deny its general meaning,[6] or extend its general meaning to the consensus among the mainstream Western economics (such as the Washington Consensus). For example, many economists are unwilling to believe in the feasibility of combining socialism with a market economy. Therefore, recognizing the success of China's reform and opening-up will inevitably come to the conclusion that this is the success of capitalism in China.

Steven Zhang firmly believes that China's reform is heading toward capitalism, and he prided himself on predicting early that China will follow this path and be "successful."[7] Huang Yasheng summarized China's reform as capitalism with Chinese characteristics.[8] According to the seemingly self-explanatory logic, what is consistent with it is the reason for the success of the reform, and what is inconsistent with it is used as the basis for making a pessimistic judgment on the reform. Based on a similar framework, a book about China's reform simply summarized it as *How China Became Capitalist* while advocating China's experience. The authors argued that economic transformation in China is an excellent case of Hayek's theory of "unintended consequences of human action."[9]

On the basis of the European traditional dichotomy that human social phenomena included natural results that had nothing to do with human behaviors and the results designed by mankind, Hayek proposed a phenomenon in the middle position; that is, the unexpected result of human behaviors.[10] Regardless of the general value of this dichotomy, explaining China's economic reform with this method is not only a historical nihilistic attitude but also quite close to dogmatic methodology. It regards the institutional innovation activities of thousands of people (urban and rural residents and laborers, entrepreneurs, government and their staff) with the same goals and incentives as nothing. Therefore, such interpretation is undoubtedly not in line with the actual reform orientation and process in China, and it is not conducive to generalizing Chinese wisdom with general significance and deriving Chinese solutions for reference.

Indeed, China's economic system reform did not have a blueprint at the beginning, and it did not determine the direction of establishing a socialist market economy even before the 14th National Congress of the Communist Party of China in 1992. However, given that reform and opening-up aim to improve social productivity, comprehensive national strength, and people's living standards, the logical clues are quite clear for the problems to be solved at each stage of the reform, as well as the sequence and process to advance reform. Therefore, when we review and summarize the course of reform and opening-up in accordance with the thinking method of "unified historical logic and theoretical logic,"[11] it will make it easier to draw conclusions that are consistent with historical facts and inherent logical self-consistency.

Economic development is a complete process that has a beginning and an end, goes from the surface to the center, and combines inside with outside rather than a simple splicing of many independent processes in time and space.

First, the economic level and structural state of any space unit (country or region) at any point in time are the result of past development and the starting point for future development. Where it is from and how it determines the present appearance is something people today cannot choose. However, what the current state is and how one understands today can determine the future; knowing the past is a necessary condition to know today. Choice is very important, and the right choice depends on the right understanding of history and reality.

Second, the economic development of a country or a region takes place in a specific political and economic environment, and it is inevitable to have an interdependent and interactive relationship with the outside world. Therefore, both the successful and unsuccessful experiences in a country or a region are not only the result of its cognition of the outside world but can also become public goods that enhance human knowledge.

Economists are diligently and tirelessly exploring the answer to the rise and fall of a country and how the later-moving developed economies catch up with the first-mover economies. The practice of reform and opening-up in China is the largest and most successful institutional change and innovation in human history. It will eventually realize the complete historical evolution from prosperity to decline to prosperity with a population of 1.4 billion, thus achieving the greatest miracle of human social development.

This chapter provides a logically complete exposition and analysis framework as far as possible. On the premise of referring to relevant achievements, starting from practical experience, it explains why the opportunity of catching up was missed before the reform, briefly describes the reform process according to the logic of combining theory with history, and then tries to answer the following questions: Given the initial conditions of China's economic reform, once the system constraints are lifted, how will the factor accumulation level, allocation efficiency, and potential growth rate be improved? At the development stage of China's economy, how can its driving force of growth be changed, what kind of reforms can achieve new growth momentum, and how can such reforms be promoted?[12]

China's reform and opening-up, in many respects, undoubtedly has the nature of institutional change in the general sense, but in the meanwhile it has its own distinct characteristics. As a model country that has gone through various types and stages of economic development, China has successively solved a series of problems facing economic development, becoming a treasure trove of experiences about reform, opening-up, development, and sharing. Therefore, economists engaged in studying China also have the responsibility to be the tellers of this success story to sublimate these experiences into theories that are of significance for other developing countries and at the same time make due contributions to the theoretical innovation of economics and the conversation of discourse power.

Missed convergence opportunity under the planned economy

At a development stage with a very low income level and hence a huge catch-up potential, it is feasible to adopt planned means to achieve material capital and human capital accumulation to some extent,[13] and sometimes it even has a higher resource mobilization effect than a system that adopts the free market model but cannot effectively regulate economic activities by legal means. In addition, the economic planning approach mainly implemented by administrative means can also achieve a certain degree of effective (but not efficient) resource allocation to serve specific goals, such as the strategic goals of prioritizing heavy industry.

For example, in 1980, China's per capita gross national income (GNI) or per capita gross domestic product (GDP) ranked fourth from the bottom of more than 100 countries with data, but the average number of years of education for people over 25 years old ranked 62nd among 107 countries with data; life expectancy at birth ranked 56th among 127 countries with data.[14] Although the low per capita income level represented a low capital factor endowment, China had strong resource mobilization ability during the planned economy period, and it achieved a high rate of capital accumulation. During the period from 1953 to 1978, China's accumulation rate reached an average of 29.5%, significantly higher than the world average.[15]

However, the planned economy cannot perfectly create the necessary institutional conditions for economic growth and realize efficient resource allocation and effective incentives. The growth theory and economic history evidence about the rise and fall of a country show that in typical human economic activities, resource scarcity is not doomed to the failed development, and the unique resource endowment does not necessarily guarantee successful development (such as the famous hypothesis of the "resource curse"). Whether economic development is successful or not is closely related to the choices of the resource allocation system and incentive mechanism, and hence, the efficiency of resource allocation and incentive effectiveness are closely related to the development results.

Transnational economic research and China's experience in the planned economy have proven that under the traditional economic system model, the exclusion of market mechanisms leads to the macro inefficiency of resource allocation, the lack of incentive mechanisms leads to the micro inefficiency of economic activities, and the absence of reward and punishment systems hurts the working enthusiasm of workers, farmers and managers. The growth of the production factor, including human capital, achieved under the government's strong resource mobilization was largely offset by the negative growth of total factor productivity, which failed to transform to good economic growth performance. In particular, resource misallocation led to the malformation of the industrial structure, the achievements of scientific and technological progress were not used in industries related to people's livelihood, and people's living standards could not be improved along with economic development.

After the founding of the People's Republic of China, China experienced a change of population reproduction from high birth rate, high death rate, and low growth to high birth rate, low death rate, and high growth in the 1950s, almost at the same period when the planned economic system was formed, which meant that the process of economic involution was completed. According to the logic, China's economy should enter the development stage of the dual economy. According to Lewis's definition and the situation in China, the most typical feature of the development stage of the dual economy was a serious surplus labor force in agriculture.

Subsequently, starting in the late 1960s, the birth rate began a downward trend, and the natural growth rate of the population dropped significantly, which meant that demographic conditions conducive to economic growth, that is, a potential demographic dividend, gradually formed. On the one hand, with capital accumulation and the industrialization process, surplus labor was transformed into a cheap production factor, which could be reflected as a country's comparative advantage and competitive advantage under open conditions; on the other hand, the nature of unlimited supply of labor also constituted a series of other factors conducive to growth, which could support rapid growth of the catch-up type.

However, since there was a strong and anxious desire to promote industrialization and catch up with developed countries, furthermore with a misled understanding of industrialization and limited choices, such as insufficient accumulation and consumption capabilities under the conditions of the peasant economy, it became the choice at that time to implement a forced accumulation strategy of prioritizing heavy industry and to build an institutional model that relies on centralized planning to allocate resources. At the same time, China's economic development during this period inevitably deviated from its potential comparative advantages. It can be seen that the disadvantage of the planned economy model implemented before the reform was that a series of institutional factors led to resource misallocation, and they were mutually locked with ineffective incentive mechanisms, leading to low productivity and growth performance and forming a vicious circle.

Justin Yifu Lin and others summarized the traditional economic system as a three-in-one model, that is, under the premise of implementing the strategy to give priority to heavy industry, the first task is to form a macro policy environment that violates comparative advantages and distorts product and factor prices to achieve industrialization accumulation as soon as possible; then, they construct a highly planned system for resource allocation and abandon the market mechanism; to further construct a micromanagement system corresponding to it, which is shown as state-owned enterprises occupying the absolute dominant position in industry, and the people's commune is realized in agriculture and workers' remuneration and efforts are decoupled from human capital, the assigned plan is fully implemented by the operator, and the investment is in the form of appropriation when revenue and expenditure are financially unified. The enterprise is not constrained by the budget with no competitive pressure, resulting in insufficient incentives and low micro-efficiency.[16]

Spence argued that the global economy began an era of great convergence in approximately 1950.[17] Although the research and statistics of growth economists indicated that the global economy did not show a trend of convergence at least before the 1990s, some European countries that were once underdeveloped, Japan, and the Four Asian Tigers took advantage of this period to catch up with developed economies. However, China missed this opportunity to catch up.

As China's actual economic growth rate was slower than the average level of the corresponding income group during this period, the gaps between its per capita income and the average levels of developed countries, other developing countries, and the world average widened. According to data from the World Bank and calculated in constant 2010 US dollar prices, China's actual per capita GDP during the period of 1960 to 1978 had a low starting point, and its growth rate was slower than that of other economies, leading to a widening gap (see Figure 5.1).

Whether from the domestic perspective of improving people's lives or international comparisons from the perspective of national strength, China's development performance during this period was not satisfactory. Due to rapid population growth, the accumulation-to-consumption ratio was seriously imbalanced, and the per capita income level grew very slowly until the eve of reform and opening-up. During this period, China's economy was

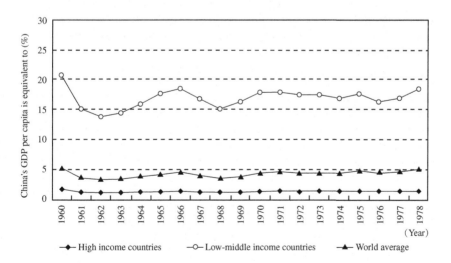

Figure 5.1 China failed to catch up before the reform and opening-up

emphatically closed. In 1978, total imports and exports accounted for only 9.7% of GDP, of which 47.2% were exports, and more than half were primary products. It was not until 1983 that the actual utilization of foreign capital and foreign direct investment were US$22.6 billion and US$9.2 billion, respectively.

From the perspective of economic structure and productivity change, it can also be explained that the implementation of the planned economy mode leads to low efficiency of resource allocation and poor economic development performance. According to statistics, the proportion of China's agricultural labor force in 1952 was 82.5%. According to the logic of dual economy development, an abundant labor force can delay the diminishing returns to capital and maintain a high rate of return on capital. With the advancement of industrialization, surplus labor can be transferred from agriculture to non-agriculture, and the efficiency of resource reallocation can be obtained.

At the same time, in the mid-1960s, the dependency ratio of the population declined, mainly the dependency ratio of children and adolescents, which theoretically formed a demographic dividend that was beneficial to capital accumulation and human capital improvement. However, these favorable factors for economic growth in that period were not fully utilized due to the misallocation of resources.

We can also analyze the components of China's per capita GDP growth rate to see the characteristics of economic growth before the reform and opening-up. Zhu Xiaodong estimated that in the average per capita GDP growth rate of 2.97% per annum from 1952 to 1978, the contribution of the labor participation rate was 3.63%, the contribution of the capital-output ratio was 116.15%, and the contribution of average human capital was 52.25%. During this period, the growth rate of total factor productivity was negative, and its contribution to per capita GDP growth was −72.03%.[18] Meanwhile, there was no fundamental change in the industrial structure during this period. In 1977, the proportion of the agricultural labor force was still as high as 74.5%.

Logic and process of the reform and opening-up

According to the general law, a country needs to solve the problems of accumulation and allocation of material capital and human capital institutionally to achieve successful economic development. This involves issuing mechanisms, signals, efficiency, and incentives. Starting from a planned economic system, the above problems could not be solved. There are many obstacles that need to be overcome to initiate the initial reform. To be feasible politically and operational in practice, it must meet at least three conditions. First, only when reform brings benefits to specific laborers, microeconomic units, and social groups can it form the basic motivation to launch reform. Second, such reform does not directly conflict with the interests of any other social groups; that is, it should be a so-called Pareto improvement. Third, such reform potentially launches a key change of gear, thereby promoting reforms in other fields of the logical chain. However, this last condition is often unknown in advance.

Realizing the household contract system in agriculture and abolishing people's communes are most in line with the preconditions of the abovementioned reforms, starting in the late 1970s, the reform of the household contract responsibility system was quietly piloted in some regions. This kind of spontaneous reform experiment was not limited to Xiaogang Village or Fengyang County in Anhui Province, as mentioned above, but had already appeared in a large number of rural poverty-stricken areas in Anhui, Sichuan, and Inner Mongolia provinces before the Third Plenary Session of the Eleventh Central Committee of the Communist Party of China.

In just a few years in the early 1980s, such reform of the agricultural management system was quickly completed when the central government's policy evolved in several stages from acquiescing to the status quo, allowing experiments in remote and poverty-stricken areas to implement it in the whole country. By the end of 1984, all the production teams and 98% of rural households in the country had adopted the household contract responsibility system, and the people's commune system was later formally abolished.

This reform solved the long-lasting problems of agricultural labor and business incentives in one fell swoop. While farmers obtained the residual claim right, it correspondingly granted and gradually expanded their right to allocate production factors and their autonomy in business activities. In the short period from 1978 to 1984 when the household contract responsibility system was implemented, the yield per unit area of grain increased by 42.8%, the total output increased by 33.6%, and the agricultural value added achieved an actual increase of 52.6%.

According to econometric analysis, 46.9% of the increase in agricultural output during this period was contributed by the system change of the household contract responsibility system.[19] In the same period, the per capita income of farmers achieved a nominal increase of 166%. When the poverty standard increased from 100 yuan to 200 yuan per person per year, the absolute impoverished population in rural areas decreased from 250 million to 128 million.[20] Such change also greatly increased the supply of agricultural products to cities, creating conditions to abolish the food coupon system in a few years.

From some previous analyses, it is believed that in China's economic reform in the early 1980s, only the rural reform was remarkable, centered on the household contract responsibility system, while there was no substantial reform in the urban economy.[21] In fact, this is a mistake in observation. Reforms with similar approaches and effects also occurred in state-owned enterprises. The bonus system was resumed in enterprises in 1978, which was actually about decentralization and reforming the wage system to solve the issue of employee labor incentives and involved the relation between employees and the enterprise. At the same time, enterprise reforms began with decentralization and interest concessions as the main content, focusing on solving the incentive issue of enterprises and their operators and touching the relation between enterprises and the market and the state.

In summary, enterprise reform, being the core of urban economic reform, is carried out along three main lines, which are shown in both the successive relation in time and the coexistence relation in space.

The first was to start with granting and continuously expanding the operational autonomy of state-owned enterprises and to gradually construct a vigorous business entity and finally establish a modern enterprise system; that is, the reform of the corporate system. Beginning in 1979, pilot programs were carried out to expand enterprise autonomy, and the scope of the pilot was continuously expanded until full coverage was achieved. Enterprises were given a series of autonomous rights, such as salary increases, bonus payments, hiring and dismissal of employees, material procurement, product sales and pricing, and the use of self-owned funds.

As a deepening and institutionalized exploration of the reform of decentralization and interest concessions, various patterns were successively trialed, such as the factory director (manager) responsibility system, the corporate contract system, the asset contract management system, the leasing system, and the shareholding system. By the end of the 1990s, with the advancement of restructuring major enterprises and relaxing control over small ones, it became the basic direction for the reform of state-owned enterprises to carry out the reform of the corporate system in accordance with the requirements of the modern corporate system.

The second was to redefine the relation between state-owned enterprises and the state. The initial reform was characterized by the state's decentralization and interest concessions to enterprises. Such reform measures were adopted as retained profit, tax for profits, and grant-to-loan swap to strengthen the corporate responsibility as the main body of the market economy and adjust the state's management of state-owned enterprises. In 1988, the State-owned Assets Administration Bureau was established in the State Council. On March 16, 2003, the State-owned Assets Supervision and Administration Commission were established to perform the responsibilities of investors on behalf of the state. Their supervision covers the state-owned assets of enterprises under the central government (excluding financial enterprises). Local governments also set up corresponding institutions to manage the state-owned assets of local enterprises. At present, the reform being promoted is aimed at strengthening state asset supervision by focusing on capital management, reforming the authorized operation system of state-owned capital, setting up a number of operating companies for state-owned capital, and supporting the transformation of qualified state-owned enterprises into state-owned capital investment companies.

The third was to allow and encourage the development of a non-state-owned economy, restructure major enterprises and relax control over small ones, and introduce foreign direct investment, which provided state-owned enterprises with competitive pressure and an operating impetus. During the reform of the property rights system and governance structure, competition among enterprises under diverse forms of ownership and the formation of mixed ownership played a key role in making state-owned enterprises become market entities and paying more attention to improving efficiency. From a statistical point of view, it has basically formed a pattern where multiple ownership systems and mixed ownership systems coexist for competitive development.

As of 2017, among the industrial enterprises with the turnover of main businesses exceeding RMB20 million per annum (that is, "enterprises with designated size"), the enterprises registered as state-owned industrial enterprises only generated 3.4% of the total turnover of main businesses, and the other parts (i.e., 96.6%) were generated by enterprises registered in more than 20 types, including private industrial enterprises, industrial enterprises of limited liability companies, foreign-invested industrial enterprises, and industrial enterprises of Sino–foreign joint ventures.

When incentive mechanisms are gradually formed for farmers and enterprises, correct market signals are needed to truly establish their dominant market positions and promote the rational flow and reallocation of production factors and resources. In other words, the next reform task in logic must be to correct distorted price signals by developing product and factor markets. From the planned pricing of products to the market-determined prices, from the planned distribution of products and production means to free market transactions, and from the unified allocation of production factors to the free flow through the factor market, all these key changes are mostly realized through the dual-track system, namely, the gradual transition from the planned track to the market mechanism and the decline and the growth between the former and the latter.

Through the abovementioned reform process, which accords with the logic of the transition from a planned economy to a market economy, the accumulation incentive of material capital and human capital and the market allocation mechanism have been gradually established, and the corresponding macro-policy environment has been formed. China's economic reform is multifaceted and comprehensive. However, many other important reforms can be regarded as following the abovementioned basic logic. As new problems continue to emerge and are resolved in the reform process, reforms in related fields are promoted and completed by appropriate means.

It is especially important to pay attention to the transformation of government functions or the reform of the relation among the government, enterprises, and the market. Generally, the government should gradually withdraw from directly participating in economic activities and instead assume the function of promoting social development through redistribution. Nevertheless, the Chinese government, especially local governments, has paid high attention to economic development. For a long time, it has been reflected in the competition among local governments to promote the growth of local GDP and thus enhance fiscal capability.

Such a pattern of government action played a positive role in transforming the incentives formed by reform into growth rates. At the same time, it also brought such negative effects as the government was excessively involved in direct resource allocation and hampered the functioning of market mechanisms. As China's economy enters a new normal and the reform of streamlined administration and power delegation is developing in depth, government functions are increasingly changing to fulfill the responsibilities of promoting educational development, strengthening social protection, safeguarding market order, regulating the macroeconomy, and supplying other public goods.

The relation between opening-up to the outside world and the aforementioned economic reform process can be understood from four perspectives. First, opening-up and reform are logically consistent; second, the two processes are parallel in time; third, in terms of effect, the two are mutually conditional and mutually promoting; fourth, the two take the same advancing way, that is, a gradual approach.

Through expanding international trade, introducing foreign direct investment, outbound investing by enterprises, participation in global economic governance, and actively implementing the Belt and Road construction in recent years, China has participated in economic globalization with the help of opening-up to the outside world to the greatest extent, and the degree of openness has significantly increased in various domestic economic fields. Meanwhile, opening-up has played a role in promoting a series of reform and development goals for enterprises to become the main body in competition, absorb foreign technology and management experience and cash in demographic dividends in economic growth, and gain comparative advantages in industrial development.

Cashing in demographic dividends in reform and opening-up

China's reform and opening-up have brought about high-speed economic growth, which is rare in the history of human economic development. From 1978 to 2018, China's real GDP grew at an average rate of 9.4% per annum, the fastest growth rate in the world over this period. In the 33 years before the slowdown in 2012, the average growth rate was as high as 9.9% per annum. Following it was an extraordinary and equally rapid demographic transition. According to data from the United Nations, China's total birth rate dropped from 2.5–3.0 around the beginning of the reform to the replacement level of 2.0 in the early 1990s. It has stabilized at approximately 1.5 since the late 1990s.

There is much controversy among scholars and policy researchers on the birth rate in China since the beginning of the 21st century. If calculated directly according to the census or survey data of 1% population sampling, the birth rate is incredibly low. For example, the fifth census in 2000 was 1.22, the survey of 1% sampling in 2005 was 1.34, and the sixth census in 2010 was 1.19.[22] Even after it was corrected based on the assumption that there was a certain error in the data, most scholars believe that the actual birth rate is lower than the cited data of the United Nations; that is, it has remained at 1.4 or even a lower level for many years.[23] After the Chinese government successively relaxed the birth rate, that is, in the first step, couples were allowed to have two children if the husband or wife was the sole offspring, and in the second step, all couples were allowed to have two children, the birth rate showed a slight and short rise.

Nevertheless, no matter what the birth rate is supposed to be, one unquestionable fact is that China entered a stage of demographic transition where the birth rate was below the replacement level for a quarter century. Before inevitably leading to an aging population that is not conducive to economic growth, such a rapid demographic transition will help form a demographic transition pattern in a certain period of time where there is a rapid increase in the working-age population and a significant decline in the population dependency ratio; that is, the potential demographic dividend.

The contribution of the demographic dividend to economic development has gradually attracted the attention of economists. Researchers have also observed how China enjoyed the demographic dividend during the period of reform and opening-up and have actually made an empirical estimation about the contribution of the demographic dividend to economic growth. For example, Wang Feng and Andrew Mason used the population dependency ratio as a proxy indicator of the demographic dividend and estimated that the contribution of the demographic dividend to China's economic growth was 15% between 1982 and 2000.[24] The estimation of Fang Cai and Wang Dewen, showed that the decline in the dependency ratio over the same period contributed as much as 26.8% to the growth of per capita GDP.[25]

In a standard Cobb–Douglas production function $Y = A*F(K,L) = K\alpha*(AL)^{1-\alpha}$, Y represents output (GDP) growth, K represents capital input, and L represents labor input, which can be decomposed into labor quantity and human capital. Symbol A is total factor productivity, which can be decomposed into resource reallocation efficiency and residuals. Some economists have also formed the tradition of "right-hand fighter"; that is, adding many explanatory variables that are expected to be theoretically meaningful and statistically significant on the right hand of the formula in the process of growth regression.[26]

This is an attempt to take the population dependency ratio as a proxy variable for revealing the contribution of the demographic dividend. In fact, if the demographic dividend is understood as a contributing factor to the growth rate in a broad sense, it is almost reflected in all the explanatory variables of the production function. If the contribution rate is estimated with the dependency ratio as a variable, it is at best the residual of the demographic dividend contribution.

Following dual economic theory to expand the neoclassical growth theory framework, we can make new assumptions and explanations for the contribution of the demographic dividend based on the actual experiences of East

Asian economies and China's economic development. In the following text, we will summarize the economic growth factors related to population and use the empirical evidence provided by relevant literature to show a more comprehensive demographic dividend effect.

The success of China's reform and opening-up has broken a series of expectations based on the paradigm of mainstream Western economics. As believers in the Washington Consensus devised a priori institutional goals for reforms in developing countries and transitional countries, scholars who firmly believed in neoclassical growth theories also arbitrarily set standards based on Western economic development experience to compare China's reform and development. Such an a priori argument means many documents that attempt to explain China's reform achievements fail to give convincing answers to the main and key questions.

For example, American economists Alwyn Young and Paul Krugman followed their consistent theoretical starting points and empirical methods and believed that the growth during China's reform period was similar to the East Asian economy that they criticized many years ago, which only relied on the input of capital and labor without the support of increased productivity and hence was extensive and unsustainable.[27] This judgment completely ignored China's characteristics at the development stage of the dual economy. Like their judgment on the East Asian economy, its correctness has been negated by the facts.

In addition, many researchers observed the differences in China's reform approaches, but they did not see that the choice of such a reform approach is logically related to the starting point of the reform, and therefore they neglected that China's reform and opening-up are oriented to improve the living standard of all residents, with the expansion of employment and the redistribution of labor force as the core, thus having the characteristics of shared economic development.[28]

China's reform and opening-up were launched under the background and conditions that all potential resources were used up under the planned economy. As a general growth condition, China's development potential of the dual economy and the demographic dividend, as well as the human capital endowment accumulated during the planned economy period or even earlier, which exceeded that of countries with equivalent income, began to release during the reform and opening-up, becoming the source of economic growth.

With such potential in the Chinese economy, the demographic dividend was cashed in under the reform and opening-up, which could form a high potential growth rate and furthermore achieve a high actual growth rate. If we are not confined to a certain economic theory dogma, we should not ignore the process of reform and opening-up to promote development and share China's experience in 40 years, and there is no reason to deny that such practice is fully in line with economic logic and general development laws.

First, a low and continuously declining population dependency ratio is conducive to achieving a high rate of savings, while the feature of unlimited supply of labor delays the occurrence of diminishing returns to capital, thus making capital accumulation the main engine of economic growth. Earlier studies by the World Bank found that in GDP growth from 1978 to 1995, the contribution rate of material capital accumulation was 37%.[29] However, many other later studies estimated that this contribution rate should be even higher.[30]

If we do not understand or admit the development stage of the dual economy, we will inevitably conclude that such an economic development pattern is unsustainable. However, the East Asian experience, including China, has proven that there is a Lewisian development stage of a dual economy, which has an obvious feature of unlimited supply of labor. Moreover, there are also documents that have proven that this feature of unlimited supply of labor has indeed delayed the occurrence of diminishing returns to capital for a certain period of time. For example, research by Chong-En Bai et al. showed that China's returns on capital remained at a high level in a long period of reform and opening-up; however, once the feature of unlimited supply of labor begins to disappear, for example, after crossing the Lewis turning point,[31] the returns on capital will drop rapidly.[32]

Second, the favorable demographic factor ensures that the quantity and quality of the labor force will make a significant contribution to economic growth. Most studies have noticed the contribution of a large number of labor forces to economic growth, and the econometric decomposition has proven this as well. Economists have also paid attention to the contribution of human capital. For example, Whalley and Zhao estimated an 11.7% contribution of human capital. If it was put into consideration that the enhanced education level had the effect of improving productivity, the contribution could be increased to 38%.[33] However, people often ignore the relation between labor quality and population structure, and therefore the human capital factor is not regarded as an important part of the demographic dividend.

A favorable population structure ensures that there are continuously new entrants to the labor force. For developing countries, the overall human capital of the labor force is mainly improved through this incremental approach. China has shown a particularly outstanding performance in this regard. For example, according to data from the China Urban Labor Survey (CULS) in 2010,[34] rural migrant laborers had an average of 9.5 years of education, and urban local laborers had an average of 12.1 years, but rural migrant laborers and urban local laborers had median ages of 33 and 40 years old, respectively. When young rural migrant laborers replace older urban laborers, the overall education level of the employed population is improved.

In Figure 5.2, we show the age distribution of the two groups and the years of education by age. Taking 0 as the base point, the upper part of the figure reflects the age structure of rural migrant laborers and years of education by age group, and the lower part of the figure reflects the age structure of urban local laborers and years of education by age group. It can be seen from the figure that because rural migrant laborers are younger and there is a higher

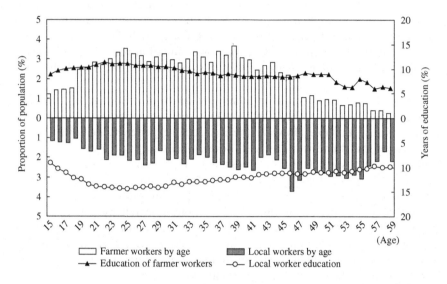

Figure 5.2 Rural migrant laborers and laborers with urban household registration: Distribution by age and years of education

level of education in certain age groups, they will replace urban laborers who withdraw from the labor market year by year, which can increase the overall human capital of the labor force. For example, the rural migrant laborers in the group aged 21–25 have 13.3 years of education. This group replaces the urban local labor force in the group aged 55–59 (with 10.1 years of education), and there is a significant effect to increase the overall years of education of the urban labor force.[35]

Third, whether it is the entry of a new growing labor force or the movement of long accumulated urban and rural surplus labor among industries, sectors, and regions, it is a structural adjustment in line with the path of productivity improvement. It will create resource reallocation efficiency, becoming the main component of total factor productivity and labor productivity.

For example, in earlier studies, the World Bank further divided total factor productivity into resource reallocation efficiency and residuals. The former referred to increased productivity brought by the transfer of the labor force from low-productivity sectors (agriculture with surplus labor and overstaffed state-owned enterprises) to sectors of higher productivity (non-agricultural industries and start-ups). It is estimated that such resource reallocation efficiency contributed 16% to economic growth.[36] According to the estimation of Fang Cai and Wang Dewen, when the labor force transferred from agriculture to non-agricultural industries, it brought an increase in total factor productivity, contributing as much as 21% to economic growth.[37]

It can be seen that China's 40 years of fast growth performance is the result of the reform and opening-up to stimulate the factor endowment advantage at a specific stage of development, that is, to transform the demographic dividend into a high potential growth rate at the development stage and actually into rapid economic growth by improving micro-incentive mechanisms, correcting price signals, developing product markets, and removing institutional barriers to the production factor flow, transforming the government's economic functions, introducing technology, capital and competition through opening-up, and exploring the international market. From the perspective of factor supply capability and resource allocation efficiency potential, econometric analysis reveals that the potential annual growth rate of China's economy was an average of 9.7% from 1979 to 1995 and 10.4% from 1997 to 2010.[38]

Finally, in sharp contrast with the employment trend in the United States and other developed countries during globalization,[39] China has achieved an overall expansion of urban and rural employment, a higher level of labor allocation structure, and balanced growth in employment in trade sectors and non-trade sectors, while reform and opening-up promote rapid economic growth. While employment expands continuously and the labor force is reallocated, it has promoted industrial structural changes and improved resource allocation efficiency, so labor income has increased greatly, and urban and rural residents have participated in and shared the development results of reform and opening-up.

According to the National Bureau of Statistics, during the same period when total employment in urban and rural areas increased from 402 million in 1978 to 776 million in 2017, the proportion of the agricultural labor force fell from 69.6% to 27.0%. According to the estimation based on actual conditions, the true proportion of the agricultural labor force was likely to be 10 percentage points lower than the statistical data.[40]

China has experienced the widening of the income gap reflected by various indicators, but in general, its urban and rural residents have shared the fruits of reform and opening-up and economic development at different periods through three channels or effects, which has won the Chinese people's support for reform and opening-up and has also created huge domestic consumption demands. The first is the effect of expanded employment quantity. This has created more jobs to develop labor-intensive industries. Although the income gap has widened, the income of all income groups has improved significantly. The second is the effect of an improved wage rate and employment quality. After reaching the Lewis turning point, the wages of ordinary laborers and thus the income of low-income families increased at a fast pace. Since 2009, there has been a continuously narrower trend for both the Gini coefficient of residents' income and the income gap between urban and rural areas. The third is the effect of the enhanced redistribution policy. It is represented in the efforts of the central and local governments to promote the equalization of basic public services. Such logic and the process of reform and opening-up have formed a virtuous circle of development.

Conclusion

Looking back on the 70-year history of economic construction and the 40-year development process of reform and opening-up in the People's Republic of China, abstracting successful experiences and even unsuccessful lessons into development and transformation theories with Chinese characteristics is not only the need for theoretical innovation but also necessary for judging the current development stage, understanding the nature of new tasks facing reform and looking forward to China's economic prospects. Most economists admit that during the 40 years of reform and opening-up, China's economy has mainly undergone two important changes, namely, in terms of the institutional model, transforming from a planned economy to a market economy, and in terms of the growth type or the development stage, transforming from dual economic development to neoclassical growth. In fact, there is also a rapid demographic transition occurring in parallel with these two processes; that is, the change from the high birth rate stage to the low birth rate stage, which remains stable in the latter stage and brings many new things.

The rapid economic growth brought about by reform and opening-up can be seen as a process in which reforms continue to create an appropriate institutional environment for production factor accumulation and effective allocation, thereby fulfilling the demographic dividend. Logically speaking, it was not possible for China's economy to change its past growth trajectory without the sufficient condition of reform and opening-up, and it was not possible for the growth rate at least from 1978 to 2010 to be so high without the necessary condition of demographic dividend.

To date, the reforms of incentive mechanisms, corporate governance structures, price formation mechanisms, resource allocation models, opening-up systems and macro-policy environments have all been proposed and promoted in response to special institutional requirements at a certain stage of economic development. Looking at the present and looking forward to the future, the focus, difficulty, advancing approach, and even orientation of reforms should also be adjusted with changes in the development stage. On the one hand, as China has entered the stage of moving from an upper-middle income country to a high-income country, the pattern of economic growth should change to be productivity-driven; on the other hand, the closer it is to a mature and better-defined stage of the socialist market economy system, the more difficult the reform will be.

With China's economy crossing the Lewis turning point characterized by labor shortages and rising wages, the demographic dividend is rapidly disappearing, past economic growth factors are weakening, the potential growth rate is falling, and the extraordinary growth rate can no longer be maintained. We have observed a series of factors that cause a decline in the potential growth rate of China's economy, including the following: labor shortage causes wages to rise too fast, which exceeds the supporting capacity of labor productivity growth; the rapid increase in capital–labor ratio causes a large drop of returns on investment; the reduction of new entrants to the labor force slows down the improvement of human capital; the slowdown of rural labor transfer weakens the resource reallocation effect; and the growth rate of total factor productivity declines.

It can be seen that China's economy has entered a new normal characterized by a decline in growth rate, industrial restructuring, and accelerated transformation of development patterns. Fang Cai and Lu Yang estimated that the potential growth rate of China's economy dropped from approximately 10% before 2010 to 7.6% during the 12th Five-Year Plan period (2011–2015) and 6.2% during the 13th Five-Year Plan period (2016–2020).[41] Subsequently, the potential growth rate will continue to decline and will not return to the average value until China is fully modernized.[42] To date, the trajectory, rhythm, and trend of actual growth slowdown have confirmed the prediction. This puts forward urgent requirements to adjust the industrial structure, and the response to challenges should be based on deepening economic reform.

According to the growth theory expectation and the development experience in various countries, growth slowdown is almost inevitable to change from catch-up development of the dual economy to neoclassical growth at the forefront of technology.[43] However, it varies greatly from country to country at which percentage the potential growth rate will decrease and at which speed the actual economic growth will slow down, and it will also lead to completely different long-term consequences.[44] As far as China is concerned, only by deepening the economic system reform, promoting the transformation of development patterns, tapping the potential of traditional growth drivers, cultivating new growth drivers, maintaining a reasonable potential growth rate, and realizing real growth of medium to high speed can it avoid falling into the middle-income trap and achieve the goal of national modernization.

Generally, in the face of an economic system that is short of incentive and is therefore inefficient, reform starts with breaking the insufficient micro-incentives in the vicious circle, so it is easy to promote reforms in the path of Pareto improvement and then change the method of resource allocation to correct the pattern of resource misallocation. As the reform advances in depth, there are fewer opportunities for Pareto improvement not to harm any group. This requires not only a firm political determination to advance reform but also political wisdom to properly handle contradictions.

China's further reform is facing several difficulties. First, reform will inevitably make in-depth adjustments to the interest structure, so it will encounter resistance and interference from vested interest groups. Second, in the competition process of survival of the fittest, some laborers and operators will get into real trouble. Third, the cost bearer of the reform and the gainer of the reform benefits do not exactly correspond to each other, causing the incompatibility of incentives. In the face of such difficulties, we should focus on sharing reform costs and reform dividends, redefining the fiscal expenditure responsibilities required to establish a new system, and providing necessary compensation to the damaged parties, especially providing social policy support for workers.

Many studies have shown that reform and non-reform will create completely different prospects for China's economic growth. For example, the study of Cheremukhim et al. took the economic growth performance during the period from 1978 to 2012 and the period from 1966 to 1975 as the reference for reform and non-reform, respectively, and simulated China's economic growth in 2050, showing a huge difference between the two.[45]

Generally, reform and growth are not in a substitution relation of either one or the other. Reform has an obvious effect of promoting economic growth. The experience and logic of China's reform and opening-up reveal that the reform dividend will eventually be reflected in promoting economic growth and improving people's living standards. We will describe the reform process more deeply in certain aspects in the following chapters and will also explain the expected reform dividend in more details.

Notes

1 Xi Jinping: *Secure a Decisive Victory in Building a Moderately Prosperous Society in All Respects and Strive for the Great Success of Socialism with Chinese Characteristics for a New Era: A Report Delivered at the 19th National Congress of the Communist Party of China*, Shanghai: People's Press, 2017, pp. 18–19.
2 For example, in a book on China's economic transformation, 45 Chinese and foreign authors conducted a detailed analysis of the effects of reforms from the field of economics. See Loren Brandt and Thomas G. Rawski (eds.), *China's Great Economic Transformation*, Cambridge: Cambridge University Press, 2008.
3 For example, see Ronald Coase and Ning Wang, *How China Became Capitalist*, London: Palgrave Macmillan, 2012; Justin Yifu Lin, Cai Fang, and Zhou Li, *The China Miracle: Development Strategy and Economic Reform* (revised edition), Hong Kong: Chinese University Press, 2003; Jinglian Wu, *China Economic Reform*, Shanghai: Far East Publishers, 2003.
4 Alwyn Young, Gold into the Base Metals: Productivity Growth in the People's Republic of China during the Reform Period, *Journal of Political Economy*, Vol. 111, No. 6, 2003, pp. 1220–1261.
5 For example, see Alwyn Young, Gold into the Base Metals: Productivity Growth in the People's Republic of China during the Reform Period, *Journal of Political Economy*, Vol. 111, No. 6, 2003, pp. 1220–1261; Paul Krugman, Hitting China's Wall, *New York Times*, July 18, 2013.
6 Jeffrey Sachs, *Lessons for Brazil from China's Success*, transcript, São Paulo, November 5, 2003.
7 Steven Cheung, *The Economic System of China*, Beijing: China CITIC Press, 2009.
8 Huang Yasheng, *Capitalism with Chinese Characteristics: Entrepreneurship and the State*, Cambridge: Cambridge University Press, 2008.
9 Ronald Coase and Ning Wang, *How China Became Capitalist*, London: Palgrave Macmillan, 2012.
10 Friedrich Hayek, *Studies in Philosophy, Politics and Economics*, London: Routledge and Kegan Paul, 1967, Chapter 6.

11 Engels summarized this way of thought in Karl Marx's Preface and Introduction to *A Contribution to the Critique of Political Economy*: "The train of thought must begin at the same point as the beginning of this history, and its further progress will be nothing but the reflection of the historical process in an abstract and theoretically consistent form; a corrected reflection but corrected in accordance with laws yielded by the actual historical process itself, since each factor can be examined at the point of development of its full maturity, of its classical form" (*Marx and Engels, Selected Works, Volume 2*, Shanghai: People's Publishing House, 1995, p. 43).

12 In the following chapters, we will describe how the corresponding parties react to the changed incentives and opportunities in the process of reform and opening-up, thus playing the leading role.

13 For example, see Loren Brandt, Debin Ma, and Thomas G. Rawski, From Divergence to Convergence: Reevaluating the History behind China's Economic Boom, *Journal of Economic Literature*, Vol. 52, No. 1, p. 93.

14 See Cai Fang, *Demystifying China's Economy Development*, Beijing and Berlin: China Social Sciences Press and Springer-Verlag, 2015; Thomas Rawski, Human Resources and China's Long Economic Boom, *Asia Policy*, Vol. 12, 2011, pp. 33–78.

15 Justin Yifu Lin, Cai Fang, and Zhou Li, *The China Miracle: Development Strategy and Economic Reform* (revised edition), Hong Kong: Chinese University Press, 2003, p. 71.

16 See Justin Yifu Lin, Cai Fang, and Zhou Li, *The China Miracle: Development Strategy and Economic Reform* (revised edition), Hong Kong: Chinese University Press, 2003.

17 Michael Spence, *The Next Convergence: The Future of Economic Growth in a Multispeed World*, New York: Farrar Straus and Giroux, 2011.

18 Zhu Xiaodong, Understanding China's Growth: Past, Present, and Future, *Journal of Economic Perspectives*, Vol. 26, No. 4, pp. 103–124. Except for a few studies, most studies support the conclusion that China's total factor productivity growth rate was negative before the reform and opening-up. For example, refer to Anton Cheremukhim, Mikhail Golosov, Sergei Guriev, and Aleh Tsyvinski, *The Economy of People's Republic of China from 1953*, NBER Working Paper, No. 21397, 2015; Yang Jianbai, Speed, Structure, Efficiency, *Economic Research Journal*, Vol. 9, 1991; Dwight H. Perkins, China's Economic Growth in Historic and International Perspective, *China Economic Quarterly*, Vol. 4, No. 4, 2005.

19 Justin Yifu Lin, Rural Reforms and Agricultural Growth in China, *American Economic Review*, Vol. 82, No. 1, 1992, pp. 34–51.

20 Cai Fang, *Demystifying the Economic Growth in Transition China*, Beijing: China Social Sciences Press, 2014, p. 5.

21 Huang Yasheng, *Capitalism with Chinese Characteristics: Entrepreneurship and the State*, Cambridge: Cambridge University Press, 2008.

22 Guo Zhigang, Wang Feng, and Cai Yong, *Low Fertility Rate and Sustainable Development of Population in China*, Beijing: China Social Sciences Press, 2014, p. 21.

23 Guo Zhigang, Wang Feng, and Cai Yong made a detailed and convincing discussion in the book *Low Fertility Rate and Sustainable Development of Population in China* (Beijing: China Social Sciences Press, 2014).

24 Wang Feng and Andrew Mason, The Demographic Factor in China's Transition, in Loren Brandt and Thomas G. Rawski (eds.), *China's Great Economic Transformation*, Cambridge: Cambridge University Press, 2008, p. 147.

25 Cai Fang and Wang Dewen, China's Demographic Transition: Implications for Growth, in Ross Garnaut and Song Ligang (eds.), *The China Boom and Its Discontents*, Canberra: Asia Pacific Press, 2005.

26 T.N. Srinivasan and Jagdish Bhagwati, *Outward-Orientation and Development: Are Revisionists Right?* Economic Growth Center Discussion Papers, No. 806, Yale University, 1999.

27 Young once bluntly pointed out: "With minimal sleight of hand, it is possible to transform the recent growth experience of the People's Republic of China from the extraordinary into the mundane." Out of this preconception, he denied the substantial increase and contribution of productivity in China's economic growth. See, Alwyn Young, Gold into the Base Metals: Productivity Growth in the People's Republic of China during the Reform Period, *Journal of Political Economy*, Vol. 111, No. 6, 2003, pp. 1220–1261.

28 See Cai Fang (ed.), *Transforming the Chinese Economy, 1978–2008*, Leiden and Boston: Brill, 2010, Introduction, for detailed discussions.

29 World Bank, *China 2020: Development Challenges in the New Century*, Oxford University Press, 1998.

30 For example, Cai Fang and Zhao Wen, When Demographic Dividend Disappears: Growth Sustainability of China, in Masahiko Aoki and Jinglian Wu (eds.), *The Chinese Economy: A New Transition*, Basingstoke: Palgrave Macmillan, 2012.

31 The Lewisian dual economy development is characterized by an unlimited supply of labor with constant wages, and a continuous shift from agriculture to non-agricultural industries. Therefore, once labor shortages and wage increases occur steadily, we call this point of time the Lewis turning point. For discussions on when China reached the turning point, please see Cai Fang, *Demystifying China's Economy Development*, Beijing and Berlin: China Social Sciences Press and Springer-Verlag, 2015.

32 See Chong-En Bai, Chang-Tai Hsieh, and Qian Yingyi, *The Return to Capital in China*, NBER Working Paper, No. 12755,2006; Chong-En Bai and Qiong Zhang, An Analysis of China's Capital Return Rate and Its Influencing Factors, *The Journal of World Economy*, Vol. 10, 2014.

33 John Whalley and Xiliang Zhao, *The Contribution of Human Capital to China's Economic Growth*, NBER Working Paper, No. 16592, 2010.

34 The survey was conducted by the Institute of Population and Labor Economics of the Chinese Academy of Social Sciences from the end of 2009 to the beginning of 2010 when the data on the labor force were collected in the six cities of Shanghai, Wuhan, Shenyang, Fuzhou, Xi'an, and Guangzhou. The survey followed the principle of random sampling by stages, and 700 urban households and 600 households of migrant population (rural migrant laborers) were selected in each city.

35 See Cai Fang, Guo Zhenwei, and Wang Meiyan, New Urbanization as a Driver of China's Growth, in Song Ligang, Ross Garnaut, Cai Fang, and Lauren Johnston (eds.), *China's New Sources of Economic Growth, Vol. 1: Reform, Resources, and Climate Changes*, Canberra and Beijing: ANU Press and Social Sciences Academic Press, 2016.

36 World Bank, *China 2020: Development Challenges in the New Century*, Oxford University Press, 1998.

37 Cai Fang and Wang Dewen, Sustainability of China's Economic Growth and Labor Contribution, *Economic Research Journal*, Vol. 10, 1999.

38 Cai Fang and Lu Yang, The End of China's Demographic Dividend: The Perspective of Potential GDP Growth, in Ross Garnaut, Cai Fang, and Song Ligang (eds.), *China: A New Model for Growth and Development*, Canberra: ANU Press, 2013, pp. 55–74.

39 Michael Spence and Sandile Hlatshwayo found that during the period from 1990 to 2008, a large number of the lower value-chain manufacturing industries in the United States moved offshore, causing a loss of corresponding jobs. The non-tradable service sector accounted for the vast majority of new employment during this period, thus coming to the conclusion that "The US economy is destroyed by industrial migration." See Michael Spence and Sandile Hlatshwayo, *The Evolving Structure of the American Economy and the Employment Challenge*, Working Paper, Maurice R. Greenberg Center for Geoeconomic Studies, Council on Foreign Relations, March 2011.

40 Cai Fang, Reform Effects in China: A Perspective of Labor Relocation, *Economic Research Journal*, Vol. 7, 2017.

41 Cai Fang and Lu Yang, The End of China's Demographic Dividend: The Perspective of Potential GDP Growth, in Ross Garnaut, Cai Fang, and Song Ligang (eds.), *China: A New Model for Growth and Development*, Canberra: ANU Press, 2013, pp. 55–74. Although scholars and institutions predicted different numbers, the mainstream perception is that China's potential growth rate has slightly declined.

42 Pritchett and Summers believed that any growth rate above the mean is abnormal, and "regression to the mean" is the law. According to their logic, the so-called "mean" here is the average growth rate of the world economy. The estimates of Cai Fang and Lu Yang indicate that China's potential growth rate will still be higher than 3%until 2050. See Lant Pritchett and Lawrence H. Summers, *Asiaphoria Meets Regression to the Mean*, NBER Working Paper, No. 20573, 2014; Cai Fang and Lu Yang, Take-off, Persistence, and Sustainability: Demographic Factor of the Chinese Growth, *Asia & the Pacific Policy Studies*, Vol. 3, No. 2, 2016, pp. 203–225.

43 For example, see Robert J. Barro, *Economic Growth and Convergence, Applied Especially to China*, NBER Working Paper, No. 21872, 2016; Barry Eichengreen, Donghyun Park, and Kwanho Shin, *Growth Slowdowns Redux: New Evidence on the Middle-income Trap*, NBER Working Paper, No. 18673, 2013.

44 Barry Eichengreen, Donghyun Park, and Kwanho Shin, *When Fast Growing Economies Slow Down: International Evidence and Implications for China*, NBER Working Paper, No. 16919, 2011.

45 Anton Cheremukhim, Mikhail Golosov, Sergei Guriev, Aleh Tsyvinski, *The Economy of People's Republic of China from 1953*, NBER Working Paper, No. 21397, 2015.

6 Background, logic, and contributions of rural reform

Introduction

As we all know, China's rural reform represented by implementation of the household contract responsibility system marks the starting point of China's economic reform. However, the effect and significance of this reform or subsequent rural economic reforms have been underestimated. In most cases, references to the household contract responsibility system as the starting point of China's economic reform are about the chronological order of reforms. A thorough understanding of the household contract responsibility system's impact on subsequent rural reform and further on China's reform and opening-up policy and its development and sharing effects must be based on a clear understanding of the historical background and theoretical logic of the system's substitution for the people's commune system.

The reform related to agriculture, rural areas, and the well-being of farmers involves many sectors, so it is the object of economic research and the source of nourishment for economic development. Theoretical construction of issues such as lease, industrial evolution, dual economic structure, and labor mobility has been conducted by economics, especially by development economics. However, economists have so far not had the opportunity to examine and test these theoretical hypotheses comprehensively on the basis of complete experiences.

That is to say, the integrity of China's reform and development practice starting from the countryside not only provides an unprecedented experiential basis for development economics, but also naturally makes revolutionary contributions to it. A complete development process has its causes and effects, and the experiential logic therein also has its ins and outs. To fully reveal the complete meaning of China's reform and development experience, especially its implications to the world, we must explain clearly why there was the people's commune system, why the system was bound to fail, and what logical chain the reform must follow when reviewing and theoretically explaining the history.

The greatest significance of the rural reform starting from the household contract responsibility system is that it marks the beginning of the dual

DOI: 10.4324/9781003329305-8

economy development process in China. Moreover, in the following 40 years, a series of reform and opening-up measures and processes were logically targeted at the development of dual economy. The development of dual economy has crossed the key turning point, i.e., the Lewis turning point, but has not yet ended.

As explained in Chapter 4, agricultural involution is a common economic development stage in all countries. Despite its nature of traditional agriculture, it is no longer regarded as staying in the Malthusian trap because of the opportunity of its steering towards dual economic development. Nevertheless, each country may adopt a different model when experiencing the dual economic development stage. One is called the classical model; that is, squeezing out and polarizing small-scale peasant economies by industrial mass production. The other is the East Asian model; that is, Kuznets process in a gradual way according to the rhythm of agricultural surplus labor transition.

Since these two models are premised on the role of market mechanisms and are incompatible with planned economy, a third model, agricultural collectivization, has been adopted in the practice of promoting a highly centralized planned economy in the Soviet Union, Eastern European countries, and China. In this way, small-scale peasant economies have been merged into large-scale agricultural production and management by virtue of the coercive force of the state. The theoretical basis of this model is that as there is great potential for scale economy in agricultural production, collectivization can utilize scale economy and will not cause market differentiation for farmers, conforming to the ideal model of public ownership.

However, collective agriculture has a natural defect, namely, it cannot provide an incentive mechanism for productive labor and may lead to low efficiency at a micro level. At the same time, collective farms or people's communes, as part of the planned economy system, and collective agriculture, as part of the planned economy, cannot solve the problem of effective allocation of resources at a macro level. This is why the agricultural management system has failed in all countries, paying a heavy price for human resources and material factors of production, and finally becoming the object of reform.

In view of the fact that all chapters in Part I of this book have paved the way for China's economic development in history and theory, this chapter attempts to adopt a narrative method of unifying historical logic and realistic logic when reviewing and summarizing the rural reform and its continuous impact. For this purpose, it is necessary to clarify in advance possible doubts on two common reflection methods and on the method to be adopted.

As for the traditional system formed during the planned economy period, the most common saying is that we have copied the Soviet model. Despite many commonalities and similarities in the socialist planned economy model, this simple copying theory has underestimated the problem-oriented consciousness of Chinese leaders. Actually, a system is designed in most cases to achieve a specific goal or to solve a specific problem. For example, the people's commune system differed greatly from the collective farms in the Soviet Union, and there was a big difference in their implementation patterns.

Another argument related to this is that the formation of a certain system was the result of a political or hot-headed decision. For example, people's communes or their embryonic forms radically established in some areas were even glorified by then Chairman Mao Zedong because of their superficial effects and conformance to the ideology of a higher degree of public ownership. Mao's slogan that "the people's commune system is good" became a nationwide mobilization order. This slogan could hardly stand up to the scrutiny of facts. If we fully understand the relevance and consistency before and after the event, we can see that even if it was a wrong choice and we had paid certain price for it, there was indeed some inherent logic and economic theory or idea in the decision-making process, rather than it being the result of a blind, arbitrary, or random decision.

There was an internal logic promoting agricultural collectivization, e.g., exploring a way to eliminate traditional agriculture and move toward dual economic development under the planned economy condition, but how can we be sure that decision-makers truly understood this logic, and how can we integrate a complex theoretical model with a highly realistic policy decision?

Economic theory is the abstraction of regular reality, and a theoretical model should be the logical basis for policy-making. whether the theory is correct or not, and whether its explanatory power is large or small, it has reflected specific reality and responded to specific problems. Therefore, even if decision-makers did not know or understand a certain theory, they were faced with practical issues that had puzzled several generations or even more than a dozen generations. That is, there is no difference in the depth of thinking between a theorist and a practitioner, except that the former has adopted terminology and formatted or modeled expressions.

In fact, the Soviet Union had also faced an agricultural reality of involution before implementing agricultural collectivization. A. Chayanov, a well-known expert on farmers' issues, described in detail the characteristics of Soviet Russian farmers' family farms by analyzing the data obtained from a large-scale survey. To reveal the difference between family farms and capitalist farms, he depicted, in his important book *Farmers' Economic Organization*, the special nature that the scale of this kind of family farm was determined by the relationship between family consumption demand and family labor force, and also disclosed some basic characteristics of the involution of agriculture.[1]

First, the family farm tends to regress to the mean value due to its inconspicuous differentiation. Chayanov provided data on the change in land distribution from 1882 (starting year) to 1911 (ending year) (Figure 6.1), which we can generally understand according to the following interpretation of data. First, farmers with a smaller scale in the starting year tended to expand their farm scale, while farmers with a larger scale in the starting year tended to shrink their scale. Second, assuming that the "mean value" was generated by the three middle land scales (3–6 Emu, 6–9 Emu, and 9–12 Emu; 1 Emu = 1.09

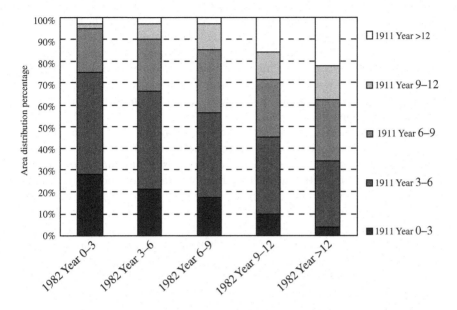

Figure 6.1 Farmers' differentiation in the czarist Russia era

hectare) of the five types of farmers, all farmers of any farm scale tended to regress to the mean value, regardless of their starting year.

Second, Chayanov's description of the peasant family labor force's self-development concluded that the degree of such self-development depended immensely on the pressure from the family consumption demand. Due to the mismatch between population and means of production (land), family consumption only to sustain daily life had forced family labor to invest more working time and increase labor intensity until the physiological limit of workers started to inhibit. He also discovered that the demographic birth rate was endogenous in the family economy scale, i.e., the Malthusian inhibition law.

Third, the motivation of the peasant family labor force's self-development also meant more intensive farming on the limited land. That is, in order to meet the rigid demand of household consumption, it was necessary to improve the effective utilization of the labor force, so farmers would take more soil improvement measures that could hardly be taken under the conditions of capitalist farms. This is a classic rational response to the involution of agriculture.

On the basis of such a small-scale peasant economy, it was logically possible to make the choice of agricultural collectivization in order to guide Soviet agriculture towards the imagined road of socialized mass production. Moreover, this policy was supported by some economic theories at that time. A representative proposition came from Preobrazhensky (Евгений Алексеевич Преображенский), an authoritative economist of the Communist Party of the Soviet Union, who advocated socialist primitive accumulation by expropriating small-scale farming.[2] He explained that after the revolutionary victory in a country, the more backward the economy is, the more it is necessary to forcibly accumulate from non-socialist elements; the more developed the economy is, the more it needs to rely on the surplus products of the socialist elements themselves.

The logic is that when agriculture remains in a state of non-socialist economic sectors, it will be forced to become the source of primitive accumulation. It should also be transformed into a socialist economic sector as soon as possible so as to shift toward the self-accumulation of socialist economic sectors. Preobrazhensky forecast three prospects of the small-scale production (small-scale peasant economy), i.e., maintaining a long-term status of small-scale production, being capitalized, and being united into a socialist sector. He certainly chose the third way and advocated increasing socialist factors. Indeed, the subsequent Soviet collective farm was actually a mixture of (land) state ownership and (other means of production) collective ownership.

Another theory came from Chayanov himself. An analysis of farmers' internal organization concluded that the small-scale farmers' family farm was economically reasonable. However, Chayanov admitted that, given the existence of capitalist production mode, farmers' family farms and capitalist farms reacted in different ways to the same external environment. He also knew about the difficulty of farmers' family farms; for example, their labor intensity often reached their physiological limit in order to meet the rigid demand of family consumption. In addition, family farms were likely to be differentiated, although this was not typical phenomenon.

Obviously, Chayanov did not deny scale economy. However, when writing *Farmers' Economic Organization*, he envisioned methods of applying scale economy in agriculture based on the connection between agricultural products as raw materials and other industries, which intended to bring farmers' farms into the process of vertical integration of agriculture through the institutional form of cooperatives, and guide agricultural economy to the track of planned economy. This helped avoid the horizontal integration process that may lead to polarization.

When he published *The Most Suitable Scale of Agricultural Enterprises* in 1922 and reprinted *Farmers' Economic Organization* in 1925, Chayanov advocated that the smaller family farm was the most economical unit. However, in 1929 when the agricultural collectivization began in the Soviet Union, Chayanov became an advocate of large-scale agricultural operations. He argued that American mechanical technologies such as crawler tractors, combine harvesters, and heavily loaded trucks had furnished large-scale mechanized farming with an overwhelming advantage over all other forms of agricultural organizations. He even demonstrated that 100,000 hectares was the most suitable size of farms specialized in growing wheat.[3]

The change of Chayanov's status from a representative figure advocating family farms to an advocator of large-scale agricultural operations may be thought of as the result of political speculation or certain political pressure. While such political factors' influence cannot be ruled out, and this assumption was more logical at that time and place, a conclusion could be deduced from Chayanov's theoretical logic: once there was large agricultural machinery, the scale economy would enjoy great popularity and the farm size would be getting bigger and bigger.

The combination of above two theories would highlight the concept of collectivization—the only way to eliminate the involution of agriculture under a planned economy. There already emerged its key feature: "large scale, combination of workers, peasants, businessmen, students and soldiers, and integration of government and society," as illustrated by the people's commune system that had emerged later. Apparently, whether from the policy choice of agricultural collectivization or from the inevitable failure of the people's commune system with numerous drawbacks, the similarity between China and the Soviet Union in practice originated from the commonality of problems to be solved in both countries, although each later encountered inner contradictions in development path and destination. This finally led to a series of reforms. In China, the people's commune system was substituted by the household contract responsibility system.

The implementation of the household contract responsibility system was not a one-off event but marked the beginning of China's reform and opening-up across the country. In the following chapters, we will explain how the reform has transformed the necessary conditions for economic growth into actual high-speed growth from the perspective of the complete process of labor force exiting from low-productivity sectors, moving between urban and rural areas, regions, and industries, and entering high-productivity sectors in cities. The later part of this chapter describes how the agricultural surplus labor force "exits" from low-productivity agriculture and rural industries under the background of the decline in agricultural share, observes and reviews corresponding rural reforms and their processes and results, summarizes its implications for development economics, and proposes policy suggestions for further reform and development in the future.

Rise and fall of the people's commune system: utopian experiment

After the land reform was implemented in China, approximately 700 million *mu* (1 *mu* = 0.0667 hectares) of arable land was distributed free of charge to approximately 60–70% of landless or land-insufficient farmers in response to the farmers' call for "land to the tillers." According to a buzzword at that time, the rural areas consisted of the capitalist ownership of rich peasants and the ownership of numerous individual peasants after the land reform.[4] That is to say, by expropriating landlords' land and turning landless farmers and tenant farmers into individual farmers, land reform solved the disadvantages of centralized land rights and polarization of farmers' lives, increased other means of production of farmers, and mobilized their initiative in agricultural production. For example, the total grain output grew 47.4% from 1949 to 1953.

However, land reform failed to change the agricultural economic pattern composed of small-scale peasant economies. In essence, therefore, China's agriculture after land reform has undoubtedly continued its long-term involution characteristics: the planting structure became more labor-intensive as labor force was intensively put into a very small amount of land to maximize the mobilization of auxiliary family labor, thus leading to diminishing labor remuneration.[5] According to a survey after land reform in China, the small-scale peasant economy formed at that time was of a very limited size, and there was limited potential for expanding reproduction without modern input factors (Figure 6.2). From the perspective of decision-makers, there was no way out for this kind of individual peasant economy but to wane to a close.[6]

From the external environment, this also put forward requirements for changes in the agricultural economic system. The first "Five-Year Plan" began in 1953, during which the overall task of economic construction was to gradually transform China from a backward agricultural country into a powerful industrial country. To achieve this goal, the state government established the strategy of giving priority to the development of heavy industry. To speed up industrial accumulation, it was necessary to reduce the cost of heavy industry development by lowering labor costs; that is, implementing a low wage system. Accordingly, it was necessary to lower the price of agricultural products and ensure the supply of agricultural products. This is why three major systems emerged, i.e., the unified purchase and marketing of agricultural products, the household registration system, and the people's commune system.

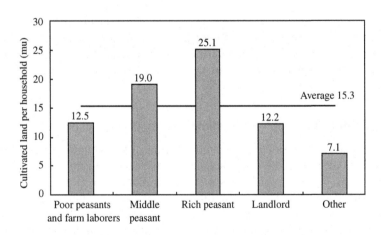

Figure 6.2 Farmers' average possession of farmland after land reform

The system of planned purchase and supply of grain came into being in 1953. With the addition of other important agricultural products, a system of unified purchase and marketing of agricultural products was formed for long-term implementation. If agricultural production could not obtain reasonable income, the outflow of rural factors of production, especially the outflow of labor force, may occur. In order to avoid such outflows and ensure normal progress of agricultural production, it was necessary to make institutional restrictions on the flow of rural production factors, including capital and labor force.

In 1953, in view of the large number of farmers flowing to cities, which aroused worry about unemployment in cities and about adverse consequences on agricultural production, the Central Committee of the Communist Party of China issued the *Instructions to Discourage Farmers from Blindly Rushing into Cities*, and deployed six measures to prevent farmers from leaving the countryside and persuade migrants to return home. In 1958, the Standing Committee of the National People's Congress passed the *Regulations of the People's Republic of China on Household Registration*, stipulating that "citizens who move from rural areas to cities must hold the employment certificate of the urban labor department, the admission certificate of the school, or the certificate of permission to move in from the urban household registration authority, and apply to the household registration authority of the place of permanent residence for emigration."[7] This marks the official formation of the household registration system in which residents are managed separately according to their urban and rural residences.

The completion of land reform throughout China was followed by agricultural cooperation, which had evolved from mutual aid cooperative groups, agricultural production cooperatives (primary cooperatives), and advanced agricultural production cooperatives to people's communes. Among them, mutual aid groups and primary cooperatives featured farmers' voluntary production cooperation, and advanced cooperatives meant cultural collectivization. The whole process tended to accelerate, and the change in production relations obviously exceeded the requirements of productivity.

In 1952, when nationwide land reform had basically ended, 39.9% of the total number of farmers in the country participated in mutual aid groups for agricultural production, while only 0.1% joined agricultural production cooperatives (all primary cooperatives). By 1955, the proportion of farmers participating in mutual aid groups had increased to 50.7%, and the proportion of farmers participating in primary cooperatives had increased to 14.2%, which were the main forms of agricultural cooperation.

Later on, however, the number cooperatives and collectivization had increased at an extraordinary speed. The proportion of farmers participating in agricultural production cooperatives increased to 80.3% at the beginning of 1956 and reached 96.3% at the end of that year. Among them, the proportion of farmers participating in advanced cooperatives suddenly increased from 30.7% at the beginning of the year to 87.8% at the end of the year.[8] Starting in the summer of 1958, the original 740,000 agricultural production cooperatives in China had been merged into more than 26,000 people's communes by the end of that year, which included more than 120 million peasant families, accounting for more than 99% of the total number of farmers in China.

The organization of people's communes aimed to accelerate industrialization, which had been hurting farmers' enthusiasm for production and labor due to its nature of "large scale, combination of workers, peasants, businessmen, students and soldiers, and integration of government and society," which resulted in the lack of a normal incentive mechanism. The failure of the public canteen experiment had also caused malnutrition among the masses and brought about disastrous losses to agricultural production.

Grain production is taken as an example. The total output dropped sharply from 197.66 million tons in 1958 to 136.51 million tons in 1961, and the output per unit area dropped greatly from 1,549kg per hectare in 1958 to 1,124kg per hectare in 1961, down 31% and 27% respectively. As the national economy was still dominated by agriculture and the added value of agriculture, which accounted for more than a third of GDP, a serious reduction in agricultural production had caused a sharp decline in national economy, with zero growth in real GDP in 1960 and significant negative growth in 1961 and 1962.

Judging from the special historical conditions at that time, the Great Leap Forward (a left-wing aggressive social production campaign launched nationwide in 1958–1960) was initiated as a realistic need to accelerate the industrialization of the country, but it was based on the theoretical belief in the large scale, combination of workers, peasants, businessmen, students and soldiers, and integration of government and society. The word "large" here expresses a firm belief in scale economy. In fact, the reason for prevailing boastfulness and falsely reporting and exaggerating the propaganda of grain output was also based on this belief. Just as American-style large-scale agricultural machinery made it necessary to have a farm scale of 100,000 hectares, the utilization of solar photosynthesis made it no longer impossible to produce 5,000kg per *mu*.

For example, the Enlarged Session of the Political Bureau of the Communist Party of China (CPC) Central Committee held in August 1958 (also known as Beidaihe Conference) was focused on steel production and the establishment of people's communes. It was believed at the meeting that merging and transforming smaller agricultural production cooperatives into larger people's communes was an inevitable trend for the rapid development of rural production. On this basis, the goal set by the meeting for the Great Leap Forward in agricultural production for that year was increasing the total grain output by 60% to 90% and the cotton output would at least double over the previous year.[9]

In 1961, the central government began to adjust national economy, downsize capital construction, and put under control the development of industry, especially heavy industry, which, to a certain extent, had reversed the trend of unbalanced industrial structure. In rural areas, the production units were downsized to form a "team-based three-level ownership" system, i.e., three-level ownership of communes, production brigades, and production teams, with the production team taken as the basic accounting unit featuring independent accounting, self-financing, and direct distribution of production and income.

As a result of this adjustment, the ultra-large scale of 6,700 members in each commune formed in 1958 was adjusted, and by 1961, there were six million production teams with an average size of 30 members, which became the foundation of the people's commune system. The people's commune system remained unchanged, and central government still maintained its control over agricultural production, distribution, and consumption of agricultural products, but this adjustment to the scale of production units at that time was also of great significance to restoring agricultural output to a certain extent.

This adjustment and its effect had also inspired us to understand from today's perspective why the scale economy theoretically existing in the people's communes could not be actually utilized in reality. First, the nature of agricultural means of production and the actual level of equipment at that time were far from enough to match such a large-scale economic unit. Second, the special nature of agricultural production determined that the connection between the labor process and the final result was not close, so it was difficult to judge the degree of effort and quality of work of workers in each specific labor stage, and the larger the scale of an economic unit, the greater the difficulty of labor supervision and evaluation. This resulted in the phenomenon of loafing on the job or dawdling along in the process of collective labor, which could hardly be prevented in the system.

Although the "three-level ownership and team-based three-level ownership" system was established and stabilized, the incentive defects of the people's commune system had not been fundamentally remedied. Especially after agricultural collectivization, farmers or commune members were deprived of their "right to exit," and there were no means to curb the natural drawbacks of the labor incentive mechanism.

Under the people's commune (production team) system, the production team predetermined the work point standard for each labor force. At the end of the year, the total income calculated according to the output of the whole production team was deducted from material expenses to form net income, and the value of each work point was calculated according to all recorded work points. A commune member would be distributed a portion of income corresponding to the work points he had earned. Since the work points for one day had been predetermined, how much or little effort a member made would only affect the final output of the entire production team, and the loss apportioned on each member would have nothing to do with the degree of effort as long as the production team leader could not identify who had caused the loss.

In a production team composed of n persons, for instance, one person can be 100% loafing on the job, but the output loss caused from him is only 1/n;

in contrast, another person who has gone all out to work can only get 1/n of the output increment he has contributed. Economists thus believe that this incentive mechanism naturally encourages laziness. This explanation is certainly in line with the logic of economic rationality, and it has been generally accepted for many years. However, it makes an inconvincible assumption that a lazy strategy has been formulated from the very beginning because everyone (i.e., every member of the production team) was born with the character of haggling over every ounce, cheating, and even being selfish.

To make a precise explanation, we should discard the filter of traditional economics that only focuses on material factors to the neglect of human ones and observe the common behavior of the prevalent "loafing on the job" in combination with the mismatch of resources at the macro level, the inefficiency of production units and the lazy behavior of some workers. First, at the level of the national economy, heavy industry was prioritized regardless of actual national conditions, and at the level of agricultural policy, the policy of "taking grain as the key link to ensure an all-round development" was implemented, resulting in macro misallocation of resources. Second, micro inefficiency as a result of blind guidance in production undoubtedly reduced the total output. Finally, after all, some people loafed on the job during collective labor by taking advantage of the difficulty of supervising agricultural labor. This led to the fact that the actual production results of the production team eventually differed greatly from the possible maximum output.

In the 1970s, China was the poorest country in the world with its gross national income per capita lower than the average level of poor countries in Africa. Therefore, the agricultural possible maximum output at that time was only a lowest survival level. With the actual output significantly lower than the possible maximum output, the distributable surplus output of the production team could no longer meet the needs of food and clothing after excluding the required state purchase quotas. On the whole, according to the poverty standard of 100 yuan income per person per year, 250 million rural people in China lived below the subsistence level in 1978.

At the micro level, if the distribution results of the production team were converted into nutritional standards such as calories, the actual consumption of people exerting themselves to work during collective labor could hardly be compensated in many cases. If industrious team members spared no effort to work in the production team but could not obtain necessary compensation, they would not be able to maintain reproduction due to the imbalance between the expenditure and intake of calories. It often happened at that time that the labor force did not earn enough food rations after one year of work, that is to say, the physical expenditure caused by labor could not be compensated by the "calories" earned. For this reason, in the case of moral hazard, some people would formulate the strategy of loafing on the job, but in most cases, this was an inevitable result of a series of repeated contests.

When envisaging the reform, some leaders had also made very realistic judgments. According to Guangyuan Yu's recollection, at the Central

Working Conference before the Third Plenary Session of the Eleventh Central Committee of the Communist Party of China, Dengkui Ji (then member of the Political Bureau) pointed out that a farmer's grain ration at that time was less than 300kg, i.e., they were living on short commons.

This conclusion should not be directly inferred from the laziness of human nature, although the labor mode and incentive mechanism of the production team under the traditional Chinese system can be summarized as loafing on the job. On the one hand, the contest for the need for survival has resulted in a vicious circle between insufficient labor enthusiasm and low agricultural output. On the other hand, whenever the production team leader was forced to occasionally try the way of short-term contract work, e.g., stipulating that a laborer could finish a day's work after clearing a pigsty or shoveling a ridge of land, the laborer would often finish the work at an unimaginable speed when thinking for a while about the direct correspondence between his work results and underpaid work points. This also implies that the reform under the all-around responsibility system has long been used or prepared among farmers and grassroots cadres to varying degrees.

How to create exit conditions in rural reform

The household contract responsibility system, which had been implemented nationwide since the early 1980s, was often called "fixing output quotas for individual households"; more exactly, it should be the "household-based contract system" (or the "all-round responsibility system"). There is a common point between the system of fixing output quotas for individual households and the household-based contract system: collectively owned land was contracted to farming households according to the size of their population and labor force, and the collective set output quotas for contracted land and would no longer arrange unified collective labor activities or intervene in the production process. The difference between the two is that farmers are allowed to possess all surplus products after paying agricultural tax, satisfying the unified and fixed state purchase and delivering the amount retained by the collective, so there is no longer unified distribution by the production team. Eventually the household contract responsibility system was widely implemented throughout the country in the form of a household-based contract system.

If this form of reform is compared with the concept that already has a more mature analytical framework in economics, it can be concluded that the system of fixing output quotas for individual households is more similar to a "sharecropping" form by which only part of extra output (according to a fixed proportion) is attributed to the contractor, while the household-based contract system is closer to a "fixed rent" form by which all the extra output is attributed to the contractor. Studies have proven that the latter has a more obvious and straightforward incentive effect on production activities.

Therefore, the household contract responsibility system achieved a miraculous effect because it empowered farm contractors with the "claimants right on residual," i.e., they were allowed to possess all surplus grain once they had delivered enough tax grain and paid in full the amount retained by the collective, which had significantly improved the effect of agricultural labor and production incentives. Early literature has already made an authoritative explanation of this reform effect and actually estimated its quantitative range.[10]

However, if this reform was designed just for the incentive effect, it would merely mean that it is only the return of the production possibility frontier, and its agricultural yield-increasing effect would be a one-off effect on overall economic growth. This has greatly underestimated the rural reform's macro contributions and lost sight of the logical relationship between subsequent reforms and initial reforms.

In fact, when farmers were entitled to the claimants right on residual, that is, they had the right to freely dispose of the output increment gained by extra effort, they would gradually get the right to freely allocate production factors. After the household-based land contract system was implemented, there emerged a saying about the "dual-level management" by farmers and production teams; in fact, however, the purchase and input of means of production as well as the allocation of labor force and working time were entirely decided by farmer contractors themselves. The enhancement of labor enthusiasm and labor efficiency resulted in a significant increase in output and a noticeable decrease in the labor time spent on per unit land area (Figure 6.3), thus disclosing the hidden phenomenon of labor surplus in the past. It can be said that only when farmers had the autonomy to control labor factors could they begin to "exit" from low-productivity sectors.

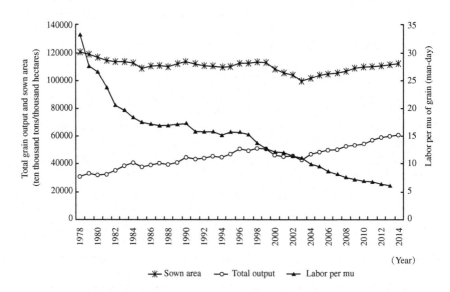

Figure 6.3 Changes in total grain output, sown area, and labor use

Therefore, from the perspective of the ultimate reform effect, if the change of incentive mechanism was of revolutionary significance in the initial stage for mobilizing labor enthusiasm and thus greatly improving agricultural output, the right of farmers to allocate production factors would have a more grand and long-term effect on subsequent economic development.

The implementation of the household contract responsibility system has undoubtedly promoted labor efficiency measured from a personal point of view through the incentive mechanism, and correspondingly explicated the phenomenon of surplus labor force in agriculture and low marginal productivity, thus promoting the labor force's exit. However, the exit of labor force was a continuous process composed of different stages, ranging from one-sided grain production to diversified farming, to all-round development of agriculture, forestry, animal husbandry, and fishery, and then to township enterprises, small towns, and cities at all levels, each step of which means exit from an existing low-productivity sector. Since the effect of the reform on the household contract responsibility system is a one-off, the driving force for labor exit from low-productivity sectors must be supported by further reforms.

In fact, after the emergence of the one-off effect of the reform of the household contract responsibility system, policy-makers and researchers have observed fluctuations in both agricultural production and farmers' income. From 1980 to 1984, while the household contract responsibility system was rapidly promoted, the purchase price of agricultural products increased significantly as never seen before (e.g., the producer price of agricultural products increased by 22.1% in 1979). Under this incentive effect, the total grain output increased at an average annual rate of 2.2% under the condition that the use of labor and the sown area were obviously reduced. In the following four years, however, while the use of labor and the sown area were very stable, the total grain output decreased at an average annual rate of 1.8% (Figure 6.3). The change before and after the one-off effect of the reform of the household contract responsibility system has revealed the characteristics of the reform effect in this period.

As a positive response to this situation, as early as in the late 1980s, relevant researchers put forward a proposition of "the second step of rural reform," while practitioners made various attempts and the government also issued many reform measures. These studies and attempts were far less influential than the household contract responsibility system, so they have not occupied a prominent position in academic research literature, and some of them have faded from our memory.

However, all these reforms, from a micro perspective, are local experiments that farmers carried out to further increase their income; from a macro perspective, they have been recognized or encouraged by governments at all levels aimed at ensuring the stable growth of agriculture; and from a historical perspective, many of them are also related to today's reforms. Next, we will take the land system reform as an illustrative example.

The household contract responsibility system has made equal division of land in accordance with different weights given to each farmer based on the number of population and labor force. Thus, a narrow scale of land management has formed due to less land per capita (or labor per capita) in rural areas. What's more, as one land plot differs in quality from another, in many cases, each household should be given the same collocation of quality-varying land plots for the sake of fairness when dividing the land, thus further thinning the land.

As the phenomenon of surplus agricultural labor force came out, there emerged the need to utilize scale economy while there was an increasing pressure of labor force transfer, resulting in the need for land circulation. In fact, this is an institutional demand that requires a mechanism to promote land circulation. At that time, the institutional demand was not so much to realize a certain degree of scale operation as to create conditions for the exit of surplus labor.

There were two forms of institutional innovation at that time. The first is farmers' spontaneous negotiation on subcontracting the contracted land. Since subcontracting land actually transferred the rights (claimants right on residual) and responsibilities (taxes, unified purchase and acquisition and collective retention) of the contracted land at the same time, the subcontracting "price" of land was determined in different regions according to different conditions; that is, the relative components of rights and responsibilities. The second is the collective's redivision of the right to land contractual management. The typical form is called "two-field system"; that is, the land is divided into a grain-ration field and a responsibility field. The former is still equally distributed according to the size of population and labor force, while the latter is operated by large-scale bidding.

It can be seen that the reform aimed at promoting land circulation actually started very early, and with the continuous transfer of agricultural labor force, the reform experiment in this area has been uninterrupted. Today, the land subcontracting system is more perfect, the mode is more diversified, and the scale and scope of land subcontracting are significantly expanded. In order to promote land circulation and effective allocation of land resources, the reform separating rural land ownership, contractual management rights and management rights has been actively promoted since the 13th Five-Year Plan (2016–2020). By the end of June 2016, more than 70 million out of 230 million farming households in China have carried out land circulation, accounting for more than 30% of all farming households, and the figure of coastal developed provinces exceeded 50%.[11]

Declining share of agriculture as a result of development

For a period of time, discussions in the economic literature on the contribution of agriculture to economic development tended to be less common. Early classical literature summarized agriculture's contributions to economic development from the perspective of resource transfer. For example, some scholars summarized the contribution of the labor force, capital, and foreign exchange in addition to the directly observable product contribution or the possible market contribution of a large agricultural population.[12] According to this logic, the land contribution made by agriculture to non-agricultural industries and urbanization after the improvement of agricultural productivity should also be discussed. These are factor contributions made by agriculture to overall economic development as they were very significant, and some of them are still important today.

Before the reform and opening-up, in order to implement the strategy of giving priority to the development of heavy industry and the planned economy, the three systems such as the unified purchase and marketing system of agricultural products, the people's commune system and the household registration system had tightly confined the rural labor force in agricultural production. As surplus labor force could not be transferred, the contributions made by the labor force were not so prominent as to be discussed. Since the reform and opening-up, the surplus labor force has been transferred on a large scale.

The number of outbound rural laborers in cities increased from 38.9 million in 1997 to 173 million in 2018, accounting for more than one third of all urban employment at present. In addition, more than 100 million rural laborers were engaged locally in non-agricultural employment. The number of migrant workers who transferred locally and left their villages and towns reached 288 million in 2018, meeting the huge labor demand for the development of non-agricultural industries.

As early as in the planned economy period in which the level of agricultural productivity was extremely low and hundreds of millions of rural people failed to have adequate food and clothing, the state managed to realize large-scale transfer of capital from rural areas to cities and from agriculture to industry by virtue of price scissors between industrial and agricultural products and agricultural taxes. According to a summary of economists' estimates, in the decades of planned economy period, China obtained a total of approximately 600–800 billion yuan of industrial accumulation from agriculture through various channels.[13]

This one-way mobility of agricultural and rural resources to non-agricultural industries and cities had not been reversed even a long time after the reform. Some scholars estimated that during 1980–2000, a surplus of 1.29 trillion yuan (at constant prices in 2000) was absorbed from agriculture through various channels for industrial development. From the perspective of rural–urban relationships, approximately 2.3 trillion yuan of funds flowed from rural areas to urban sectors in the same period.[14]

Similarly, agricultural, forestry, animal husbandry, and fishery products had occupied an important share of total exports for a long time. For example, the export of primary products (which can be regarded as agricultural products in general), excluding fossil fuels, lubricants, and related raw materials, accounted for more than 20% of the country's total exports until 1990. Under the condition of an early foreign exchange shortage, this foreign exchange contribution is indeed very significant.

On the premise of improving agricultural productivity, and with the promotion of industrialization in various places, arable land had also been largely converted into non-agricultural industries. We cannot see this trend by directly observing the change in arable land area in China. According to statistics, the arable land area in China increased by 36.56 million hectares in 2016 as compared with 1983, with an increase rate of 37.2%. In fact, this was caused by statistical errors.

In Figure 6.4, the results of the first and second national land surveys showed a large jump in arable land data in 1996 and 2009 respectively. However, on the basis of the number of each new caliber, the arable land area diminished afterward.

However, the actual contribution of rural reform to economic growth cannot be accurately understood only from the abovementioned summary based on factor contribution. On the one hand, the contributions of some of these factors still represent the urban bias or industrial bias in the development policy, which is also the object of reform. On the other hand, with the occurrence of a relative decline in agricultural share and the role of other factors, these contributions will inevitably decline or even disappear, so it seems that agriculture and rural areas can no longer make significant contributions to economic development.

First, as a result of the transfer of surplus labor force, the number and proportion of agricultural labor force have been greatly reduced. Since the vast

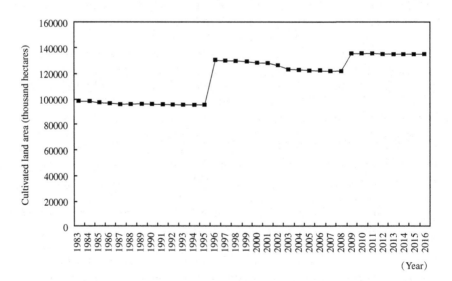

Figure 6.4 Change in arable land areas in China

majority of the newly growing rural labor force has chosen to go out to work for many years, the aging problem of the farming labor force has emerged. As a result of the demographic transition, the number of newly growing rural labor force has also begun to decrease. For example, the total rural population aged 16–19 peaked in 2014, and then showed a negative growth. As the trend of demographic transition is irreversible, the labor contribution of agriculture to economic growth will gradually wane or even vanish in the future.

Second, as industrial and agricultural products should and in fact tend to be exchanged on an equal footing, even the tendency to protect agriculture is becoming increasingly obvious, and the share of agricultural added value in the national economy is becoming smaller and smaller, the capital contribution of agriculture to economic growth will also vanish. After complete abolition of the agricultural tax in 2006, it became normal for the government to implement the policy of "giving more and taking less" or "cities supporting countryside and industry nurturing agriculture" for agriculture, rural areas, and farmers. At the same time, the export of agricultural, animal husbandry, and fishery products has long been insignificant, and the foreign exchange contribution of agriculture is no longer a phenomenon worth mentioning.

Third, as a powerful measure to ensure food security, the central government has implemented the strictest farmland protection policy, drawing a "red line" between arable land and basic farmland. At least in terms of denotation, the space for land transfer from agriculture to non-agriculture is very limited, and the land contribution of agriculture to economic growth is no longer worth advocating As shown in Figure 6.4, the shrinking farmland after 2009 has slowed down as compared with the previous farmland.

In development economics literature, Lewis and other economists also highlighted that while making factor contributes to economic development (capital and labor), agriculture had more importantly brought about changes in economic structure. Kuznets discovered the essence behind this structural change phenomenon, i.e., the continuous improvement of labor productivity. Therefore, Masahiko Aoki called the change of industrial structure characterized by the transfer of agricultural labor force and the decline of relative share the "Kuznets process."[15]

The fundamental feature of this structural change was the long-term downward trend of the agricultural share (output value and employment). The whole process of China's reform and opening-up to promote development and sharing has always been accompanied by the declining agricultural share. For example, Figure 6.5 illustrates the growth and decline trend of the contribution rate of three industries to economic growth. It meets the theoretical expectation and is obvious from experience that since the 21st century, the contribution rate of agricultural added value to GDP growth has been 5% or less.

Although the decline in the proportion of the agricultural labor force seriously lags behind that of the agricultural output value, the decline of the proportion of agricultural labor force is still very significant. According to

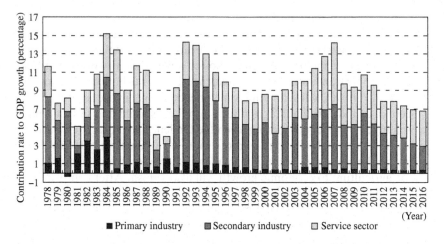

Figure 6.5 Changes in the contribution rates of three industries to GDP

the National Bureau of Statistics, the proportion of agricultural labor force decreased from 70.5% in 1978 to 27.0% in 2017. According to the author's estimates, the currently proportion of agricultural labor force is likely to be approximately 10 percentage points lower than this official figure.[16]

Moreover, reform and opening-up and development sharing are two processes with cause–effect relationships. They are mutually conditional and promote each other; that is, on the one hand, the reform allows the labor force to exit from the low-productivity sector, promotes its mobility between urban and rural areas, between regions and between industries, and then eliminates the institutional obstacles for it to enter the high-productivity sector in cities, making the process of declining agricultural share a real "Kuznets process." Among them, a series of measures in rural or agriculture-related reforms have played a role in allowing and promoting surplus labor to "exit" from agriculture and rural areas. On the other hand, it is precisely because of the process of declining agricultural share that employment expansion and productivity improvement are integrated. Reform and opening-up not only lead to high-speed growth, but also make this development result fully shared.

People often think that in the early stage of rural reform, the agricultural output value or added value increased rapidly, and its proportion in the national economy increased. This is in fact only a superficial phenomenon caused by the rising prices of agricultural products. If the influence of price factors was excluded, there was actually no increase in the proportion of agricultural output value. That is to say, the downward trend of agricultural share appeared almost from the beginning of the reform. Moreover, this process of declining agricultural share was also a process of resource reallocation.

Figure 6.6 illustrates the average annual real growth rates of added value of planting, forestry, animal husbandry and fishery, secondary industry, and

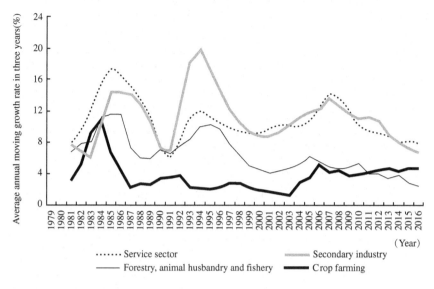

Figure 6.6 Growth trend of the added values of various industries

tertiary industry, which have been smoothed to a three-year moving average growth rate. Among them, the added value of planting, forestry, animal husbandry, and fishery is an approximate index calculated according to the added value of the primary industry, and the share of the two sectors in the agricultural output value is used as the weight. As shown in Figure 6.6, from the late 1970s to the early 1980s, during the rapid implementation of the household contract responsibility system, the added value of agriculture once increased rapidly but did not exceed the growth rate of the secondary and tertiary industries. A comparison of the growth rates of several industries shown in the figure has concluded some meaningful characteristics, as summarized below.

First, the planting sector initially slowed down, while forestry, animal husbandry, and fishery saw the first round of decline after rapid growth much later than planting, and the first lowest point of planting growth occurred in 1985 while that of forestry, animal husbandry, and fishery occurred two years later, in 1987. This shows that before the employment opportunities in non-agricultural industries were created, forestry, animal husbandry, and fishery played a role in absorbing the surplus labor force in the planting industry. With the increase of employment opportunities in rural non-agricultural industries, the proportion of rural labor force engaged in agriculture, forestry, animal husbandry, and fishery has obviously decreased since 1985, and the number of labor force engaged in non-agricultural industries has greatly increased. This period was exactly the peak of booming development of township enterprises.

According to date from National Bureau of Statistics, the output value of township enterprises accounted for less than a quarter of the total rural social output value in 1978. After nearly ten years of rapid development, it exceeded the total agricultural output value for the first time in 1987, accounting for 52.4% of the total rural social output value.[17] According to another data source, during 1980–1985 and 1985–1990, in terms of nominal growth caliber, the industrial output value of township enterprises increased by 2.59 times and 2.31 times respectively, while the total industrial output value of state-owned enterprises increased only by 60.95% and 1.07 times respectively during these two periods. By 1993, the proportion of township enterprises in the total industrial output value of the whole society had slightly exceeded that of state-owned enterprises.[18] Since then, the forms of ownership have become diversified and the non-public economy has been further expanded.

Second, the changing trend of forestry, animal husbandry, and fishery in agriculture is different from that of the planting industry, but is more consistent with the growth rate of the secondary and tertiary industries, indicating that while the share of agriculture is declining, agriculture has also experienced industrial structure adjustments, as a starting point, the resource allocation structure inclined to the grain and planting industry. It was not until 2003 when China's economy crossed the "Lewis turning point" that the growth rate of its output value dropped significantly due to a more serious labor shortage encountered by forestry, animal husbandry and fishery with higher labor intensity, with their annual growth rate converging once again to that of the planting industry.

Finally, since the beginning of the reform, the adjustment of industrial structure characterized by the decline of agricultural share was also initiated, and the added value growth rate of the secondary industry and tertiary industry has always been faster than that of the primary industry. Especially after Deng Xiaoping's talks given during his inspection tour in the south in 1992, the growth rate of non-agricultural industries was even higher, leaving the primary industry far behind. This is reflected not only in the relative growth trend of the output value of the three industries but also in the relative changing trend of employment in the three industries. The result is a continuous decline in the share of agricultural output value and employment.

This change in industrial structure, the "Kuznets process," has produced obvious efficiency of resource reallocation, and made great contributions to the improvement of labor productivity during the period of reform and opening-up. Moreover, the effect of resource reallocation has not shown a declining trend so far. This problem will be further discussed in Chapter 8.

Return of scale economy

The destination of Chinese agriculture is an unavoidable problem. Many developed agricultural countries have the advantage of abundant land and natural resources, forming large-scale and highly mechanized modern agriculture. However, East Asian economies that have similar resource endowments to China, such as Japan, South Korea, and Taiwan, have mostly adopted agricultural protectionism policies, hindering the role of price mechanisms and narrowing the scale of agriculture. Even if these countries can be regarded as having realized agricultural modernization in terms of material and equipment levels, they will always find it difficult to improve their agricultural competitiveness.

China is a country with a large population, and the per capita cultivated land is far below the world average level. The development of agricultural modernization is a very special problem. According to the general law, the improvement of agricultural labor productivity is the fundamental symbol of modernization. However, the scale of land operation has become an obstacle to further improvement of agricultural labor productivity. Can we sidestep the problem of scale in agricultural operations that is inevitable in practice and controversial in theory?

In discussions about China's agricultural economy, two traditional theories are very popular: (1) scale economy has its particularity in agriculture based on Schultz's theory, and (2) agriculture has industrial weakness, which is generally accepted by theoretical and policy circles. The extent to which problems existing in China's agricultural economy are influenced by these two theoretical viewpoints is also a problem worthy of in-depth discussion. The following discussion shows that these two viewpoints have so far exerted adverse effects on theoretical discussion and practical adjustment of China's agricultural policy orientation.

The myth of the "false indivisibility" of agricultural production factors

Theodore W. Schultz took tractors as an example to prove that the indivisibility of production factors, which was the basis for the existence of economies of scale, did not exist in agriculture, i.e., the so-called "false indivisibility."[19] He pointed out that tractors could be manufactured according to different specifications and models, very large or very small, to meet the cultivated land area. Furthermore, he actually extended the "false indivisibility" derived from tractors to other production factors. For example, he believed that part-time farming, as a mode of agricultural labor allocation, could even make workers "divisible."

Of course, his view that farm size could not determine the basic economic characteristics of traditional agriculture or modern agriculture was correct. He also acknowledged that it was more reasonable to use small or large tractors when the relative price of labor was lower or higher, but on the whole, he overgeneralized and absolutized the particularity of the scale economy in agriculture.

This theory focused on demonstrating that the scale economy in agriculture was not very important. In the early 1980s, when the household contract system was implemented in Chinese agriculture (that is, the large-scale production team operation was broken down into small family operations), this theory was used to endorse the legitimacy of the reform. In the development stage of China's agriculture at that time, it was proven that this theory was a very important and powerful theoretical basis. However, after China's agriculture had accomplished the staged tasks of safeguarding food supply and raising farmers' income, a small operation scale would undoubtedly hinder the use of agricultural machinery.

Observation of some real agricultural management examples has demonstrated how small-scale agricultural management increased transaction costs, thus causing losses to the scale economy. On the surface, commercial or cooperative services of agricultural machinery enabled farmers to purchase socialized services of agricultural machinery service companies or cooperatives rather than purchase agricultural machinery by themselves, which could continue to maintain the "false indivisibility" hypothesis of agricultural machinery.[20] However, the combination of production costs and transaction costs in agricultural operation has demonstrated that the scale of agricultural operation has become a realistic constraint to the improvement of agricultural production efficiency.

First of all, one viewpoint about the false indivisibility of agricultural production factors was that small-scale farmers did not have to own agricultural machinery, but purchased socialized agricultural machinery services. However, the narrow average household size and the scattered distribution of land plots have limited the use of large-scale agricultural machinery services. Theoretically, the small scale of agricultural machinery services could be expanded by cooperation between contracted farmers operating adjacent land plots. Nevertheless, the household-based land contracting and management may allow farmers to plant varieties of crops, and the negotiation between one contracting farmer and another in adjacent plots was undoubtedly very difficult, which would inevitably increase the transaction cost of purchasing agricultural machinery services.

Second, a scale economy also existed in farmers' activities of purchasing means of production and related services before, during, and after production. The use of scale economy necessitated a certain ability and incentives in order to bargain, collect information, evaluate results, and pay the corresponding transaction costs. However, the small scale of land area and operation would inevitably increase transaction costs and reduce incentives. For example, farmers used to face many options in the seed market. In the face of shoddy or even fake seeds, farmers would not be willing or able to spend time, energy, and financial resources on effective identification and choice of seeds.

Finally, similar to the "quantitative paradox" about the weak position of small farmers' negotiations in political economy,[21] a small-scale operation would be ineffective as regards generating an inducing mechanism for technological change. The relative scarcity of production factors or the market demand can always change anytime and anywhere.

During large-scale land operation, the change in relative scarcity of production factors or the market demand would form a guiding signal through changes in relative factor prices or in production and operation costs to induce technology to change in the direction of saving scarce factors or meeting market demand. For a narrow operation scale, however, farmers could find it difficult to respond effectively to market signals. For example, raising taxes could reduce the use of pesticides and correspondingly increase the cost of agricultural production. Large farms may use lamplight to trap and kill pests. However, it was difficult for household-based farmers to reach an agreement on inducing a land plot's pests onto another plot for centralized extermination, which also prevented the use of alternative technologies.

Discussions on the "theory of weak agricultural industry"

For a long time, most Chinese agricultural economists have regarded the "weakness" of agriculture as a self-evident premise and the basis for protecting agriculture, but it has not been verified by studies. There are three reasons for this.[22] First, agriculture is a process in which natural reproduction and economic reproduction are intertwined, and the labor force is not fully utilized during production. Second, agriculture is affected by stronger natural factors, leading to uncertainty of production results. Third, on the one hand, the supply of agricultural products has a "cobweb effect" to some extent; on the other hand, after entering a certain stage of development, the elasticity of agricultural product income will be less than 1, resulting in the lack of stable guarantee for producers' income.

Obviously, the above three reasons are nothing more than repeating the old tune of traditional ideas. Under modern financial and insurance systems and higher product market forms, coupled with necessary government regulation functions, these three aspects are at least difficult to become powerful arguments for agricultural "weakness."

More convincing discussions were not focused on the universality of agricultural weakness but on comparison of countries engaging traditional types of agriculture, particularly those characterized by high man–land ratio, with New World countries of superior land endowment generating a static reason—i.e., the theory of agricultural comparative advantage—and a dynamic reason—i.e., the theory of agricultural labor force proportion. A combination of these two theories has formed the theory of Chinese agricultural particularity to some extent.[23]

According to this point of view, first of all, China's agricultural resources endowment could hardly rival such countries as the United States and Australia, and second, it is not easy to relocate an excessively large-scale agricultural labor force all at once. Therefore, the general path of expanding the operation scale seems impassable, and it is still necessary to use international rules to subsidize and protect agriculture more or less.

Experiential research on agricultural protection in international economic circles has both supported and denied the theory of Chinese agricultural particularity. For example, according to econometric analysis made by Masayoshi Honma and Yujiro Hayami, the lower a country's agricultural comparative advantage, the higher the country's protection level of agriculture; meanwhile, as the decrease of agricultural share meant that the non-agricultural population had an increased ability and willingness to subsidize agriculture, the level of agricultural protection would increase with the decreasing proportion of agricultural labor force or output value.[24]

In the final analysis, however, it was an indisputable fact that agricultural protection led to efficiency loss, so the level of agricultural protection would not be improved blindly. Experience has shown that when the proportion of the agricultural labor force fell to 6–8% or the proportion of agricultural output value fell to approximately 4%, there would emerge a turning point at which the agricultural protection level stopped ascending. This means that agricultural subsidy or "support by industry sector" was a phenomenon at a specific development stage, while the "theory of weak agricultural industry" tended to break the stage boundary and fix or perpetuate agricultural subsidy and protection.

For example, according to Yujiro Hayami's division, Japan's agriculture had also experienced stages of food shortage and poverty, but it did not enter the stage of agricultural production mode according to logic; instead, it turned to the other side of the forked road, i.e., implementing the agricultural protection policy.[25] Even after reaching the critical point of declining agricultural share, Japanese agriculture was still advancing under protection. A series of Yujiro Hayami's studies began with the loss of efficiency and welfare arising from agricultural protection, hoping to guide the agriculture of Japan and other economies to the stage of adjustment aimed at improving efficiency. Many countries that were once considered short of comparative advantages in agriculture had finally created a more efficient and competitive mode of agricultural production.

How to develop agriculture in countries short of comparative advantages is not a simple industrial policy issue, but it also involves issues in relation to social aspects, people's livelihoods, and food security. After all, the modern agricultural production mode is the foundation for solving the above problems as a whole. In particular, whether agriculture should be protected as a weak industry does not depend on farmers' expectations and government's wishes in the final analysis; instead, it is restricted by a series of factors that do not depend on human will, such as the maximum of international agricultural product prices, the minimum of domestic agricultural product production costs, the yellow line of WTO rules, and the red line of land resources. In addition to seeking all available solutions, it is undoubtedly an unavoidable path to expand the scale of agricultural operation and curb the diminishing return on capital.

The status quo of China's agricultural operation scale

Since the mid-1980s, farming households have become the basic operational unit of China's agriculture as a result of the implementation of the household contract responsibility system. The land originally cultivated by the production team was distributed, following the tying principle of good and bad land plots, to each peasant household according to a certain proportion of the number of family members and labor force. In order to consolidate reform achievements, the central government enacted a law establishing household management as the basic agricultural management system, and extended the contract period to 30 years.

In this case, the scale of land is extremely small, and the land of each household is often scattered. However, the division of this plot also leads to the reduction of arable land utilization rate due to too many roads, ridges, and ditches. Moreover, even if there was inherent requirement of land concentration due to a shortage of labor, it was difficult to substantially expand the scale of land management because the existing household registration system made it hard for farmers to change their permanent residence, not to mention the abandonment or extensive cultivation of farmland caused by the separation of households and land and the inability to achieve land circulation and concentration.

The American writer Henry David Thoreau described a self-sufficient agricultural production mode in *Walden*: "if one would live simply and eat only the crop which he raised..., he would need to cultivate only a few rods of ground [a square rod is approximately 25.3 square meters], and that it would be cheaper to spade up that than to use oxen to plow it." As shown in Table 6.1, the average land size of Chinese farmers was far smaller than that of developed countries in Europe and America, Eastern European countries, Latin American and African countries, and even significantly smaller than that of Asian neighbors. The land plots of each farming household in China were scattered in several different positions, usually five or six plots or even more on average,[26] which was almost the same as the situation described by Thoreau.

It should be noted that the land sizes of Chinese farmers in Table 6.1 were the result of the first agricultural census in 1997. China conducted the second agricultural census in 2006, but did not issue any comparable information, resulting in lack of access to available figures on the average land size of farmers, so only the data of the first agricultural census were provided in the table to facilitate comparison. It can be expected that since the first agricultural census, the Chinese central government has made great efforts to promote land circulation, bringing about great change in the situation.

For example, according to figures provided by Xiwen Chen, the land circulation has been promoted in recent years through policies encouraging separation of land contract right from land management right. Of the 1.3 billion

Table 6.1 International comparison of average farm (farmer) size

	Year of census	Average size (ha)	China equivalent (%)
China	1997	0.67	100.0
South Asia:			
Pakistan	2000	3.09	21.8
India	2000/2001	1.33	50.6
Developed countries:			
Japan	2000	1.20	56.2
France	1999/2000	45.04	1.5
U.S.	2002	178.35	0.4
UK	1999/2000	70.86	0.9
Africa:			
Namibia	1996/1997	2.99	23.3
Uganda	2002	3.25	20.7
Eastern Europe:			
Hungary	2000	6.67	10.1
Romania	2000	2.93	23.0
Latin America:			
Nicaragua	2000/2001	31.34	2.1
Brazil	1996	72.76	0.9

Source: Food and Agriculture Organization of the United Nations, *2000 World Census of Agriculture: Main Results and Metadata by Country (1996–2005)*, Rome: FAO, 2010.

mu of contracted land, approximately 380 million have been circulated and 940 million have not, with the former accounting for approximately 28%. From the perspective of farming households, approximately 170 million households did not have their land transferred and only 60 million had some or all of their land transferred, accounting for 26%.[27] In addition, according to a sample survey covering different periods, the ratio between farming households cultivating their own contracted land and those cultivating transferred land changed from 97:3 in 1996 to 81:19 in 2008.[28] Farmers operate a larger proportion of transferred land. This undoubtedly means that there is a trend of land concentration and that the scale of operation has been expanded.

Nevertheless, there are also some studies that do not support the conclusion of expanding scale of farmers' land operation. For example, according to a survey on rural land in China that selected farmers' samples from Jiangsu, Sichuan, Shaanxi, Jilin, and Hebei Provinces, from the average level of all samples in these provinces, the size of farmers' land operation expanded from 0.59 hectares in 2007 to 0.62 hectares in 2013, only a slight increase.[29] Researchers who conducted the survey claimed that the data were nationally representative. Regardless of data credibility, the average size of farmers' operation obtained by the survey was even smaller than that of the national agricultural census in 1997.

A World Bank study defines farmers with less than 2 hectares of arable land as small land holders,[30] so farmers with only approximately 0.6 hectares can undoubtedly be called ultra-small land holders. Pursuant to international standards, the land scale of China's agriculture and the resulting agricultural operation scale are obviously very small. This is an indisputable fact to date. This situation has hindered farmers from improving agricultural production efficiency at the micro level, and constituted an obstacle to the modernization of China's agricultural production mode as a whole.

Empirical test on China's agricultural development stage

Some researchers have attempted to estimate the agricultural production function and describe the changes in China's agricultural development stage from an empirical perspective. However, due to the large discrepancy between the agricultural labor input data used in the econometric model and the actual situation, the degree of change was often underestimated, resulting in inaccurate judgments on the agricultural development stage. This conclusion tended to cover up severe problems and new challenges facing China's economy.[31]

As data of the material and service costs and the number of workers in the national agricultural product cost–benefit survey were reflecting the actual input, Cai Fang and Meiyan Wang utilized these data for quantitative analysis in an attempt to solve the problems in previous estimates and avoid corresponding misjudgments.[32] Three grain crops—japonica rice, corn, and wheat—were adopted to estimate China's agricultural production function, and the marginal productivity of capital and labor of three crops was calculated according to the estimation results (Table 6.2), from which some conclusions can be drawn.

First of all, until reform effect came out in 1984, China's agriculture had been in the stage of solving the problem of food shortages, featuring a dual

Table 6.2 Marginal productivity of capital and labor (kg)

	1978–1984	1978–1990	1991–2006	2007–2013
Japonica rice				
Marginal productivity of capital	9.461	8.422	6.732	6.186
Marginal productivity of labor	−1.369	0.219	4.306	11.261
Corn				
Marginal productivity of capital	10.177	9.351	8.273	6.672
Marginal productivity of labor	0.589	2.378	6.005	19.206
Wheat				
Marginal productivity of capital	6.537	6.126	5.624	4.953
Marginal productivity of labor	−0.366	0.361	2.322	20.070

Source: Fang Cai and Meiyan Wang, From Poor Economy to Scale Economy: Challenges to China's Agriculture from Changes in Development Stages, *Economic Research Journal*, Vol. 5, 2016.

economy mode and very low marginal labor productivity. From 1978 to 1984, crops such as japonica rice and wheat saw a negative marginal productivity of labor, while corn saw a near-zero marginal labor productivity, consistent with Lewis's hypothesis of "zero-value labor." Corresponding to a lower stage of development in the shortage of modern production factors, the higher marginal productivity of capital was in line with theoretical expectations.

Second, during 1978–1990, there emerged an obvious decreasing trend of marginal capital productivity and an increasing trend of marginal labor productivity of the three food crops. Especially during the period from 2007 to 2013, the marginal capital productivity of japonica rice decreased by 27%, and the marginal capital productivity of corn and wheat decreased by 29% and 19% respectively. Correspondingly, the marginal labor productivity of japonica rice increased 50 times in the same period, and the marginal labor productivity of corn and wheat increased by seven times and 55 times respectively. The increase in marginal labor productivity of three food crops was much higher than the decrease in marginal capital productivity.

Finally, it was observed that, after the Lewis turning point, the marginal capital productivity of China's agriculture continued to decline, thus indicating that under the condition of relative scarcity of production factors and changes in relative prices, the narrow scale of agricultural operation had become a restrictive factor, resulting in diminishing returns on capital and declining returns on investment. According to Schultz's theory and its policy implications, the key to transforming traditional agriculture was the introduction of modern production factors. However, this kind of new production, factors requires a critical minimum operating scale in order to realize efficient allocation.

Conclusions

Over the past 70 years, with the failure of the people's commune experiment and the success of the rural economic reform, China has experienced twists and turns in its general economic development stage, and has been closer to the whole process of dual economic development. At the same time, China has verified the indispensable role of reasonable economic systems and mechanisms in production power, labor incentives, scale economy utilization, and resource allocation.

The status quo of China's agriculture remains a small-scale household-based management mode. Although this mode of production is not a simple reappearance of the involution of agriculture before reform and opening-up, it is still far from modern agriculture. On the one hand, free mobility of labor and the extremely low comparative income of agriculture made agriculture unable to improve productivity by the means of intensive involution. On the other hand, the current land system and household registration system still hinder the transfer of land and can hardly centralize land plots in the hands of the most productive operators in order to make full use of scale economy. The only way to realize modernization of agriculture and rural areas and break the cycle of agricultural production mode is to break through the stable and balanced state of agriculture and improve labor productivity by expanding the land operation scale.

The rapid economic growth in the period of reform and opening-up was accompanied by a prominent phenomenon: significant decline in agricultural share. This phenomenon has also led to important changes in the way agriculture contributed to economic development in the traditional sense. The relative importance of factor contribution has declined, and the effect of resource reallocation characterized by labor transfer has become the most significant contribution mode.

This Kuznets process and its related reforms took place around the exit of labor from low-productivity sectors, the labor mobility between urban and rural areas, regions and industries, and the labor entry into high-productivity urban sectors and non-agricultural industries. In the meantime, the main line of rural reform was creating motive force and mechanism conditions for surplus labor to exit from low-productivity agriculture and rural industries.

According to the general law and international development experience, there is huge potential for China's rural labor force transfer, and accordingly, the rural reform aimed at releasing surplus labor force is far from complete. From the development stage of China's economy, we can see whether the proportion of agricultural labor force is still high according to international comparison. By comparing the proportion of China's agricultural labor force with that of other upper-middle-income countries with their GDP per capita higher than that of China, we can see that the proportion of China's agricultural labor force is still much higher than the arithmetic average of these countries.[33] That is to say, if China wants to enter the ranks of high-income countries in the near future, it must significantly narrow the gap with these countries in terms of the industrial structure feature of employment distribution.

The unfinished reform should be systematic and all-round, but, whether it is from the logic of this chapter or from the problem-oriented principle, defining rural reform to promote labor exit helps China to make efforts on currently urgent tasks and clarify urgent tasks of further reform.

History is not only similar, but also periodic. The use of agricultural scale economy in economic development was also manifested as constantly returning to the starting point. However, regardless of the agricultural production mode itself or from the external environment, each starting point was brand-new. In the development stage of transition from upper-middle-income countries to high-income countries, China is currently facing a new challenge of how to realize agricultural scale economy, which requires China to embark on a special road of development in line with national conditions and the general laws.

The strategy of rural vitalization initiated in the report of the 19th National Congress of the Communist Party of China has fully deployed policy requirements and implementation strategies based on reform so as to realize urban–rural integration and agricultural and rural modernization. The foresight of this strategy lies in close combination of the fundamental solution to issues relating to agriculture, rural areas and the well-being of farmers with the long-term sustainable development of the entire Chinese economy. Therefore, the proper meaning of implementing this strategy is undoubtedly improving agricultural labor productivity by expanding the land operation scale and further creating conditions for agricultural labor to exit from low-productivity employment.

Notes

1 See A. Chayanov, *Farmers' Economic Organization*, Beijing: Central Compilation & Translation Press, 1996. After Keynes's visit to the Soviet Union in 1925, he came to the conclusion that the population growth was so fast that it caused mounting pressure on the means of survival. See Isaac Deutscher, *The Prophet Unarmed: Trotsky 1921–1929*, Beijing: Central Compilation & Translation Press, 2013, p. 168.

2 See Евгений Алексеевич Преображенский, *New Economics: An Attempt to Theoretically Analyze Soviet Economy*, Hong Kong: SDX Joint Publishing Company, 1984.

3 Naum Jasny, *Socialized Agriculture in the Soviet Union: Plans and Results, Volume I*, Beijing: The Commercial Press, 1965, p. 29.

4 Xing Su, *Socialist Transformation of China's Agriculture*, Shanghai: People's Publishing House, 1980, p. 11.

5 See Huang Zhongzhi, Development or Involution? Great Britain and China in the 18th Century: Comment on Kenneth Pomeranz's *Great Divergence: Europe, China and Development of Modern World Economy*, *Historical Research*, Vol. 4, 2002.

6 This is a researcher's reading note after studying Mao Zedong's *On Agricultural Cooperation*. See Xing Su's Struggle between Socialism and Capitalism in Rural China after Land Reform, *Economic Research Journal*, Vol. 7, 1965.

7 Institute of Contemporary China Studies, *Chronology of the History of the People's Republic of China (1958)*, Beijing: Contemporary China Publishing House, 2011, p. 30.

8 Su Xing, *Socialist Transformation of China's Agriculture*, Shanghai: People's Publishing House, 1980, p. 156.

9 Institute of Contemporary China Studies, *Chronology of the History of the People's Republic of China (1958)*, Beijing: Contemporary China Publishing House, 2011, p. 538.

10 See, e.g., Justin Yifu Lin, Rural Reforms and Agricultural Growth in China, *American Economic Review*, Vol. 82, No. 1, 1992, pp. 34–51; John McMillan, John Whalley, and Zhu Lijing, The Impact of China's Economic Reforms on Agricultural Productivity Growth, *Journal of Political Economy*, Vol. 97, No. 4, 1989, pp. 781–807.

11 Information Office of the State Council, *Policy Interpretation of the Opinions on Separation of Rural Land Rights*, November 3, 2016, www.scio.gov.cn/34473/34515/Document/1515220/1515220htm.

12 Pei-kang Chang, *Agriculture and Industrialization: The Adjustments that Take Place as an Agricultural Country Is Industrialized*, Cambridge, MA: Harvard University Press, 1949; Bruce F. Johnston and John W. Mellor, The Role of Agriculture in Economic Development, *The American Economic Review*, Vol. 51, No. 4, 1961, pp. 566–593

13 Cai Fang, *Economics of People's Livelihood: An Analysis of Issues Relating to Agriculture, Rural Affairs and Farmers and Employment*, Beijing: Social Sciences Academic Press, 2005, p. 78.

14 Huang Jikun, Keijiro Otsuka, and Scott Rozelle, *The Role of Agriculture in China's Development*, presented at the workshop "China's Economic Transition: Origins, Mechanisms, and Consequences," Pittsburgh, November 5–7, 2004.

15 Masahiko Aoki, The Five Phases of Economic Development and Institutional Evolution in China, Japan and Korea, in Masahiko Aoki, Timur Kuran, and Gérard Roland (eds.), *Institutions and Comparative Economic Development*, Basingstoke: Palgrave Macmillan, 2012, pp. 13–47

16 See Cai Fang, *China's Economic Growth Prospects: From Demographic Dividend to Reform Divide*, Cheltenham, UK: Edward Elgar, 2016.

17 National Bureau of Statistics, *Series Analysis Report on 50 Years of New China (6): The Rise of Township Enterprises*, 1999, www.stats.gov.cn/ztjc/ztfx/xzg50nxlf xbg/200206/t20020605_35964html.

18 Cai Fang, *Economics of People's Livelihood: An Analysis of Issues Relating to Agriculture, Rural Affairs and Farmers and Employment*, Beijing: Social Sciences Academic Press, 2005, p. 108.

19 Theodore W. Schultz, *Transforming Traditional Agriculture*, Chicago and London: University of Chicago Press, 1983, pp. 110–127

20 The phenomenon that Chinese farmers increased their purchase of professional mechanized services has just shown that large tractors and their self-contained farm tools are no longer irrelevant but necessary for agricultural production at this phase.

21 According to this theory, the interest group of peasants has numerous members, but it is precisely because of a series of factors related to this "quantitative" characteristic that makes them difficult to communicate when they perform collective actions. See Mancur Olson, *Logic of Collective Action*, Shanghai: People's Publishing House, 1995.

22 For example, Fan Gao, Basis, Connotation and Change Path of China's Agricultural Weakness, *Social Sciences in Yunnan*, Vol. 3, 2006.

23 For example, Chen Xiwen, Focus Issues of China's Agricultural Development, *Agriculture Machinery Technology Extension*, Vol. 7, 2015.

24 Masayoshi Honma and Yujiro Hayami, The Determinants of Agricultural Protection Levels: An Econometric Analysis, in Kym Anderson and Yujiro Hayami (eds.), *The Political Economy of Agricultural Protection*, Sydney: Allen & Unwin, 1986, Chapter 4.

25 Yujiro Hayami, *Japanese Agriculture under Siege: The Political Economy of Agricultural Policies*, New York: St.Martin's Press, 1988

26 Gao Liangliang, Huang Jikun, and Scott Rozelle, Rental Markets for Cultivated Land and Agricultural Investments in China, *Agricultural Economics*, Vol. 43, 2012, pp. 391–403.

27 Yao Yuan, Han Miao, *Chen Xiwen's Talks about Land Circulation: Avoid Random Land Division and Allow Farmers to Make Independent Choices*, 2015, http://news. xinhuanet.com/fortune/201503/06/c_1114552132htm.
28 Gao Liangliang, Huang Jikun, and Scott Rozelle, Rental Markets for Cultivated Land and Agricultural Investments in China, *Agricultural Economics*, Vol. 43, 2012, pp. 391–403
29 Ji Xianqing, Scott Rozelle, Huang Jikun, Zhang Linxiu and Zhang Tonglong, Are China's Farms Growing?, *China & World Economy*, Vol. 24, No. 1, 2016, pp. 41–62.
30 Quoted from Ji Xianqing, Scott Rozelle, Huang Jikun, Zhang Linxiu, and Zhang Tonglong, Are China's Farms Growing?, *China & World Economy*, Vol. 24, No.1, 2016, pp. 41–62.
31 For example, Ryoshi Minami and Ma Xinxin estimated the agricultural production function using the number of agricultural labor force published by official statistics, and came to the conclusion that China has not yet reached the Lewis turning point. See Ryoshi Minami and Xinxin Ma, The Turning Point of Chinese Economy: Compared with Japanese Experience, *Asian Economics*, Vol. 50, No. 12, 2009, pp. 2–20. Up to now, there have been many observers who have come to similar conclusions while failing to figure out the changes in the number of agricultural labor force. In view of this, Cai Fang introduced and discussed the actual situation of labor use in agriculture, and made a re-estimation based on the existing research. See Cai Fang, *China's Economic Growth Prospects: From Demographic Dividend to Reform Divide*, Cheltenham, UK: Edward Elgar, 2016.
32 Cai Fang and Wang Meiyan, From Poor Economy to Scale Economy: Challenges to China's Agriculture from Changes in Development Phases, *Economic Research Journal*, Vol. 5, 2016.
33 Cai Fang, Has the Potential of Agricultural Labor Transfer Been Exhausted?, *Chinese Rural Economy*, Vol. 9, 2018.

7 Urbanization in the development of reform and opening-up

Introduction

China's reform and opening-up has brought unprecedented high economic growth. In the period from 1978 to 2018, China's real GDP grew at an average annual rate of 9.4%, the fastest and longest-lasting growth rate in the world in this period. It cannot be ignored that China's urbanization rate was also the fastest in the world in the same period.

In this period, China's urbanization rate ascended from 17.9% to 59.6% at an annual rate of 3.1%, not only much faster than the average level of high-income countries (0.33%) and low-income countries (1.39%), but also significantly faster than the more comparable average level of "late demographic dividend countries" in the same demographic transition stage (1.75%)[1] and than the average level of upper-middle-income countries in the same economic development stage (1.65%). In this period, 25.6% of the increase in the world's urban population came from China. However, China's urbanization was closely related to its economic growth in this period; to a considerable extent, the former was the latter's realization mode, i.e., turning the necessary condition of demographic dividend into realistic economic growth. These two "miracles" were actually one and the same thing.

Some studies on China's rapid growth either ignored the necessary conditions for economic growth,[2] thus crippling their explanatory power for China's rapid economic growth for 40 years, or simply denied the existence of such necessary conditions,[3] resulting in continued bad-mouthing of China's economy, regardless of their repeated misjudgments.[4] Moreover, the failure to properly find out the necessary conditions for China's economic growth also led to an overemphasis on the demand perspective of economic growth and neglect of the supply perspective, giving rise to misreading and misjudgment of China's economy from at least two aspects as below.

First, due to their inability to accurately understand the characteristics of unlimited labor supply in China's dual economy development stage as well as the Chinese characteristic manner that this endowment was transformed into comparative advantage, some economists in the world, when facing the international competitiveness acquired by China's labor-intensive manufacturing,

DOI: 10.4324/9781003329305-9

challenged and even tried to revise the principle of comparative advantage[5] that they had believed in for 200 years, or simply gave up their self-evident oath of "firm belief in free trade." For this purpose, they attributed the imbalance of the world economy or the polarization of Western countries, especially of the American society, to China's development mode, resulting in economic and trade frictions against China with the increasing tendency of populist politics and protectionist policies.

Second, some Chinese and foreign economists cannot accurately understand the supply-side driving force of China's rapid growth and the changes accompanying the development stage. Faced with the slowdown of China's economic growth, they tend to look for answers from the demand side, or come to the suggestion that the driving force of economic growth needs to shift from export to consumption. These suggestions seem reasonable, but they cannot prescribe the right medicine or draw the conclusion that the government needs to increase the stimulus to investment, in an attempt to rely on demand to return to the previous growth rate. Based on this kind of awareness of intentionally or unintentionally ignoring the supply-side factors of economic growth, ignoring the development conditions and their changes, the policies suggested by them were tantamount to seeking fish from the wood.

Understanding the high coincidence between the reform and opening-up period and the special stage of population transition can better explain the necessary conditions for China's economic growth. During 1980–2010, China's working-age population aged 15–59 grew at an average annual rate of 1.8%, while the dependent population outside this age range basically stayed in a state of zero growth (−0.2%). The scissors gap formed by the two types of population growth was also manifested in the continuous decline in the population dependency ratio, which created a unique demographic window of the population in this period.

China's unique and now-or-never demographic dividend was manifested not only in the sufficient labor supply but also in almost all explanatory variables on the right side of the overall production function equation describing economic growth. First, a low and declining dependency ratio was conducive to the realization of a high savings rate, while the unlimited supply of labor delayed the occurrence of diminishing returns on capital, thus making capital accumulation the main engine of economic growth. Second, favorable demographic factors have ensured outstanding contributions made by sufficient quantity of labor force and its improved quality to economic growth. Third, the interindustry, intersector, and interregional mobility of surplus labor and redundant workers in the low-to-high order of productivity has brought about the resource reallocation efficiency and become a main component of total factor productivity.

Economists' decomposition of China's economic growth factors seemed to involve conventional production factors and the productivity contribution. However, once they understood the meaning of demographic factors to these conventional variables, all relevant studies have actually tested the above hypothesis and certified that the demographic dividend was a necessary condition for China's rapid growth.

However, realistic evidence has been provided either by China before the reform and opening-up or by other countries that are characterized by similar demographic transitions but have never achieved any outstanding growth performance, showing that the necessary conditions alone are not enough for development that also need an effective incentive mechanism for the accumulation of production factors and an economic system for the allocation of production factors so as to transform favorable demographic structure features into corresponding economic growth.

In other words, economic reform was the sufficient condition for China to realize its own potentialities. Understanding both the necessary conditions and sufficient conditions[6] helps make a scientific explanation of China's economic growth, and enables us to better understand the growth process in the past 40 years, correctly judge the current economic situation, make an accurate outlook for the future, and reveal relevant policy implications.

The demographic transition from rural to urban areas promoted by China's rapid urbanization as well as the reallocation of the labor force from agriculture to non-agricultural industries in the past 40 years have illustrated how relevant reforms eliminated the institutional obstacles hindering the mobility and reallocation of production factors, and transformed favorable demographic features into high economic growth, significant structural adjustment, and profound social changes. Therefore, the process of urbanization and the institutional reform, structural transformation, growth contribution, and sharing effect revealed in the process may become an all-around epitome of the whole process of reform, opening-up, and development sharing.

This chapter describes urbanization with Chinese characteristics as a process of reform and development from three aspects: the "exit" of labor force from low-productivity agriculture and rural industries, the "mobility" of labor force between agriculture and non-agricultural industries, between urban and rural areas, and between regions, and the "entry" of labor force into cities, sectors, and society in terms of residence, employment, and social identity. The three most representative historical moments (events) are selected to reflect the magnificent historical picture of China's reform and opening-up, and attempts to summarize relevant characteristic facts from the perspective of economics as staged efforts to upgrade Chinese experience to Chinese wisdom.

In any economy with a potential demographic dividend, even if it is fully utilized, this favorable development condition will eventually decline or even vanish with time. China is also in this stage of development. Accordingly, the functions of various factors of economic growth will inevitably change, not only in the sense of relative degree, but also in the reversal of direction.

For example, under the condition of negative growth of the working-age population, the contribution of the labor force to economic growth may become negative, which is the most obvious situation, while the changes in the contribution made by other growth factors such as material capital, human capital, and total factor productivity are more complicated. In any case, the traditional source of growth will eventually turn to a new and more sustainable source of growth. For this reason, this chapter also expands the general characteristic facts, and puts forward some policy suggestions to shape the new connotation of urbanization through reform in order to gain new growth momentum.

Three historical moments of reform

Although the historical process took place continuously according to internal development logic, some important historical events often appeared independently, forming a symbolic node connecting the past with the future, which is of milestone significance in the whole historical process. In the process of China's reform and opening-up, there were countless time nodes with such symbolic significance.

This chapter focuses on urbanization in the period of reform and opening-up. Therefore, we have chosen three events that can generally reflect the starting point, advancement process and tipping point of urbanization, i.e., historical events that have important turning points and strong narrative characteristics and are easy to express with economic concepts, so as to connect various periods, different fields and independent plates with these classic moments according to the internal logic of the whole reform, and embody the unity of historical logic and theoretical logic when describing the reform process.

Historical moment 1

Fengyang County, Anhui Province, is located on the Huaihe River that is the natural boundary between north and south China. Fengyang is the hometown of the Emperor Taizu of the Ming Dynasty Zhu Yuanzhang, but the Fengyang flower-drum dance is even more well-known. Since the Ming and Qing dynasties, Fengyang has been famous for its perennial calamities and extreme poverty due to frequent occurrences of flood, drought, and locust plagues. Hordes of victims fled to beg for food with flower drums on their backs, so Fengyang flower drum became a cultural symbol of poor Fengyang County. However, by the end of the 1970s, Fengyang was only a microcosm of the poverty caused by the people's commune system. In 1978, there were 250 million people in absolute poverty whose annual per capita income in rural areas was less than RMB100 yuan.

One day in December 1978, farmers in Xiaogang Village got ready to go out to beg for food as they had done for many years. However, the year 1978 was destined to be an unusual year. From December 18 to 22, the Third Plenary Session of the Eleventh Central Committee of the Communist Party of China was held in Beijing, which re-established the Party's ideological line of emancipating the mind and seeking truth from facts, and decided to shift the priorities of the whole Party's work to economic construction, laying a theoretical foundation for reform and opening-up.

Xiaogang villagers may not know the convening of this meeting and what was discussed at the meeting. In fact, the documents adopted at the meeting did not explicitly affirm any reform practice. However, the political atmosphere was quite different than before. Villagers felt that there was a different choice from fleeing the famine and begging for food, and began thinking of abandoning the production team's mode of labor. This was a move against the world in that era. As a result, heads of 18 peasant households signed and pressed their fingerprints in red ink on a written pledge, unanimously deciding to implement fixed output quotas for individual households and bear the possible political consequences.

The system of fixing output quotas for individual households or the household-based contract system was referred to collectively as the household contract responsibility system. In fact, while farmland in Xiaogang Village was divided and distributed to individual households as 18 peasant households had done, this experiment was also carried out in many places all over the country, especially in Sichuan, Anhui, and Inner Mongolia. This system was implemented throughout the country in the following years and led to the abolition of the people's commune system.

At the beginning of 1980, only 1.1% of the production teams in China implemented the household contract responsibility system, which increased to 20% by the end of the same year. By the end of 1984, this mode of operation covered 100% of the production teams and 97.9% of the peasant households. This rural reform broke preliminarily through the traditional planned economic system. The disruptive institutional innovation in Xiaogang Village was regarded naturally as the pioneering practice of China's economic reform.

The direct purpose of implementing the household contract responsibility system was to improve the incentive mechanism for agricultural production and labor, and to give farmers autonomy in land management and the right to claim surplus products. Furthermore, after this incentive mechanism was improved and its remarkable effect of stimulating agricultural growth appeared, the core content of this reform was giving peasant householders the autonomy in allocating production factors. That is to say, with the explicit surplus of labor force in agriculture, the labor force began to exit from low-productivity agriculture and turn to non-agricultural industries and rural areas, and the scale of transfer gradually increased from small to large.

Historical moment 2

As early as in 1979 when the reform was initiated, Deng Xiaoping proposed that Chinese policy-makers should establish special export zones (later called "special economic zones") in Shenzhen, Zhuhai, and Shantou in Guangdong Province and Xiamen in Fujian Province. In 1984, a number of open coastal cities were established in succession. In 1988, Hainan Province was established as a special economic zone. Several years later, what effect, experience, and implications have these special economic zones and open coastal cities provided for the reform and opening-up of China as a whole?

On January 17, 1992, Deng Xiaoping, who was 88 years old and had retired from his leadership position, boarded the southbound train and began his trip to the south for more than one month. From January 18 to February 21, Deng visited Wuchang, Shenzhen, Zhuhai, Shanghai, and other places, among which Shenzhen and Zhuhai were the earliest special economic zones while Shanghai was the largest open coastal city. What was written in the history of China's reform and opening-up was a series of important talks made by Deng on his way south.

As a summary of the south tour talks that were most impressive and targeted to China at that time and later became the content of the guiding ideology of reform, the following key questions were answered by Deng Xiaoping.[7] First, what is reform, and for what? Reform was to establish a socialist economic system full of vigor and vitality, and to develop and emancipate productive forces. Second, how should we judge the success or failure of reform? The judgment depends on whether it was conducive to developing the productive forces of socialist society, enhancing the comprehensive national strength of socialist countries, and improving people's living standards. Third, how should we accelerate the pace of reform? Market is an economic means that exists either in a capitalist country or in a socialist one. These talks conveyed an important message, i.e., what Deng had always required: we should accelerate the pace of reform and opening-up, and unwaveringly adhere to the strategic thinking that only development counts.

Deng Xiaoping's talks were inspiring and received a positive response from China's top leadership. Since then, the pace of reform and opening-up has accelerated. Either observations of economic growth indicators or observations of economic export-oriented indicators such as foreign direct investment growth and export growth can help find the remarkable launching role of Deng Xiaoping's south tour talks. The rapid development of export-oriented labor-intensive manufacturing industry in coastal areas has created a large number of jobs and huge demand for rural labor.

It was from this time that the transfer of agricultural labor force was no longer just surplus-driven, but was added with new demand pull. At the same time, the institutional obstacles hindering the transfer of agricultural labor force were eliminated, e.g., cancellation of the coupon-based system, extension of the scope and scale of labor mobility, and removal of tangible obstacles to living and employment in cities and towns at all levels.

Historical moment 3

The household registration system enacted in 1958 was designed to incorporate the residence and employment of population into the national plan, restricting free migration and mobility of population and labor force between regions, especially between urban and rural areas. Researchers' and observers' understanding of this system at one time (if not still so) tended to be simplistic because they thought that this single population registration system could solve all problems and limit the migration and mobility of population to the extent as desired by the central government.

This leads to two misleading results. First, we cannot see that many policies and institutional forms supporting the household registration system play the same role of restricting the flow in the periphery; second, we cannot see that the related policy reform gradually hollows out the connotation of the household registration system and weakens its function, so it is also a process of household registration system reform.

On March 17, 2003, Sun Zhigang, a 27-year-old graphic designer who worked in Guangzhou after graduating from university, was questioned by the police on the street and then held in a detention center in Guangzhou because he did not apply for a temporary residence permit. During his stay at the center, he died unnaturally three days after he had been beaten by medical staff and some inmates.

After the incident was exposed, it shocked the whole country. After the incident, 12 parties were sentenced (including one death penalty) and 20 public servants were subject to administrative punishment. The central government paid a lot of attention to this case. Realizing the institutional drawbacks caused by the problem, it abolished the State Council's *Measures for Detention and Repatriation of Urban Vagrants and Beggars* three months later, which had been implemented for 20 years, and replaced it with the *Measures for Relief and Management of Vagrants and Beggars in Cities*.

The change in the implementation goal and connotation of government laws and regulations from "detention and repatriation" to "relief" marks a major breakthrough in the institutional environment for exit, mobility, and entry of labor force. The household registration system has confined the rural population to the countryside in terms of geographical region, to farming in terms of employment, and to farmland in terms of workplace. This system was realized through a series of supporting systems such as the people's commune system and the coupon-based system. The abolition of the people's commune first entitled peasants to be employed in other industries, while the abolition of the coupon-based system expanded the geographical scope of rural labor transfer. Therefore, this round of institutional reform represented by the Sun Zhigang incident actually included a series of such breakthroughs, which was an important turning point of urbanization.

The author took the income gap between urban and rural areas at the beginning of rural reform in 1978 as a benchmark to predict that the next fundamental institutional change related to the relationship between urban and rural areas would occur when the income gap between urban and rural areas returned to this benchmark level—that is, one or two years after the publication of the article.[8] Afterward, the author treated the year 2004 as the year when China's economy reached the Lewis turning point, and pointed out that this turning point was not only marked by labor shortages and wage increases for ordinary workers, but also accompanied by a series of institutional changes and policy adjustments.[9] The removal of barriers to urbanization was beyond all doubt the most historical series of measures among these changes.

Characteristic facts of urbanization with Chinese characteristics

The above three historical events selected from the course of reform and opening-up in the past 40 years respectively represented how reform could remove institutional obstacles to the exit, mobility, and entry of labor force. Narration and review of these three events could only help observe and understand some of many perspectives in the reform process, and would not lead to a one-sided understanding of reform.

Economic development is composed of total growth and structural change. Productivity is an important source of growth, but its core is allocation efficiency. Structural change is directly based on the "Kuznets process." Therefore, promoting the mobility of production factors, especially of the labor force, is the key to development and urbanization. The purpose of reform is to change the incentive mechanism inhibiting development, and to eliminate institutional obstacles hindering rational allocation of resources, especially obstacles to the exit, mobility, and entry of the labor force. Summarized below are three characteristic facts of urbanization with Chinese characteristics (also China's reform process to a large extent).

Fact 1: Incentives in agriculture and thus the improvement of productivity are the premise of labor withdrawal.

The people's commune system is the source of all institutional drawbacks under the planned economy. As referred to in Chapter 6, the strategy of giving priority to the development of heavy industry led to the deviation of resource allocation from the comparative advantage at that time,[10] and the one-sided agricultural policy that took food grain as the key link also led to misallocation of resources in the agricultural economy. The form of collective labor in agriculture led to low efficiency of micro-production links, and to tremendous efficiency loss of total output. The institutional irreversibility caused by the people's communes deprived peasants of their right to exit from low-efficient organizational forms, and some commune members loafed on their jobs during collective labor, taking advantage of the difficulty of supervising agricultural labor.

All these led to the fact that the agricultural economy under the people's commune system had an extremely low production possibility frontier and substantially deviated from the production possibility frontier. This means that a laborer sparing no effort could scarcely get the reward needed for food and clothing, i.e., the imbalance between calorie expenditure on labor and calorie intake from distribution, so he could not maintain simple reproduction, let alone expand reproduction. As a result, the "free rider" problem would inevitably become a common phenomenon, and low incentives would certainly lead to extremely low productivity.

The rapid popularization of the household contract responsibility system is not only the result of government permission and policy promotion, but also the result of the vast peasantry's initiative choice when they saw the real effect of improved output and labor productivity. The most thorough household-based contract system was designed to assign collective land to all households according to the number of their family members and labor force, by which, all extra outputs besides agricultural tax, unified purchase quantity and collective retention to be paid as required in the contract agreement would be the discretionary income of peasant households.

This change in incentive mechanism has broken the "free rider" paradox of collective labor and significantly improved the labor productivity of agriculture, forming a sharp contrast to long-term stagnation or even retrogression of productivity. For example, the average annual growth rates of agricultural added value and grain output per unit area increased from 0.9% and 3.1% during 1975–1980 to 9.9% and 7.2% during 1980–1984 respectively. Accordingly, the rural poverty incidence declined drastically.

Most early studies focused on observing the remarkable effect of the household contract responsibility system on the increase in agricultural production from the perspective of improved incentives. If we look at the connection between this step of reform and the later development process, we can see a more important fact: the improved incentives led to exaltation of the agricultural labor productivity, creating the necessary conditions for the transfer of labor to non-agricultural industries and areas outside rural areas. The complete abolition of the people's commune system inevitably caused by the implementation of the household contract responsibility system was the first institutional breakthrough in labor transition.

China's reform and development promoted each other. As the transformation of the market-oriented economic system intertwined with the Lewis dual economy development, the labor transition has not only broken institutional shackles but also absorbed surplus agricultural labor, thus it became the beginning of the Kuznets process while the agricultural labor productivity being much lower than that of non-agricultural industries was the Todaro's "pushing force" in development economics.

Albert Hirschman's "exit" emphasized the action choice taken by the parties due to their dissatisfaction with the organization.[11] This concept is only used here in one half of its sense; that is, it is really necessary to achieve institutional breakthroughs before the agricultural labor force can obtain the right to exit. On this premise, in the other half of its sense, this chapter focuses on describing a fact that the improved agricultural labor and production incentives made the surplus of labor force come out, thus starting the actual exit from low-productivity agriculture. In the latter sense, the "exit" process had a more general meaning of development economics. If both meanings were considered, there would be an exit process with Chinese characteristics that unified reform and development.

Fact 2: Labor mobility was promoted by economic growth and expansion of non-agricultural employment

The rapid growth of China's economy during the reform period was not merely a return to the old normal growth (or production possibility frontier). In fact, the window of population opportunity formed in this period has helped China's economy to form a higher potential growth rate in terms of factor accumulation and allocation and productivity improvement.

With the release of this potential growth capacity by the system reform, and with the cooperation of demand factors (the ever-increasing consumption demand caused by the expansion of urban and rural employment and the increase of income, the huge investment demand caused by economic growth, and the external demand obtained from opening to the outside world), the potential growth rate can be changed to a real high growth. Therefore, reallocating labor to employment areas with higher productivity or promoting labor mobility was key to realizing demographic dividend.

Under the condition of a planned economy, the three systems (people's commune system, household registration system, and coupon-based system) confined rural labor force to collective labor of production teams, not allowing industrial transfer and interregional mobility. The surplus of labor force became prominent rapidly as micro incentives were improved. In the mid-1980s, approximately 30–40% of China's rural labor force was surplus, and the absolute number of surplus labor force was as high as 100 million to 150 million.[12] The pressure on transition of surplus labor force facilitated the removal of a series of institutional obstacles, and finally enabled reallocation of labor force.

According to many studies represented by Todaro, the resultant force of the rural pushing force and urban pulling force shaped the process and characteristics of labor mobility. The motive force and direction of China's labor mobility were determined by the surplus of agricultural labor force in a specific period and by the demand for labor force created by non-agricultural industries. The migration of agricultural surplus labor force has successively experienced the reallocation process from "food grain as the key link" to diversified economy, from single planting industry to all-round development of agriculture, forestry, animal husbandry, and fishery, from agriculture to township enterprises, and from "staying away from home but not leaving hometown" to entry small towns and even large and medium-sized cities.

However, China's special mission was aimed to fulfill institutional transformation from a planned economy to a market economy while undergoing the process of labor reallocation. Previous studies observed various institutional factors in the process of labor migration, but China's reform, as a case of comprehensive economic system transformation, was faced with a more arduous reform task and more complicated reform process. This is why the Chinese experience is also more inspiring.

The following key reforms have breakthrough significance for promoting labor mobility. First of all, due to substantial increase in the output of agricultural products, peasants were allowed to engage in long-distance transport and self-marketing of agricultural products in 1983, breaking through the geographical restrictions on employment for the first time. Second, the government allowed peasants in 1988 to get employed in neighboring cities and towns on their own, breaking through the barriers between urban and rural employment for the first time. Finally, with the abolition of the coupon-based system (including grain coupons) in the early 1990s, rural laborers no longer encountered tangible obstacles in entering cities and towns at all levels for residence and employment.

According to National Bureau of Statistics data, the number of rural laborers who had been away from their villages or towns for six months or more reached 173 million in 2018, of which 78.2% dwelled and got employed in cities and towns. Combination of these data with the change of urban and rural employment structure helps us see the effect of the Kuznets process. According to estimates different from official data,[13] the proportion of agricultural labor force decreased from 70.5% in 1978 to 18.3% in 2015. The largest labor mobility in the history of human peace and the resulting reallocation of resources have made remarkable contributions to China's rapid economic growth and substantial improvement of labor productivity.

Fact 3: Removing institutional obstacles to promote entry of labor force into urban sectors

There was no free mobility of labor between urban and rural areas in the planned economy period because rural population and labor were not allowed to migrate freely to cities. Therefore, the industrial structure got stuck in a rut for a long time, with the proportion of agricultural labor force staying at a high level. In the meantime, urban residents' employment was fully guaranteed, and almost all of them were absorbed by the state-owned economy and collective economy.

For example, in 1978, employees in state-owned sectors accounted for 78.3% of all urban employees. Plus collective sector employees, the employment of two public-owned sectors occupied a proportion of 99.8%. When rural laborers migrated into cities and towns, they had been employed by emerging non-public sector enterprises for a long time. It was the development of urban labor market and the reform of employment system in state-owned sectors that had removed the barriers to rural laborers' entry into urban sectors, so that rural labor force could be reallocated among various industries and enterprises across urban, rural, and regional boundaries.

If the traditional system was designed to set up exit obstacles for the agricultural labor force in order to ensure that agriculture could make product contributions and capital contributions to industrial accumulation under the condition of unequal exchange, the entry barriers set by this system exclude migrant workers from employment in urban basic public services, so as to fully guarantee the employment of urban residents. Accordingly, the order by which two kinds of obstacles were gradually removed was also determined by mutual promotion between various reforms and by the requirements of the economic development stage.

In the 1980s, township enterprises were still main sectors absorbing rural laborers migrating into urban areas. After 1992, the labor-intensive manufacturing industry in coastal areas, especially the non-public sectors, developed rapidly and began to absorb the rural labor force migrating across regions, forming the first rush of migrant workers. Until the late 1990s, state-owned enterprises carried out drastic and absolute reforms of the employment system when faced with huge difficulty in business operations, breaking the "iron bowl" of employment that had existed for decades. As laid-off workers were provided with certain social security, they needed to be re-employed through the labor market; meanwhile, the newly grown labor force also needed to choose their own jobs. There thus formed the mechanism of market allocation of labor resources.

This led to an unexpected result, i.e., migrant workers were provided with increasingly equal opportunities for competitive employment. Nevertheless, the development of the labor market to this point has also resulted in separation between access to the labor market and the rights and interests of basic public services within the city.

In 2018, of the 288 million migrant workers who had experienced employment transfer, 40% were employed in their own towns, 60% left their own towns (of which 78.2% entered cities at all levels and 44.0% moved across provinces), and 27.9% were employed in manufacturing, 18.6% in the construction sector and 50.0% in the tertiary industry. In recent years, the proportion of laborers migrating from rural areas in all urban employment has exceeded a third. Migrant workers secured an adequate supply of labor force in the urban economy by virtue of their large population and age advantages (more than half of them were under 40 years old). Therefore, China's characteristic urbanization in the reform period was the way to realize high economic growth and enjoyed the same reputation as this growth miracle, writing a splendid chapter in economic history.

In 2010 when China's total economic volume surpassed Japan and became the world's second largest economy, China's demographic transition also crossed a turning point: the growth of the working-age population reached its peak and then entered a negative increment stage. The decline in the population dependency ratio hit the bottom and then curved up sharply.

The trend of this demographic change on the one hand had an adverse impact on the potential growth rate and on the actual growth rate in terms of labor supply, human capital improvement, returns on capital, and reallocation of resources,[14] and on the other hand, tended to slow down the urbanization pace. During 2010–2017, despite the increasing urbanization rate, the annual increase rate decreased at an annual rate of 6.7%, and the annual growth rate of the urbanization rate fell from 3.33% to 2.04%.

From the perspective of demographic trends, the rural population aged 16–19 has seen a negative growth since it peaked in 2014. Since population in this age group was equivalent to graduates from rural junior and senior high schools and was the main source of the annual increment of migrant workers in cities, the declining total size of this part of population has inevitably reduced the annual increment of migrant workers. It is thus clear that the slowdown of urbanization was purely caused by demographic factors.

According to the general law of development, the urbanization rate also increases with the increasing per capita income level. Therefore, China will have a long way to go to improve the urbanization rate in the process of entering the ranks of high-income countries. Judging from the urbanization rate index, there was a gap of several percentage points for China to reach the average level of 65% in its income group (upper-middle income countries classified by the World Bank), while the average level of urbanization rate in high-income countries was as high as 84%.

In the past 40 years, China's characteristic urbanization, which featured removal of institutional barriers to promote the exit of labor from low-productivity sectors and mobility across urban and rural areas, regions, and industries, and realizing its entry into high-productivity sectors, was an effective experience in the development stage of dual economy. With the demographical transition and the change in economic development stage, these experiences should be updated according to their inherent logic so as to promote the transition of urbanization from high-speed expansion to high-quality improvement. Next, the new connotation of urbanization with Chinese characteristics will be outlined from three aspects.

How to improve agricultural labor productivity

When we look back on the process of reform and opening-up, the motivation of agricultural labor exit has been discussed largely from the perspective of stimulating related productivity improvement. At the current stage, it is necessary to discuss how to improve agricultural labor productivity from the perspective of changing the agricultural production mode.

The contribution of rural reforms discussed in previous chapters to the national economy involved nothing but improvement of the agricultural labor productivity. During 1978–2017, the average agricultural added value of each labor force calculated at constant price, i.e., agricultural labor productivity, increased by 6.26 times, with an average annual growth rate of 5.2%.

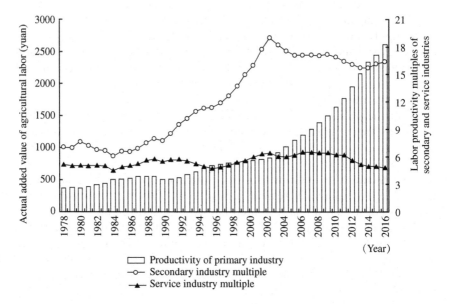

Figure 7.1 Agricultural labor productivity and its relationship with non-agricultural industries

The growth characteristics of agricultural labor productivity observed from different periods also reflected the staged features of reform and development (Figure 7.1).

During 1980–1984 when the household contract responsibility system was increasingly widespread, the agricultural labor productivity increased rapidly. However, due to the one-off effect of this reform, the improvement of agricultural labor productivity has slowed down since the mid-1980s. After Deng Xiaoping's south tour talks in 1992, the development of manufacturing industry in coastal areas produced a large demand for labor force, thus accelerating the migration of the surplus labor force and pushing the agricultural labor productivity to its peak. Soon afterward, urban state-owned enterprises' reform of reducing staff and increasing efficiency increased the employment pressure, resulting in a slowdown in the transition of the agricultural labor force and in improving productivity.

After China joined the World Trade Organization in 2001, the demand for labor in the export-oriented manufacturing industry increased again. In 2004, China's economy saw the Lewis turning point. The labor shortage and wage increase of unskilled workers became normal, which once again accelerated the improvement of agricultural labor productivity. This speed has been maintained for many years and shows no trend of slowdown.

The substantially improved agricultural labor productivity has laid a foundation for the migration of labor force from rural areas and for acceleration of the urbanization of permanent residents. In fact, it is also the basic guarantee for China's rapid economic growth during the whole period of reform and opening-up. The demographic dividend was realized on this basis, which could be manifested by adequate supply of labor and fast improvement of the quality of the labor force (human capital). A low population dependency ratio is conducive to a high savings rate and capital accumulation. Sufficient supply of labor force helps delay the diminishing returns on capital, safeguards high returns on investment, and transfers surplus labor to improve the efficiency of resource reallocation, so as to boost the total factor productivity.

Despite fast improvement of the agricultural labor productivity, even faster than the secondary and tertiary industries in some years especially after the Lewis turning point, it has not outperformed the labor productivity in non-agricultural industries as a whole, and failed to significantly narrow the gap between agricultural and non-agricultural labor productivities. For example, in the period from 1978 to 2017, the average added value of labor in the secondary industry actually increased by 7.5% on an annual basis, much faster than the increase in agricultural labor productivity. The average added value of labor in the tertiary industry actually increased by 5.0% on an annual basis, slower than the increase in agricultural labor productivity, but it was not slow enough for agriculture to catch up with or even surpass the tertiary industry, so that the labor productivity gap between agricultural and non-agricultural industries remained.

For example, in 1978, the labor productivity of the secondary industry and the tertiary industry was 7.0 times and 5.1 times that of the primary industry respectively; afterward it was reduced to a lower level, but it had also reached a very high level, e.g., the average labor added value of the secondary industry and the tertiary industry was 19.0 times and 6.4 times that of agriculture respectively in 2003. In 2017, the labor productivity of the secondary and tertiary industries was still 16.4 times and 4.8 times that of agriculture respectively. This situation constituted an obstacle to the coordinated development of urban and rural areas and to the sustainable and healthy growth of China's economy, urgently requiring major breakthroughs.

Since the beginning of the 21st century, the Chinese government has implemented a series of policies benefiting farmers, increased financial investment in agriculture and direct subsidies to producers, and carried out the reform to achieve separation of the land ownership, the contracting rights and the management rights, thus creating the institutional conditions for land circulation.

However, the policy relating to agriculture, rural areas, and farmers was more orientated to the change from "taking more and giving less" to "giving more and taking less" than to transforming the agricultural production mode and realizing agricultural modernization. Modernization of the agricultural production mode, on the one hand, is bound up with the improvement of the industry's own development ability and competitiveness, and on the other hand, paves the way for labor mobility and improvement of the resource reallocation efficiency. Therefore, the policy relating to agriculture, rural areas, and farmers should focus more on the production mode itself, and the government's investment should be orientated to expanding the scale of land operation.

When the author proposed, debated, and studied the Lewis turning point, his main job was to make a judgment regarding the arrival of the first Lewis turning point, and the main changes he faced were labor shortages and wage increases. Some scholars mistakenly believed that the Lewis turning point was marked by the equality of labor marginal productivity between agricultural and non-agricultural industries, so they denied the arrival of the Lewis turning point. In order to avoid confusing different concepts, the author intentionally skirted around the second turning point in the previous discussion.

The paradox of labor productivity convergence became increasingly prominent after the first turning point, because previous attention was concentrated on solving the problem of a surplus labor force and extremely low marginal productivity of agricultural labor, and thereafter on the growth of agricultural output under given labor input. This raises an important topic worth discussing, i.e., the relationship between agricultural labor productivity and labor transfer, which is closely related to the second turning point in theory. Now it is the right time to discuss the arrival of the second turning point, although it is not necessary to make such a judgment.

Figure 7.2 shows the whole process of dual economy development from surplus labor transfer to disappearance of unlimited labor supply. In the figure, OYX stands for the curve of total agricultural output. A surplus labor

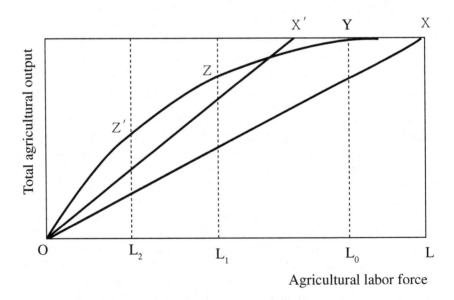

Figure 7.2 Stages and characteristics of agricultural labor transfer

force existed at the starting point of this development process. OL represents the total labor force initially used. Labor transfer moves from L to the left, and the marginal productivity of labor is zero until the point L_0. From the total output curve, the marginal productivity of labor starts to be positive from the left of point Y, that is, the slope of each point on the curve is greater than 0. Therefore, the L_0 or Y point represents the first Lewis turning point. After that point, with continuous transfer of labor force, the marginal productivity of labor ascends gradually and approaches the average productivity of labor represented by the slope of OX curve until it reaches L1 point of labor force transfer (corresponding to Z point on the output curve), i.e., the second Lewis turning point. At this point, the marginal productivity of labor is equal to the average productivity of labor, i.e., the slope of Z point is parallel to OX. This is the so-called second Lewis turning point (or commercialization point), marking the end of dual economy development. If the labor force continues to transfer thereafter, the marginal labor productivity will be greater than the average productivity of labor, and the wages in agriculture will no longer be the sharing of the average productivity of labor determined by the system, but will be determined by the marginal productivity in labor market.

Starting from the first Lewis turning point, as the marginal productivity of the labor force is no longer zero, further transfer requires improvement of the (average) labor productivity; if otherwise, this turning point will be become the food shortage point as predicted by Gustav Ranis and John C.H. Fei.[15] It is thus clear that this turning point is very important. Previously, labor transfer improved labor productivity, but thereafter, it was required that the modernization of production mode lead to the improvement of labor productivity in order to support continuous transfer of labor force.

This shows that the requirement of improving agricultural labor productivity has been constantly increasing with the process of labor transfer. After the second Lewis turning point, the development of dual economy became Solow-style neoclassical growth and was no longer the focus of discussions by development economists including Lewis. However, the issue of agricultural labor productivity is so important that economists who truly care about economic development itself instead of being content with constructing theoretical models must pay enough attention to it. From the first turning point to the second turning point and even thereafter, the issue of labor productivity must be highlighted in whichever stage.

The author therefore added a curve OX' in Figure 7.2 to represent the increasing average productivity of agricultural labor on the basis of OX. In this case, the transfer of agricultural labor supported by the improvement of labor productivity can continue. It can be seen from the figure that the labor force further transfers from L1 to L2, which corresponds to Z' on the total output curve, and the tangent of this point is parallel to the new average labor productivity curve OX'. In other words, the decline in the share of agricultural employment is endless. At present, the average proportion of the agricultural labor force in high-income countries with per capita gross national income of more than US$12,300 as defined by the World Bank is only 4%. The continuous active improvement of agricultural labor productivity was supported by this continuous labor transfer or by the decline of agricultural employment share.

In previous studies, the author demonstrated that China had seen the Lewis turning point in 2004.[16] As this turning point was characterized by the shortage of supply and wage increases of ordinary workers, it did not mean that the marginal productivity of agricultural and non-agricultural labor was equal; therefore, the Lewis turning point mentioned here was actually the so-called first turning point in development economics. Since then, the trend of labor shortages and wage increases has intensified, even a negative growth of the working-age population after 2010, and the feature of unlimited labor supply has been disappearing rapidly.

Does this mean that China's economy sees a second turning point? From an economic point of view, this is of course a question that must be answered by empirical research. However, this question is difficult to answer from an operational perspective.

In essence, taking zero marginal productivity of agricultural labor as the basis for judging the first turning point and taking marginal productivity of agricultural labor equal to that of non-agricultural industries as the basis for judging the second turning point are both theoretical definitions, but this is not the case in a statistical sense. After all, estimating a production function does not mean perfectly depicting economic activities themselves. Various institutional arrangements and other interference factors can make statistical representation deviate from economic reality.

On the other hand, as far as economic reality is concerned, it is not necessary to judge whether the turning point is coming by estimating the marginal productivity of labor. After all, economic reality, especially the real performance of the labor market, is more reliable than the coefficient in the production function estimated by economists.

First of all, the first turning point could prove itself by the general shortage of labor force that has never happened before, especially the resulting wage increase of ordinary workers. The reason why it is necessary to identify whether this turning point is coming is that it marks a completely different stage of dual economy development, or more accurately, marks the end of dual economy development as an important stage of development, thus having a brand-new meaning for economic and social policies.

Second, the arrival of the second turning point will be eventually manifested by the fact that agriculture is no longer an industry that exports labor, and the entry and exit of employed people is no longer a trend but a normal career choice as two-way mobility with non-agricultural industries anytime and anywhere.

Moreover, the turning point is actually only a characteristic summary of the facts of economic development by economists, and its policy meaning lies in understanding the most prominent problems in a specific development period and in finding ways to break the constraints. Therefore, discussing the second Lewis turning point does not mean that it is necessary to make a judgment on whether it will come or not. This book does not intend to estimate the marginal labor productivity in agricultural and non-agricultural industries, but observes the decline of agricultural employment share as a continuous process, so as to reveal the theoretical and practical points and corresponding policy implications at different stages.

The general law of development shows that there are three ways to improve labor productivity. The first is to promote the deepening of capital. The capital-labor ratio should be increased by expanding capital investment input. The effect of the growing output per labor can be realized when each worker is equipped with more machinery and equipment. The second is to improve human capital. The improvement of workers' education level or skills can increase the output per labor under the condition that other factors remain unchanged. The third is to improve the total factor productivity. The labor output is increased using inputs more efficiently under the condition that the input level of production factors remains unchanged.

There is no doubt that these paths have been followed by the improvement of agricultural labor productivity. At the same time, such improvement has also been affected by the characteristics of this industry and subject to problems existing in the current system.

First of all, after the Lewis turning point, the level of agricultural mechanization has been greatly improved, which is an important driving force for the improvement of agricultural labor productivity. For example, in the period from 1978 to 2017, the total power of agricultural machinery increased at an average annual rate of 5.6%. With the shortage of the labor force in rural areas, the requirement of improving labor productivity has become increasingly urgent. During 2003–2017, the number of large and medium-sized agricultural tractors and their supporting farm tools with labor-saving functions increased by an average annual rate of more than 14%. This is not only a typical process of labor-saving technological change caused by labor shortages but also conforms to the general law of capital deepening.

However, the substantial increase in material input to agriculture has also brought about a decline in the returns on investment. The diminishing returns on capital are a regular phenomenon in economics due to restrictions from other production factors. Agricultural production is mainly determined by inputs of capital, labor and land. Although the characteristic of unlimited supply of labor force gradually disappears, up to 27% of the agricultural labor force only produces an agricultural added value accounting for 7.6% of GDP, indicating that labor factors have not yet constituted a constraint on agricultural development.

Land is indeed a limited and scarce production factor in China; nevertheless, land here does not mean the total amount of arable land resources but the scale of land management. Due to unsmooth land circulation and low level of centralized management, the land scale managed by each peasant household in China is small and scattered. In Chapter 6, we have discussed in detail the problem that the small scale of land management leads to a significant reduction in returns on investment.

Second, human capital has been significantly improved with the improvement of the education level of China's working-age population. However, due to the distortion of rural labor allocation, the human capital of agricultural labor tends to weaken due to the distorted allocation of rural labor. Under the current household registration system and labor mobility, the labor force registered in rural areas is divided into two groups: those who choose to stay in rural areas, most of whom can be regarded as the agricultural labor force, and those who go out to work and become migrant workers within or outside their own towns.

Generally, the labor force transferred out of agriculture is young and has a high level of education. For example, in 2018, among all migrant workers, 52% were under 40 years old and 83% held an educational degree above junior high school. Among them, migrant workers who left their villages and towns looked more like productive population. On the contrary, the labor force staying in rural areas to work in agriculture was characterized by older age and lower education level. It was because of the existence of the household registration system that the family members of peasant households were separated from each other in economic activities and employment areas according to their respective productive characteristics, thus becoming the institutional reason for distorted allocation of rural labor force.

Finally, the total factor productivity can be improved by institutional reform, technological innovation, and resource reallocation. Reform in the past 40 years has laid a dynamic incentive mechanism for agricultural production and management, and great progress has been made in agricultural scientific research and technology popularization and application. At present, the greatest constraint on reform is that land resources cannot move fully among operators and are not concentrated in the hands of the most capable operators to achieve more effective allocation.

As the phenomenon of surplus agricultural labor force came out in the late 1980s, there emerged the demand to utilize scale economy while there was an increasing pressure on labor force transfer, resulting in the need for land circulation. In fact, this was an institutional demand that required a mechanism to promote land circulation.

Through years of exploration, farmers, autonomous organizations, and local governments have also gained a lot of experience. The report of the 19th National Congress of the Communist Party of China proposed that improving the system of separating "three rights" (ownership, contracting rights, and management rights) of contracted land was the result of the practical experience of these institutional innovations, which had been treated as the orientation of rural land reform. In addition, the expansion of the land management scale is also mutually conditional and restrictive with the speed and stability of agricultural labor transfer.

It is thus clear that a small land management scale is the law of diminishing returns to capital restricting the improvement of agricultural labor productivity; however, incomplete labor force transfer has restricted the improvement of agricultural labor productivity in terms of human capital accumulation and total factor productivity.

Policies used to promote problem-solving from the above two directions can be found in the *Opinions on Establishing and Perfecting the Institutional Mechanism and Policy System of Urban–Rural Integration Development* promulgated by the Central Committee of the Communist Party of China and the State Council on April 15, 2019, including: first, deepening reform of the household registration system in an effective and orderly manner, and removing restrictions on urban settlement except for several megacities; and second, improving the system of separating "three rights" relating to rural contracted land, and equally protecting and releasing land management rights on the premise of protecting collective ownership and farmer contracting rights according to law. Only by implementing these two requirements can we maintain continuous improvement of agricultural labor productivity and strongly support the integration of urban and rural development.

From horizontal mobility to longitudinal mobility

China's economic development has reached such a stage that labor mobility should shift from horizontal mobility to longitudinal mobility caused by horizontal mobility. With the increasingly mature urban and rural labor markets, migrant workers have moved in a larger geographical range from central and western regions to coastal areas and from rural areas to cities at all levels.

For example, of 173 million migrant workers who left their villages and towns for six months or more in 2018, 44% moved across provincial boundaries. The proportion of migrant workers moving across provinces in the central region was as high as 60.6%, while that in the western region was 49.6%. In fact, this proportion was even higher in previous years. With the transfer of manufacturing industry from coastal areas to the central and western regions, more employment opportunities have emerged in the central and western regions. In addition, the shortage of labor force has led to the aging of migrant workers, to the increasing opportunity cost and psychological cost of staying away from home, and to the ascending proportion of labor mobility inside province.

Sufficient labor transfer and mobility and expanding scope of mobility have begun to narrow the income gap between urban and rural areas and the wage gap between regions. The ratio of urban residents' income to rural residents' income decreased from the highest level of 2.67 in 2009 to 2.32 in 2018. The average wage of migrant workers in the central and western regions in 2018 was equivalent to 90.2% and 89.1% of the average wage in the eastern regions respectively, indicating a trend of equating wage levels in different regions.

However, this just explains the effect of horizontal mobility of labor force. In regard to social mobility, a complete process should be such that the expansion of horizontal mobility gives individuals and families in different positions of social stratification more opportunities to climb up the ladder of social hierarchy, i.e., the longitudinal mobility represented by the change of social identity.

Generally speaking, horizontal mobility is a prerequisite for longitudinal mobility, but it does not necessarily lead to longitudinal mobility. We can regard the probability of a social group realizing longitudinal mobility as a function of the following factors. The first is the demographic characteristics of population group including human capital, such as demographic characteristics, years of education, skills, etc. The second is the nature and status of their employment. The third is opportunities that they can obtain to get promoted. The fourth is whether their state is stable or dynamic.

In general, despite great improvements achieved for migrant workers in these aspects, the household registration system has prevented them from becoming urban citizens; therefore, their employment and life in cities have shown many weak characteristics as compared with the urban household registration population, thus making them face greater obstacles in social integration, opportunity acquisition and promotional probability. Therefore, they are still at a disadvantage in social longitudinal mobility. By a descriptive statistical analysis of the results of this sampling survey,[17] we can observe from several aspects as follows.

The first is the nature of employment. Under the current system and social environment, the category, unit type, ownership nature, and industry characteristics of job sectors can to a certain extent reveal the position and promotional expectations of specific labor groups in the social hierarchy. From this point of view, migrant workers have greatly improved as compared with six years ago (2016 to 2010). Over time, although the social status of migrant workers has improved, the gap between migrant workers and urban registered residents is still very significant.

When the entry into administrative and public institutions, public-owned enterprises, and large-scale enterprises is taken as an indicator of longitudinal mobility, migrant workers still face the gap with the urban registered population while improving in these aspects. For example, the proportion of migrant workers employed in administrative and public institutions is only 2.5%, while the proportion of urban registered residents is as high as 17.8%. The proportion of migrant workers employed in state-owned enterprises or collective enterprises is 7.4%, while that of urban registered residents is 24.5%. The proportion of migrant workers employed in enterprises with more than 20 employees is 45.7%, and that of local residents is 73.5%.

The second aspect involves labor remuneration, social security, and other benefits. Compared with six years ago, the average wage of migrant workers has increased significantly from RMB2,855 yuan in 2010 to RMB4,965 yuan in 2016, with an increase of 73.9%. Meanwhile, the wage gap between migrant workers and workers with urban household registration also narrowed. In 2016, the average wage of workers with urban household registration was RMB5,528 yuan. If we look at the median wage, the migrant workers' wage has doubled in six years, already equivalent to the level of urban registered workers.

As can be imagined, however, the employment stability of migrant workers is still not satisfactory. The proportion of migrant workers who signed labor contracts has increased from 24.1% to 39.0%, but is still 31.4 percentage points lower than that of urban registered workers. The proportion of migrant workers participating in social insurance has greatly increased, but it is still significantly lower than that of urban registered workers. the self-rent ratio of migrant workers' housing is very high (Table 7.1) since they have never obtained allocated housing, have no equal access to subsidized housing, and have no ability and expectation to buy commercial housing.

The final aspect is human capital endowment. Similar to other demographic characteristics, the average education level of migrant workers has also improved, despite a certain gap with local workers in cities (Table 7.2). This can be clearly seen from a rough estimation of the average number of years of education per capita. However, it may be particularly noted that migrant workers' education tends to be slightly polarized, i.e., the education level of those having received primary school education or below has not decreased, that of those having received junior high school and senior high school education has decreased, and that of those having received junior college and above has increased significantly. This actually reflects the changing trend of the age composition of migrant workers; that is, with the decrease of the number of new graduates from rural high schools and junior high schools, the age replacement speed of migrant workers slows down and tends to age. Therefore, on the one hand, young people are becoming increasingly educated; on the other hand, the proportion of migrant workers who are older and less educated has increased, forming the current distribution of human capital.

Table 7.1 Social insurance participation rate of migrant workers and urban local workers (%)

	Migrant workers		Local workers
	2010	*2016*	
Social endowment insurance	10.84	32.52	10.84
Health insurance	9.43	31.48	9.43
Unemployment insurance	7.17	25.76	7.17
Injury insurance	8.55	27.53	8.55
Proportion of self-rented houses	79.61	76.09	79.61

Source: Calculated based on CULS data in 2017.

Table 7.2 Educational composition of migrant workers and urban local workers (%)

| | Migrant workers | | Urban local workers |
	2010	2016	
Primary school and below	14.0	14.5	14.0
Middle school	52.3	43.2	52.3
Senior high school or secondary technical school	25.0	22.3	25.0
Junior college and above	8.8	19.9	8.8
Years of education (year)	9.9	10.5	9.9

Source: Calculated based on CULS data in 2017.

Note: The years of education were estimated by the author according to the following assumptions: six years for "primary school and below," nine years for "junior high school," 12 years for "senior high school or secondary technical school," and 15.5 years and 18 years for "junior college and above" for migrant workers and urban residents respectively (because it is assumed that migrant workers have more junior college students in this group, and urban residents have more graduate students in the whole group).

In addition, the service industry is divided into lower-skilled, medium-skilled, and higher-skilled industries. A larger proportion of migrant workers are employed in medium-skilled and higher-skilled industries than they were six years ago (comparing 2016 with 2010). However, as compared with the employment of urban registered workers, migrant workers are still more concentrated in lower-skilled industries. For example, the employment proportion of migrant workers in higher-skilled industries increased from 9.6% in 2010 to 15.0% in 2016, but it was still 23.6 percentage points lower than that of urban registered workers.

At a more macro level, the following facts also show that migrant workers have not received opportunities for sufficient longitudinal mobility. In 2018, the average monthly wage of migrant workers was RMB3,721 yuan, and that of those who left their villages and towns was RMB4,107 yuan. Considering their family support coefficient, this income has reached the standard of middle-income groups in the usual sense according to some definitions.[18] However, due to restrictions from the household registration system, they have no equal access to the basic public services in cities, and their consumption tendency cannot be developed because of worries, so they cannot be regarded as middle-income groups in a true sense.

Similarly, due to the household registration system, the children of migrant workers either stay in their hometown to become left-behind children, or migrate with their parents to become migrant children, so they can hardly obtain adequate opportunity and quality of compulsory education, thus leading easily to intergenerational occupational solidification and social hierarchical solidification. In addition, migrant workers are faced with unstable living and employment expectations as well as low desire and few opportunities for training, thus their space for career development is greatly reduced.

In order to play the function of urbanization in enhancing social mobility, it is necessary to promote the longitudinal mobility of population and families on the basis of horizontal mobility of labor force. Social (longitudinal) mobility, which reflects the degree of social equity, is the comprehensive result of a set of social policies and an important basis for policy adjustment. In order to achieve the social policy goal of significantly improving the income distribution, narrowing or even eliminating the difference in basic public services, the most critical link and the most obvious focus of the expected effect are to promote migrant workers and their families into middle-income groups in a true sense by meeting the needs of basic public services and eliminating shortcomings in the system and mechanism of population mobility.

Promote institutional reform on migrant workers' household registration

Of 173 million migrant workers in 2018, 78.2% entered cities and towns at all levels, with a total of 135 million persons. The problem now is that their entry into cities and towns is seen mainly as temporary workers, not as permanent residents. Judging from the problems that need to be solved in China at present, it is increasingly urgent to realize this change of entry status.

In today's China, the key to enhancing the longitudinal mobility of the labor force is to open the door for migrant workers to enter the urban employment sector and integrate into social life at a higher level and to a deeper extent. Generally speaking, at a certain stage of economic development, the labor market itself can bring about the sharing of development achievements. For example, in the period of dual economy development, with continuous expansion of employment in the process of industrialization, workers' participation in non-agricultural industries can be greatly increased, and family income can be increased by becoming wage-earning workers. When economic development steps over the Lewis turning point, ordinary workers and low-income families can benefit from wage increases.

However, with the economic development becoming increasingly characterized by neoclassical growth, the accumulation of production factors is more strictly restricted, and the space for reallocation of production factors is obviously reduced. Accordingly, the institutional reform no longer has the nature of "Pareto improvement." In general, at this time, either the process of creative destruction is needed to improve productivity, or suffering will be inevitably created by the reform, the improvement of income distribution and equalization of opportunities increasingly need to rely on redistribution policies.

Under China's special national conditions, on the one hand, there is still room to improve income sharing opportunities, and on the other hand, it is necessary to gradually increase the protection level of social policies, both of which depend on building the ladder of social longitudinal mobility while further dredging the horizontal mobility channels of labor force. The key measure to break institutional and mechanism barriers that hinder these two mobility directions is to reform the household registration system. This system not only means that entry is not sufficient, but also is a series of other institutional bases that lead to inequality in basic public services.

The reform of the household registration system is not monolithic, nor is it without remarkable breakthroughs from beginning to end. If the household registration system is regarded as composed of a "kernel" and "periphery," this reform has been actively promoted on the periphery. For example, it is precisely because of the successful reform of the people's commune system, coupon-based system, and urban employment system that the long-term employment and residence of migrant workers in cities have been realized, increasing the urbanization rate of the resident population.

Up to now, the household registration system is still playing its role in hindering stable settlement and employment of the transferred labor force in cities. The speed of urbanization is unprecedented, but the reform of household registration system has adopted a gradual way. Their rhythms have not completely synchronized with each other. Migrant workers and their families who go out all the year round are counted as permanent urban population, but they have not obtained urban "*hukou*" (registered household), which makes this urbanization process present a "coming and going" mode of life-long employment cycle of migrant workers at the micro level. Only by promoting and completing reform of the household registration system with the "citizenization" of migrant workers as the core can labor transfer continue and migrant workers and their families settle down in cities.

However, the fact that migrant workers cannot become urban residents in the full sense shows that the reform has not yet affected the core of the household registration system. Therefore, migrant workers entering cities are deemed as employees but not yet as registered residents. According to statistics, there has always been a gap between the urbanization rate of the resident population and that of the registered population. The former was 58.5% and the latter was 42.4% in 2017.

If reform of the household registration system, which promoted urbanization in the past 40 years, has followed a path from "periphery" to "kernel," now we need to focus on tackling key problems and achieve breakthroughs in the "kernel." It is difficult to take the most critical step in reform of the household registration system, i.e., "citizenization" of migrant workers, because of the asymmetric relationship between reform benefits and reform costs. Studies show that reform of the household registration system can significantly improve the potential growth rate of China's economy by increasing the efficiency of labor participation and resource reallocation in non-agricultural industries.[19] This means that the reform of the household registration system can produce obvious reform dividends.

However, this tangible reform dividend cannot be obtained by the local government in an exclusive way that is directly responsible for paying the reform cost, thus leading to the incentive incompatibility between the central government and the local government in promoting the reform. Therefore, the key to promoting reform of the household registration system and realizing the entry of migrant workers and their families into cities as citizens lies in the top-level design of the reform by the central government to innovatively arrange the sharing of reform costs and benefits, and form incentive compatibility.

Considering that the potential benefits obtained from the reform of the household registration system can have a huge positive external effect on the sustainable growth of China's economy and the improvement of social fairness and justice in China, this reform actually has the nature of public goods nationwide at the highest level. Therefore, the central government should assume greater expenditure responsibility to pay for necessary reform costs, which can become the tipping point for truly promoting reform and achieving results.

Conclusions

China's economic reform, which started in the late 1970s, has gradually eliminated the institutional barriers to the accumulation and allocation of production factors, and created sufficient conditions for China's rapid economic growth. The specific population transition stage has been highly coincident with the reform period, which provides necessary conditions for rapid growth. Urbanization with Chinese characteristics is a carrier that integrates reform, development, and sharing into the same process and transforms the potential growth rate into a miracle of economic development.

The exit of agricultural surplus labor force from low-productivity agriculture as well as its mobility between urban and rural areas, between regions and between industries and its entry into the high-productivity urban sector have constituted the process and connotation of urbanization with Chinese characteristics, which provides a useful perspective to explain the success story of China's economic development, enhance its general significance of development economics, and reveal the logic of further reform and development.

First, let us look at the implications of these experiences for China's sustainable development. The experience of urbanization with Chinese characteristics shows that China's economic development has been achieved through the reform of traditional systems. It created micro-incentives and obtained macro-efficiency, which conforms to almost all the laws of economic growth, structural adjustment, and social change. However, it is closely combined with China's national conditions, corresponding to China's economic development stage, demographic transition stage and institutional heritage. Following the same logic, the successful experience can be carried forward.

In the meantime, great changes have taken place in China's economic development stage, which objectively requires China to adapt to the changed situation and update the connotation of existing experience in order to complete the unfinished tasks of reform, urbanization, and economic development.

Second, let us look at the more general meanings of these experiences. Each country has its own unique necessary conditions for economic development. This chapter highlights necessary conditions rather than the comparative advantage of economic growth, because necessary conditions are richer in connotation and more circumspect in denotation than comparative advantage. In practice, necessary conditions only need to consider supply-side factors, without considering the demand-side and cyclical factors, so they can be grasped concretely.

From this point of view, China's reform and development experience represented by urbanization can answer the following questions and thus solve problems of general development. First, reform can help tackle the incentive problem of production factors accumulation and the reallocation mechanism of production factors, thus transforming necessary conditions into actual economic growth. Second, based on reallocation of the labor force to promote fuller employment, reform, opening-up, development, and sharing are integrated to win consensus and support of the whole society for reform and enable it to continue to advance. Finally, the change of development stage and constant adjustments of reform priorities and development mode are intended to maintain and create new conditions for economic growth.

However, to say that urbanization is a beneficial thing lies in the fact that the process, as the embodiment of the general law of development, should have the quality of keeping pace with the times; in other words, in different development stages and in the face of different development tasks, it can play a unique role in integrating the goals of economic and social development. After fulfilling the task of serving as a carrier of resource reallocation and helping China realize its demographic dividend in the period of rapid growth, urbanization at a higher stage of development needs to perform functions of economic integration and social integration, so as to push China across the middle-income trap and overcome growing pains. However, no matter how the task priority changes, the next stage of urbanization should still take resource reallocation as a red line and aim to improve labor productivity.

Notes

1 The World Bank defines the country category of "late dividend countries" as follows: the fertility rate was at or above the replacement level in 1985, while the proportion of working-age population (aged 15–64) decreased or remained unchanged during 2015–2030. See the World Bank Group and International Monetary Fund, *Global Monitoring Report 2015/2016: Development Goals in an Era of Demographic Change*, Washington, DC, 2016, p. 268.
2 For instance, Loren Brandt and Thomas G. Rawski (eds.), *China's Great Economic Transformation*, Cambridge: Cambridge University Press, 2008.

3 Alwyn Young, Gold into the Base Metals: Productivity Growth in the People's Republic of China during the Reform Period, *Journal of Political Economy*, Vol. 111, No. 6, 2003, pp. 1220–1261

4 Paul Krugman, Hitting China's Wall, *New York Times*, July 18, 2013

5 For example, Paul Samuelson, Where Ricardo and Mill Rebut and Confirm Arguments of Mainstream Economists Supporting Globalization, *Journal of Economic Perspectives*, Vol. 18, No. 3, 2004, pp. 135–146.

6 Considering that some readers may be more concerned with formal logic than China's economy, it is stressed here that reform and opening-up will certainly lead to an economic growth in line with potential growth capacity, so reform and opening-up are a sufficient condition; nevertheless, without demographic dividend, the potential growth rate would not be so high; for this reason, there would not be high economic growth as we have seen in the past few decades.

7 Deng Xiaoping, Talking Points in Wuchang, Shenzhen, Zhuhai, Shanghai and Other Places, in *Selected Works of Deng Xiaoping, Volume III*, Beijing: People's Publishing House, 1993, pp. 370–383.

8 Cai Fang, Urban–Rural Income Gap and Critical Point of Institutional Reform, *Social Sciences in China*, Vol. 5, 2003.

9 Cai Fang, *China's Economic Growth Prospects: From Demographic Dividend to Reform Dividend*, Cheltenham, UK: Edward Elgar, 2016

10 Yifu Lin et al revealed that the people's commune system was an inevitable institutional arrangement to implement the strategy of giving priority to the development of heavy industry. See Justin Lin, Cai Fang, and Zhou Li, *The China Miracle: Development Strategy and Economic Reform* (revised edition), Hong Kong: Chinese University Press, 2003, Chapter 2.

11 Albert Hirschman, *Exit, Voice, and Loyalty: Responses to Decline in Firms, Organizations, and States*, Cambridge, MA: Harvard University Press, 1970.

12 J.R. Taylor, Rural Employment Trends and the Legacy of Surplus Labor, 1978–1989, in Y.Y. Kueh and R.F. Ash (eds.), *Economic Trends in Chinese Agriculture: The Impact of Post-Mao Reforms*, New York: Oxford University Press, 1993.

13 Cai Fang, How has the Chinese Economy Capitalized on the Demographic Dividend during the Reform Period?, in Ross Garnaut, Song Ligang, and Cai Fang (eds.), *China's Forty Years of Reform and Development: 1978–2018*, Canberra: ANU Press, 2018

14 Cai Fang and Lu Yang, The End of China's Demographic Dividend: The Perspective of Potential GDP Growth, in Ross Garnaut, Cai Fang, and Song Ligang (eds.), *China: A New Model for Growth and Development*, Canberra: ANU Press, 2013, pp. 55–74.

15 Gustav Ranis and John C.H. Fei, A Theory of Economic Development, *American Economic Review*, Vol. 51, No. 4, 1961, pp. 533–565.

16 Cai Fang, *China's Economic Growth Prospects: From Demographic Dividend to Reform Dividend*, Cheltenham, UK: Edward Elgar, 2016, Chapter 10.

17 In 2016, the Institute of Population and Labor Economics of the Chinese Academy of Social Sciences conducted the China labor force survey (CULS) in six cities: Shanghai, Wuhan, Shenyang, Fuzhou, Xi'an, and Guangzhou. In Shanghai and Guangzhou, the target sample size includes 700 local registered households and 500 immigrant households. In Shenyang, Fuzhou, Wuhan, and Xi'an, the target sample size includes 600 local registered households and 400 immigrant households.

18 Cai Fang, How to Cultivate Middle-income Groups, in *Chinese Story to Chinese Wisdom*, Sichuan: People's Publishing House, 2019, pp. 219–230.
19 Cai Fang and Lu Yang, The End of China's Demographic Dividend: The Perspective of Potential GDP Growth, in Ross Garnaut, Cai Fang, and Song Ligang (eds.), *China: A New Model for Growth and Development*, Canberra: ANU Press, 2013, pp. 55–74.

8   Resource reallocation effect of reform

Introduction

China has gone through 40 years of reform and opening-up since 1978, when the Third Plenary Session of the Eleventh Central Committee of the Communist Party of China was convened. Confucius said, "at 40, I no longer suffered from doubt," so the summary of reform and opening-up at 40 years should be different from that at 20 and 30 years. A more complete course and more precise facts will help us to form a clearer and more profound understanding. In particular, more abundant empirical evidence can not only help answer the relationship between reform and economic growth but also help explain the relationship between reform contents and methods and growth performance and its extent.

The previous chapter describes the urbanization process with distinct Chinese characteristics, and we still need to extract more general connotations. One example is that people should have sufficient experience and take a profound historical perspective to thoroughly analyze in what aspects and to what extent the urbanization process with Chinese characteristics provides momentum for the fast-growing reform period, hence drawing conclusions of general significance.

To date, a wealth of literature has been accumulated in economics to discuss China's economic reforms. Generally, domestic scholars have first-hand information, and they have contributed to the literature describing the reform process or summarizing experiences in an econometric way. In addition to econometric research, some foreign influential studies have tried to connect China's reforms with general development and the law of institutional change from a comparative perspective, thus receiving more attention.

As the core process of reform to promote development and sharing, urbanization has a resource reallocation effect. In this regard, many influential studies have insufficient explanatory power because they have not fully revealed the resource reallocation effect of reform. Meanwhile, we can also take related research paradigms as the benchmark to see if economics with resource reallocation will have a stronger explanatory power for the development and sharing of China's reform and opening-up.

DOI: 10.4324/9781003329305-10

Believers in the Washington Consensus gave a priori institutional target models to China's reform. Some scholars simply apply neoclassical growth theory to arbitrarily set criteria based on Western economic development experiences. In this way, they try to conclude after comparison whether China's reform has been thorough and successful, China's growth can be regarded as a "miracle," and whether it is sustainable.

For example, with their consistent theories and empirical methods, Alwyn Young and Paul Krugman believed that the growth during China's reform was extensive and unsustainable, and it was similar to the East Asian economy criticized by them many years ago.[1] Such a judgment has completely ignored the characteristics of China's dual economic development stage, which has been denied by facts just as their judgment on the East Asian economy. These researchers have not only failed to understand the role of unlimited supply of labor in preventing the law of diminishing returns to capital but also ignored the effect of resource reallocation to raise total factor productivity.

Another defect of the research is that it has not fully revealed that China's reform has followed an inherent logic and taken unique approaches. Some researchers have tried to illustrate China's reform approach[2] or acknowledge the success of China's reform approach in the face of facts and international comparison results,[3] but they have often failed to explain why people's lives have improved significantly or why there was a huge income gap during China's reform and opening-up. They allow such incompleteness in interpretation to exist and often list achievements and existing problems in a way of a proviso.

Only when the process of resource reallocation is clear can we explain the economic growth miracle and the fact of improving people's livelihoods. Although there are many factors affecting income distribution, the factor price equalization effect produced by resource reallocation will eventually play a role. In addition, the gradual reform is successful because it can freely reallocate the inefficient inventory without a severe impact on the parties involved and transform it into a source of economic growth. This in turn supports the reform to continuously advance and enhance the political consensus on reform and opening-up.

Barro and others have long defended the neoclassical growth theory. They incorporated a series of variables, including institutional factors, into the growth regression as one of the factors of conditional convergence.[4] However, the institutional variables in their model may not be consistent with the institutional factors that are the targets of China's economic reform. For example, institutional factors often use the proportion of government expenditure in the model as a proxy variable for inappropriate intervention. This may be a negative factor for some developing countries, but one important feature for China's rapid growth during reform and opening-up is that the government has played an active role. Therefore, it has made a wrong prediction of China's economy to simply apply the so-called law of convergence.[5] Even though some models have explanatory power for China's economy, they only partially see the necessary conditions for convergent growth and fail to see the most critical core—the resource reallocation effect—so that it cannot explain the source of China's rapid growth.

Some economists have seen China's favorable demographic conditions and revealed the role of demographic dividends in growth,[6] but eventually they failed to elaborate the mechanism of Chinese-style dual economic development, and they also failed to elaborate how the favorable demographic structure is transformed into demographic dividends and then transformed into rapid economic growth.

Such research lacks the perspective of the economic development stage. It starts with the neoclassical growth theory but does not understand that the dual economic development stage with the unlimited supply of labor has the special source of growth—the demographic dividend. Especially it does not understand how China's demographic dividend is transformed into the growth source, so it cannot deduce a theoretically consistent explanation about the contradiction between the economic growth performance driven by factor input and the seemingly unsustainable growth approach.

The theory of structural evolution law is a tradition of development economics. Kuznets, Chenery, and others started this tradition and revealed the significance of industrial structural reform led by increased productivity for economic development,[7] and Masahiko Aoki also applied it to East Asian economic research, including China, and agreed with the Kuznets process of China's economy.[8] Such research focuses more on experience and is less confined to a priori conclusions and inherent prejudices. However, even if such structural evolution law is widely accepted, there are still huge national differences in reality. Hence, a comprehensive study of China and an understanding of the unique evolutionary path are still missing.[9]

Focusing on making up for the existing research and based on China's economic development stage and its changes during the reform, this chapter explains the relevant reform processes from the perspective of labor resource reallocation and empirically reveals the resulting economic growth and structural adjustment effect. In particular, it tries to answer the sufficient conditions, mechanism, structural perspective and stage changes for China's economic development miracle and its implications for further reform and development.

Why is resource reallocation important?

Researchers have conducted many studies on China's reform and opening-up and its economic growth performance. The economic literature usually focuses on answering the three questions of why China's rapid economic growth occurs, how the reform is advanced and where economic growth performance in the statistical sense comes from. The third question of "where does it come from" has been discussed in detail in Chapter 5. Here, we mainly answer the questions of "why" and "how," to understand the significance of resource reallocation from the occurrence of rapid growth and its promoting mechanism.

Answering the question of "why" is to elaborate why the Chinese economy has achieved unprecedented rapid growth during the reform; that is, the relationship between reform and growth performance. The documents on development economics, institutional economics, and growth theory have all revealed that the institutional environment conducive to protecting property rights and promoting competition and the proper definition of government functions will be beneficial to economic growth and be helpful for countries at a low development level to converge toward living standards in developed countries. Therefore, it is foreseeable that the reform of the economic system increases growth speed since it aims at identifying the key factors hindering development and correcting them and furthermore eliminates or weakens the disadvantages of the traditional system.[10]

Most studies agree that growth performance is the result of reform and opening-up; that is, China improved its incentive mechanism at the micro level, corrected price signals, developed product markets, removed institutional barriers to the flow of production factors, and introduced technology, capital, and competition through opening-up, so it enhanced its potential growth capacity at the development stage and realized actual growth. For example, in a book on China's economic transformation, 45 Chinese and foreign authors reached a consensus that the remarkable achievements in China's economy should be attributed to the major change from the planned economy to the market mechanism, from single public ownership to the coexistence of multiple ownerships, and from isolation to participation in economic globalization.[11]

The planned economy model was implemented in China before the reform. The shortcomings lie in the fact that a series of institutional factors not only damaged the incentive mechanism for managers and laborers but also led to inefficient, invalid, and even wrong allocation of resources. When the traditional system was first formed, China as a whole had completed the economic involution and accumulated a large amount of surplus labor in agriculture and formed a dual structure society and an unbalanced resource allocation pattern. The dual economic development characterized by labor migration should be begun in China.

However, the strong desire to catch up with industrialized countries, coupled with the misleading understanding of industrialization and limited choice space, led China to choose the planned economic system, which hindered the flow of production factors and Kuznets industrial structure evolution. Such a pattern of resource misallocation in turn defines inefficient incentive mechanisms, causing low productivity and low growth performance and forming a vicious circle.

Generally, in the face of an economic system that lacks an incentive mechanism for a long time, thus inhibiting the efficiency of resource allocation, it is easy to push forward the reform by Pareto improvement and then change the method of resource allocation and correct the pattern of resource misallocation, starting with breaking the micro-incentive deficiency in this vicious circle. China's economic reform in the past 40 years has basically been carried out along this path, thus realizing the demographic dividend, changing the potential growth rate of China's economy, and realizing the rare high-speed growth in human history. This is the economic principle that reform unleashes the productive forces and promotes growth.

Answering the question of "how" reveals the unique approach of China's reform in a comparative way. Early observation emphasized that this reform path pays attention to the convergence between the old and the new, such as Barry Naughton's famous expression that the new system "grows out of the plan,"[12] has the gradual nature of the reform, and focuses on incremental reform,[13] to distinguish it from the transition of other former planned economy countries, such as the "shock therapy" adopted by Russia and Poland to simultaneously promote the liberalization of prices and the privatization of state-owned enterprises. Furthermore, researchers have also observed that China's reform has not only ensured the people's basic livelihood while not causing a decline in economic growth, but the reform itself is also characterized by improving the living standards of all residents.[14]

Correspondingly, there is an important issue about the inclusiveness of China's development. It is often ignored by researchers, and illogical conclusions are drawn. Most scholars have noticed that with the increase in the overall income of Chinese residents, unequal income distribution has shown an upward trend, and this inequality of income distribution is still at a very high level so far.

According to the data released by the National Bureau of Statistics, the Gini coefficient of Chinese people's income in 2018 was 0.474. Some scholars believe through their own research results that there is actually a much larger income gap among the Chinese people. For example, after Wang Xiaolu attempted to obtain complete data at the rich and poor ends of the income distribution, he revealed a large amount of off-the-books income that was not included in statistics,[15] and Gan Li et al. calculated the Gini coefficient in 2010 as high as 0.61.[16]

Various indicators have reflected income inequality, so we should surely admit that there is indeed a widening income gap during the reform and opening-up, and China has a relatively high income gap according to international standards. However, in general, Chinese urban and rural residents have separately or simultaneously shared the economic growth results in different ways at different periods in the process of economic development.

The following facts cannot be ignored to obtain a correct understanding of sharing in China's reform and opening-up.[17] First, in the trend of a widening income gap, all income groups have experienced rapid income growth. Second, it may be helpful to identify the extreme values at the high and low ends of various income groups, but it is not appropriate for making international comparisons because income statistics information at both ends is missing in various countries. In fact, there are technical problems in China's income survey, which underestimates the income of rural households and overestimates the income of permanent urban residents, thus exaggerating the urban–rural income gap. Finally, the indisputable evidence of China's inclusive development lies in the fact that hundreds of millions of people have shaken off absolute poverty and created a world-recognized achievement in poverty alleviation.

At the typical dual economic development stage, the unlimited supply of labor hinders the improvement of the wage level, but it maintains and strengthens the comparative advantages and international competitiveness of labor-intensive industries and creates more jobs. There is a significant increase in employment in non-agricultural industries, thus enhancing the income of urban and rural residents and benefiting families in all groups.

International scholars have generally observed that in recent decades, the United States and many other developed countries have had little experience in increasing employment. David Autor et al. observed the polarization of the US labor market, i.e., there was a quick increase in high-skilled jobs and low-skilled jobs, and there were fewer jobs in the middle. Laborers were "downgraded" to low-skilled jobs who used to work at the middle-skilled task but had no college training.[18] Michael Spence and Sandile Hlatshwayo concluded that during the period 1990–2008, there was less new employment in the United States, and almost none came from tradable sectors such as manufacturing.[19]

In sharp contrast to these observations, China's non-farm employment has not only expanded substantially but also maintained a balance between the tradable sector and the non-tradable sector, with an average annual growth of 6.9% and 4.7%, respectively, during the period 2004–2013. Considering that the growth rate was calculated on the basis of the non-farm employment being underestimated by approximately 20% in 2013, the actual employment growth would be even more prominent.[20]

China's economy reached the Lewis turning point characterized by labor shortages and rising wages in 2004. Before that, the income gap widened significantly, but it did not become polarized, and the income levels of all income groups increased. After that, the wages of ordinary workers and thus the income of low-income families accelerated. Since 2008, all indicators have shown a narrowing trend of the income gap.

At the same time, when it reached the Lewis turning point, the central and local governments significantly promoted the implementation of redistribution policies. A prominent approach is to establish the subsistence security system and the basic pension system for rural residents. There is an adequate supply of basic public services, and urban and rural residents and regional and social groups enjoy more equal access to basic public services, which has expedited the construction of the labor market system. All these have significantly enhanced the sharing of economic development.[21] Reform related to the household registration system has been accelerated, and the policy environment for labor mobility has improved greatly as well.

Labor migration and allocation

Reform that is conducive to the production factor flow, especially labor mobility and reallocation, involves many areas at the micro and macro levels. When reform is described simply in chronological order, it is difficult to theoretically and logically highlight the significance of a certain reform in resource reallocation. We can just directly observe the result that during the reform, a series of system barriers were removed through institutional reforms and policy adjustments, and workers were able to leave their original low-productivity employment fields, move geographically among industries, and enter new and higher-productivity employment fields according to the market signals of employment opportunities and relative incomes.

When Masahiko Aoki divided development stages based on the experience of East Asia (mainly China, Japan, and the Republic of Korea), he proposed a Kuznets stage (or K stage for short) characterized by changes in the industrial structure.[22] Other scholars have also admitted that as a typical feature of the structural changes in Asian economies, the movement of labor has promoted resource reallocation efficiency,[23] and it has become an important component of total factor productivity and hence labor productivity growth during China's reform and opening-up.[24] It has made a significant contribution to the economic growth in the period.[25]

Reform in related fields has removed a series of institutional barriers and promoted labor reallocation among industries and regions in the direction of increasing productivity. This has made China's economic growth since the reform undergo a Kuznets process; that is, resource allocation efficiency has continuously improved, becoming an important part of total factor productivity and supporting the rapid growth in this period. In this sense, the results of economic reform in the past 40 years are an organic combination of total economic increase and industrial restructuring.

Below, based on previously published research results, we empirically observe the situation of labor force transfer and the effect of resource reallocation brought by this reform.[26]

According to the general law of economic development, agricultural output and employment share decline with the increase in per capita income. After 30 years of economic development, demographic changes, and the accompanying expanded employment, the total employment in China's urban and rural areas increased from 402 million in 1978 to 775 million in 2015.

Meanwhile, as a result of the large-scale movement of agricultural labor, the proportion of employment in the primary industry fell from 70.5% to 28.3%, and the proportion of employment in the secondary and tertiary industries increased from 17.3% and 12.2% to 29.3% and 42.4%, respectively. When the total GDP grows rapidly, the value added in non-agricultural industries grows faster, and the labor force is reallocated. The three industries show different productivities and increasing speeds, but aggregate labor productivity has increased greatly.

However, before data are used to further demonstrate this process and results, we need to revise the official statistics to a certain extent and form a data series that corresponds to the official data.

First, the total employment in urban and rural areas before 1990 is flattened to a certain extent. Official statistics show that there was an abnormal jump in the total level of employment in 1990, it increased by 17% from 553 million in 1989 to 647 million in 1990. Such a sharp increase in employment did not actually occur in one year but was adjusted based on the data of the fourth census in 1990.

Since there is no sufficient basis to explain and properly deal with this abnormal value, we flatten it; that is, the one-time sharp increase in employment in that year was properly spread to the years from 1978 to 1989, and official statistics are still used in subsequent years after 1990.

Second, the number and proportion of agricultural labor have been lowered based on the assumption closer to the real situation. Several considerations have made us believe that the proportion of agricultural labor in the official data is too high. First, there is still the judgment that there is a large amount of surplus labor in agriculture, which is inconsistent with the mass migration of labor during the reform and opening-up. Second, while China's economy grows fast and industrial structure experiences dramatic changes, the proportion of agricultural labor declines at a speed less than half that of Japan and the Republic of Korea in the corresponding period, so it is difficult to make logical sense. Third, previous studies have provided much evidence or discovered that the proportion of agricultural labor in China is abnormally higher than theoretical expectations[27] or believed that the proportion of agricultural labor in statistics has been overestimated since the early years.[28]

A previous study re-estimated the actual agricultural labor in 2009 by reasonably amending the definition of agricultural labor by the National Bureau of Statistics, indicating that official data overestimated the proportion of agricultural labor by approximately 13.4 percentage points.[29] This result is highly consistent with the estimates made by Loren Brandt and Zhu Xiaodong, who used data from other sources.[30]

Based on this result, the chapter evenly spreads the overestimated official data in 2009 to the previous and subsequent years. Specifically, taking 2009 as the benchmark, we equally spread the agricultural labor considered to be overestimated to the previous years and readjust the data for subsequent years according to the level of overestimation. It can be concluded that the actual proportion of agricultural labor in 2015 was 18.3%, which was at least 10 percentage points lower than the official figure.[31] The difference between the statistical data and the adjusted data is apportioned to the data of the secondary industry and the tertiary industry according to the corresponding weight.

In this way, we can compare official statistics and adjusted data with the world average and the national average in different income groups (Table 8.1). According to the statistics released, the employment distribution among

Table 8.1 International comparisons of labor distribution in the three industries (%)

Countries and regions	Primary industry	Secondary industry	Tertiary industry
China (statistical data)	28.3	29.3	42.4
China (adjusted data)	18.3	33.4	48.3
China (ILO)	28.9	23.7	47.3
World average	29.6	21.5	48.9
Low-income countries	68.5	8.3	23.2
Lower-middle-income countries	40.4	21.3	38.3
Upper-middle-income countries	23.9	24.0	52.1
High-income countries	3.1	22.5	74.3
High-income economies in East Asia	4.1	35.3	60.3

Source: ILO (2017), the National Bureau of Statistics in previous years and the author's estimates.

Notes: The first two lines are values from the statistical data and from the adjusted data, and other values are estimated by international labor organizations through the models.

China's three industries is characterized by an atypical structure, which is especially shown as an excessively high proportion of agricultural labor and a low proportion of labor in the tertiary industry. On the other hand, the adjusted data results are more in line with expectations for the institutional reform and restructuring effects, but compared with high-income countries and regions, the proportion of agricultural labor is still too high, and the proportion of employment in the tertiary industry is still low.

Labor productivity growth and its source

Upon examining the process and effects of labor reallocation, we calculate the actual value added in the three industries each year through the value-added deflator by industry and obtain the overall labor productivity and the labor productivity by industry. Since the sum of the deflated industrial value added is greater than the actual GDP, we use the former as the proxy data for the actual GDP each year. Therefore, we have two sets of data on the total employment number, the respective employment number in the three industries, the respective actual value added in the three industries, and the time series data of the sum of GDP. On this basis, we can calculate aggregate labor productivity and labor productivity in the three industries.

As shown in Figure 8.1, according to statistics, China's labor productivity (per labor GDP) actually increased by 16.7 times from 1978 to 2015, of which primary industry increased by 5.5 times, secondary industry increased by 13.5 times and tertiary industry increased by 5.2 times. Calculation based on the adjusted data shows consistent changes, but it just shows that primary industry has a greater labor productivity growth.

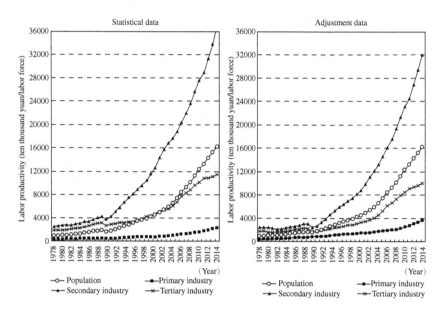

Figure 8.1 Overall labor productivity and labor productivity by industry

It is worth pointing out that after 40 years of industrial restructuring and increases in aggregate labor productivity, the labor productivity gap among the three industries, especially between primary industry and secondary industry, has not narrowed. According to statistics, the percentage of labor productivity in primary industry equivalent to that in secondary industry decreased from 14% to 6% during the period 1978–2015, and the percentage equivalent to that in tertiary industry increased from 19% to 28%. The percentage of labor productivity in tertiary industry, equivalent to that in secondary industry, shrank from 73% to 31%. Even from the perspective of adjusted data, such a productivity gap had roughly similar changes.

There are usually two methods to decompose the sources of labor productivity to observe the components and their relative contributions, which have different focuses.

In the first method, the sources of labor productivity are decomposed into total factor productivity, capital–labor ratio, and human capital contributions from the perspective of functionality. For example, the estimates of Louis Kuijs show that from 1978 to 1994, China's labor productivity increased by 6.4% per annum, and the above three factors contributed 46.9%, 45.3%, and 7.8%, respectively.[32] From 1995 to 2009, labor productivity grew at an average rate of 8.6% per annum, and the three factors contributed 31.4%, 64.0%, and 3.5%, respectively.

In the second method, the sources of labor productivity are decomposed into contributions from different sectors or industries from the structural perspective, such as contributions by the primary industry, secondary industry, and tertiary industry. It is relatively easy to obtain the data required by the latter calculation, and it has a relatively simple estimation method with intuitive and concise conclusions. Once used properly, its explanatory power can cover the former to a certain extent.

In their comparison and research on labor productivity growth in Asian manufacturing, Marcel Timmer and Adam Szirmai provided a calculation formula to decompose the factors for labor productivity growth,[33] and we can use it to decompose the contributions of the three industries to aggregate labor productivity and the contributions of labor transfer among the three industries to aggregate labor productivity; that is, the reallocation effect. The formula is as follows:

$$LP^t - LP^0 = \sum_{i=1} \left(LP_i^t - LP_i^0 \right) S_i^0 + \sum_{i=1} \left(S_i^t - S_i^0 \right) LP_i^0$$
$$+ \sum_{i=1}^{3} \left(S_i^t - S_i^0 \right) \left(LP_i^t - LP_i^0 \right)$$

where LP denotes labor productivity, subscript i denotes 1, 2, and 3, which means the three industries, S_i denotes the share of labor in a certain industry, and o and t denote the beginning and end of the investigation, respectively.

The left side of the equals sign denotes the growth of aggregate labor productivity. The first term on the right side of the equation denotes the contribution of labor productivity growth to the overall productivity by industries. The second and third terms denote the contributions of industrial structural changes to aggregate labor productivity. The second term denotes the static shift effect; that is, the contributions of labor to industries with higher labor productivity at the beginning of the period, and the third term denotes the dynamic shift effect; that is, the contributions of labor to industries with higher labor productivity growth rates.

We calculate the entire period and stages according to the statistics. Since the adjusted data have been flattened, they are only used to calculate this period and are not used for the calculation of stages (Table 8.2). According to the previous information, it is known that among the three industries, the labor productivities in the secondary industry and the tertiary industry were significantly higher than that of the primary industry at the beginning of the reform, and the productivity increase during the entire reform was greater than that of the primary industry, while the secondary industry was more prominent.

The calculation results show that in the increase in aggregate labor productivity from 1978 to 2015, the contribution to labor productivity growth by industry is greater than that by structural changes. Among the structural change effects, the dynamic effect is the main contributor, while the static effect contributes less.

We can see from the calculations about the three periods, i.e., from 1978 to 1990, from 1991 to 2003, and from 2004 to 2015, the effects on structural changes are prominent in the first and third periods. Among the structural

Table 8.2 Labor productivity growth in China and decomposition of its contribution (%)

	Total labor productivity growth	Contribution rate within the industry	Contribution rate by structural changes	Among which: static effect	Dynamic effect
1978–2015	1671.3	55.1	44.9	4.6	40.2
	(1671.3)	(56.0)	(44.0)	(5.5)	(38.6)
1978–1990	77.5	60.8	39.2	25.8	13.4
1991–2003	205.2	86.2	13.8	7.0	6.8
2004–2015	173.5	66.9	33.1	15.9	17.2

Source: China Statistics Yearbook 2016 from the National Bureau of Statistics and the author's calculation.

Notes: Numbers in brackets are estimated based on the adjusted data.

changes in the first period (39.2%), the static effect contributed significantly, accounting for 25.8 percentage points. In the middle period, the contribution by the industry was in an absolute dominant position. In the third period, the contribution rate by structural changes returned to a high level again.

With the decomposition method of Barry Bosworth and Susan Collins, we can further observe the contributions of the three industries to the increase in overall labor productivity.[34] With this method, the contribution of each industry can be displayed separately, and the residual other than the contribution of the three industries to aggregate labor productivity can be used as a measure of the effects out of resource reallocation. The calculation formula can be expressed as:

$$G_0^t = \sum_{i-1} G_{i,t}^0 S_i^0 + R$$

where $G_o{}^t$ is the growth rate of labor productivity during the investigation period, subscript i is 1, 2, and 3, denoting three industries, S_i denotes the proportion of value added in a certain industry, and o and t denote the beginning and end of the investigation, respectively. R is a residual term, equivalent to the part of aggregate labor productivity growth not explained by industrial labor productivity growth.

We take such a rough method to estimate labor productivity growth (average labor value added) in primary, secondary, and tertiary industries and the contribution percentage point of the residual term to the growth rate of aggregate labor productivity (per labor GDP) (Table 8.3). We still divide the reform into three periods, representing the period when the reform unleashed the potential for improvement in resource allocation, the period when economic growth and structural adjustment steadily advanced, and the period after the Lewis turning point. Meanwhile, we mainly use official statistics for calculations. The adjusted data are only used to observe the entire period, not for the calculation of the stages.

Table 8.3 Contributions to labor productivity from the three industries and by reallocation (%)

	Average annual growth rate	Contribution rate by primary industry	Contribution rate by secondary industry	Contribution rate by tertiary industry	Contribution rate by allocation
1978–2015	8.08	17.73	44.22	15.39	22.66
	(8.08)	(21.86)	(42.53)	(14.53)	(21.08)
1978–1990	4.90	15.65	34.46	16.57	33.32
1991–2003	9.75	7.44	61.30	16.71	14.55
2004–2015	9.58	6.68	48.69	20.27	24.36

Source: China Statistics Yearbook 2016 from the National Bureau of Statistics and the author's calculation.

Notes: Numbers in brackets are estimated based on the adjusted data.

It can be seen from the calculation results in Table 8.3 that the average annual growth rate of aggregate labor productivity from 1978 to 2015 was 8.1%. From the perspective of the stage, the growth in the first stage was relatively slow, and it increased significantly in the following two stages. Therein, the contribution by the primary industry declined steadily, with less than one percentage point in each stage; the contribution of the secondary industry increased significantly, becoming the largest contributor to labor productivity growth in each stage; the contribution by the tertiary industry also increased, but its contribution was significantly lower than that of the secondary industry; the resource reallocation also contributed significantly, but it performed very poorly in the middle period. No significant difference was found when using adjusted data to calculate the entire period.

Preventing the inverse Kuznets process

After enjoying the demographic dividend and achieving rapid growth, the Chinese economy has experienced several landmark turning points since the beginning of the 21st century. First, there was a lack of migrant workers in the Pearl River Delta region in 2004, which led to nationwide labor shortages and rising wages that have continued to the present day. Since this phenomenon conforms to the classic definition of dual economic development theory, we call it the Lewis turning point. Second, the working population aged 15–59 increased to a peak in 2010 and then entered a negative growth stage, and the aging of the population accelerated accordingly. We call this the turning point for the demographic dividend to disappear. Third, the rural population aged 16–19, as the main component to move to cities, reached its peak in 2014 and subsequently entered negative growth. We call this the turning point of labor migration deceleration.

These three turning points are actually concluded from three different observation perspectives in the same process, and they also reflect the three stages of this process, which results in the accelerated disappearance of the demographic dividend. Correspondingly, reversal changes have happened to the variables related to demographic factors and conducive to economic growth, which will inevitably lead to a slowdown in economic growth. This phenomenon is within expectation, reflecting the inevitability of changes in economic development stages. Researchers and decision-makers have also realized that the traditional economic growth factors have weakened, requiring the transformation of the economic growth drivers as soon as possible from being production factor-driven to being labor productivity-driven.

However, there are two issues worthy of attention. First, while observing the dual economic development stage, we should recognize two important factors that maintain the unlimited supply of labor from the perspective of inventory and increment: one is a large amount of surplus labor accumulated in agriculture, and the other is the rapid growth of the working age population. The occurrence of labor shortages is just the result of demographic factors, but the surplus labor has not been fully absorbed. Second, after the Chinese economy has crossed a series of turning points, whether it can realize the transformation of growth kinetic energy depends on the adjustment of a series of related factors.

We are accustomed to saying that the 30-year rapid growth during the reform and opening-up is attributed to the necessary condition of the demographic dividend. The author has repeatedly tried to prove this conclusion with the results of econometric estimation. We should also see that all kinds of factors can only change to growth drivers through continuously raising agricultural labor productivity when they are related to demographic characteristics and conducive to the supply and allocation of production factors to promote rapid economic growth. A large-scale transfer of labor across regions and across industries and the resulting increase in labor supply and resource reallocation efficiency must be built on the improvement of agricultural labor productivity.

In dual economic development, there are two different mechanisms to raise dominant agricultural labor productivity. Before the Lewis turning point and a series of other turning points, agricultural labor productivity passively increased. In the period of the planned economy, the people's commune system and the household registration system hindered labor mobility, so a large amount of surplus labor was accumulated in agriculture. From then on, the improvement of agricultural labor productivity depends on how much surplus labor can be absorbed by the development of non-agricultural industries and urbanization.

After the aforementioned turning points, agricultural labor productivity should be raised more with its own efforts by enhancing agricultural production methods. In other words, the increase in agricultural labor productivity will determine not only whether Chinese people have enough food but also how fast, how long, and how far labor migration can go.

After decades of agricultural labor migration, we cannot say that the surplus labor in agriculture has been completely transferred. In terms of agricultural equipment and material input, the potential of agricultural labor productivity is far from being fully realized. Once the potential to raise such labor productivity is identified, agricultural labor still has a huge potential to transfer. The international comparison based on the development stage of China's economy in Table 8.1 proves that there is still a high proportion of agricultural labor in China.

Let us take a problem-oriented approach to answer the question of whether agricultural labor should continue to transfer. In recent years, the agricultural labor movement has slowed down significantly. For example, the average annual growth rate of migrant workers leaving their hometowns dropped significantly from 7.1% in the period 2000–2009 to 1.9% in the period 2009–2018. The prominent problems of labor shortages and rising wages have significantly weakened the comparative advantage and competitiveness of the manufacturing sector, which has long been successful due to the resource endowment of abundant labor.

This means that the existing manufacturing capacity and investment increment will inevitably shift outward. While some manufacturing sectors have been relocated from the coastal areas to the central and western areas, another part that cannot be ignored has transferred to countries with low labor costs.

A direct consequence is that the growth of the manufacturing sector has slowed, and its proportion has fallen. Although the proportion of the manufacturing sector may not fully reflect one country's industrialization degree and industrial level, the change in its proportion can reveal the industrialization trend. The experiences of various countries show that national industrialization does not follow a straight trajectory, but it follows an irregular inverted U-shaped curve.

For example, the ratio of manufacturing added value to GDP usually goes through a gradual rising process at first. After reaching a certain stage of development, the ratio reaches its peak and then slowly decreases (Figure 8.2).[35] The proportion of China's manufacturing sector reached its peak at 36.8% in 1996. However, it did not drop significantly in the following decade but remained relatively stable. After 2006, the proportion dropped all the way from 36.2%.

Is the decline in the proportion of China's manufacturing sector a natural phenomenon, or is it of a premature nature? The decline in the proportion of the manufacturing sector may result from the natural evolution of the industrial structure at a high industrialization stage, or it may be premature "deindustrialization" when conditions are not yet ready. Many countries have achieved important positions in the development of the manufacturing sector, but they have experienced a decline in the proportion of manufacturing, so people can learn from their experiences and lessons. We will compare China's situations with two groups of countries.

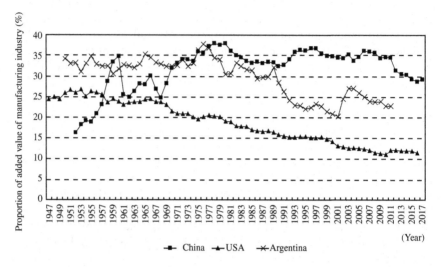

Figure 8.2 International comparisons for declining proportion of manufacturing

In the first group, we refer to the United States and Japan as developed countries. As early as 1953, the value added in the US manufacturing sector began to decline when it accounted for 26.8% of GDP. At 2010 constant prices, the then per capita GDP in the United States was US$16,443, and the proportion of agricultural labor in the total labor dropped to 7%. The proportion of Japan's manufacturing sector began to decline at the level of 34.1% in 1970, its per capita GDP reached US$18,700, and the proportion of agricultural labor was 19%. The two countries both entered the ranks of high-income countries at the turning point when the share of the manufacturing sector declined, and agricultural output and labor share were both low.

In the second group, we take the Latin American countries of Argentina and Brazil for comparison. The proportion of the manufacturing sector in Argentina began to decline at 37.9% in 1976, when the per capita GDP was US$7,292 and the proportion of agricultural labor was 15%. The proportion of the manufacturing sector in Brazil began to decline at the level of 30.3% in 1980, when the per capita GDP was US$8,317, and the proportion of agricultural labor was as high as 38%. In other words, the proportion of the manufacturing sector in both countries started to decline when it was both at the upper-middle-income level.

The decline in the proportion of manufacturing in the first category of countries mentioned above is a natural process. After the decline in the proportion of GDP, the manufacturing sector has held a more important position in the global value chain. The labor productivity of the entire economy has continued to increase, and it has maintained its status as a developed manufacturing country thus far. The decline in the manufacturing proportion in the second category of countries is an immature process. After the proportion of the manufacturing sector declined, the upgrading of the manufacturing sector was not successful, international competitiveness declined, and labor productivity growth failed to support sustained and healthy economic growth. Judging by per capita GDP standards, many such countries have not yet entered the ranks of high-income countries.

We can therefore summarize the following experiences and lessons. First, per capita GDP as a landmark indicator reveals that the highly industrialized traditional source is gradually declining at a certain development stage. When industrialization turns to a stage with innovation and upgrading as its connotation, it is inevitable to see the declining proportion of the manufacturing sector. Second, when the proportion of agriculture drops to a lower level, it means that there is no longer pressure for the transfer of surplus agricultural labor, and tertiary industry is also at a high-end position. Therefore, the declining proportion of the manufacturing sector will not lead to the reverse Kuznets process; that is, a decrease in labor productivity. Third, the declining proportion of the manufacturing sector will never mean the decreasing importance of the industry. In contrast, the new industrialization stage is a critical period for the manufacturing sector to climb up the value chain ladder.

In contrast to international experience, the decline in China's manufacturing proportion has come too soon. When its proportion reached its highest point in 1996, China's per capita GDP was only US$1,335 at 2010 constant prices, it had just crossed the threshold of lower-middle-income countries, and the proportion of agricultural labor was as high as 51%. When the proportion of manufacturing started to decline in 2006, the per capita GDP was only US$3,069, it was still in the ranks of lower-middle-income countries, and the proportion of agricultural labor was still as high as 43%.

When China's per capita GDP reached US$7,329 in 2017, the proportion of manufacturing fell to 29.3%, and the proportion of agricultural labor was 27%. From the perspective of the development stage and the features of industrial structure, there was a larger gap with the United States and Japan when the proportion of manufacturing declined, and it was closer to the level when the proportion of manufacturing in Argentina and Brazil began to decline. That is, even if the proportion of China's current manufacturing industry is too high and needs some adjustment, the current level should still be used as a warning line to stop the downward trend.

The effort to prevent premature deindustrialization is, on the one hand, to reserve enough time for the upgrading of the manufacturing industry to a technology-intensive high-end industry and to transfer surplus agricultural labor, develop the service industry, and increase labor productivity and, on the other hand, to reserve sufficient space to innovate core technologies, enhance core competitiveness and gain a new position in the global value chain at a higher end of the industry. Without this necessary time and space, the inverse Kuznets phenomenon may occur.

The stage when labor migration is not finished yet

Undoubtedly, it is not possible for a country to always enjoy the demographic dividend in its economic development, and the feature of unlimited labor supply will eventually disappear. Correspondingly, the increase in total factor productivity is a long and sustainable source of economic growth. The question is whether the potential for labor migration in China is truly exhausted and whether there is still room to improve the labor supply and reallocate it. In the text below, we will put China in a more targeted international perspective to compare and use data to answer the empirical question.

Based on available data, we have marked the relationship between the per capita GDP and the proportion of agricultural labor in 89 countries and regions in Figure 8.3. Figure 8.3a and Figure 8.3b both try to reveal the same fact. First, Figure 8.3a shows that the proportion of agricultural labor decreases with the increase in per capita income. This comes from the general law of development economics (economists are so decisive about its effect that this law is also called the iron law), that is, the agricultural share declines as the economic development level improves. Second, Figure 8.3b is from a zoomed graph drawn with the same data to highlight China's position.

Figure 8.3 shows that relative to the development stage, China's agricultural labor still occupies a relatively high share. Even based on the author's re-estimated figures, for example, the number and share of agricultural labor are approximately 10 percentage points lower than the figures shown here, but they are still at a relatively high level. Furthermore, it is of great urgency to continue to reduce the share of China's agricultural labor.

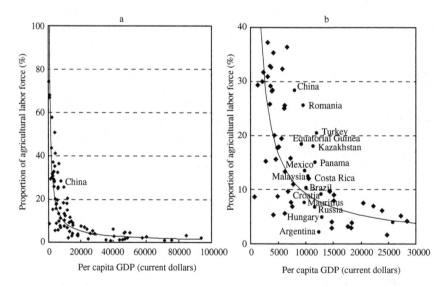

Figure 8.3 Economic development level and proportion of agricultural labor

China is in the process of transition from the ranks of upper-middle-income countries to the ranks of high-income countries. In Figure 8.3b, the author marks the countries in the range where the per capita GDP in 2015 was above China's level and fell below US$13,000 (at that time, approximately US$12,600 was defined by the World Bank as the dividing line between middle income and high income). Therein, the share of agricultural labor in all countries is significantly lower than that of China. When the arithmetic average of 14 countries without China is calculated, it can be seen that the entry ticket to enter the ranks of high-income countries is that the share of agricultural labor drops to approximately 12.6%. In other words, if China wants to catch up with this level, it needs to further reduce by 15.7 percentage points. Even based on the share of agricultural labor estimated by the author, there is still an approximately 6 percentage point reduction for China.

If the per capita income of these countries is regarded as the goal of catching up in the next few years, they should also be taken as a direct reference for the transformation of employment structure. In other words, when China is developing toward a high-income country, one unavoidable task is to further reduce the share of agricultural labor.

The question is as follows: Why did labor migration in China slow down when the share of agricultural labor was still high? On the surface, the slowdown in labor migration seems to be an exception to the law of declining agricultural share as the economic development level increases. The management of excessively small-scale land slows the increase in agricultural labor productivity and restricts the decline in the share of agricultural labor. This is the explanation for the "exception." Therefore, it is possible to find the constraints of China's economy, especially the agricultural sector, to further break the bottleneck of labor migration.

In the literature of development economics, there are three classical labor migration (mobility) models, and they were originally proposed by Arthur Lewis, Michael Todaro, Gustav Ranis, and John Fei. Such models are both consistent and complementary to each other.[36] It should be pointed out that for their own purposes, these three models theoretically illustrate the entire process of labor migration, and they do not correspond to different development periods or migration stages.

However, each model differs in the most prominent contribution points. For example, the Lewis model emphasizes that the marginal productivity of agricultural labor is zero, so the industry can obtain a sufficient supply of labor at a constant wage level in the expanding process; the Todaro model emphasizes the push (from rural areas) and pull (from cities) of labor migration as well as how the balance of various forces influences the migration process; the Fei-Ranis model emphasizes the importance of increasing agricultural labor productivity after the first turning point (or "food shortage point" as they call it).

Only in this sense, to better summarize and depict some characteristic facts and corresponding challenges in the process of China's labor force transfer, we seize the most prominent contribution points of each model and divide the labor force transfer or transfer process into different stages. "Lewis migration," "Todaro migration," and "Fei-Ranis migration."[37]

The first stage is Lewis migration. The stage is featured with zero marginal productivity of agricultural labor. Therefore, the wage level of the transferred labor has always remained unchanged so that reduced labor will not have an adverse effect on agricultural production. Therefore, labor migration during this period is "unconditional." In China, migration began in the early 1980s, that is, the period when the household contract system was locally explored and then promoted nationwide, and ended in 2004, when the first Lewis turning point characterized by labor shortage and rising wages or the food shortage point had arrived.

The survey with the consistent standard on the number of migrant workers who left their own villages and towns can be traced back to 1997.[38] We have made certain amendments to make it connected with the continuous data released by the National Bureau of Statistics since 2001 (Figure 8.4); we can also obtain the monthly wage data of migrant workers after 2001. There were no available wage data before, and according to the statement of a responsible person of the National Bureau of Statistics about a survey in 2004, there was no substantial increase in the wages of migrant workers in the previous 20 years, and it was only approximately 600 yuan.[39]

Based on the approach, we assume an average wage level of migrant workers in 1997 and make it connected with the actual survey data in 2001 at an annual growth rate of 1%. In this way, taking 2004 as a turning point,

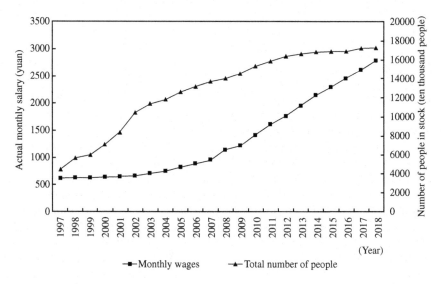

Figure 8.4 Changes in the number of rural migrant workers and actual wages

we can observe unchanged features of unlimited labor supply and wages before 2004 and a decreasing trend of labor supply and rapidly rising wages after 2004.

The second stage is Todaro migration. After crossing the first Lewis turning point, the marginal productivity of agricultural labor became positive, but it was still less than the average labor productivity. As there remains a strong demand for transferred labor in the non-agricultural industry, labor shortages and wage increases continue to exist. After the first Lewis turning point in 2004, China's labor migration was at this stage. In Figure 8.4, the slow growth of the unskilled labor supply represented by migrant workers and the accelerated rise of wages properly depicts the characteristics of this stage of labor transfer.

At this time, the phenomenon of replacing labor with capital already appeared in agriculture, improving agricultural labor productivity and raising non-agricultural wages at the same time. In addition, the flow of the labor force is restricted by a series of institutional factors, and it is often not in the desired direction. For example, the urban policy of excluding migrant laborers based on the household registration system has generated adverse effects that are not conducive to labor mobility. Therefore, at this stage, it is necessary to promote the reform to ensure the smooth flow of laborers.

The third stage is Fei-Ranis migration. After overtaking the second Lewis turning point, the marginal productivity of agricultural labor was greater than the average labor productivity. According to the theoretical hypothesis, at this stage, the marginal productivity of labor in agriculture and non-agricultural industries has been equal, labor mobility seems no longer a systematic and one-way flow from agriculture to non-agricultural industries, and there is no room for corresponding resource reallocation, but it should have been a two-way flow, so there is no need to divide a special stage of labor migration.

However, there are two reasons why we still need to pay attention to this stage and even to pay attention to this stage in advance. First, to achieve seamless connection between different development stages, it is necessary to break through the theoretical division of development stages and blur its boundaries in reality. Second, in fact, in high-income countries, there is almost no lower limit for the decline in the proportion of the agricultural labor force, and even the equal marginal productivity of labor in various industries is only of theoretical significance.

Therefore, we can expect that agricultural labor will continue to transfer substantially. The stage is named "Fei-Ranis migration" for the purpose of emphasizing that it must rely on the modernization of agricultural production methods and the improvement of labor productivity to support and drive labor migration. Therefore, to realize the modernization of agricultural production methods and break the situation that agricultural labor productivity fails to converge with non-agricultural industries, we start to discuss this stage as the foothold, but we aim to emphasize that this task runs through all stages.

Conclusion

Since 1978, China's economic reform has made substantial progress in many fields, gradually removing the institutional obstacles that hinder the flow of the labor force so that the surplus labor force under the dual economy can gradually obtain the right to withdraw from the original allocation pattern, the right to reallocate according to the productivity principle, and the right to enter sectors with higher productivity and growth rates. While material capital and human capital have been accumulated to their maximum, labor reallocation has significantly improved productivity and has become an important contributor to rapid economic growth.

This chapter summarizes the reform process in related fields from the perspective of labor reallocation. It analyzes the source of labor productivity growth during the reform from a quantitative perspective, revealing the total contribution of the three industries, their respective contributions, and the contributions of labor reallocation in the process. Although this analysis path is only one approach to study the effect of reform and cannot replace the research conducted under other frameworks, on the one hand, the perspective of resource reallocation is indispensable for economic development research, and on the other hand, the study in the chapter also confirms the basic conclusions of other studies from its own perspective. More importantly, research from the perspective of resource reallocation helps us to understand the source of China's economic growth in the future when resource endowments change.

As China entered a demographic change stage with low birth rates for a long time, the relationship between labor supply and demand changed from quantitative changes to qualitative changes. After overtaking the Lewis turning point in 2004, the supply-side conditions of China's economic growth changed, which is shown as the working-age population reached the peak and the decline of the population-dependency ratio hit the bottom in 2010. The demographic dividend on which high growth depends has begun to disappear at a fast rate, so the growth model supported by capital accumulation and labor input is no longer sustainable, and economic growth will increasingly be driven by labor productivity growth.

Meanwhile, since the total number of laborers available for transfer decreases, the previous obvious effect of resource reallocation has shown a weakening trend, and it has become increasingly difficult to promote productivity. The factors of labor productivity improvement obtained by decomposition in this chapter can provide useful enlightenment for exploring the potential of productivity improvement in the future.

There is still a huge gap among the productivities of the three industries, especially between agriculture and non-agricultural industries. This fact means that there is a great potential to increase agricultural labor productivity, and the efficiency of reallocating resources can still be expected. As the rural population aged 16–19 entered negative growth in 2014, the labor migration from rural areas to cities slowed down significantly. However, since there are differences in productivity among industries, it is possible to continue to increase overall labor productivity by further improving the policy environment for labor migration, preventing the premature decline of the proportion of the manufacturing industry, and eliminating the unsustainable factors in labor productivity growth in the secondary industry, such as excessively depending on the increase of the capital–labor ratio.

The first is to increase the incentives for agricultural labor transfer through the household registration system reform. Comparisons show that the current share of China's agricultural labor is lower than the average level of upper-middle-income countries, but there is still a considerable gap with the average level of high-income countries and that of high-income economies in East Asia. This means that there is still a necessity and urgency for China to further reduce the share of agricultural labor, which is the goal and task of structural change in the future.

The second is to break through the constraints of the ultrasmall agricultural operations scale. One of the reasons why land cannot be transferred to form ultrasmall-scale agricultural operations is that the household registration system prevents the complete transfer of the labor force. From the composition of migrant workers, we can see that incomplete transfer has been an obstacle to land circulation. In 2017, 40.0% of the 287 million migrant workers transferred to employment in non-agricultural industries in their own towns, and they could also take care of agricultural production; 46.6% were family members who left their towns for employment, but their family members were still working in rural areas; Only 13.3% of the whole families migrated out of the town,[40] and they may have been willing to transfer the land.

The third is to rely on total factor productivity to maintain the sustainable increase in industrial labor productivity. In the case of labor shortages and rising wages, companies have to increase labor productivity by capital instead of labor. However, if the process cannot be coordinated with such factors as the quality of workers, an excessive increase in the capital–labor ratio will lead to diminishing returns to capital.

Japan has provided lessons on this aspect. After it lost the demographic dividend, the Japanese economy relied excessively on capital investment instead of total factor productivity to continue to increase labor productivity. The contribution of the capital–labor ratio to labor productivity increased from 51% during the period 1985–1991 to 94% during the period 1991–2000, while the contribution of total factor productivity decreased from 37% to −15%, resulting in a decline in potential growth capacity.[41]

Under the circumstances that the transfer from agricultural labor to non-agricultural industries has significantly slowed down, the labor reallocation among industries in the secondary industry and that among enterprises in an industrial sector are the force driving innovation and development, and it is also an important source to raise total factor productivity. Productivity differences among enterprises in the same industry mean that production factors have not yet reached the optimal allocation. Therefore, after the end of the dual economic development stage, the increase in productivity is driven more by the process of entry, exit, rebirth, and death of enterprises—that is, the process of creative destruction—in a way that promotes the transfer of production factors to more efficient enterprises. Studies have shown that in developed countries such as the United States, the contribution to productivity increases from such sources is as high as a third to a half,[42] while there is still a huge potential in China in this field.[43]

Finally, we should adhere to the productivity principle of resource reallocation. In reality, the level of labor productivity among the three industries is not on the order of No. 1, No. 2, and No. 3. Generally, the labor productivity of the tertiary industry is higher than that of the primary industry, but it is far lower than that of the secondary industry. For example, based on the value added in the average production of labor, if the productivity of the secondary industry is 1, the labor productivity of the primary industry and the tertiary industry in 2018 was only 0.19 and 0.76, respectively.

Therefore, the transfer of labor from agriculture to the service sector will undoubtedly lead to an increase in productivity, but the transfer of labor from the manufacturing sector to the service sector does not necessarily bring about an overall increase in productivity. In recent years, while the proportion of the manufacturing industry has decreased and the proportion of employment in tertiary industry has increased, labor productivity has been hovering. Therefore, to promote the development of the service industry and increase its proportion, we need to follow the principle of productivity improvement, focusing on modern service industries with high productivity and rapid growth.

Notes

1 Alwyn Young, Gold into the Base Metals: Productivity Growth in the People's Republic of China during the Reform Period, *Journal of Political Economy*, Vol. 111, No. 6, 2003, pp. 1220–1261; Paul Krugman, Hitting China's Wall, *New York Times*, July 18, 2013.
2 Justin Lin, Cai Fang, and Zhou Li, *The China Miracle: Development Strategy and Economic Reform* (revised edition), Hong Kong: Chinese University Press, 2003; Barry Naughton, *Growing Out of the Plan: Chinese Economic Reform, 1978–1993*, Cambridge: Cambridge University Press, 1996.
3 Jeffrey Sachs, *Lessons for Brazil from China's Success*, transcript, São Paulo, November 5, 2003.
4 Robert J. Barro and Xavier Sala-i-Martin, *Economic Growth* (second edition), Cambridge, MA: MIT Press, 2004.
5 Robert J. Barro, *Economic Growth and Convergence, Applied Especially to China*, NBER Working Paper, No. 21872, 2016.
6 Wang Feng and Andrew Mason, *The Demographic Factor in China's Transition*, in Loren Brandt and Thomas G. Rawski (ed.), *China's Great Economic Transformation*, Cambridge, New York: Cambridge University Press, 2008.

7 Simon Kuznets, *Economic Growth of Nations: Total Output and Production Structure*, Beijing: The Commercial Press, 1985; Hollis B. Chenery and Moises Syrquin, *Patterns of Development 1950–1970*, Washington, DC: Economic Science Press, 1988.

8 Masahiko Aoki, The Five Phases of Economic Development and Institutional Evolution in China, Japan, and Korea, in Masahiko Aoki, Timur Kuran, and Gérard Roland (eds.), *Institutions and Comparative Economic Development*, Basingstoke: Palgrave Macmillan, 2012, pp. 13–47.

9 Hollis B. Chenery and Moises Syrquin, *Patterns of Development 1950–1970*, Washington, DC: Economic Science Press, 1988, p. 14.

10 Loren Brandt and Thomas G. Rawski (eds.), *China's Great Economic Transformation*, Cambridge: Cambridge University Press, 2008, p. 9.

11 Loren Brandt and Thomas G. Rawski (eds.), *China's Great Economic Transformation*, Cambridge: Cambridge University Press, 2008, p. 9.

12 Barry Naughton, *Growing Out of the Plan: Chinese Economic Reform, 1978–1993*, Cambridge: Cambridge University Press, 1996.

13 Justin Lin, Cai Fang, and Zhou Li, *The China Miracle: Development Strategy and Economic Reform* (revised edition), Hong Kong: Chinese University Press, 2003.

14 Cai Fang (ed.), *Transforming the Chinese Economy, 1978–2008*, Leiden and Boston: Brill, 2010, Introduction.

15 Wang Xiaolu, *Strategical Thinking on National Income Distribution*, Beijing: Xuexi Publishing House/Hainan Publishing House, 2013.

16 Gan Li, Yin Zhichao, Jia Nan, Xu Shu, Ma Shang, and Zheng Lu, *China Household Finance Survey Report 2012*, Chengdu: Southwestern University of Finance and Economics Press, 2012, p. 153.

17 See Cai Fang, *China's Economic Growth Prospects: From Demographic Dividend to Reform Dividend*, Cheltenham, UK: Edward Elgar, 2016, Chapter 10.

18 David H. Autor, Lawrence F. Katz, and Melissa S. Kearney, *The Polarization of the U.S. Labor Market*, NBER Working Paper, No. 11986, 2006; David H. Autor, Work of the Past, Work of the Future, *AEA Papers and Proceedings*, Vol. 109, 2019, pp. 1–32.

19 Michael Spence and Sandile Hlatshwayo, *The Evolving Structure of the American Economy and the Employment Challenge*, Working Paper, Maurice R. Greenberg Center for Geoeconomic Studies, Council on Foreign Relations, March 2011.

20 A detailed comparison and data description will be provided in Chapter 12.

21 See Cai Fang, *China's Economic Growth Prospects: From Demographic Dividend to Reform Dividend*, Cheltenham, UK: Edward Elgar, 2016, Chapter 11.

22 Masahiko Aoki, The Five Phases of Economic Development and Institutional Evolution in China, Japan, and Korea, in Masahiko Aoki, Timur Kuran, and Gérard Roland (eds.), *Institutions and Comparative Economic Development*, Basingstoke: Palgrave Macmillan, 2012, pp. 13–47.

23 Margaret S. McMillan and Dani Rodrik, *Globalization, Structural Change and Productivity Growth*, NBER Working Paper, No. 17143, 2011.

24 Barry Bosworth and Susan Collins, *Accounting for Growth: Comparing China and India*, NBER Working Paper, 12943, 2007.

25 Du Yang, On Labor Market Changes and the New Economic Growth, *China Opening Journal*, Vol. 3, 2014.

26 Cai Fang, Reform Effects in China: A Perspective of Labor Reallocation, *Economic Research Journal*, Vol. 7, 2017.

Narrative of reform, opening-up, development, and sharing

27 International Monetary Fund, Asia Rising: Patterns of Economic Development and Growth, in *World Economic Outlook*, September 2006, pp. 1–30.

28 For example, Thomas Rawski and Robert Mead, On the Trail of China's Phantom Farmers, *World Development*, Vol. 26, No. 5, 1998, pp. 767–781.

29 Cai Fang, Du Yang, and Wang Meiyan, Demystify the Labor Statistics in China, *China Economic Journal*, Vol. 6, No. 2–3, 2013, pp. 123–133.

30 Loren Brandt and Zhu Xiaodong, *Accounting for China's Growth*, Working Paper, No. 395, Department of Economics of University of Toronto, 2010.

31 With the new release by the National Bureau of Statistics, in general we can still judge based on the latest update that the actual proportion of agricultural labor is 10 percentage points lower than shown in statistics.

32 Louis Kuijs, *China Through 2020: A Macroeconomic Scenario*, World Bank China Research Working Paper, No. 9, 2010.

33 Marcel P. Timmer and Adam Szirmai, *Productivity Growth in Asian Manufacturing: the Structural Bonus Hypothesis Examined*, Structural Change and Economic Dynamics, No. 11, 2000, pp. 371–392.

34 Barry Bosworth and Susan Collins, *Accounting for Growth: Comparing China and India*, NBER Working Paper, No. 12943, 2007.

35 Data for calculations in the section are mainly from the World Bank database and Marcel P. Timmer, G.J. de Vries, and K. de Vries, Patterns of Structural Change in Developing Countries, in J. Weiss and M. Tribe (eds.), *Routledge Handbook of Industry and Development*, London: Routledge, pp. 65–83.

36 See Arthur Lewis, Economic Development with Unlimited Supply of Labor, *Manchester School*, Vol. 22, No. 2, 1954, pp. 139–191; Gustav Ranis and John C.H. Fei, A Theory of Economic Development, *American Economic Review*, Vol. 51, No. 4, 1961, pp. 533–565; M.P. Todaro, A Model of Labor Migration and Urban Unemployment in Less Developed Countries, *American Economic Review*, Vol. 59, No. 1, 1969, pp. 138–148.

37 For the sake of understanding, readers can refer to Figure 7.2 in Chapter 7 where the decline in each phase corresponds to a certain section and the turning point for changes at important phases is marked.

38 Cai Fang, *Scientific Development Philosophy and Sustainability of Economic Growth*, Shanghai: Zhonghua Book Company, 2009, p. 147.

39 Li Deshui, Economic Reasons for the Lack of Migrant Laborers, *People's Daily Online*, 2005, http://politics.people.com.cn/GB/1027/3149315.html.

40 National Bureau of Statistics, *The National Report on Migrant Worker Monitoring and Survey 2015*, 2016, www.stats.gov.cn/, provided the data about the whole-family migration for the period 2010–2014 in an earlier version, and no such information has been provided since then. The author estimates that the migrant population was 38.25 million in 2017 based on the then proportion and the average annual growth speed.

41 Asian Productivity Organization, *APO Productivity Data Book 2008*, Tokyo: Asian Productivity Organization, 2008.

42 Lucia Foster, John Haltiwanger, and Chad Syverson, Reallocation, Firm Turnover, and Efficiency: Selection on Productivity or Profitability?, *American Economic Review*, Vol. 98, No. 1, 2008, pp. 394–425.

43 Chang-Tai Tsieh and Peter J. Klenow, Misallocation and Manufacturing TFP in China and India, *The Quarterly Journal of Economics*, Vol. 124, No. 4, 2009, pp. 1403–1448.

9 China's concept and practice of poverty alleviation and its global contribution

Introduction

During Deng Xiaoping's visit to Japan in 1978, he took the well-known Shinkansen train. When the reporter asked about his feelings, he said concisely and sincerely, "Fast, truly fast!"[1] In the 40 years since then, China's reform and opening-up, initiated by Deng Xiaoping, have created a rare miracle in the history of the world economy in the aspects of developing economy, getting rid of poverty, enhancing national strength, and improving people's living standards. Any outside observer, when commenting on this, will be happy enough to repeat Deng Xiaoping's concise statement.

Both professional researchers and broader observers have unanimously praised China's achievements in economic development. It is rare to hear doubts, especially in regard to the speed of China's economic growth. However, there is no consensus on the reasons, processes, and results of China's economic growth. Some scholars may have biased observations and even misunderstandings.

For example, many economists failed to accurately grasp the general nature of China's economic reform and even underestimated the importance of certain basic conditions for economic growth, thus misjudging sustainable economic growth. There are also different views on whether China's economic development is fully inclusive. Some researchers deny the existence of such full inclusiveness based on the change of unequal income distribution indicators.

Due to the aforementioned misunderstanding, some researchers make specious judgments about the demand-side factors of China's economic growth; that is, deny the important role of domestic demands, especially consumer demands, and even draw unreasonable conclusions and policy implications. Under these circumstances, even though some observers who sincerely admire China's achievements in poverty reduction cannot regard poverty reduction effects and economic development achievements as one process with consistent logic, they understand the poverty alleviation experience and growth models in a combined way.

There is a famous saying from John Maynard Keynes: "Practical men, who believe themselves to be quite exempt from any intellectual influence, are

DOI: 10.4324/9781003329305-11

usually the slave of some defunct economist." In reality, there are indeed two late economists who have been quoted by contemporary researchers and have had a considerable influence on evaluating China's economic development experiences. However, in terms of the reform and opening-up process in the past 40 years and the resulting development and shared results, regardless of whether these late economists are right in ideology, it often leads to distorted views of facts when applied to explain China's experiences. Nevertheless, such influence is also of academic value since it can accidentally trigger deeper discussions.

Let us first examine the influence of Friedrich Hayek. It is said that one contribution of this Austrian economist has been to expand people's way of thinking. Based on the traditional dichotomy that divides social phenomena into natural results completely free from human behavior intervention and results intentionally made by humans, he identified the third type, i.e., the unexpected consequences of human unintended behaviors.[2]

Such economists as Huang Yasheng, Steven Cheung, Ronald Coase, and Ning Wang have shown theor appreciation for China's reform and opening-up and the resulting development achievements. Either explicitly quoting Hayek's argument or being unconsciously affected by the concept, they have actually regarded the Chinese experience as an excellent case of such "unexpected consequences of human behaviors" theory.[3] In other words, whether they are unable to see themselves as outsiders or are unwilling to see due to prejudices, they do not have enough understanding of the fundamental starting point of China's reform and opening-up.

At the moment when Deng Xiaoping praised the Japanese Shinkansen train as "truly fast," he had already drawn an important conclusion: Poverty is not socialism. Obviously, the goal of getting the Chinese people out of poverty and continuously improving their living standards has been the aim of reform and opening-up from the very start, and it has run through the whole course. Later, in his famous Southern Talks, Deng Xiaoping put forward the "three benefits" criteria—with developing productive forces, enhancing national strength, and improving people's living standards as the principles of reform—which have been well implemented since then. Since the 18th National Congress of the Communist Party of China, socialism with Chinese characteristics has entered a new era. It is the cornerstone of Xi Jinping's thought on socialism with Chinese characteristics in the new era to adhere to the people-centered development philosophy and take the general people as the main body of reform and development and the main body of sharing and ultimate beneficiary as well. Obviously, China's 40 years of reform and opening-up is by no means an "unintentional behavior," and the economic growth and poverty reduction miracle are not "unintended consequences."

During research on income distribution in China's reform period, economists found a rising trend of unequal income indicators, such as the Gini coefficient. Therefore, they believe that China's development in this period lacked sharing. This argument is not only theoretically inconsistent but also misread and misunderstood in the statistical sense. In addition, it will be difficult to make a consistent explanation of the poverty reduction achievements if one cannot correctly understand the shared nature of China's development. More importantly, the facts in this regard and the logic behind them are undoubtedly the strongest evidence to prove that the reform practice is purposeful and self-conscious. This chapter will clarify and explain this statement.

Let us look at the influence of Hollis Chenery. The former chief economist of the World Bank believes that certain development conditions can work alone in the short term to promote economic development when other conditions are not yet available.[4] Under this influence, there is a research tendency to list the basic conditions for China's economic development, and it is believed that each development condition has different importance in terms of promoting economic growth, so reforms that create different development conditions also have different significance.[5]

Some researchers even believe that only the rural reform centered on the household contract responsibility system was remarkable in China's economic reform in the early 1980s, and they unfairly commented on other reforms.[6] Even if people have correctly observed that reform has solved the problem of incentives to stimulate economic growth, because they cannot see the overall logic of the reform and its internal relations, and they do not know the necessary conditions of economic growth in this period, they can easily regard the growth effect of the reform as a one-time return to the production possibility boundary, thus denying the long-term sustainability of economic growth. Krugman and Young are representatives of this view.[7]

In fact, if China's dual economic development process is explained with the hypothesis of neoclassical growth theory without clarification that the period of reform and opening-up coincides with a specific demographic window of opportunity, not only will the potential growth rate of China's economy and its sustainability on the supply side be underestimated, but the important role of consumer demands will be unclear, and there will be no consistent explanation of the demand side factors.

Scholars and observers at home and abroad have generally agreed that China has achieved rapid economic growth during the reform and opening-up and have also seen the role of reforms in improving the incentive mechanism. China's achievements in poverty reduction during this period have also been highly appreciated and valued by the international community. However, since there is not much research on reforms in other fields, especially reforms to promote resource reallocation, researchers cannot establish a consistent inherent connection among reforms, development and sharing from a theoretical and logical perspective. Theorists will be embarrassed when explaining China's successful practice of poverty reduction. This is also why the research literatures on economic transformation, economic growth, and poverty reduction and development are independent from each other.

Economists may not know or may have forgotten a passage from another late economist, Karl Marx. He said, "But what distinguishes the worst architect from the best of bees is this, that the architect raises his structure in imagination before he erects it in reality."[8] Every step of reform and opening-up and every development and shared achievement can very well prove this passage, and it is also fully embodied in the "three benefits" and people-centered development philosophy.

This chapter briefly describes how China's economic reform has transformed the historical heritage of underemployment and demographic transition into a source of economic growth. While maintaining rapid growth for more than 40 years, China's reform has reflected shared development and achieved remarkable achievements in poverty reduction.

We first reveal that economic development characterized by labor reallocation has a shared nature since it promotes employment and increases labor income, and we further elaborate on the reform aimed at improving people's living standards and the people-centered development philosophy. The Chinese government has continuously implemented a poverty relief strategy for poor rural residents, has continuously innovated and upgraded the strategy along with the changes at different stages, and has broken the myth of diminishing marginal effects on poverty alleviation. Finally, the chapter attempts to reveal the world significance of China's poverty alleviation concept and practice, look to the future poverty alleviation pattern, and make proposals on policies.

Broad and shared fast growth

In the long period of 40 years from 1978 to 2018, China's GDP grew at an average annual rate of 9.4%. With a 17-fold growth in labor productivity, the consumption level of urban and rural residents increased by more than 16 times over the same period. Obviously, such economic development achievement is not without reason. It not only conforms to the well-known general law of economic development but also clearly reflects the uniqueness of China's experience. There is no theoretical or empirical evidence to say that economic growth will inevitably lead to a reduction in poverty, but making a cake big is an indispensable prerequisite for dividing the cake.

For example, we can see clearly from international comparison that on the one hand, China's rapid economic growth corresponds to significant poverty alleviation effects; on the other hand, more moderate economic growth in upper middle-income countries (excluding China) corresponds to a relatively mediocre poverty reduction effect (Figure 9.1).

In the past 40 years of reform and development, China has experienced a very unique demographic transition for at least 30 years (1980–2010), shown as continuously rapid growth of the working-age population aged 15–59 (with an average annual increase of 1.68%), while the dependent population outside the age range remains constant (decreasing at an average annual rate of 0.01%). It poses a sharp contrast between the average situation in developed

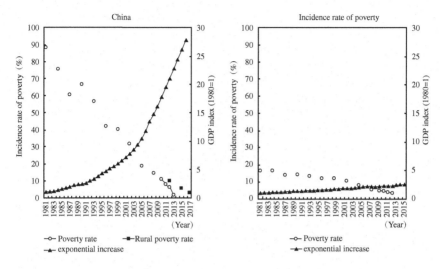

Figure 9.1 Relationship between economic growth and poverty alleviation effect in international comparison

countries, i.e., an average annual growth of 0.44% for the working-age population and an average annual growth of 0.47% for the dependent population, and the average situation in developing countries excluding China, i.e., an average annual growth of 2.44% for the working-age population and an average annual growth of 1.43% for the dependent population. This means that China now has the demographic characteristic of "there are more workers and fewer dependents," and it is in a demographic window of opportunity conducive to economic growth.

In the early stage of reform and even over a longer duration of time, obviously no one realized such a potential demographic dividend. Instead, researchers and policy-makers regarded a large population and labor surplus as a historical burden and treated it as a huge challenge. In fact, the one-child policy started to be strictly implemented in 1980, at the beginning of the reform and opening-up. In retrospect, it was inevitable that such understanding had historical limitations, but the corresponding policy measures and reform measures may not be without purpose and positive effects.

Whether the strict family planning policy to control the population is meritorious or not, and how effective, after all, it has accelerated the population to change to a certain extent from high birth rate, low death rate, and hence high growth rate to low birth rate, low death rate, and hence low growth rate. It enabled China's demographic dividend to be released earlier. We will not discuss this in detail but examine how reform promotes labor transfer, achieving the effect of improving economic growth and expanding employment.

In the face of the widespread poverty in rural areas in the initial period and the phenomenon of labor surplus after the implementation of household contract system, the most important thing in the subsequent rural reform is to create the full flow of production factors from the system and mechanism, to promote the rural production factors with labor as the core to withdraw from industries with low productivity and low return rate, and to transfer to industries with higher productivity and income. The reform carried out according to this logical thread has never stopped and continues to this day.

First, it was the most thorough major reform in rural areas to abolish the people's commune system that had lasted for more than 20 years. When the household contract responsibility system was quickly implemented throughout the country, the *Constitution of the People's Republic of China* officially defined the villagers committee as a self-governance organization of villagers after the amendment at the end of 1982; the Central Committee of the Communist Party of China and the State Council issued the *Notice on Separating Government Administration from Social Organizations and Establishing Township Governments* in 1983, requiring separating government administration from social organizations and setting up township governments. Correspondingly, administrative villages were established at the previous production brigade level, and villagers' groups were established based on production brigades. The villagers' self-governance system in rural areas, together with the basic rural management system centered on the household contract responsibility system, has fundamentally established the right of rural households to allocate production factors independently under the premise of land under collective ownership, and the reform has yielded overall and long-term benefits.

Second, policies to restrict labor allocation have gradually loosened, and barriers to labor transfer among production activities, among the three industries, and between urban and rural areas have been successively removed. At the beginning, the rural labor force transferred from purely planting grains to diversified management, from a single planting industry to agriculture, forestry, animal husbandry, sideline production, and fishery, and from agriculture to village and township enterprises that "enable farmers to depart farming but stay in hometowns," and later they moved to small towns and even large and medium-sized cities to be employed in non-agricultural industries.

Just as in the process of promoting the household contract responsibility system, the term "can" in the CPC Central Committee's documents has played a key role (for example, "can be contracted to households") in removing institutional obstacles of labor mobility, and it is also reflected as "allowed" in a series of policies. For example, in 1983, farmers were allowed to be engaged in long-distance trafficking and self-sales of agricultural products, which for the first time broke the geographical restrictions on employment; in 1988, farmers were allowed to bring their own rations and work in neighboring cities and towns, which for the first time broke the barriers of employment in urban and rural areas; in the early 1990s, food coupons and other ticket systems were abolished, and rural migrant labor was allowed to live and work in cities and towns at all levels.

Third, the household registration system and a series of relevant institutional reforms have gradually rolled out, enabling labor transfer and flow in a wider scope. Such reform is mainly reflected in two aspects. First, state-owned enterprises and the urban employment system are reformed to promote the development of the labor market, and second, built on the household registration identity of residents, the different social security systems between rural and urban areas gradually develop toward being integrated and equalized.

In the late 1990s, the employment system was reformed to break the "lifelong employment" of state-owned enterprises. It once led to large-scale unemployment and severe urban poverty, but the labor allocation was transferred from the planning system to the market mechanism in the process. Meanwhile, a social security system was established in the city. These reforms subsequently have a chain effect. On the one hand, rural migrant laborers have obtained fairer opportunities to compete for employment. On the other hand, the construction of the social security system has gradually expanded to rural areas to greatly improve the coverage of urban and rural residents.

In retrospect, the aforementioned reforms advanced a clear logical line. That is, by enabling the surplus rural labor force and the redundant employees of urban enterprises to withdraw from inefficient allocation, they will flow between urban and rural areas, between regions, between industries and between enterprises and be reallocated, thus entering the field of higher productivity and transforming the demographic dividend into high-speed economic growth through factor accumulation and resource reallocation. A study shows that among the 16.7-fold labor productivity growth (per labor GDP) from 1978 to 2015, 44% was contributed by such reallocation of labor resources.[9]

Looking back at the reform process and its effect on promoting economic growth, we can see how the reform has gradually removed the institutional barriers that hinder the flow of production factors and transformed the rural surplus labor and redundant workers in urban enterprises, which are the heritage of the planned economy, into favorable growth factors. To put it plainly, it has transformed the favorable demographic factor at the special demographic transition stage into a demographic dividend, thus realizing rapid economic growth.

From the perspective of system reform and economic development, we can see that inclusiveness and sharing are their inherent nature. That is, the whole process of economic growth is accompanied by an increase in the labor participation rate in non-agricultural industries and the expansion of employment. Through this redistribution effect and quantitative effect, the income of workers and their families is increased, thus improving the living standard.

Needless to say, Chinese society experienced a widening income gap. At the same time, we should admit that the widening income gap shown in relevant indicators contains an overestimation related to statistical factors. Moreover, we are concerned about the overall sharing nature of economic growth in the reform and opening-up, so it is necessary to analyze the stage problems and the trend problems separately. Only in this way can we neither underestimate achievements nor gloss over problems.

Based on the declining proportion of labor remuneration in GDP, some studies conclude that the income distribution situation has deteriorated. Judging from the indicator, it indeed showed a downward trend from 2003 and reached its lowest point of 45.8% in 2011. However, the proportion subsequently increased year by year and regressed to 51.1% in 2015. Some scholars have explained that the decline in this proportion is partly caused by the decline in the share of agriculture, which has high labor remuneration, and therefore it does not fully mean the income distribution has deteriorated.[10] Such observation suggests that we should take into account the regular change of declines in the agricultural share and re-understand the sharing nature of the reform and development process.[11]

During economic development, it is a recognized law that agricultural output and employment share decline irreversibly. During the decline in the agricultural share, both the early experience in developed countries and the reality in developing countries have shown that the decline in the agricultural employment share is left behind that of the output share.[12] This characteristic is more prominent in China due to institutional factors such as the household registration system. Nevertheless, the proportion of agricultural labor dropped significantly after all.

According to the National Bureau of Statistics, the proportion of agricultural labor dropped from 70.5% in 1978 to 27% in 2018. The author's research concludes that the current proportion of agricultural labor is likely to be another 10 percentage points lower than the official figure.[13] Obviously, this is the result of the large-scale transfer of rural labor to urban non-agricultural industries.

Such large-scale labor transfer realized in a relatively short time has helped form a typical Lewisian dual economic development process. As a result, migrant laborers obtain jobs paid higher than their income from farming, reducing the rural poverty level as a whole and creating the effect of narrowing the urban–rural income gap. On the one hand, even if the wage rate remains unchanged, expanding the scale of labor mobility can significantly increase the income of rural families. On the other hand, rural poor households can significantly increase the family's per capita net income by means of being employed elsewhere. For example, a study shows that migrant workers can increase the per capita net income of rural poor families by 8.5% to 13.1%.[14] In the text below, we will summarize some important facts about how migration helps reduce poverty.

First, household surveys in the official statistical system before 2013 were conducted independently in urban and rural areas, so rural households who migrated with whole families and members of rural households who went out to work were often obviously excluded from the urban sample due to being not in the sampling, and on the other hand, they were largely excluded from the survey coverage of rural household sampling because they were no longer treated as rural permanent residents owing to being long absent. Based on surveys in some areas, some researchers estimated the incomes of migrant workers that were missed in urban and rural household surveys. The results showed that the problems in the sampling and definition of household surveys in the official statistical system led to the disposable income of urban residents being overestimated by 13.6% on average and the net income of rural residents being underestimated by 13.3% on average. As a result, the urban–rural income gap was on average overestimated by 31.2%.[15]

We know that the income gap is often caused by various factors. Accordingly, the index to describe the degree of income inequality is also statistically decomposable. By decomposing the contributing factors to the income inequality index, studies have found that in the overall income gap measured by the Theil index, the contribution rate of the urban–rural income gap is between 40% and 60%.[16] Therefore, once the overestimated urban–rural income gap is corrected statistically, the overall degree of income inequality (for example, measured in the Gini coefficient) will decrease accordingly.

In addition, some studies have estimated extremely high indicators of income inequality, arousing attention from public opinion.[17] Although such research has its own special value, the conclusion drawn has been greatly discounted because the method used focuses on digging for extreme statistical values. Generally, income distribution follows a normal distribution. It is often difficult for statistical surveys to collect accurate information when observing the two ends of the sample, namely, the richest and poorest. The problem with survey statistics is common in statistical systems in all countries. Obviously, the Chinese numerical value from such a special estimation method cannot be simply compared with the statistics published by other countries, nor can it be used to make general inferences.

Second, although the transferred laborers have not seen a significant wage rise in a certain period of time, it has led to a significant increase in the total wage income of rural households and correspondingly a higher proportion since the labor participation rate in non-agricultural industries has increased and rural laborers have been more adequately employed. For example, no substantial increase was seen in the wages of migrant workers from 1997 to 2004, but as the scale of labor migration increased from less than 40 million people to over 100 million people, the total wages earned by migrant laborers achieved an average annual increase of 14.9%. Therefore, even when the wage income of rural households is underestimated, its proportion in rural households' net income has increased significantly from 24.6% to 34.0%.[18]

Third, the Chinese economy met with the Lewis turning point in 2004. As the characteristics of the dual economy gradually disappeared, labor shortage has become normal, and it has significantly improved the negotiating position of laborers in the job market and accelerated to improve the wages of ordinary laborers and the income of low-paid families.

For example, the actual wages of migrant workers increased at a rate of 9.6% from 2003 to 2018. The rising wages of ordinary workers, a feature of the Lewis turning point, have accordingly promoted the arrival of the income gap peak. If the trend can continue, it may become a Kuznets turning point in income distribution.

However, it is a question worthy of consideration whether the trend can continue. The income gap of urban–rural residents calculated at constant prices (the ratio of urban residents' income to rural residents' income) continued to decline from the highest point of 2.67 in 2009 to 2.32 in 2018, totaling a decrease of 13.1%, while the Gini coefficient of national income decreased from the highest point of 0.491 in 2008 to the lowest point of 0.462 in 2015 among recent years, but then it rebounded to 0.474 in 2018.

The income of rural residents has grown faster than that of urban residents, so the urban–rural income gap has maintained a narrowing trend, while the Gini coefficient has rebounded. This fact shows that first, the urban–rural income gap has contributed less to the Gini coefficient, and further observation and research should be done to determine corresponding measures to narrow the income gap; second, it may not meet the Kuznets turning point to rely solely on the labor market, and various redistributive social policies have become increasingly indispensable.

Not only has the social security coverage of urban workers and residents been greatly improved, but since 2004, the government has extended the focus of social security system construction to rural areas, and the social protection policies of cities have increasingly covered migrant workers and their accompanying family members, as well as unemployed people. The construction of the labor market system and social security system has been accelerated, and economic development and social development are more coordinated, which further highlights the extensive inclusiveness contained in the Chinese experience.

Finally, coinciding with the arrival of the Lewis turning point, the central government and local governments have put more effort into implementing the redistribution policy. They have advanced to adequately and equally supply basic public services to further improve the sharing of economic development. Not only has social security covered more urban employees and residents, the government has extended the focus of the social security system to rural areas since 2004, and social guarantee policies in cities have increasingly covered migrant workers and their accompanying family members and unemployed people. The accelerated construction of the labor market system and social security system and more coordinated economic and social development have highlighted the broad inclusiveness embedded in China's experience.

Poverty reduction practices and effects during the reform period

It is undoubtedly the key to solving poverty that the reform and opening-up has promoted rural economic development and the overall rapid growth of the national economy, expanded employment and increased labor remuneration. However, economic development is a necessary condition but not a sufficient condition to improve income distribution. As observed by economists on a global scale, although economic development can reduce poverty, it does not naturally produce a "trickle-down effect."

Therefore, implementing a special poverty alleviation strategy is indispensable to achieve the goals of sharing and poverty reduction. China's achievements in poverty reduction are closely linked with the special poverty alleviation strategy implemented and its effectiveness. Against the backdrop of 40 years of reform and opening-up, China's rural poverty reduction process can be observed in three stages, including the unannounced actual poverty reduction process and the clearly announced implementation process of the poverty alleviation strategy.

The period from the early 1980s to the mid-1980s marked the first stage of poverty reduction. There was no clearly announced poverty alleviation strategy during this period. The overall reform of the rural economic system was the main force promoting the rapid development of the rural economy and national economy in the period. The overall income growth of rural residents was the main factor for poverty reduction in the period. The reform of the basic rural management system greatly mobilized farmers' enthusiasm for production. The vitality of the rural economy was comprehensively strengthened by raising the prices of agricultural products, accelerating the adjustment of the agricultural structure and industrializing rural areas. It also created more opportunities for rural laborers with higher human capital endowments to get rid of poverty and become better off by expanding employment channels.

From 1978 to 1985, the national agricultural value added increased by 55.4%, agricultural labor productivity improved by 40.3%, and the composite purchase price index for agricultural products increased by 66.8%. During the same period, with the rapid growth in the output of agricultural products, the per capita net income of farmers increased by 2.6 times. Their per capita calorie intake increased from 2,300 kcal per person per day in 1978 to 2,454 kcal in 1985. During the same period, although the poverty standard doubled, the rural population living below the absolute poverty line dropped from 250 million people to 125 million people, and the proportion in the rural population fell to 14.8%; the impoverished population decreased by 17.86 million people per year on average.

The period from the mid-1980s to the end of the 20th century could be regarded as the second stage to implement poverty reduction, and it was also the starting stage for the officially announced poverty alleviation strategy. The government set up special poverty alleviation agencies, arranged different kinds of special funds, formulated relevant preferential policies, carried out a thorough reform of the traditional relief-type poverty alleviation, and defined the development-oriented poverty alleviation policy. The series of policies and measures helped to carry out planned, organized, and large-scale development-oriented poverty alleviation. The poverty alleviation work at this stage could be regarded as the government's poverty alleviation efforts for specific people in rural areas. There are two special experiences that should be specially mentioned.

First, after the overall concept of regional development-oriented poverty alleviation was determined, the central government formulated unified standards and defined a number of national key poverty-stricken counties to centrally use poverty alleviation funds and effectively support the impoverished population. Based on the standard of the annual per capita net income of farmers in 1985 being less than 1,150 yuan in counties, the government identified 592 key poverty-stricken counties in 1986, accounting for nearly one-fifth of the county-level administrative units nationwide. Since then, the standards on impoverished counties have been adjusted accordingly along with economic development, especially the improvement of economic conditions in impoverished areas.

Second, the state formulated, promulgated, and implemented the Seven-Year Program for Lifting 80 Million People out of Poverty in 1993. The program strived to concentrate efforts to basically solve the problem of food and clothing for the 80 million poor people in rural areas across the country in the last seven years of the 20th century. The program hoped to achieve the greatest poverty alleviation effect in a relatively short time by utilizing the strong mobilizing force and high consensus in Chinese society in a special way of effort. In the three years from 1997 to 1999, every year, eight million poor people solved the problem of food and clothing, achieving the fastest poverty reduction in rural areas since the 1990s and pushing the round of poverty alleviation to a climax.

The results from implementing the program showed that the rural poor population had decreased by 50 million in seven years, and the poor incidence rate had reduced from 8.7% to 3.4%. From 1986 to 2000, the per capita net income of farmers in national key poverty-stricken counties increased from 206 yuan to 1,338 yuan, and the national poor population decreased from 131 million to 32.09 million. Various social undertakings in contiguous poor areas have improved. For example, with great efforts in the period, the ownership rates of infrastructures such as transportation, communications, electricity, and schools in poverty-stricken areas were very close to those of non-impoverished areas.

As China completed the Priority Poverty Alleviation Program and basically achieved the expected goals, its poverty alleviation strategy entered its third stage in 2001. Under the government's poverty alleviation efforts in previous stages, the overall distribution of rural poverty has greatly changed with more obvious regional characteristics. In the economically developed eastern regions, the poverty incidence rate has reduced significantly, and poverty is mainly seen in the central and western regions with harsh natural conditions. According to this new distribution feature, the central government identified 592 key counties for national poverty alleviation in the central and western regions. In 2002, the absolute poor population in key counties accounted for 62.1% of the country's total population of poverty, and the low-income population accounted for 52.8% of the country's total population of poverty.

Since 2000, the poverty incidence rate in rural areas has basically remained at a constant level. In the following ten years, the poor population has been reduced by 5.21 million. The increase in the poverty alleviation funds invested by the state every year means that the regional development plan has not had obvious poverty alleviation effects as before. Long-term poverty caused by such natural conditions as geography and climate, as well as the ability of families and individuals, has become the main feature of rural poverty— marginalized poverty.

The new situation calls for a major adjustment of poverty governance measures; that is, it is difficult to benefit the marginalized poor population by promoting regional development and the industrial development of poor areas. Even in poor counties, the spatial differentiation between the poor population and the non-poor population has become gradually obvious. It has increasingly been a serious problem whether regional economic growth can truly benefit the poor and whether the poverty alleviation fund is used for the real poor. In view of this, only when poverty alleviation policies and measures are more focused and the poverty alleviation fund is used more efficiently can poverty alleviation resources truly benefit the poor population.

In 2001, the CPC Central Committee and the State Council formulated, promulgated and implemented the *Outline for Development-Oriented Poverty Alleviation for China's Rural Areas (2001–2010)* (hereinafter referred to as the *Outline*). An outstanding feature of the *Outline* is to provide assistance to poverty-stricken villages, and accordingly, the implementation method is called the "poverty alleviation strategy at the village level." Beginning in 2001, the work was conducted based on poverty-stricken villages within each county. Based on various economic and social indicators from production, living, and geographical environments, key poverty-stricken villages were identified within poverty-stricken counties, with a total of 148,000 key poverty-stricken villages identified across the country. In this way, it not only specified the poor areas but also carefully identified the poor group, thus improving the efficiency of targeted poverty alleviation.

During the period, poverty alleviation at the village level demonstrated a significant effect. During the implementation of the *Outline*, the income growth of farmers in key poverty-stricken villages was significantly higher than the average level of poverty-stricken counties and higher than the national average. In all poverty-stricken villages, farmers where the poverty alleviation strategy at the village level worked achieved an income growth of 8–9% higher than farmers without such a strategy. In the period, various social undertakings in poverty-stricken areas also made great progress. Significant improvements have been made in poor villages in terms of productive infrastructure and living service facilities, and related indicators improved are much higher than the average level of poverty-stricken counties.

As the national poor population had further declined by the end of 2010, China was the first to achieve the goal of halving the impoverished population in the United Nations Millennium Development Goals. China then began to implement the *Outline for Development-Oriented Poverty Alleviation for China's Rural Areas (2011–2020)*, which identified contiguous areas with special difficulties as the focus of poverty alleviation. It will provide more powerful policy guarantees and financial support for poverty alleviation in these areas.

In the *Outline*, contiguous poor areas with special difficulties were established. The contiguous poor areas with special difficulties are the key areas for poverty alleviation. They include areas such as Liupan mountain area, Qinba mountain area, Wuling mountain area, Wumeng mountain area, rocky desertification areas in Yunnan, Guizhou, and Guangxi Provinces, mountainous border in western Yunnan, south of the Greater Khingan mountains, Yanshan mountain-Taihang mountain area, Lvliang mountain area, Dabie mountain area, and Luoxiao mountain area, as well as Tibet, the Tibetan areas in the four provinces, and the three prefectures in southern Xinjiang that have been covered with special policies,.

Meanwhile, the state raised poverty alleviation standards above the internationally accepted standards, demonstrating that the government has increased its responsibility for poverty alleviation, included more rural low-income population into the scope for poverty alleviation, and given greater support to poverty-stricken areas and people and enhanced investment in and support for contiguous poor areas with special difficulties. The new special fund for poverty alleviation from the central treasury is mainly used for contiguous poor areas with special difficulties.

Since the 18th National Congress of the Communist Party of China, China has made new achievements in shaking off poverty as if fighting a new battle by stepping up its efforts to implement the poverty alleviation project, carrying out targeted poverty alleviation, classifying to support poverty-stricken families. Under higher poverty standards, the rural impoverished population decreased from 98.99 million people in 2012 to 16.6 million people in 2018, with an average annual decrease of 13.73 million, breaking the "gradually decreasing law" of diminishing marginal poverty alleviation effects in this field.

The 13th Five-Year Plan, implemented since 2016, has defined a grander goal for poverty alleviation, that is, to lift all poverty-stricken people in rural areas out of poverty, eliminate poverty in all poor counties, and eradicate regional poverty in accordance with the current poverty alleviation standard (to be adjusted with price index and other factors, it is estimated that the per capita annual income in 2020 will be less than 4,000 yuan) by 2020.[19] In fact, 28 impoverished counties eliminated poverty in 2016 through legal procedures, achieving a breakthrough in shaking off poverty in impoverished counties and being a good start to complete the goal for poverty alleviation by 2020.

The global significance of China's poverty reduction effect

Since the reform and opening-up, China has not only achieved the fastest economic growth in the world and improved people's living standards to the greatest extent but also achieved the world's largest scale poverty alleviation and reduction. In 1978, according to the poverty standard set by the Chinese government at that time, i.e., 100 yuan per person per year, there were 250 million rural poor people below the subsistence level, accounting for 30.7% of the total rural population. In 1984, the poverty alleviation standard was raised to 200 yuan per person per year, the impoverished population dropped to 128 million, and the poverty incidence rate dropped to 15.1%.

After that, China began to implement a development-oriented poverty alleviation strategy. While poverty standards continued to rise, the impoverished population continued to decrease. According to the poverty alleviation standard of 1,274 yuan per person per year in 2010, the rural poor population decreased from 94.22 million people in 2000 to 26.88 million people in 2010. Correspondingly, the poverty incidence rate dropped from 10.2% to 2.8% (Figure 9.2).

In 2011, the central government greatly raised the national poverty alleviation standard to 2,300 yuan based on the constant price of 2010, which was 92% higher than that in 2009. With the introduction of the new standard, it has covered China's poor population from 26.88 million people in 2010 to 128 million people. According to the internationally comparable purchasing power parity method, the new poverty alleviation standard is equivalent to US$1.8 per person per day, which is above the international poverty standard

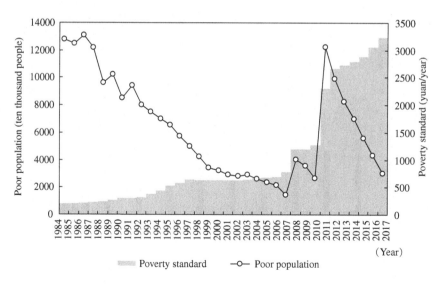

Figure 9.2 Poverty standard and changes in the impoverished population

of US$1.25 per day set by the World Bank in 2008. Under the new standard, the rural poor population has continued to decrease drastically (as shown in Figure 9.2). In the six years from 2012 to 2018, a total of 82.39 million rural poor people were lifted out of poverty, and the poverty rate calculated based on the new standard dropped from 10.2% to 1.7%.

China has been hailed internationally for its great achievements in development-oriented poverty alleviation and overall completion of the Millennium Development Goals ahead of schedule. It is generally believed that China's achievement in poverty alleviation has a profound impact on the international community. It has directly contributed quantitatively to global poverty reduction and has also provided an experience model for developing countries and even the whole world to refer to.

During the period 1981–2015, the poverty-stricken population in the world as defined by the World Bank standard—that is, the population with a daily income of less than US$1.9 (2011 constant price)—decreased from 1.893 billion to 753 million, while the population in China decreased from 878 million to 9.599 million in the same period (Figure 9.3). In other words, China's direct contribution rate to global poverty alleviation is 76.2%. This is China's great contribution to the international development-oriented poverty alleviation cause, and it is also a great contribution to the human civilization and progress cause.

Beneficial knowledge and concepts that have been proven in practice are specific types of public goods. Therefore, it is undoubtedly the main way for China to contribute more to mankind to elevate China's successful practical experience or its story to China's wisdom and provide it to developing

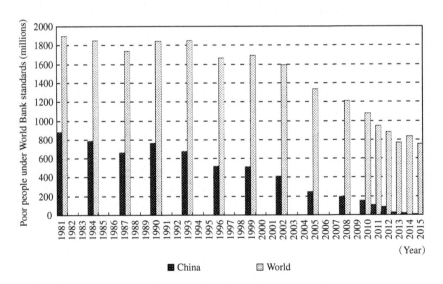

Figure 9.3 Reduction in world poverty population and China's contribution

countries as a possible development path to choose. Obviously, China's wisdom is reflected in China's successful experience of poverty reduction.

Deng Xiaoping's "three benefits" reform standard and Xi Jinping's people-centered development thought have ensured that the reform, opening-up, development, and sharing became a whole, with inherent logic between them and inevitable causality. In this overall relationship, the implementation of the poverty alleviation strategy is an important part of realizing the concept of sharing and improving people's livelihood. It is the conscious action of the Chinese people rather than the unintentional action and the initiative of the government and society rather than just the trickle-up effect of the market.

Below, taking breaking the law of diminishing the marginal effect of poverty alleviation as an example, we show that people-centered development thought is the core of Chinese wisdom and the Chinese plan.

Researchers and practitioners have generally observed a phenomenon of diminishing marginal effects from poverty alleviation practices in various countries in the world. Some even call it a "law"; that is, with the promotion of poverty alleviation and the reduction of the poverty population, it will be increasingly difficult for the last part of the small-scale impoverished population to eliminate poverty. The reason is that they live in areas with poor ecological, production and living conditions and have demographic characteristics of inadequate labor capability, such as disability, disease, old age, and low education level. Therefore, the last mile of shaking off poverty is very difficult, so most developing countries and even many developed countries have failed to conquer this stubborn bastion of poverty.

From the practice of poverty alleviation since the reform and opening-up, we can see that in the process of the continuous reduction of the rural poor population in China, we also constantly encounter this phenomenon of diminishing marginal effect. As shown in Figure 9.2, poverty alleviation standards are constantly improving. However, at every stage so far, although poverty alleviation efforts have not been weakened at all, the poverty alleviation problem of the last small number of rural poor people has not been completely solved.

From the poverty alleviation practice since the reform and opening-up, we can see that China has encountered the phenomenon of diminishing marginal effects from time to time when the rural poor population continues to decrease. As shown in Figure 9.2, poverty alleviation standards are constantly improving. However, although poverty alleviation efforts have not weakened at all at each stage, the last small number of rural poor people has not been completely lifted out of poverty.

We can take the growth of the special fund for poverty alleviation from the central treasury in recent years and its poverty reduction effects as an example to understand the phenomenon of diminishing marginal effects of poverty reduction. The number of rural poor people reduced by per 100 million yuan of the central treasury's poverty alleviation fund fell from 878,000 in 2011 to 317,000 in 2014 and further down to 68,000 in 2017.[20]

In the field of material production, once investment activities encounter diminishing marginal returns, the investment usually stops and shifts to other areas. However, poverty alleviation is an investment in people and is different from ordinary investment activities. Obviously, it should not follow the law of material investment. However, it is undoubtedly the most significant Chinese characteristic to persist in poverty alleviation investment in practice. During the period 2010–2017, the special fund for poverty alleviation from the central treasury still grew steadily at an average annual rate of 21.3%.

Only from the people-centered as the fundamental starting point can we make such unremitting efforts to help the poor and make a solemn commitment to get rid of poverty completely. From then on, the reduction of poverty is the return of investment in poor people, and the "law" of diminishing marginal effects of poverty alleviation does not apply to China. Since the goal of building a moderately prosperous society in all-around way in 2020 is approaching, the task of "leaving no one behind" is becoming increasingly arduous and realistic. The CPC Central Committee has made a solemn commitment and strategic and tactical deployment of lifting all rural poor people out of poverty under the current standards.

Under the guidance of the people-centered development ideology and in the process of reform, opening-up, development, and sharing, China has implemented a special strategy for rural poverty alleviation. The achievements and main experiences of poverty alleviation and reduction can be summarized in the following aspects.

First, it has given full play to the institutional advantages of concentrating nationwide resources and mobilizing social forces to the greatest extent, achieving poverty alleviation in all aspects and throughout society. As early as the mid-1980s, a standing leading organization for poverty alleviation was set up at the central government level. Poverty alleviation has not only become an established strategy and has been consistently implemented, but it has also set unique key tasks and goals at each stage in the form of the *Seven-Year Program for Lifting 80 Million People out of Poverty* and the *Outline for Development-Oriented Poverty Alleviation for China's Rural Areas*. Special funds for poverty alleviation have been included in the budgets of the central and provincial governments, and the overall scale has continued to increase.

In addition, urban and rural subsistence allowances, social assistance, and other social protection mechanisms were established, the charity undertaking was developed, and the paired mechanism of poverty alleviation was improved, which has been a supplement to the poverty alleviation strategy and has formed synergies. Since the reform and opening-up, especially since the 18th National Congress of the Communist Party of China, the whole Party, the whole country and the whole society have been mobilized to perform targeted poverty alleviation and reduction, which has become a world-renowned experiment with social intervention.

Second, with the changes in the economic development stage, the focus of poverty alleviation has continuously adjusted so that policies and measures have focused more on the impoverished population. As the impoverished population has increasingly concentrated in vulnerable areas and disadvantaged families, the poverty alleviation strategy has also changed accordingly from initially implementing the regional development-oriented poverty alleviation strategy to identifying key poverty-stricken counties at the national level and then to establishing key poverty-stricken villages to implement the poverty alleviation strategy at the village level until a file is created for each impoverished family, and the support measures are directly targeted to the individual. For the marginalized poor population in different situations, the government has helped them eliminate poverty through policy measures such as supporting production and employment, relocating and resettling immigrants, guaranteeing subsistence allowances, and providing medical assistance.

In addition, at a more macro level of regional development, regional coordinated development strategies such as the western development strategy and the rise of Central China implemented in 2000 have removed barriers for the rural poor population to eliminate poverty in terms of human capital, infrastructure, and institutional mechanisms. Under the regional development strategy, macro and micro measures at all levels have been taken to precisely target poverty alleviation areas, key poverty alleviation counties, key villages and poverty-stricken households.

Finally, the experience and lessons learned at each stage have absorbed into the new stage of the poverty alleviation strategy and then formed and continuously improved the working mechanism. From the perspective of the overall and final goals, the Chinese government's poverty alleviation work has gone through hardships and achieved remarkable results. In the exploring process, there are successful experiences and lessons worth learning. Such experiences and lessons have been adequately reflected and absorbed into a new round of strategic thinking to gradually form an effective working mechanism. Since the 18th National Congress, the following working mechanism has been established: adhere to the central coordination, provincial responsibility, and implementation by cities and counties; strengthen the responsibility system of party and government leaders with overall responsibility; adhere to the pattern of large-scale poverty alleviation; pay attention to the combination of poverty alleviation with ambition and wisdom; carry out in-depth cooperation in poverty alleviation between the east and the west; and focus on tackling the task of poverty alleviation in deep poverty areas.

Conclusion

In the context of reform and opening-up, China has achieved the largest poverty reduction in human history in 40 years and has also made tremendous contributions to reducing the world's poor population through shared economic development and special poverty alleviation strategies. In his keynote speech at the opening session of the World Economic Forum Annual Meeting 2017, President Xi Jinping quoted Henry Dunant, founder of the

International Red Cross, "Our real enemy is not our neighboring country, and it is hunger, poverty, ignorance, superstition and prejudice." For today's world, the quote still remains pertinent.

According to World Bank data, there were still 753 million people in the world with a daily income less than US$1.9 (purchasing power parity in 2011) in 2015, and 36.4% of these poor people lived in low-income countries, with only 8.4% of the world's population. In view of this, the *2030 Agenda for Sustainable Development*, released in 2015, still listed "eliminating all forms of poverty in the world" as the top of the 17 Sustainable Development Goals. Therefore, China's practice of poverty alleviation and reduction is undoubtedly a successful exploration of developing rules in human society. The resulting Chinese story, China's wisdom and approach should become the common spiritual wealth of China and the vast developing countries.

There is no end to practice and exploration. We firmly believe that as long as we adhere to the correct guiding ideology and given working methods, we will surely get the last rural poor population out of poverty and achieve the goal of a moderately prosperous society in all aspects while "leaving no one behind" before 2020. However, there is no end to safeguarding and improving people's livelihood, and there is only a continuous new starting point. This is also true for poverty alleviation and reduction. We should work on the following aspects and plan ahead to explore the "upgraded version for post-2020" for the poverty alleviation strategy.

First, we should maintain stable and sustainable policies and consolidate the poverty alleviation results. In the final stage of lifting all the rural poverty-stricken people out of poverty, we need to make every effort. After the goal is reached, there are still arduous tasks to be done to consolidate the results achieved and prevent any large-scale relapse into poverty. Achieving the goal of poverty alleviation is not the same thing as forming the ability of stable poverty alleviation. It is normal for farmers whose income level is close to the poverty line to have a higher probability of returning to poverty.

For example, the per capita disposable income of rural households in the lowest 20% income group in 2017 was 3,302 yuan, which was only slightly higher than the poverty standard of the year (3,242 yuan). Farmers in the income group may relapse into poverty by either long-term factors, such as slowdown in the growth of migrant laborers caused by changes in the rural population, or cyclical factors, such as fluctuations in the prices of agricultural products. Therefore, the policy must grasp the dynamic balance between shaking off poverty and relapsing into poverty so that the rate of shaking off poverty will always be greater than that of relapsing into poverty.

Second, we should pay close attention to and actively respond to new factors that cause poverty. With the deepening of population aging, the population of the elderly and the disabled will expand, which will lead to an increase in the group of people suffering from disabilities and form a new source of impoverished population. Aging itself and the consequent disability problems will all lead to the loss or weakening of labor ability. As young and middle-aged laborers migrate to work, the degree of aging is more serious in rural areas than in cities.

For example, the data from a 1% population sampling survey in 2015 show that the proportion of the population aged 65 and above in the total population (aging rate) is 7.7% in urban areas and as high as 10.1% in rural areas. Correspondingly, it poses a severe challenge to consolidate the poverty alleviation results, so we should not only make strategic responses to population aging but also adjust our existing poverty alleviation method and working mechanism over time.

Third, we should deal with the phenomenon of risk-impact poverty. Generally, periodic impacts such as financial crises cannot be avoided, the resulting poverty will appear repeatedly, and there is no room for slack in the fight against poverty. Farmers are particularly vulnerable to various risks. Among the disposable income of rural households in 2017, wage income and net operating income accounted for as much as 78.4%, and these two parts of incomes are greatly affected by market risks. In particular, low-income farmers whose income level is close to the poverty line are more susceptible to various external impacts. For example, in addition to the phenomenon of the macroeconomic cycle, impoverished farmers are particularly vulnerable to natural risks from agriculture, risks related to the agricultural product market, laborers' migrant environment, and changes in labor supply and demand.

Finally, we will explore long-term sustainable strategies for poverty reduction. Even though it will not last forever, it can be said at the least that poverty will exist for a long time. There is a long-lasting debate in the theoretical circle about absolute poverty or relative poverty. Some people divide poverty into absolute type and relative type. For China's "post-2020 period," relative poverty will exist for a long time, and there are different mechanisms to cope with and eliminate absolute poverty. Innovation is needed to transform institutional mechanisms. Others advocate setting different absolute poverty standards according to the development stage or income level. For example, since October 2017, the World Bank has set PPP income standards for low-income countries, lower middle-income countries, upper middle-income countries, and high-income countries at constant prices in 2011 as absolute poverty lines at US\$1.9/day, US\$3.2/day, US\$5.5/day, and US\$21.7/day, respectively.[21]

It is worth pointing out that establishing another poverty standard for middle-income countries and high-income countries is not a higher level of poverty alleviation but a higher cost to achieve the same poverty alleviation effect at different stages of development. According to World Bank data, China's GNI per capita was US\$9,470 in 2018, a level close to the upper line level among upper middle-income countries.

If purchasing power parity of US\$5.5 is applied as the poverty standard, we will still face the arduous task of poverty reduction even though all rural impoverished people are lifted out of poverty according to "China's current standards" (between US$1.9 and US$3.2 and 4,000 yuan in 2020). If China's per capita GNI exceeds the threshold between middle-income countries and high-income countries (such as US$12,235) in 2020 or later,[22] we will obviously encounter more difficult challenges.

Notes

1 Ezra E. Vogel, *Deng Xiaoping and the Transformation of China*, translated by Feng Keli, Hong Kong: SDX Joint Publishing Company, 2013, p. 303.
2 Friedrich Hayek, *Studies in Philosophy, Politics and Economics*, London: Routledge and Kegan Paul, 1967, Chapter 6.
3 For example, see Huang Yasheng, *Capitalism with Chinese Characteristics: Entrepreneurship and the State*, Cambridge: Cambridge University Press, 2008; Steven Cheung, *The Economic System of China*, Beijing: China CITIC Press, 2009; Ronald Coase and Ning Wang, *How China Became Capitalist*, London: Palgrave Macmillan, 2012.
4 Hollis B. Chenery and Alan M. Strout, Foreign Assistance and Economic Development, *The American Economic Review*, Vol. 56, No. 4, 1966, pp. 679–733.
5 For example, Loren Brandt and Thomas G. Rawski (eds.), *China's Great Economic Transformation*, Cambridge: Cambridge University Press, 2008, p. 9.
6 For example, Huang Yasheng, *Capitalism with Chinese Characteristics: Entrepreneurship and the State*, Cambridge: Cambridge University Press, 2008.
7 See Alwyn Young, Gold into the Base Metals: Productivity Growth in the People's Republic of China during the Reform Period, *Journal of Political Economy*, Vol. 111, No. 6, 2003, pp. 1220–1261; Paul Krugman, Hitting China's Wall, *New York Times*, July 18, 2013.
8 Karl Marx: *Capital, Volume I*, Shanghai: People's Publishing House, 1975, p. 202. Of course, not all economists ignore the argument of Karl Marx. In fact, Wu Jinglian cited the passage in the preface of his book to illustrate the internal logic of the reform and opening-up process. See Fan Gang, Yi Gang, Wu Xiaoling, Xu Shanda, and Cai Fang (eds.), *Twenty Years for Fifty Economists*, Beijing: China CITIC Press, 2018.
9 Cai Fang, Reform Effects in China: A Perspective of Labor Reallocation, *Economic Research Journal*, Vol. 7, 2017.
10 Bai Chong-En, Qian Zhenjie: *Who Has Eroded Residents' Incomes? An Analysis of China's National Income Distribution Patterns*, Social Sciences in China Press, 2009 (5).
11 For example, from the demand structure of economic growth, the proportions of agricultural output, agricultural labor, and rural population have all fallen sharply, so declining proportion of rural residents' consumption contribution is a rational result.
12 Christopher B. Barrett, Michael R. Carter, and C. Peter Timmer, A Century-Long Perspective on Agricultural Development, *American Journal of Agricultural Economics*, Vol. 92, No. 2, 2010, pp. 447–468.
13 See Cai Fang, *China's Economic Growth Prospects: From Demographic Dividend to Reform Dividend*, Cheltenham, UK: Edward Elgar, 2016.
14 Du Yang, Albert Park, and Sangui Wang, Migration and Rural Poverty in China, *Journal of Comparative Economics*, Vol. 33, No. 4, 2005, pp. 688–709.

15 Gao Wenshu, Zhao Wen, and Cheng Jie, How Rural Labor Flow will Influence the Statistics on Income Gap of Rural and Urban Residents, in Cai Fang (ed.), *Reports on China's Population and Labor (No. 12): Challenges during the 12th Five-Year Plan Period: Population, Employment and Income Distribution*, Beijing: Social Sciences Academic Press, 2011, pp. 228–242.

16 For example, see Ravi Kanbur and Xiaobo Zhang, *Fifty Years of Regional Inequality in China: A Journey through Central Planning, Reform, and Openness*, United Nations University WIDER Discussion Paper, No. 50, 2004; Guanghua Wan, Understanding Regional Poverty and Inequality Trends in China: Methodological Issues and Empirical Findings, *Review of Income and Wealth*, Vol. 53, No. 1, 2007.

17 For example, Wang Xiaolu focused on discovering the huge hidden income of high-income people not included in the statistics, while Gan Li estimated a Gini coefficient of as high as 0.61. See Wang Xiaolu, Report 2013 on Off-The-Books Income and National Income Distribution, *Comparative Studies*, Vol. 5, 2013; Gan Li, Yin Zhichao, Jia Nan, Xu Shu, Ma Shang, and Zheng Lu, *China Household Finance Survey Report 2012*, Chengdu: Southwestern University of Finance and Economics Press, 2012.

18 Cai Fang, Du Yang, Gao Wenshu, and Wang Meiyan: *Labor Economics: Theory and China's Reality*, Beijing: Normal University Publishing Group, 2009, p. 220.

19 In fact, in addition to the "current standards" in currency, the poverty allevi-ation goals also include specific material standards, "Two Assurances and Three Guarantees"; that is, assurances of adequate food and clothing, and guarantees of access to compulsory education, basic medical services, and safe housing for impoverished rural residents.

20 Zhu Ling and He Wei, Forty Years' Poverty Reduction in the Chinese Industrialization and Urbanization, *Studies in Labor Economics*, Vol. 4, 2018.

21 Francisco Ferreira and Carolina Sanchez, *A Richer Array of International Poverty Lines, Let's Talk Development*, October 13, 2017, http://blogs.worldbank.org/deve lopmenttalk.

22 Regarding the classification criterion on new poverty lines, see the World Bank Data Team, *New Country Classifications by Income Level: 2018–2019*, July 1, 2018, http://blogs.worldbank.org/opendata/new-country-classifications-income-level-2018-2019.

10 Understanding the deceleration of China's economic growth

Introduction

Since the reform and opening-up policy was implemented in the late 1970s, China's economy has achieved rapid growth for more than 30 years, with an average annual growth rate of 9.9% from 1978 to 2011. There were many economic fluctuations during the period, and the growth rate dropped to a low level several times; for example, the economic growth rate was below 8% in 1989 and 1990 after it exceeded 9% in 1982. However, in most years, this was generally an unprecedented period of rapid economic growth.

In view of the fact that the Chinese government has long regarded it as the bottom line for actual growth target to "guarantee 8%" (to ensure that the economic growth rate is no less than 8%),[1] we therefore take the starting year of continuously below 8%, namely 2012, as a turning point for significant economic deceleration. After the growth rate dropped to 7.7% in 2012 and 2013, it further dropped to 7.3% and 6.9% in 2014 and 2015 and 6.7%, 6.8%, and 6.6% in 2016, 2017, and 2018, respectively.

After China's economic growth slowed down, understanding the new normal growth rate became a focus of debates among economists at home and abroad. People also tried to use various weapons in the economic theories in the debate, forming a situation of different views but with no consensus. In general, these different views reflect the influence of three economic paradigms. In the following text, we will take the views of some of the most influential economists as examples to briefly introduce and comment on them and lay a background for the positive elaboration in other parts of the chapter.

The first paradigm is the "Phillips trade-off." The well-known "Phillips curve" in economics, considered one of the ten principles in economics by American economist N. Gregory Mankiw, believes that there is a trade-off relationship between the inflation rate and unemployment rate at least in the short term. It is used as an analytical framework to understand China's economic slowdown, meaning to treat deceleration as a cyclical issue.

Justin Yifu Lin explained the slowdown of China's economic growth from the demand side (and therefore cyclical reasons). After the financial crisis, the sharp reduction in net exports led to a reduction in demand; thus, economic

DOI: 10.4324/9781003329305-12

growth slowed down.[2] With the help of the identity of the national economy used by macroeconomists to analyze the cycle problem caused by demand-side factors, namely, $Y = C + I + G + (E-M)$, or the so-called "troika" analysis method,[3] the composition of GDP is decomposed from consumer demand (C), investment (I), government consumption (G) and net export (E−M), and then relevant policy paths and policy instruments are found. Based on the logic, once the demand bottleneck is broken, i.e., to further strengthen the investment stimulus, as suggested by Justin Yifu Lin, the cycle will be solved, and the Chinese economy can still return to its original track and achieve a high growth rate, such as 8%.

By taking the percentage of an economy's per capita GDP equivalent to the US level as the criterion to judge the development stage, Justin Yifu Lin found that China's per capita GDP was equivalent to 20% of that of the United States. Therefore, such a development stage was equivalent to the year 1951 in Japan and the year 1967 in Singapore, the year 1975 in Taiwan, and the year 1977 in ROK. The data show that these economies have achieved economic growth rates of 9.2%, 8.6%, 8.3%, and 7.6%, respectively, in the 20 years after reaching the milestone. Hence, it is concluded that the Chinese economy still has fast-growing potential.

However, such a method of comparing economic development stages ignores the effect of demographic factors on economic growth and China's feature of "getting old before getting rich." Economic history shows that when the demographic transition is at a stage of a continuously growing working-age population and a relatively decreasing population dependency ratio, the demographic factor is conducive to achieving fast economic growth, thus forming a sufficiently high potential growth rate. This is the so-called demographic dividend. Before 2010, China was in the period of reaping the demographic dividend, so the potential growth rate and the actual growth rate were both very high; afterwards, as the demographic dividend quickly disappeared, the potential growth rate fell, leading to a fall of the actual growth rate.

In other words, corresponding to the level of per capita GDP, China's demographic transition is extremely fast, and the turning point of losing demographic dividends has come even earlier. Since fast economic growth before deceleration has been highly dependent on demographic dividends for more than 30 years and demographic dividends quickly disappear early at a fast pace, it is necessary to understand the potential growth rate of the Chinese economy from the supply-side perspective. In comparison with Justin Yifu Lin's research, it will inevitably conclude inconsistent forecast results, leading to very different policy implications. This also denies the cyclical factor explanation of China's economic slowdown.

The second paradigm is "Kahneman regression." As a behavioral economist, Kahneman proposed a "regression to the mean" phenomenon that is of great help to understanding economic phenomena.[4] It has also been used by some economists to explain China's economic slowdown. For example, Lant Pritchett and Lawrence H. Summers argue that any above-average growth is abnormal, and it will eventually regress to the mean according to the rule of law.[5]

According to the author's logic, the so-called "mean" here is the average growth rate of the world economy. There is also another source of this understanding, the famous Galton's Fallacy. Just as the average height of the members of an extended family cannot stay abnormal over a long period of time, it tends to regress toward the average level of the overall population. The same statistical pattern is followed in economic growth. According to their forecast, China's economic growth will fall to 5.01% between 2013 and 2023 and further fall to 3.28% between 2023 and 2033—the so-called "mean."

Summers once firmly said that developed countries face problems on the demand side rather than the supply side. Specifically, he himself put forward the argument of "secular stagnation" and attributed the problem to the very low "neutral" real interest rate, so the traditional monetary policy could not do what was needed.[6] We are inclined to Summers's judgment, but his and his collaborators's opinion that China's economy "will regress to the mean" is more than just an excessive and inappropriate inference of this kind of "secular stagnation."

Like these two scholars, claiming that a superficial statistical law cannot be avoided anytime and anywhere is tantamount to drowning the protracted and colorful growth practices of many countries in a set of superficial data, especially ignoring the catch-up characteristics of developing countries. Since the logic fails to answer the past catch-up economies such as Japan and the Four Asian Tigers, and why China has achieved rapid economic growth in the past 30 years, and it has not provided a reasonable interpretation about China's economic deceleration, the prediction of "regression to the mean" is not convincing.

Furthermore, once the methodology is used to predict the growth percentage of China's economy in the next 20 years, it is like making a shoe with average sizes of thousands of men, women, and children in the world and claiming that this average size can be applied to any living individual. It is obviously a methodological mistake of "dogmatism and diffidence," so we cannot expect it to provide targeted policy implications.

The third paradigm is the "Solow convergence." China has been in a process of economic growth convergence in the past few decades, so the paradigm is targeted, and it will naturally lead to relevant explanations for the deceleration in economic growth. For example, Robert Barro concluded a prediction similar to Summers before 2016 that China's economic growth rate will soon fall significantly to a range of 3–4%, making it impossible to achieve the expected growth target of 6–7% defined in the 13th Five-Year Plan period (2016–2020).[7]

Barro's basis comes from the "conditional convergence" hypothesis and its analytical framework. In his growth regression model, the determinants of economic growth are divided into two categories: one is the convergence effect, with the initial per capita GDP (in the log) as independent variables, and the other is a group of explanatory variables (or X variables) to determine the steady-state growth. After countless growth regressions, he is convinced that he has come to an "iron law of convergence"; that is, a country cannot converge with more advanced economies or in its own steady state at a rate that differs from 2% for a long time. Since China's economy has accomplished a growth rate significantly faster than predicted in the model, it is unlikely to maintain the previous growth momentum in the future according to the iron law.

With the increase in per capita income and the narrowing of convergence space, the deceleration in economic growth is undoubtedly in line with the general law. However, even if people agree with Barro's framework of convergence analysis, in addition to the "iron law of convergence," there are still many X variables that affect the economic growth rate. Barro also admitted that when it is specific to a single economy, there may be unique X variables or special factors in the sense of a state, which make it different from the so-called "iron law" or "the mean value." In extreme cases, Barro and his collaborators have included more than 100 explanatory variables into the growth regression model and found them all to be significant.[8]

The story of China's economic growth is both of general meaning and of unique meaning. Ignoring or neglecting its unique factors will lead to underestimating China's economic growth potential and misjudging its deceleration time and extent. For example, due to the incorrect selection of explanatory variables and their values, Barro forecasted China's per capita GDP growth in 2015 to be 3.5%, which was much lower than the actual growth rate of 6.9% that year. In fact, after comparing his forecast of China's per capita GDP growth in each period with the actual situation, we can see that there are always huge differences.

Barry Eichengreen and his collaborators also use the convergence paradigm as the analytical framework, but they do not agree that there is a certain iron law of economic growth deceleration.[9] They have made special efforts to identify the country-specific factors relating to deceleration in economic growth and total factor productivity. These authors found that an economy usually experienced two slowdowns when per capita GDP calculated by purchasing power parity in 2005 was on average in the range of US$10,000–11,000, and in the range of US$15,000–16,000.[10]

In a 2013 paper, Barro et al. identified a number of universal factors related to deceleration, such as the "regression to the mean" effect related to convergence, disappearance of the demographic dividend caused by the aging population, lower returns from excessive investment rates, and the undervaluation of the exchange rate preventing the industrial structure from climbing to a higher technological ladder. It also pointed out some factors to reduce the deceleration probability and extent, such as better human capital reserves.[11] Although they failed to clarify the causal relationship between some of these factors and the deceleration itself and did not completely distinguish cyclical factors from growth factors, they drew an important and instructive conclusion in 2011. The decline in total factor productivity can explain 85% of economic growth deceleration.

Misjudging the reasons for China's economic deceleration and failing to adequately clarify China's future economic growth potential are all because the above traditional paradigm-based views did not fully illustrate the reasons for China's economic growth and did not make an accurate judgment on the development stage of the Chinese economy. The previous chapters have expounded on the reasons for economic growth. The following parts of the chapter will try to illustrate the current deceleration in China's economic growth based on historical logic and then look forward to the future.

Why do economists insist on the cyclical perspective?

Some of the problems encountered in economic life are local and occasional short-term disturbances, which are usually the research objects of economic cycle theory. Some are long-term, global and inevitable according to certain laws, which are the research objects of economic growth theory or economic history. To understand the latter situation, people need to have a deep sense of history in thinking to maintain a clear understanding and strategic determination in judgment and then choose and adopt correct countermeasures in actions.

Because the research paradigm is dominated by Western mainstream economics, which is based on developed economies that have been in steady growth for a long time, this is usually the most accustomed way of thinking for economists to explain the slowdown of economic growth from the perspective of cycles. Macroeconomics empirically sums up various manifestations and forms of the economic cycle and theoretically provides various analytical frameworks to observe economic cycle phenomena. In the policy toolbox, there are 18 weapons that can be used to implement countercyclical measures.

In the history of economic theory, people have found from their own observations that there has been a short cycle of 3–4 years in different periods, called the Tvede cycle; the middle cycle of 9–10 years, called the Juglar cycle; the medium and long cycles of 20–25 years, called the Kuznets cycle; and the long cycle of as long as 50–60 years, called the Kondratiev cycle.[12] During the economic development of capitalist countries, various types of economic cycles occur alternately or coincide with economic crises, which cannot be avoided. For this reason, crises or cyclical issues have become a catalyst to give birth to macroeconomics and a long-lasting subject in the development of discipline.

When the potential growth rate is regarded as a steady state of economic growth to be supported by improving the potential of the production factor endowment and the total factor productivity at a given stage of economic development, a negative growth rate gap usually means that there will be cyclical disturbances on the demand side so that the actual growth rate cannot reach the potential growth rate, and production factors are not fully utilized. At this time, it often occurs that production capacity is not fully utilized, such as cyclical unemployment. In contrast, when the actual growth rate exceeds the positive growth rate gap caused by the potential growth rate, it will result in an overheated economy, which is usually shown as inflation or economic bubbles.

In most cases, the economic cycle is caused by the impact on the demand side. Regardless of the internal impact or external impact, once the disturbance impact causes a shortage of aggregate demand to such an extent that the actual growth rate is significantly lower than the potential growth rate, it will form a growth rate gap. Most macroeconomists believe that under this situation, macroeconomic policies to stimulate aggregate demand, either accommodative monetary policies or expansionary fiscal policies, can be adopted in conjunction with other policies, such as industrial policies or even regional policies, due to their countercyclical functions to stimulate economic growth and achieve the effect of eliminating the growth rate gap.

Despite unprecedented high-speed growth, China's economy has also experienced several cyclical decelerations in the reform and opening-up, accordingly forming a growth rate gap. Our estimates indicate that China's potential growth rates in the periods of 1979–1994 and 1995–2010 were 9.66% and 10.34%, respectively.[13] The growth rate gap for each year can be obtained by subtracting the corresponding average potential growth rate from the actual growth rate over the years during the period.

Calculations show that in the 30-odd years before 2010, China's economic growth generally experienced three fluctuation cycles, forming four troughs, that is, the largest growth rate gap, namely, −4.42% in 1981, −5.82% in 1990, −2.72% in 1999, and −1.13% in 2009. Interestingly, the duration between every two troughs is approximately nine to ten years, which is in line with the generally accepted Juglar periodic characteristics (Figure 10.1).

Looking back on the economic development course in the reform and opening-up, we can see that during the several economic growth decelerations, the phenomenon of insufficient utilization of production factors has logically appeared; for example, it has been manifested as a severe employment impact many times. Similarly, although the specific form and intensity of each time were different, in general, macroeconomic policies intervened in the way of stimulating economic growth, eventually reaching a smooth cycle to make the actual growth rate regress to the potential growth rate.[14]

After 2012, the situation was obviously different. Since 2012, China's economy has significantly decelerated, and the GDP growth rate has been in a downward trend. According to past experience, assuming that the potential growth rate is still 10%, when the actual growth rate declines year by year from 2012 to 2018, there will be a gradually increasing growth rate gap of approximately 2–3 percentage points. However, our estimates and forecasts indicate that China's potential growth rate fell to an average of 7.55% during the 12th Five-Year Plan period and 6.20% during the 13th Five-Year Plan period. If it

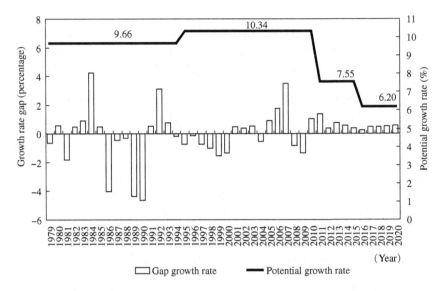

Figure 10.1 Gap between the potential growth rate and growth rate in the Chinese economy

is compared with the actual growth rate, there will be no growth rate gap. Why is there such a steep decline in the potential growth rate of China's economy?

Justin Yifu Lin listed significant deceleration of economic growth in many countries after the financial crisis and asked rhetorically: If the deceleration in China's economic growth is not a cyclical factor, why does it occur that many countries decelerate together?[15] Indeed, similar to every crisis in history, deceleration in economic growth will inevitably occur. In most cases, economic growth after a crisis will not rebound naturally and quickly like plucking a string.[16]

The financial crisis in 2008 rapidly led to negative economic growth in many countries around the world. Only one year after it rebounded, it fell into a state of long sluggish recovery again. However, just as influenza has brought many patients with the same symptoms, it cannot be denied that the patients may have had different diseases. A large number of countries were affected by the financial crisis and fell into a state of cyclical deceleration. This does not prove that all countries that have suffered deceleration are facing cyclical and demand-side impacts.[17]

While countries are experiencing the impact of the international financial crisis, China has undergone changes in the demographic transition stage. The demographic dividend that has long supported fast growth has quickly disappeared. From the perspective of changes in the demographic transition stage, the demographic transition in China has shown a completely different trend from most economies in the world during the 30 years after 2010 and before 2010. The birth rate at a certain stage of demographic transition declined significantly. As a result, China's working-age population aged 15–59 grew at an average annual rate of 1.8% from 1980 to 2010, while the dependent population outside the age range was basically at zero growth state (−0.2%).

In the same period, whether taking developed countries as a whole or developing countries excluding China as a whole, the relative growth trend of the working-age population and dependent population is far less favorable than that in China. For example, in the same period (1980–2010), the growth rates of the working-age population and the dependent population were almost the same on average in developed countries, while as seen on average in developing countries excluding China, the working-age population grew faster, but the dependent population also grew significantly. After 2010, the growth of China's working-age population has turned from positive to negative, and the dependency ratio of the population has turned from declining to rising. However, in other countries, especially developing countries, there has not been such an obvious turning point. Therefore, the deceleration of economic growth should be understood from different demographic transition characteristics.

Justin Yifu Lin made a rhetorical question in his review: If China's economic growth rate is higher than the potential growth rate, there should be inflation. However, we have not seen inflation. Indeed, based on observations and estimates, it is found that the actual growth of the Chinese economy after 2008 does have a tendency to be slightly higher than the potential growth rate, which is shown as a positive growth gap in Figure 10.1. Why can the inflation rate remain at a low level?

To answer this question, we should first clarify the relationship between the growth gap and inflation. With the help of the existing economic theory, we can understand that the economic growth rate and thus the utilization of production factors have a certain causal relationship with the inflation level at least to a certain extent (for example, in the short term). In other words, just as unemployment will occur when there is a negative growth gap, inflation will occur once the actual growth rate is higher than the potential growth rate, that is, when there is a positive growth gap.

Economists generally believe that inflation ultimately occurs when the currency in circulation exceeds actual demands, and economic overheating or a positive growth gap also means excessive issuance of currency. However, in a more mature modern economy, currency over-issuance or excess liquidity may lead to a far more complicated consequence than the general inflation denoted by the consumer price index.

The economic development practice at home and abroad shows that if an economy's government or macroeconomic regulatory authorities adopt excessive stimulus policy measures, there will be excessive currency supply and excess liquidity. Under these circumstances, inflation can be observed. This is why we will see that the US Federal Reserve will adopt an inflation targeting system to raise interest rates and shrink the balance sheets without hesitation when economic growth performance improves and the unemployment rate drops to a low level and more actively withdraw from the quantitative easing policy.

Nevertheless, excessive issuance of currency is manifested not only in the increase in the inflation rate but also more often in the inflation of asset prices. Fundamentally, the excess currency issued will always be utilized. When there is no strong demand in the real economy for general product manufacturing (which usually means that the actual growth rate is consistent with the potential growth rate), such excess liquidity will inevitably shift to fields such as real estate, the stock market and financial management, and then it will not only contribute to inflation in asset prices but also become the cause for financial instability and systemic risks. For example, the two recent economic recessions in the United States happened when the traditional inflation rate was relatively stable and there was a destructive rise in asset market prices.[18]

The phenomenon is more likely to occur when the economic development stage and thus the comparative advantage changes. For example, since the late 1980s, the demographic window of opportunity has gradually closed in Japan, and the comparative advantage of manufacturing has rapidly disappeared. However, the government did not acknowledge and was not willing to accept the declining potential growth rate, so it implemented continued stimulus policies, resulting in excessive issuance of currency and excess liquidity. In the absence of investment enthusiasm and willingness to lend in the manufacturing sector and with a sluggish derivative demand in infrastructure construction, excess liquidity caused by easing policies flowed into nonreal economies such as real estate, the stock market, overseas assets, and even the art market. Eventually, a huge economic bubble was accumulated until it finally burst approximately 1990, and the Japanese economy has since fallen into its "lost" ten years, 20 years, and even 30 years.

After China experienced inflation in the mid-1990s, the changes in the consumer price index have generally been stable and have been at a relatively low level in recent years. However, people can see the trend of loose monetary policy from various economic phenomena. For example, the ratio of the M_2 money supply to nominal GDP (also known as the Marshall K value) increased from 0.81 in 1990 to 1.34 in 2000, 1.76 in 2010, and 2.04 in 2017.

This means that the current macroeconomic situation is characterized by ever-increasing monetary quantities to promote economic growth. In the case of rising labor costs and rapid loss of comparative advantage in manufacturing, excessive currency tends to flow to investment fields that have nothing to do with comparative advantages and competitiveness. The result is that the overall economy is devoid of reality, and the financial sector is self-serving and self-circulating, even causing over-indebtedness and financial chaos, accumulating economic bubbles, and even brewing systemic financial risks.

Symbolic turning point when the development stage changes

In summary, we should surely pay attention to the possible demand impacts to understand the deceleration in China's economic growth. However, in view of the current situation, we should abandon the approach of finding answers in the "troika" analytical framework. Instead, the analysis should start with the production function ($Y = A*F (K, L) = K\alpha*(AL)^{1-}$).[19] In the special context of China, the analysis should give full consideration to the demographic dividend and disappeared factors and its concrete manifestation as a variable of economic growth.

Specifically, with the time of the working-age population aged 15–59 reaching its peak (and subsequently starting negative growth) as a benchmark for comparison, China's development stage in 2010 was actually equivalent to that of Japan's 1990–1995, ROK's 2010–2015, and Singapore's 2015–2020. If the dependency ratio (the ratio of the population aged 14 and below and the population aged 60 and above to the population aged 15–59) is used as a proxy indicator of demographic dividend, the years when the dependency ratios in Japan, the ROK, and Singapore rise significantly also come much later than the years defined by the per capita income level (Figure 10.2).

It can be seen from the figure that although Japan's dependency ratio dropped to its lowest point in approximately 1970, it was not until the 1990s that the dependency ratio truly began to rise significantly. The dependency ratios of the ROK and Singapore also reached a trough much earlier than China, and they stabilized at low points for a long time. Therefore, the dependency ratios in the two countries rose roughly at the same time as those of

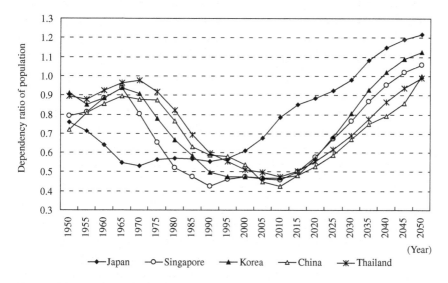

Figure 10.2 Turning point for the population-dependency ratio in East Asian countries

China and Thailand. The comparison with Japan and other developed countries in East Asia fully reveals China's characteristics of getting old before getting rich.

During the change in the demographic transition stage, or as a result, relevant signs of turning can be seen in economic reality. Specifically, China's economic development experienced the two most important turning points at the stage, thus transforming the changes in the demographic transition process into relevant changes in the economic development stage.

First, once the growing demand for laborers exceeds the labor supply, it means that the long-lasting unlimited supply of labor in China's economy no longer has outstanding characteristics, and the development of the Lewisian dual economy has entered the later stage. Therefore, we call this turning point the Lewis turning point. According to the literature of development economics and economic development experience, the turning point should not be verified by econometric methods to estimate the marginal productivity of labor but only by observing whether labor shortage and wage increase have become normal. Accordingly, 2004 can be taken as a representative year for the turning point.

Second, as the working-age population turns to negative growth and the dependency ratio turns from declining to rising, the demographic transition process has reached a leap from quantitative change to qualitative change. In other words, all variables related to demographic characteristics and helpful to rapid growth have an adverse effect on economic growth since then, leading to the rapid disappearance of the demographic dividend. We call this change the turning point for the disappearance of the demographic dividend, which occurred in 2010.

As the Chinese economy crosses the Lewis turning point characterized by labor shortages and wage increases and the turning point of the disappearance of the demographic dividend characterized by the negative growth of the working-age population and the increasing dependency ratio, the factors that used to promote economic growth do not have a significant effect. As a result, the potential growth rate falls, and the extraordinary growth rate can no longer continue.

Based on economic theories, we can expect and have thus far observed a series of factors that have led to a decline in China's potential growth rate of the economy. First, labor shortage caused wages to rise fast, which exceeded the supporting capacity of labor productivity growth; second, the rapid increase in capital–labor ratio resulted in a substantial drop in return on investment; third, the reduction of new entrants to the labor market slowed down the improving speed of human capital; fourth, the slowdown of rural labor force transfer weakened the effect of resource reallocation and reduced the growth rate of total factor productivity. The Chinese economy has entered a new normal characterized by a declining growth rate, industrial structure adjustment, and accelerated transformation of development patterns.

Our estimates show that the potential growth rate of the Chinese economy will gradually decline until China is fully modernized, that is, approximately 2050, when it will regress to the so-called Summers "mean."[20] To date, the trajectory, rhythm, and trend of actual growth deceleration have confirmed the prediction. This puts forward urgent requirements to adjust the industrial structure, and the challenge should be addressed on the basis of deepening economic reforms.

Many people believe that population is a slow variable, and the observed economic growth deceleration occurred in a short period of time; therefore, it is illogical to use demographic factors to explain the economic growth deceleration. For example, people may argue that even if the working-age population enters negative growth, the total size of the population group is still huge, and even if the dependency ratio is on the rise, it will remain low in a period of time. Questions such as this and the logic behind it are representative, reflecting a lack of thorough understanding about the working mechanism of the demographic dividend.

The demographic dividend should not be regarded as a demographic concept but should be discussed as an economic concept in the framework of long-term economic growth. Economic growth is a spot rate of change in the total economic size, denoting the relationship between the annual increment of GDP and the total amount. Although the rate of change for the total population in a given year does not necessarily directly change the economic growth rate, the supply of production factors and the improving trend of productivity at the demographic transition stage mark changes in the economic development stage, which will inevitably change the potential growth rate.

As shown in Figure 10.2, China's dependency ratio declined until 2010 and then rapidly increased after reaching the bottom of the valley. The corresponding changes in the working-age population are similar, with rapid growth before reaching the peak in 2010 and then negative growth. Such changes in demographic direction or the conversion between positive and negative signs fundamentally changed the supply capacity of labor quantity and quality, the level of savings rate and returns on capital, and the difficulty of improving total factor productivity.

To say the least, the common cases in economic history show that the inevitability of long-term trends does not often show up slowly but emerges suddenly under the action of some special short-term triggers, and the short-term trigger is often related to the failure to make correct judgments on long-term inevitability.

For example, after the 1970s, Japan's demographic dividend gradually disappeared, and economic growth began to slow down. However, Japanese economists and economic policy-makers almost unanimously believed that the deceleration was caused by demand-side factors, so macroeconomic policies turned out to be a stimulus. Especially in the 1980s, the government adopted a variety of stimulus policies, unleashing economic bubbles in various fields until the bursting of the bubbles led to a steep economic decline and long stagnant growth.

In contrast, when there were first signs of the disappearance of the demographic dividend, Singapore actively implemented policies on the supply side to maintain the sustainability of economic growth. For example, it gained time by relaxing the control over the employment of foreign laborers to postpone the demographic dividend so that its efforts to promote the increase in total factor productivity were successful, thereby stabilizing the growth speed, avoiding a sharp deceleration, and finally winning new growth sources. It has since become one of the most competitive and innovative countries in the world.

From demographic dividend to reform dividend

Economics is a science that governs society and benefits the people. Therefore, although the differences in the interpretation of economic phenomena are the normal state of economic academia, they are bound to be manifested in the meaning of policies and the consequences of policy implementation. When China's economic deceleration is understood from the demand side, the policy conclusion is to surely focus on implementing stimulating macroeconomic policies and industrial policies. Once it is recognized that China's economic deceleration mainly comes from the supply side, it can be easily inferred that the abovementioned practices can only increase the actual growth rate above the potential growth rate, and the results incurred are inconsistent with the policy intentions. In contrast, the policy efforts from the supply side are aimed at improving the potential growth rate.

According to the expectation of growth theory and the development experience of various countries, it is inevitable that the growth rate slows down when it changes from catch-up dual economic development to neoclassical growth at the forefront of technology.[21] However, the extent to which the potential growth rate decreases and the speed at which the actual economic growth slows down is quite different from country to country, hence leading to very different long-term consequences.[22] China is facing changes at this stage, so only through deepening economic system reform, promoting the transformation of development patterns, tapping the potential of traditional growth momentum, cultivating new growth momentum, maintaining a reasonable potential growth rate, and achieving medium-high real growth can it avoid being long at the middle-income stage and achieve the national modernization goal on schedule.

Many studies indicate that reform or non-reform will create completely different prospects for China's economic growth. For example, in the study by Anton Cheremukhim et al., the economic growth in the periods of 1978–2012 and 1966–1975 was regarded as the reference situation of reform and non-reform and based on this to simulate China's economic growth in 2050, indicating the huge difference between them.[23] A more important message is that there is no alternative relationship between reform and growth, and reform has an obvious effect of promoting economic growth. The experience and logic of China's reform and opening-up show that reform dividends will eventually be reflected in promoting economic growth and improving people's living standards.

The previous analysis has shown that there are two sources to improve the potential growth rate of the Chinese economy. The first is to maintain the traditional growth momentum. This does not mean maintaining the traditional pattern of factor input-driven economic development but focusing on tapping the potential of production factors, especially labor supply, and extending the demographic dividend. The second is to launch new growth drivers. This mainly implies increasing human capital accumulation and improving the growth rate of total factor productivity and the contribution rate to economic growth. These two sources of economic growth need to be developed by promoting structural reforms from the supply side, which are embodied in the following aspects.

The first is to increase laborers' participation rate in high-productivity sectors. Since almost all factors causing the decline of the potential growth rate of the Chinese economy are ultimately related to the disappearance of unlimited labor supply, increasing labor supply can significantly postpone the decline of the potential growth rate. As a result of changes in the population's age structure, the working-age population aged 15–59 has been in negative growth, and considering the current labor participation rate, the economically active population aged 15–59 has been in negative growth since 2017. Therefore, the total labor force no longer has growth potential, and the only way to tap the labor supply potential is to increase the labor participation rate.

The huge working-age population in China means that the labor participation rate of one percentage point corresponded to an economically active population of over nine million in 2015. In China's situation, there is a unique and huge potential source to improve the labor participation rate; that is, to continue to transform agricultural labor into non-agricultural labor and transform migrant laborers already employed in non-agricultural industries into urban residents. Through simulations, during the period 2011–2022, if the labor participation rate in non-agricultural industries increases by 1 percentage point each year, an additional potential growth rate of 0.88 percentage points can be obtained.[24] The greatest impetus to increase the labor participation rate in non-agricultural industries lies in reforming the household registration system and increasing the urbanization rate of the registered population, thereby stabilizing the migrant laborers to be employed in the urban economy and non-agricultural industries.

The second is to increase the total birth rate to balance the population's age structure in the future. Based on Chinese and international experiences, the decline in the birth rate is the result of economic and social development, and the childbirth policy itself can actually play a very limited role. However, given that China has implemented the family planning policy of "one child" for 35 years since 1980, it can be expected that the reform of allowing two children will increase the birth rate within a certain period of time.

It is generally believed that the current total birth rate in China is 1.5, and adjusting the childbirth policy will bring the birth rate close to the replacement level of 2.1 to a certain extent. Through policy simulation, if the total birth rate is raised to a level close to 1.8, in comparison with the situation of the total birth rate of 1.6, the potential growth rate can be increased by 0.2 percentage points between 2036 and 2040.[25] It should be particularly pointed out that as the decline in birth rate is not just the policy result, reforms aimed at balancing population development should not just be limited to adjusting the childbirth policy (we surely expect the childbirth policy will change to the stage of making decisions according to their own wishes), and it should also improve the supply system for other public services. By reducing the cost of raising children in the family, especially relieving the worries of young couples, people can decide the number of children in the family according to their own wishes within the limits permitted by the policy.

The third is to maintain the speed of human capital accumulation. Masahiko Aoki discovered from the East Asian economic development experience that any country or region, after experiencing an economic development stage characterized by Kuznetsian structural adjustment, will undergo an economic development stage driven by human capital before entering the post-demographic transition stage.[26] For China, the transition timing should be the Lewis turning point that we have already observed. This means that in terms of development stage, China has entered an era when it relies more on human capital to obtain the growth source.

In a 2016 article, Fang Cai and Lu Yang, made reasonable assumptions about the development of education and training, predicting that the overall human capital level could be improved to a certain degree so that the potential growth rate of GDP could be increased by approximately 0.1 percentage points in the future. The reform dividend is a non-ignorable factor for China's economic development under the new normal that aims to maintain a reasonable economic growth rate, such as maintaining medium-high growth in the Chinese context and avoiding prematurely falling into low-medium growth.[27]

In fact, our above simulation only considers the direct contribution of human capital. As many other studies have shown, first, educational level, as a proxy variable of human capital, can not only directly contribute to economic growth but also have the effect of improving productivity, so the total contribution rate can greatly increase.[28] Second, taking into account educational quality, the role of human capital on economic growth will further significantly improve, even more prominent than the contribution of productivity.[29]

The fourth is to increase total factor productivity and obtain a more sustainable growth source. Through theoretical expectation and existing econometric analysis (as mentioned in Cai Fang and Lu Yang's article in 2016), it can be expected that although increasing the labor participation rate in non-agricultural sectors can help improve the potential growth rate, it demonstrates a gradually weakening effect over time; however, the promotion of total factor productivity to the potential growth rate will first show an immediate effect, and then it will show enduring characteristics.

With the shift to a neoclassical growth stage, on the one hand, China's economy is increasingly relying on scientific development and technological innovation to maintain the sustainability of economic growth; on the other hand, there is still a huge space to obtain the efficiency of resource reallocation by removing institutional obstacles. In a 2013 article, the simulation of Cai Fang and Lu Zhang shows that if the average annual growth rate of total factor productivity increases by 1 percentage point during 2011–2022, the potential growth rate can correspondingly increase by 0.99 percentage points.[30]

In their 2016 article, Cai Fang and Lu Yang, made assumptions about the possible contribution effects of reforming the household registration system, education and training system, and state-owned enterprise reform to promote the labor participation rate in non-agricultural sectors and the contribution of human capital and total factor productivity. After combining different childbirth policy adjustments (hence different birth rates), they simulated possible situations to obtain reform dividends in the future. It is found that reform or no-reform and reform intensity will all make obvious differences in potential growth rates in the near and long term.

It should be noted that cyclical impacts on the demand side are inevitable for an economy at any development stage. For example, when economic globalization encounters headwinds—the rise of trade protectionism and intensification of trade friction, and even the United States initiating trade wars against China—China's economic growth and exports will be hindered, and external demands will drop significantly, which will naturally result in demand-side impacts on the macroeconomy.

However, there is a need to distinguish between the two situations. First, in the event of impacts, the decline in external demands corresponds to the decrease in the potential growth rate. At this time, there is still no need to adopt excessive stimulus macroeconomic policies. Second, when the decline in external demands has come to a level that makes real economic growth lower than the potential growth rate and full employment cannot be achieved, it is necessary to regulate macroeconomic policies to stimulate demands to ensure that the economic growth rate can regress to the potential growth rate. Given that changes in the economic development stage have altered the potential growth rate, the new potential growth rate is unknown, and the potential growth rate will decrease, making it difficult for us to judge the macroeconomic trend based on the annual growth rate change. At the moment, it is more scientific and reliable to judge the economic trend and the macroeconomic policy direction by directly observing the indicators that reflect employment status, such as investigating the unemployment rate to see if there is cyclical unemployment beyond the natural unemployment rate.

The National Bureau of Statistics releases two indicators for unemployment, namely the urban registered unemployment rate and the urban surveyed unemployment rate. The latter is usually announced at a later date. According to the author's estimates, the urban surveyed unemployment rate reached its highest point of approximately 7.6% in 2000 and then decreased year by year. Since 2008, while economic growth has not experienced cyclical changes, the surveyed unemployment rate has always remained at approximately 5%. Since the National Bureau of Statistics released the indicator, the surveyed unemployment rate has only fluctuated between 4.9% and 5.3% from January 2018 to March 2019, averaging 4.98%. Therefore, in general, the surveyed unemployment rate in China's cities and towns has basically stabilized at approximately 5% in recent years, while the registered unemployment rate has been below 4% (Figure 10.3). Therefore, what kind of labor market situation does the unemployment level reflect? What are the policy implications?

According to the definition of the natural unemployment rate (i.e., the unemployment rate not affected by cyclical factors), an analytical conclusion can be drawn that the current natural unemployment rate in China is approximately 5% for the surveyed unemployment rate and approximately 4% for the registered unemployment rate. Therefore, as long as the urban surveyed unemployment rate is no more than 5%, it means that there is no cyclical unemployment. It also indicates that the growth rate is in line with the potential growth rate and that the economy is in a state of adequate employment. In other words, there is thus far no obvious cyclical problem in China's macroeconomy. It can be said that even if economists and policy-makers have not reached a consensus on China's current potential growth rate, it can be

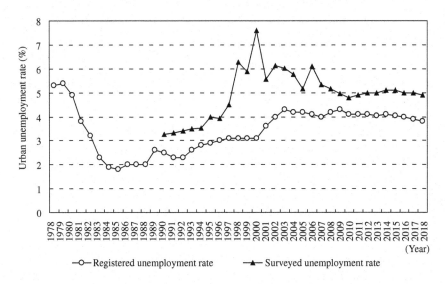

Figure 10.3 Changes in the urban unemployment rate

concluded that the economic growth rate has not fallen below the potential growth rate because the urban unemployment rate is at the natural unemployment level.

Overall, short-term impacts on the demand side will not change the development stage of the Chinese economy, which is more long-term and stable. Therefore, macroeconomic policies to deal with impacts cannot replace long-term reform-centered solutions, and the stimulus to economic growth can only be based on the changed potential growth rate. Moreover, even when loose and expansionary macroeconomic policies are implemented, it is necessary to prevent improper investment from causing over-indebtedness and reducing productivity.[31]

"Threshold trap" of high-income club

In 2018, China's per capita GDP was US$9,771. Calculated at the same growth rate, it is expected to be US$12,158 in 2020. According to the World Bank's grouping criteria, when a country's per capita GDP exceeds US$12,235, it will join the ranks of high-income countries. Therefore, is the proposition of the "middle-income trap," which has been enthusiastically discussed by researchers and policy-makers in recent years, no longer targeted at China?

Through in-depth observation of international experience, we can not only draw a conclusion that this proposition is still meaningful but also put forward more targeted new propositions. Here, we call it the "threshold trap" purely for the convenience of discussion. Such generalization is not a new concept, does not reveal a phenomenon completely different from the middle-income trap, and especially focuses on the problem that the concept of middle-income trap usually pays attention to the upper middle-income countries. To be specific, we intend to describe it in a statistical sense to see whether a country can enjoy such a new ranking once and for all when it is approaching or just entering the ranks of high-income countries.

If there is anything special here, it is trying to reveal that although a country is upgraded from the upper-middle-income group to the high-income group based on the criterion of per capita GDP of US$12,235, ultimately the classification is artificially arbitrary. For example, it is difficult to tell the substantial difference between the per capita income of US$12,234 and US$12,236. Subsequent analysis indicates that the criterion is only a threshold and is by no means a "threshold" or critical point that can assure that the country will have a certain stable status from then on.

The data used in our observation are very simple; that is, the per capita GDP in each country from 1960 to 2018 released by the World Bank at 2010 constant dollars. Our concerns here are as follows: First, what is the chance for countries that have moved into the upper-middle-income group to be among the high-income countries in a few decades? Second, what will be the subsequent economic growth performance of countries that have recently moved into the high-income group?

We first observe the situation of countries "outside the threshold." Based on available data, we select those countries that did not move into the high-income group in 1960 (US$12,000 calculated at 2010 prices) but had joined the upper-middle-income group at least by 1980 (US$4,000 calculated at 2010 prices). Among the 29 countries in line with the requirement, 14 have already been in the ranks of high-income countries since 2018.

That is, in a few decades (specifically, within 38 to 58 years), the probability is approximately half for countries to enter or fail to enter the threshold of upper middle-income countries to high-income countries. In other words, the key for the upper middle-income countries to fall into the threshold trap with a 50% probability during the period 1960–1980 is that these countries have failed to achieve the actual average annual growth rate of 2.93% in terms of per capita GDP for at least 38 years (i.e., the rate of income growth necessary to increase per capita GDP from US$4,000 to US$12,000 from 1980 to 2018).

Then, we observe the situation of countries "within the threshold." Of the 37 countries that have joined the high-income stage since 1980, 14 can be regarded as "new members," i.e., the per capita GDP of that year was lower than the average level of high-income countries (US$23,096 at 2010 prices). Therein, only Singapore and Ireland, once known as growth miracles, successfully caught up in the following years. By 2018, they have become high-income countries among high-income countries. their per capita GDP exceeds the average level of this group, respectively being US$58,248 and US$78,765 at 2010 prices. For other new members in 1980, their per capita income was still below the average of high-income countries as of 2018.

Furthermore, we can observe the economic growth performance of new members in 1980 in the subsequent periods from the perspective of convergence. In the statistical meaning of convergence, the per capita income level of a country in the initial period is inversely proportional to its subsequent economic growth rate. In Figure 10.4, we show the relationship between the per capita income of the high-income country group in the initial period and the growth rate in the observation period. From the perspective of the negative slope between the two, at least in the statistical sense, we can think that there has been a more or less catch-up relationship among countries that have joined the high-income group since 1980, thus resulting in a non-significant convergence effect.

Meanwhile, we can also see from the figure that while the developed countries show a slight convergence trend on the whole, the two groups of countries have internally shown a certain degree of divergence, whether to observe the established high-income countries alone or to observe the new members alone, and the divergence is more obvious among the new members. This means that if we only observe countries whose per capita income was lower than the average level of high-income countries in 1980, there was absolutely no negative correlation between the initial income level and the subsequent growth rate, i.e., catch-up or convergence did not occur at the same time.

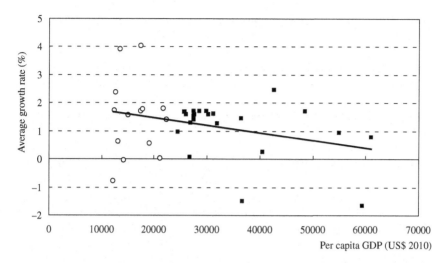

Figure 10.4 Growth rate of high-income countries

It is worth noting that among all the observed countries, four countries were in a negative growth state during the period 1980–2018, among which new members (Gabon and Venezuela) and established high-income countries (Brunei and Saudi Arabia) each accounted for half. Obviously, economists have something to say about the drawbacks of economic systems and policies in these countries, and they will not miss the perfect opportunity to take it as a typical "resource curse" case.

When economists make cautionary predictions, it does not mean that they expect their predictions to come true. Similarly, when they conceptualize an unsatisfactory situation, they only want to warn policy-makers to avoid such a situation. Either the middle-income trap or the "threshold trap" as a special case is a conceptual product of such a starting point. In other words, the state that is about to join or has just moved into the ranks of high-income countries has a more uncertain growth prospect in the state of being stable in the ranks of high-income countries.

The rapid economic growth brought by China's reform and opening-up can be seen as a process where reform continues to create an appropriate institutional environment for production factor accumulation and effective allocation, thus cashing in the demographic dividend. To date, the reforms of incentive mechanisms, corporate governance structures, pricing mechanisms, resource allocation models, opening-up systems, and macro-policy environments have all been proposed and promoted to satisfy special institutional requirements at a certain economic development stage.

However, looking at the present and looking forward to the future, we should keep the reform and adjust the focus, difficulty, promotion mode, and even orientation of development and sharing with the change of development stage. Although these tasks are not destined to become hurdles that cannot be overcome, their difficulty has indeed been greatly enhanced. From the perspective of development experiences, the emergence of these difficulties is, to a certain extent, an inevitable development law. The enhancement and inevitability of the task difficulty in the new development stage are shown in the following three aspects.

First, as China moves from an upper-middle-income country to a high-income country, it will become more difficult to maintain sustainable growth, and the economic growth pattern should change to be productivity-driven. According to an estimate,[32] during the period 1979–2010, when China's economic growth benefited from the demographic dividend, variables related to the demographic dividend contributed up to 84% in the average annual real growth rate of 9.9%. In addition to these factors, the contribution rate of total factor productivity was 16%. We need to accept the reality of the disappearing demographic dividend and the declining potential growth rate, and we do not expect to maintain the original growth rate in the future, but how to promote total factor productivity and the contribution level of total factor productivity is something related to whether China can maintain sustainable economic growth in the future before and after it joins the ranks of high-income countries. It is an arduous task and can only be accomplished with greater determination and innovation in reform and opening-up.

Second, with the maturity and finalization of the socialist market economic system, it will be more difficult to push forward the reform. Generally, in the face of an economic system that has long been less motivated and is therefore inefficient, it is easy to start reform by breaking the link of insufficient micro-incentives in the vicious circle and then promoting reform in the path of Pareto improvement, thus changing the approach of resource allocation and correcting resource misallocation. As the reform advances in depth, Pareto improvement opportunities not to harm any group will become fewer and fewer. In other words, when reform inevitably makes in-depth adjustments to the interest structure, there will be insufficient reform incentives and even resistance and interference from vested interest groups.

Especially when the cost-bearing subjects of reform and the subjects of obtaining reform benefits do not completely correspond, the promotion of reform will face the problem of incompatible incentives. In the face of these difficulties, we should focus on sharing reform costs and reform dividends, redistributing the fiscal expenditure responsibilities required to establish a new system, making necessary compensation for the injured parties, and especially providing social security to the laborers who may be impacted. This requires not only a firm political determination to advance reform but also political wisdom to properly handle conflicts.

Third, China will encounter more troubles in its further reform and development at a higher development stage. When the competitive environment of survival of the fittest with creative destruction is formed, some laborers and operators will fall into real difficulties. The improving effect of the income distribution of the market mechanism itself will be weakened; the source of productivity improvement will also shift from resource reallocation among industries to the survival of the fittest among business entities when the role of the creative destruction mechanism will be enhanced; China will participate in global value chain division at a higher development stage, and the competitive effect with developed countries will be greater than the complementary effect. This requires that under the guidance of people-centered development thought, inclusiveness should be reflected in the whole process of further reform, opening-up, and development, the redistribution of government should be strengthened, and social policies should play a supporting role.

To overcome the growing troubles, we cannot stop. For example, at the development stage, fiercer competition will have an impact on employment from time to time. If it is based on protecting jobs, it will inevitably extend to protecting enterprises, and it is difficult for uncompetitive industries and enterprises to quit; on the other hand, if the market is left to spontaneously destroy jobs, it will indeed put some laborers and their families in a difficult situation. The key to overcoming this dilemma is to change the practice of protecting jobs to protect the laborers themselves and to build a strong social protection net. The stronger the support of social policies is, the easier it will be for uncompetitive industries and enterprises to quit.

Conclusion

The slowdown of China's growth since 2012 is a new normal accompanied by changes in the population transition stage and economic development stage. Regardless of its main causes or manifestations, this deceleration is completely different from the previous cyclical phenomena mainly caused by demand-side impacts. Accordingly, the focus and priority of policies as well as the choice of policy instruments should be quite different. American economist James Tobin once said that a heap of Harberger's triangles is needed to fill an Okun gap. He talked about two economic concepts: the former refers to the welfare loss caused by monopoly, price distortion, and other institutional factors, and the latter refers to the gap between the actual economic growth and the potential growth capacity, both of which are represented by a specific reduction of the gross domestic product (GDP).

Since research resources and policy resources are scarce, we should allocate these resources to the relevant fields according to the principle of maximizing profits. Therefore, what Tobin said obviously reminds people from a utilitarian point of view that it is more meaningful to pay attention to macroeconomic issues than to institutional issues. Policy resources should be allocated to efforts to narrow the Okun gap caused by demand-side factors. Such an argument is obviously ambiguous because it does not distinguish what type of problems an economy is facing. If this argument is regarded as a general principle, obviously it not only indulges macroeconomists in excessively utilitarian pursuits but also encourages policy-makers to be lazy in thinking, hoping that stimulus policies can be effective in the short term.

The problem is that the reason for China's economic deceleration is the decline of the potential growth rate, rather than the actual growth rate being lower than the potential growth rate, so there is no obvious Okun gap. It is just a Tobin illusion to be obsessed with adopting macroeconomic policies to stimulate economic growth. It cannot maintain long-lasting effects, but on the contrary, it brings many side-effects, such as delayed reform and accumulated debts. Japan's lessons show that macroeconomic policies formulated under the illusion and made them long-term are the reason that it has fallen into the "high-income trap." Judging by the same logic as the Japanese case, once countries about to enter the ranks of high-income countries or new members in these ranks fall into this illusion, it means a larger risk of falling into the "threshold trap."

Therefore, the key for China's economy to seek long-term sustainable growth is not to use the demand-side stimulus tools that are common in macroeconomics but to focus on the supply side. We should remove the institutional obstacles that hinder the full supply and effective allocation of production factors, promote structural reform and release the institutional potential to achieve the goal of increasing the potential growth rate. Therefore, increasing the supply quantity and quality of production factors from the supply side to reduce the production cost to maintain the industrial comparative advantage, reducing the transaction cost by changing the government functions, and maintaining the policy adjustment and system reform of industries and enterprises by improving the total factor productivity all belong to the category of structural reform. The implementation of these measures should be arranged and promoted according to the expected effect of improving the potential growth rate.

Notes

1 In the Five-Year Plan and the annual plan, the target of economic growth rate is often below 8%. For example, the growth rates defined in the 12th Five-Year Plan and 13th Five-Year Plan as the expected indicators are, respectively 7.5% and 7%. However, in the actual implementation, the "8% protection" was taken as the bottom line. For example, when the Asian financial crisis and the worldwide financial crisis occurred, respectively in the late 1990s and in 2008–2009, the central government always proposed to ensure an 8% growth rate.

2 Justin Yifu Lin, China and the Global Economy, *China Economic Journal*, Vol. 4, No. 1, 2011, pp. 1–14.

3 That is, to decompose GDP from residents' consumption demand (C), investment (I), government consumption (G) and net export (E−M).

4 See Daniel Kahneman, *Thinking, Fast and Slow*, London and New York: Penguin Books, 2012, Chapter 17: Regression to the Mean.

5 Lant Pritchett and Lawrence H. Summers, *Asiaphoria Meets Regression to the Mean*, NBER Working Paper, No. 20573, 2014.

6 Lawrence H. Summers, The Age of Secular Stagnation: What It Is and What to Do About It, *Foreign Affairs*, Vol. 95, No. 2, 2016, pp. 2–9.

7 Robert J. Barro, *Economic Growth and Convergence, Applied Especially to China*, NBER Working Paper, No. 21872, 2016.

8 Robert Barro and Xavier Sala-i-Martin, *Economic Growth*, New York: McGraw-Hill, 1995.

9 Barry Eichengreen, Donghyun Park, and Kwanho Shin, *When Fast Growing Economies Slow Down: International Evidence and Implications for China*, NBER Working Paper, No. 16919, 2011.

10 Barry Eichengreen, Donghyun Park, and Kwanho Shin, *Growth Slowdowns Redux: New Evidence on the Middle-income Trap*, NBER Working Paper, No. 18673, 2013.

11 Barry Eichengreen, Donghyun Park, and Kwanho Shin, *Growth Slowdowns Redux: New Evidence on the Middle-income Trap*, NBER Working Paper, No. 18673, 2013.

12 See Lars Tvede, *Business Cycles: History, Theory and Investment Reality*, translated by Dong Yuping, Beijing: China CITIC Press, 2008.

13 Cai Fang and Lu Yang, The End of China's Demographic Dividend: The Perspective of Potential GDP Growth, in Ross Garnaut, Cai Fang, and Song Ligang (eds.), *China: A New Model for Growth and Development*, Canberra: ANU Press, 2013, pp. 55–74.

14 Cai Fang, Macro-economic Policies in Promoting More and Better Jobs in China: Issues, Evidence and Policy Option, *Studies on Labor Economics*, Vol. 3, 2015.

15 Discussion on Professor Justin Yifu Lin's viewpoints and arguments, see Cai Fang, Understanding China's Economic Growth Potential: Response to Justin Yifu Lin's Criticism on Explanation to Demographic Dividend, *Comparative Studies*, Vol. 2, 2019.

16 Carmen Reinhart and Vincent Reinhart, The Crisis Next Time: What We Should Have Learned from 2008, *Foreign Affairs*, Vol. 97, No. 6, 2018, pp. 84–96.

17 In fact, subject to cyclical impacts, many countries have shown long-lasting structural malaise, so stimulus policies cannot always be relied on to maintain long and continued growth.

18 Joseph Carson, Inflation Indices Should Add House Prices to Prevent Bubbles, *Financial Times*, December 2018.

19 In the formula, Y represents output or GDP, K and L, respectively represent capital and labor factors (can also include other production factors like human capital), and A represents technical progress or total factor productivity.

20 Pritchett and Summers believe that any above-average growth is abnormal, and it will eventually "regress to the mean" according to the rule of law. Based on their logic, the so-called "mean" is the average growth rate of the world economy. Estimates of Cai Fang and Lu Yang, show that China's potential growth rate will remain above 3% until 2050. See Lant Pritchett and Lawrence H. Summers, *Asiaphoria Meets Regression to the Mean*, NBER Working Paper, No. 20573, 2014; Cai Fang and Lu Yang, Take-off, Persistence, and Sustainability: Demographic Factor of the Chinese Growth, *Asia & the Pacific Policy Studies*, Vol. 3, No. 2, 2016, pp. 203–225.

21 For example, see Robert J. Barro, *Economic Growth and Convergence, Applied Especially to China*, NBER Working Paper, No. 21872, 2016; Barry Eichengreen, Donghyun Park, and Kwanho Shin, *Growth Slowdowns Redux: New Evidence on the Middle-income Trap*, NBER Working Paper, No. 18673, 2013.

22 Barry Eichengreen, Donghyun Park, and Kwanho Shin, *When Fast Growing Economies Slow Down: International Evidence and Implications for China*, NBER Working Paper, No. 16919, 2011.

23 Anton Cheremukhim, Mikhail Golosov, Sergei Guriev, and Aleh Tsyvinski, *The Economy of People's Republic of China from 1953*, NBER Working Paper, No. 21397, 2015.

24 Cai Fang and Lu Yang, The End of China's Demographic Dividend: the Perspective of Potential GDP Growth, in Ross Garnaut, Cai Fang, and Song Ligang (eds.), *China: A New Model for Growth and Development*, Canberra: ANU Press, 2013, pp. 55–74.

25 Cai Fang and Lu Yang, Take-off, Persistence, and Sustainability: Demographic Factor of the Chinese Growth, *Asia & the Pacific Policy Studies*, Vol. 3, No. 2, 2016, pp. 203–225.

26 Masahiko Aoki, The Five Phases of Economic Development and Institutional Evolution in China, Japan and Korea, in Masahiko Aoki, Timor Kuran, and Gérard Roland (eds.), *Institutions and Comparative Economic Development*, Basingstoke: Palgrave Macmillan, 2012.

27 Cai Fang and Lu Yang, Take-off, Persistence, and Sustainability: Demographic Factor of the Chinese Growth, *Asia & the Pacific Policy Studies*, Vol. 3, No. 2, 2016, pp. 203–225.

28 Estimates from Whalley et al. about the contribution of human capital to China's economic growth show that since increased educational level can improve productivity, the total contribution of human capital will increase from 11.7% direct contribution rate to 38%. See John Whalley and Xiliang Zhao, *The Contribution of Human Capital to China's Economic Growth*, NBER Working Paper, No. 16592, 2010.

29 Rodolfo Manuelli and Ananth Seshadri, Human Capital and the Wealth of Nations, *The American Economic Review*, Vol. 104, No. 9, 2014, pp. 2736–2762.

30 Cai Fang and Lu Yang, The End of China's Demographic Dividend: the Perspective of Potential GDP Growth, in Ross Garnaut, Cai Fang, and Song Ligang (eds.), *China: A New Model for Growth and Development*, Canberra: ANU Press, 2013, pp. 55–74.

31 When reviewing the effect of stimulus policies implemented since 2018, researchers found adverse effects like over-indebtedness and there was a negative relevance between investment rate and total factor productivity. Bai Chong-En and Zhang Qiong, China's Productivity Estimates and its Fluctuation Decomposition, *The Journal of World Economy*, Vol. 12, 2015.

32 Cai Fang and Zhao Wen, When Demographic Dividend Disappears: Growth Sustainability of China, in Masahiko Aoki and Jinglian Wu (eds.), *The Chinese Economy: A New Transition*, Basingstoke: Palgrave Macmillan, 2012.

Part III

The new scientific and technological revolution and high-level globalization

11 Globalization, convergence, and China's economic development

Introduction

The World Economic Forum with a history of nearly half a century, or the Davos Forum, which is named after being held in a ski resort in Switzerland, is famous for its topic setting getting the most extensive attention. At the beginning of 2019, the annual meeting was held with the theme of *Globalization 4.0: Shaping a Global Architecture in the Age of the Fourth Industrial Revolution*. That is, the conference theme was designed to understand and discuss the industrial revolution and globalization. To a considerable extent, the topic is related to almost all hot issues in the contemporary world, which includes many questions that have been on the minds of politicians, entrepreneurs, academic researchers, and think tank scholars for a long time.

The founder and current executive chairman of the Davos Forum, Dr. Klaus Schwab distinguished the four industrial revolutions in history from the perspective of the adopted production technology characteristics in his recently published book, and outlined a rough historical period. The First Industrial Revolution happened between 1760 and 1840 and was characterized by the use of water and steam power for mechanical production; the Second Industrial Revolution began at the end of the 19th century and continued to the beginning of the 20th century and was characterized by the use of electric power for mass production; the Third Industrial Revolution started in the 1960s and was characterized by the use of electronic information technology to promote automated production; the Fourth Industrial Revolution that is currently taking place is a revolution that breaks the physical, digital, and biological boundaries and is shown as the Internet is everywhere and mobility has been greatly improved; sensors are getting smaller and smaller but with stronger performance and cheaper cost; artificial intelligence and machine learning are on the rise; and the connotation is more extensive.[1]

In Schwab's view, globalization is a phenomenon caused by technology and innovation and the movement of ideas, people, and goods, and is therefore a global framework for industrial revolution.[2] However, he did not clearly give a complete timeframe for different versions of globalization before Globalization 4.0, as he dealt with the relationship between the Fourth

DOI: 10.4324/9781003329305-14

Industrial Revolution and Globalization 4.0. In fact, it is quite difficult to do that. Therefore, we only need to grasp the inherent connection between the industrial revolution and globalization in the way of thinking. Moreover, by doing so, it will help us express our view easily.

Nevertheless, we can still try to give a rough timeframe of the previous globalization with inverse methods and logic. The current round of economic globalization, namely, Globalization 3.0, started in the 1990s as China, India, and Central and Eastern European countries started to participate in labor division in the global value chain. The previous period, which dated back to the end of World War II, when a global economic system dominated by the Bretton Woods system was formed, can be seen as Globalization 2.0. Perhaps the period from the Age of Exploration in the 15th century to the beginning of the 20th century can be regarded as a typical period of Globalization 1.0. It can be seen with such a chronological division that globalization has experienced ups and downs and even interruptions over a large time span.

In fact, no matter whether Globalizations 1.0 through 3.0 are clearly defined and universally agreed upon, and no matter how the timeframes for different versions of globalization are defined, we can draw an undeniable conclusion: China's economic development missed the first and second industrial revolutions, as well as catch-up opportunities for Globalization 1.0 and Globalization 2.0, but seized the opportunities in the Third Industrial Revolution and Globalization 3.0. Since then, China has stood out and become the global leader and the largest beneficiary.

Since the reform and opening-up, China's successful economic development has gone through a course of 40 years, during which Chinese and foreign economists have conducted hot discussions from many aspects and given various theoretical explanations in numerous studies. Most scholars have also come to the general conclusion that the success of China's economic reform and development benefited from participating in the global division of labor. However, the in-depth study to put China's economic development in the perspective of globalization and industrial revolution in the same period is still insufficient on the whole. The changing trend of globalization and resulting severe challenges may lead to insufficient theoretical preparation for understanding the new situation and insufficient policy reserves to deal with the new situation.

The industrial revolution and economic globalization do not strictly correspond to each other in terms of time, but they are closely linked in logic. For the sake of convenience, we will discuss both historical processes in the following discussion, but we mainly start with economic globalization, although this does not mean ignoring the industrial revolution. At the same time, since our discussion focuses on China's economic development in the context of the industrial revolution and globalization, we will mainly reveal the characteristics of the previous round of economic globalization and how the Chinese economy has seized the opportunity of globalization to achieve catch-up with more advanced economies.

Regression to Ricardo: changes in globalization characteristics

David Ricardo deserves to be respected as the father of international trade theory. In other words, modern trade theory is built on Ricardo's comparative advantage principle and the "Heckscher-Ohlin-Samuelson model," which is formed by the contributions of generations of outstanding economists. According to this theory, the decisive factor for countries to trade and benefit from it is that countries have different endowments of production factors. In other words, different products contain different factor intensities; international trade is nothing else, but countries exchange their own abundant production factors for relatively scarce production factors, and then they benefit from the equivalent exchange of factor prices.

Different industries tend to use production factors of different natures. For example, traditional heavy industries contain more material capital, traditional light industry is more labor intensive, and modern information industry intensively gathers technology and human capital. Countries have different endowments on different factors, so we can foresee that international trade based on the comparative advantage principle should belong to interindustry trade.

However, what we have observed in many cases is intraindustry trade; that is, the same type of products are exchanged between countries, especially the trade of the same type of products between developed countries with homogeneous factor endowment. For example, Japan and Germany, both high-income countries, both produce cars and trade cars with each other. The situation was common in the round of globalization before the 1990s. Therefore, since then, economists have started to construct theoretical models, trying to propose new explanations for the phenomenon against the comparative advantage principle.

After World War II, the world economic system was in two separation states, shown as the separation between the East and the West and the separation between the North and the South.

First, marked by the state of the Cold War between the United States and the Soviet Union, the developed capitalist countries were separated from the socialist countries with a planned economy. There was labor division and trade among the former type of countries, and there was partial cooperation in the latter camp of countries as well, such as labor division and trade among the countries in the Soviet-led Council for Mutual Economic Assistance.

Second, some developing countries that gained independence after World War II rejected free trade with developed countries because, on the one hand, they had bitter memories of colonial trade; on the other hand, they were under the influence of radical development economics concepts such as "dependency theory" and "center–periphery theory," and there was no trade between low- and middle-income countries. Therefore, international trade in that period mainly occurred between developed capitalist countries. For example, according to World Bank data, exports of goods from high-income countries in 1960 accounted for 95.4% of the total global trade in goods, of which 70.6% of the trade took place within the high-income countries.

What is the theoretical basis for trade among developed countries with the same or similar production factor endowments? The widely accepted theory to conform to people's observations of reality is the so-called "new trade theory." According to this theory, specialized production in various countries does not give full pay to their relatively abundant production factor endowments but to make use of various increasing return effects and the network effect. Although developed countries have the same characteristics of capital factor abundance, different scales of economies and levels of supporting industries produce effects similar to comparative advantages, which can still make them gain from trade. Therefore, there are reasons for intraindustry trade to exist.

Since the 1990s, China has gradually recovered its status as a founding member of the General Agreement on Tariffs and Trade (GATT) and has made efforts to become a contracted member of the World Trade Organization (WTO) through further opening-up. The Soviet Union and Eastern European countries, Vietnam and other countries have also expanded their opening to the outside world, and emerging economies such as India have also actively participated in labor division in the international industrial chain. A landmark event was that the WTO started formal operation in 1995, replacing the GATT. The total number of member countries reached 112 that year, including countries that changed from GATT to WTO membership and many low-income countries.

These countries have huge economic scales and total labor forces, and most are middle-income or low-income countries. Taking the population of transition countries from the planned economy to the market economy as an example, the total population of China, Vietnam, Mongolia, the Soviet Union, and former European countries with the planned economy was approximately 1.63 billion in 1990, accounting for 30.8% of the world's total population. The working-age population aged 15–59 was 1.01 billion, accounting for as much as 32.8% of the world's total population. If India and Latin American countries are included, we can imagine how large the total labor force is to gradually join the global division of labor. Therefore, it is not difficult to judge that since then, world trade has gradually regressed to the Ricardian model, which is more in line with the expectation of the comparative advantage principle and is increasingly manifested as interindustry trade for exchanging production factors.

Jeffrey D. Sachs and others once did a study to directly estimate changes in the proportion of the population living in open economies. They found that the world economy after the end of World War II was generally a closed economy. It was not until 1960 that only approximately 20% of the world population lived in an open economy. In 1993, the proportion of the population was just over 50%. By 1995, as China and Russia became open economies, the population living in open economies reached 87%. If GDP is used to measure the expanding process of the open economy, the visible changing trend is also consistent.[3] In fact, the economic globalization trend after 1995 has been faster, which is reflected not only in the increase in the number of countries participating in the labor division in the world economy—for example, more than half of the WTO member states signed the contract after January 1, 1995—but also in the deepening of their participation in the global division of labor.

We can observe the impact of the aforementioned trends on the characteristics of the global trade structure more directly and clearly (Figure 11.1) when we take high-income countries as a benchmark to observe their changes as a whole in imports and exports. From the perspective of exports and imports (i.e., Figure 11.1a and Figure 11.1b), the share of trade among high-income countries rose slowly until the end of the 1980s. Since then, it has entered a period of steady decline. At the turn of the century, it began to decline at a faster pace. The total decline was more than 10 percentage points from the peak to the latest data point (2017). Changes in the opposite direction caused by the same factors can be seen from the import and export structure from high-income countries to low- and middle-income countries.

According to the flying-geese model principle in economics,[4] the development of foreign direct investment also reflects the comparative advantage principle followed by international trade. Therefore, the expanded size of global foreign direct investment and changes in regional flow are expected to be consistent with the expanded scale of global trade and pattern changes. For example, the World Bank data show that the total net inflow of foreign direct investment in low-income countries and middle-income countries in current dollars had an average annual nominal growth rate of 13.5% during the period 1970–1990 and a substantial increase to 21.4% during the period

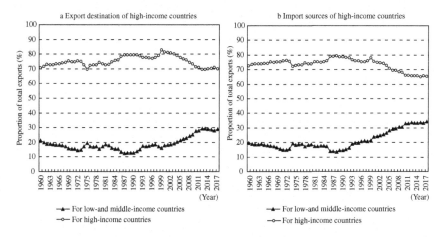

Figure 11.1 Changes of import and export directions in high-income countries

1990–2008. Since the outbreak of the international financial crisis in 2008, there has been a trend of negative growth in large fluctuations.

Different types of economic globalization have brought completely different results to the overall world economy and participating countries. Specifically, globalization is characterized by intraindustry trade, which is limited to economic countries in the developed market, and globalization is characterized by interindustry trade, including a wider type of country, which has created different price equalization effects of production factors, hence producing completely different income distribution results for countries participating in trade and the countries worldwide.

To put it simple, intraindustry trade is mainly not intended for exchanging production factors among participating countries, and therefore it does not change the relative remuneration of each country's domestic production factors; interindustry trade is essentially intended for exchanging production factors among participating countries with different factor endowments. As a result, the relative remuneration of domestic production factors in various countries has also changed.

When the international division of labor is conducted following comparative advantages, the trade between labor-rich developing countries and capital-abundant developed countries will inevitably increase the relative scarcity of labor in developing countries so that laborers can obtain higher returns, and meanwhile it will enhance the relative scarcity of capital in developed countries, resulting in higher returns for capital owners. This means that in labor-rich developing countries, the spontaneous force of the labor market will generate income distribution effects beneficial to laborers. In developed countries, although capital owners, especially multinational corporations, have obtained plentiful earnings from the round of globalization, laborers in these countries will feel hurt if there is no necessary redistribution policy.

It is generally observed that the rise of income inequality in developed countries is to a large extent caused by the increasing income share of the richest people. The wealthier the people are, the lower the share of labor remuneration in their total incomes is. For example, generally speaking, non-labor income accounts for approximately 30% of the total income in the top 10% richer people, while non-labor income accounts for approximately 50% of the total income in the top 1% richest people.[5]

It can be easily understood why some developed countries, such as the United States, have simultaneously turned to trade protectionism, leading to a policy tendency against economic globalization while nationalism and populism are on the rise. Accordingly, this round of globalization is facing its headwinds, and forces against globalization have also undergone fundamental changes, that is, shifting from late-developing countries to developed countries represented by the United States.

A controversial book from Joseph Stiglitz[6] is a masterpiece to correctly question the round of globalization from the position of underdeveloped countries. Interestingly, this Nobel Prize winner in economics reproduced the "Malthusian lag response" phenomenon, in the author's words,[7] i.e., a lagging reflection on previous history based on his long thinking and others as well as the long-accumulated experience and observations in the past when the situation has changed or even reversed. Although this kind of research is necessary and correct from the perspective of academic accumulation and lessons learned, it is no longer so timely and targeted. This means that when we study the round of globalization, we should be focused on new trends when considering the destiny of Globalization 4.0.

From club convergence to a new round of great convergence

The neoclassical growth theory represented by Robert Solow, based on the law of diminishing returns on capital, predicts that once economically backward countries obtain funds for development, they can achieve faster economic growth than developed countries. The catch up will result in converging economic development levels in all countries. Other economic development theories can also provide support for such judgment. For example, it is believed that less-developed countries can obtain assistance, investment, and ready-made technologies from developed countries, which means that they have a kind of "latecomer advantage" for development to achieve their own economic catch-up.

After World War II, many developing economies all had a strong desire to develop after achieving national independence. They created a certain degree of investment conditions by increasing the accumulation rate and receiving financial assistance. However, contrary to theoretical expectations and good wishes, most of the poor countries were still trapped in poverty for decades after the war until the late 20th century. There was no great convergence in the world economy, and the South–North wealth gap has not narrowed.

To save the neoclassical growth theory challenged by the endogenous growth theory, Robert J. Barro and other economists proposed the "conditional convergence" hypothesis; that is, in addition to the convergence factor of initial per capita income, there are also a series of factors related to economic growth that will affect the actual catch-up effect. In the econometric sense, if variables necessary for economic development are controlled, it will be possible to see the convergence result. From the reality perspective, it means that if a developing country has the necessary development conditions represented by those variables, it can achieve a faster growth rate than a developed country, thus realizing the goal of catching up.[8] These "necessary development conditions" certainly include variables such as the openness of an economy.

These studies are certainly helpful in enhancing people's understanding of economic growth and the issues of convergence or divergence. However, the explanations derived have not yet fully satisfied our curiosity at least from the following two perspectives, and the policy implications are also unclear. First, these researchers have tried to put forward hundreds of explanatory variables and found their significance during regression.[9] However, people could not conclude policy suggestions from so many factors to break the development bottleneck and obtain economic catch-up. Second, these studies try to explain why there is no worldwide convergence, which contradicts the judgment that the world has experienced a round of "great convergence" since 1950,[10] making it hard for people to tell right from wrong.

Economists discovered an interesting phenomenon during their studies on convergence or divergence; that is, although there was no overall convergence in the world economy, they did indeed find the trend of convergence within countries with some homogenous characteristics, i.e., countries with low starting points for per capita income level can grow faster in the subsequent period. Convergence among countries within the groups is often called "club convergence." In the text below, we will investigate and explain separately based on the relevant research results.[11]

The first is the situation of convergence within the club. It is found from data regression from 1950 to 1980 that there was a clear convergence among industrialized countries with high per capita incomes, resulting in a significantly narrowed gap; convergence also occurred among countries with a planned economy, including the Soviet Union, even though it was not as significant as the previous group, the gap narrowed accordingly as well. Obviously, within these two groups, there was large homogeneity among countries in terms of development conditions. Moreover, international trade was carried out more or less within the group. For example, intraindustry trade was carried out among industrialized countries based on the principle of free trade, and industrial division of labor and interindustry trade were carried out among planned economy countries based on the framework of the Council for Mutual Economic Assistance.

The second is the situation of low-income countries. During the same period, there was no sign of convergence within the low-income countries. In other words, the low starting point of the per capita income level did not provide these economies with the advantage of catching up later. As a result, the gap within the group widened after 30 years. Generally, the products produced by low-income countries are at the low end of the value chain, making it difficult to induce technological innovation. Moreover, most of these countries maintain economic closure and have little or no participation in labor division in the world economy, so they can neither share the spillover effects of technological changes from more developed countries nor obtain the factor price equalization effects from trade and foreign direct investment.

Finally, there are situations of outliers. We know that during the period, Japan and the Four Asian Tigers surpassed the developed economies with rapid growth and created the famous East Asian miracle.[12] These economies did not show the same characteristics of convergence growth as any convergence club, but they did indeed catch up with the industrialized countries. Nevertheless, the outliers seen in one model can be expected to be reasonably explained in other models. Moreover, it is precisely because there is a sample of countries that have succeeded in catching up under certain conditions that the regression model that tests the convergence of conditions can obtain the expected results.

For example, Sachs and Warner specifically took open economies as a sample for regression and found evidence of convergence.[13] To a certain extent, the research approach is similar to that of economists who advocate the conditional convergence hypothesis. In other words, since opening-up itself is closely related to taking advantage of latecomer advantages, and it works together with the domestic economic system reform, comparing open economies together is similar to taking opening-up as an institutional condition of convergence. It is similar to treating it as an explanatory variable or a control variable in the measurement process.

In fact, the worldwide great convergence—named by Michael Spence—that occurred after 1950 was the result of the club convergence among industrialized countries and economies such as Japan and the Four Asian Tigers that overtook developed countries. The argument does not exclude the conclusion of club convergence, but it can accommodate the situation of a widened gap between many low-income countries and developed countries. However, from a statistical point of view, under the above situation, an outsider is not enough to change the global pattern. During the period, there was no convergence phenomenon in the world. For example, the overall development gap expressed by the Gini coefficient did not narrow.

After understanding the reasons and mechanisms of the world economic convergence or divergence during that period, we can see that there have been many different situations since the 1990s. Measured by population distribution, while market-based economic linkages were restored among a few industrialized countries during the 1950s, most of the world's population lived in countries that chose non-market economic mechanisms for development; that is, roughly one third of the population lived in planned economies, and another 50% or so lived in countries where the government proclaimed the industrialized path. Since the 1990s, many economies have opened up. With the reform of the domestic economic system, more countries have turned to the track of the market economy.[14] The result of the reform and opening-up is shown in the economic growth performance, leading to economic growth convergence in various countries.

We can observe how the world economy has gone through a process of gap narrowing from the perspective of time change. The World Bank classifies countries into four income groups according to per capita gross national income (GNI) or per capita GDP: high-income countries, upper-middle-income countries, lower-middle-income countries, and low-income countries. We compare the per capita GDP data at 2010 constant prices in relevant groups with the world average level to observe the relative changes in per capita incomes among these country groups (Figure 11.2).

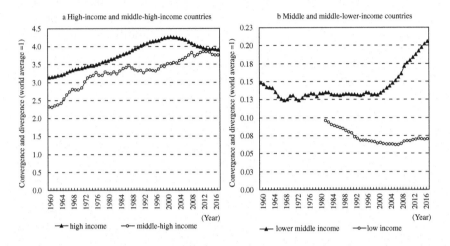

Figure 11.2 Convergence and divergence of the global economy

   The first chart in Figure 11.2 shows that the relative incomes in high-income countries continued to rise until they reached a peak in 2001. However, in the 1990s, the increase became relatively flat, and it started to fall rapidly in the 21st century. The relative incomes in upper-middle-income countries stabilized in the 1990s and subsequently rose, but the incomes began to show a downward trend in the second decade of the 21st century.
   The second chart in Figure 11.2 shows that after long being stable, the relative incomes in lower-middle-income countries have begun to rise rapidly since the 21st century. The relative incomes in low-income countries showed a declining and slowing-down trend during the 1990s. However, the downward trend has stopped since the 21st century, and it has tended to increase modestly.
   To observe the divergence and convergence characteristics in different periods more directly, we can conduct a descriptive statistical test of type-β convergence in our concern with the help of cross-country data by periods. Growth theory generally divides convergence into two types, namely, σ convergence and β convergence. The former is caused by the shrinking trend of income level diffusion among countries, and the latter is caused by lower-income countries achieving a faster growth rate.
   In Figure 11.3, we correlate the per capita GDP level of countries in 1960 and 1990 to the average annual growth rate of per capita GDP in a specific period afterwards, that is, observing the situation from 1960 to 1990 (Figure 11.3a) and the situation from 1990– to 2017 (Figure 11.3b). Obviously, the graphics represent β convergence, i.e., observe how the per capita income level at the starting point affects the subsequent growth rate. In addition, since there is no other explanatory variable to add or control

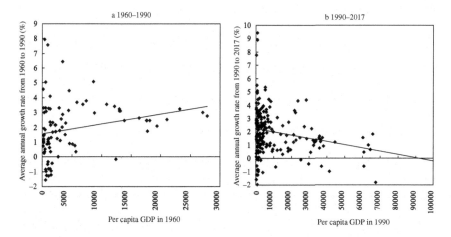

Figure 11.3 Convergence of the world economy during different periods

variable to regress, the curve shows more absolute convergence or unconditional convergence.

The per capita GDP in Figure 11.3 is shown at 2010 constant dollars. For the period 1960–1990 shown in Figure 11.3a, we obtained samples of 91 countries and regions. During the period, we did not observe a negative correlation between the per capita income level at the starting year and the subsequent growth rate; that is, no β convergence occurred. Nevertheless, there was a positive correlation between them. For the period 1990–2017 shown in Figure 11.3b, we obtained samples of 190 countries and regions, where we observed a negative correlation between the per capita income level at the starting year and the subsequent average annual growth rate. At least to the extent of descriptive statistics, we can say that β convergence occurred during the period.

A more straightforward fact is that since the early 1980s, the rate of decline of the world's poor population has gradually accelerated, after which it has become more remarkable over time. According to the World Bank data, during the period 1981–1993, the global poverty population decreased by 44.17 million, with an average annual poverty reduction of 0.2%; during the period 1993–2005, the global poverty population decreased by 516 million, with an average annual poverty reduction of 2.7%; and during the period 2005–2015, the global poverty population decreased by 577 million, with an average annual poverty reduction of as high as 5.5%. The speed of global poverty reduction since the 1990s is undoubtedly an unprecedented achievement in world economic history. As the evidence and result of worldwide convergence, the effect of poverty reduction also shows the importance of the globalization model—different types of world division of labor lead to different convergence results.

China's economic development under globalization

China is considered to be the laggard in the first and second industrial revolutions, as well as Globalization 1.0 and Globalization 2.0, but China has continuously promoted and deepened reform and opening-up since the 1980s and fully took advantage of the opportunities from Globalization 3.0, so it has achieved economic growth catch-up and gained an important position in the Third Industrial Revolution.

According to World Bank data, China's population accounted for 22.3% of the world's population, and its GDP accounted for 1.1% of the world's total in 1978. In 2017, the share of China's population fell to 18.4%, while the share of GDP increased to 12.7% at constant dollars. From 1981 to 2015, the global absolute impoverished population calculated on the basis of purchasing power parity per person per day (at 2011 dollars) decreased from 1.89 billion to 750 million, and it decreased from 880 million to 9.6 million in China, when China contributed 76.2% to the world poverty reduction. It can be said that in the round of global economic convergence since the 1990s, China's economic catch-up has made a huge contribution.

When economists ask the question of "what is done right after all" for a successful case, they are actually seeking the "basic conditions" behind the success on two levels. At the first level, they try to find the factors that significantly promote economic growth, i.e., what growth economists call the X variable. As mentioned earlier, Barro et al. found hundreds of such variables. At the second level, they try to find the basic conditions among the basic conditions, i.e., the most critical and decisive factors for economic growth when other variables can be temporarily ignored.

The late Hollis B. Chenery, the chief economist of the World Bank, and others believe that in developing countries, certain development conditions can play an independent role in a short period of time when other conditions are not yet available and then promote the formation of other conditions, thus promoting sustainable economic development.[15]

If we think that this thesis does not repel other conditions, this thesis can be used as a reference to explore what kind of development conditions have such a key role or to determine this "Chenery condition" so that a country's economic growth obtains the initial impetus to create other conditions for continued growth based on its own logic, forming a virtuous circle for economic development. To answer such questions, we need to understand China's economic development in a universal framework of development economics.

Chenery believes that foreign capital and foreign assistance have the characteristics of becoming such key development conditions. He found from fairly early experiences that effectively using foreign capital and foreign assistance can trigger technology and skill improvements and will gradually weaken a country's dependence on external resources, and then the country's economic growth can go on a sustainable track. Sachs more generally emphasized implementing opening-up and trade liberalization, thus establishing powerful direct linkages between the economy and the world system. In this way, it not only obtains such opening-up dividends as late-comer advantages and division of labor effects but also effectively promotes the domestic reform program under the pressure of international competition.[16] The famous financial commentator Martin Wolf focused his answer on the global flow of knowledge and proved that the more countries introduce external knowledge, the faster they will become a large country of knowledge with owned patents as the symbol.[17]

Exploring key conditions for economic development has ultimately focused on the important factor of opening-up, and it indicates that such a development condition is not an independent thing but a set of conditions to promote mutually and a series of events to synergize with each other. To some extent, the findings of these researchers or critics are obviously much more brilliant than those of growth economists who constructed hundreds of explanatory variables and performed four million regressions.

However, to link these discussions and their conclusions with China's development achievements in the past 40 years, we must first tell a complete story that organically integrates domestic reforms with opening-up and then look back at the factors played as "Chenery condition." To this end, let us first review the characteristics of China's most prominent resource endowments and the biggest institutional drawbacks before the reforms in the late 1970s and early 1980s.

Before the reform and opening-up, China was a country with a highly centralized planned economy. Labor enthusiasm was heavily suppressed due to a lack of incentive mechanisms, and resource misallocation led to low efficiency. Therefore, although China featured an unlimited supply of labor, it failed to initiate dual economic development, resulting in it being one of the poorest countries in the world in terms of development level. In 1978, 82.1% of the Chinese people lived in extremely impoverished rural areas, and the per capita net income of rural households was only 133.6 yuan. A total of 70.5% of the labor force in the country was engaged in agricultural production, and agricultural labor productivity was extremely low at both the absolute level and the relative level.

We can take the ratio between the value-added share and the share of employment of an industry as the industry's comparative labor productivity to calculate the agricultural comparative labor productivity. In 1978, it was only 0.39, equivalent to 14.2% of the comparative labor productivity of the secondary industry and 19.4% of the comparative labor productivity of the tertiary industry.

Therefore, it is both the starting point and the destination of reforms to form an institutional environment and a driving mechanism that can mobilize the enthusiasm of laborers, achieve full employment of excess production factors such as labor, and increase the supply and utilization of scarce production factors such as capital, thereby improving the overall resource allocation efficiency. Although China's reform did not plan a predetermined blueprint at the very beginning, the subsequent reform process was not designed by humans at all, and the ultimate achievements of the reform were not an "unintended consequence."[18] The right starting point determines the logic, path, and result of subsequent reforms.

Two fundamental problems were solved in one step by the implementation of the household contract responsibility system. First, it solved the incentive problem in agricultural production by transforming collective labor into family operations. In addition, policy measures such as drastically reducing the number of grain purchases and unified purchases, allowing farmers to rest and recuperate, and increasing the purchase prices of agricultural products greatly increased the output of agricultural products within a short period of time, increased farmers' income, and significantly reduced the incidence of rural poverty. Second, farmers were given the autonomy to allocate production factors, especially the labor force, which promoted the transfer of agricultural surplus labor and reallocated resources in accordance with the increase in labor income and the improvement of labor productivity.

The two clues of the early reforms actually laid the foundation for a series of subsequent reforms in various fields and the institutional foundation for opening to the outside world step by step. Therefore, they can be regarded as the process of creating basic conditions for development, and their logic goes through the following evolution process.

Based on the problem-oriented principle, system reforms and policy adjustments have gradually lifted the institutional barriers to the flow of production factors, promoted the large-scale transfer of labor from agriculture to non-agricultural industries, and the large-scale migration of labor from rural areas and the central and western regions to cities and coastal areas. For the largest population movement in human history in peacetime, first, it responds to the huge demand for labor from urban economic expansion and export-oriented development in coastal areas; second, due to reform deepening in related fields, China's economic growth is driven by absorbing more labor forces, thus helping reallocate resources more efficiently; finally, since the economic process and social events are people-centered, it naturally has the nature of sharing while improving efficiency and promoting growth.

From a domestic perspective, the process of reform, opening-up, development, and sharing reallocated resources and correspondingly increased total factor productivity and labor productivity; from an international perspective, it turned the most abundant production factors into industrial comparative advantages, enabling labor-intensive products to be competitive in the international market; from the perspective of domestic and international communications, it maximized the use of the abundant factor of labor and exchanged relatively scarce capital factors by introducing foreign capital and trading; from the perspective of Skopos theory, sharing is endogenous in the whole process of opening-up and development.

It can be seen that the gradual expansion of opening-up to the outside world with its own internal logic and moderate rhythm is actually predetermined by the overall logic chain of reform, opening-up, development, and sharing. In other words, in the last round of economic globalization, China became the most outstanding country for economic catch-up and a direct beneficiary of global economic convergence. Naturally, when some developed countries attempt to disrupt global supply chains and try to reverse economic globalization, China should become a defender of globalization.

Conclusion

This chapter briefly describes and analyzes the history of globalization. This indicates that economic globalization does not necessarily mean global openness and participation. Thus far, Globalization 1.0 and Globalization 2.0 observed by us are mainly the history of colonialism, and it is a globalization dominated by a single or a few colonial countries or world hegemonic countries; whether involved or excluded, and whether passive entry or active participation, the vast colonial and semicolonial countries, "peripheral" countries and developing countries have not benefited from it.

It was not until the globalization of the 1930s that the pattern of developing countries sharing dividends and reducing poverty worldwide was formed. At the same time, because many developed countries have not solved the problem of income distribution at home, the common people in these countries feel that they have not benefited from globalization, while politicians take advantage of the situation to lead conflicts to the trading partners of emerging economies, and some national leaders even acted as the instigators of anti-globalization, making radical protectionist actions in international politics and highlighting the populist color in domestic politics.

It can be seen that whether in developed or developing countries, whether at the global governance level or international relations level, two necessary conditions should be created if globalization is to truly become a propeller of global economic prosperity and be shared by all countries: the first is openness and inclusiveness to enable all countries to participate universally and equally; the second is to realize connections and interactions of domestic and international policies. In this way, opening-up measures such as foreign direct investment, international trade, and the global flow of knowledge can be linked to such domestic reforms as breaking monopolies, correcting price distortions, and removing barriers to resource allocation. It creates not only global dividends shared by all countries but also comprehensive basic conditions for economic development in all countries by virtue of the international competition environment and the world division of the labor system. In this way, all countries can realize the economic development shared by the whole population through the domestic income distribution mechanism and redistribution policy.

Similarly, the history of previous industrial revolutions also indicates that the achievements of scientific discoveries, technological progress, and revolutions in production modes will not naturally bring economic growth to countries to be shared by all residents. Only by participating in the global division of labor and competition, carrying out internal reforms to eliminate the fundamental institutional barriers, and thus cultivating key conditions to promote development can institutional innovation and technological innovation conducive to growth become the norm. Then, it will seize the opportunity of the industrial revolution, such as getting aboard the fast train of globalization to support the country's long-term sustainable growth.

Historically, China has repeatedly missed the development opportunities provided by globalization and industrial revolutions. When it came to the period parallel to Globalization 3.0, China persisted in advancing economic system reforms and opening-up, created the "Chenery conditions" for development, and achieved fast economic growth such as rarely seen in human history, thus seizing the opportunity of the Third Industrial Revolution and gradually approaching the center of the globalization stage and the forefront of a new round of industrial revolution.

China has nearly one-fifth of the world's population. Therefore, failures and lessons, successful experiences and challenges in China's economic development should not be treated as an ordinary case but also need to tap its powerful proof force and general significance: on the one hand, it is necessary to enrich and establish development economics with international vision; on the other hand, it is also necessary to continue to write a new chapter for China's development from the logic of development economics itself.

As China's economic development level is getting closer to joining the ranks of high-income countries, the deceleration in economic growth has come as expected. The fact that China is about to get through the middle-income stage does not mean that the "middle-income trap" in the empirical sense is no longer applicable. In fact, China faces a more challenging threshold trap.

This proposition also reminds us that an economy at a higher stage of economic development faces more unprecedented and severe challenges. Fast disappearing demographic dividends have weakened the traditional growth momentum, headwinds of globalization and changes in China's comparative advantages have weakened the traditional globalization dividend, and changes in labor supply and demand have weakened the market-based mechanism to improve income distribution, meaning that for the Chinese economy, the fruits that are easy to reach have been picked.

To cope with these severe challenges and growing problems, we still need to find answers from the logic of globalization and industrialization and the "Chenery conditions" for the Chinese economy to participate in globalization. When we say the demographic dividend is a prerequisite for China's economic growth, we actually mean this is why China's economy has achieved extraordinary high-speed growth, thus achieving rapid catch-up, rather than an eternal development condition.

If we emphasize the "Chenery condition" that combines the incentive effect and the resource allocation effect, we can conclude that the disappearance of demographic dividends only means the end of the rapid growth stage, while persisting in and improving "Chenery conditions" with the times, and promoting more in-depth economic reforms and more comprehensive opening-up can enable China to seize the opportunities provided by the Fourth Industrial Revolution and Globalization 4.0, hence maintaining long-term sustainable economic growth.

Notes

1 Klaus Schwab, *The Fourth Industrial Revolution*, Beijing: China CITIC Press, 2016, p. 4.
2 See Klaus Schwab, *Globalization 4.0: What Does It Mean?*, 2018, www.wefo rum.org/agenda/2018/11/globalization-4-what-does-it-mean-how-it-will-benefit-everyone/.
3 Jeffrey D. Sachs and Andrew Warner, Economic Reform and the Process of Global Integration, *Brookings Papers on Economic Activity*, Vol. 1, 1995, pp. 12–13.
4 For example, Kiyoshi Kojima, The "Flying Geese" Model of Asian Economic Development: Origin, Theoretical Extensions, and Regional Policy Implications, *Journal of Asian Economics*, Vol. 11, 2000, pp. 375–401.
5 Era Dabla-Norris, Kalpana Kochhar, Nujin Suphaphiphat, Frantisek Ricka, and Evridiki Tsounta, *Causes and Consequences of Income Inequality: A Global Perspective*, IMF Staff Discussion Note, SDN/15/13, June 2015, p. 11.
6 Joseph Stiglitz, *Globalization and Its Discontents*, translated by Yang Li and Tianxiang Zhang, Beijing: China Machine Press, 2004.
7 The life of Thomas Robert Malthus (1766–1834) happened to be at the beginning of the First Industrial Revolution, when life gradually became better. However, confined by data availability and subsequent thinking, he failed to reveal the bright prospects never experienced in the human society but extracted (long-lasting) important characteristic facts in the era before the industrial revolution. Of course, it is the lagging academic mistake that makes Malthus immortal. See Cai Fang, Why has Malthus Become the "Oldest" Economist? in *The Humble are the Wisest*, Beijing: Social Sciences Academic Press, 2017, pp. 188–196.
8 For example, see Robert J. Barro and Xavier Sala-i-Martin, *Economic Growth*, New York: McGraw-Hill, 1995.
9 Xavier Sala-i-Martin, I Just Ran Two Million Regressions, *American Economic Review*, Vol. 87, No. 2, 1997, pp. 178–183.
10 For example, see Michael Spence, *The Next Convergence: The Future of Economic Growth in a Multispeed World*, New York: Farrar, Straus and Giroux, 2011.
11 Unless otherwise specified, empirical observations of the club convergence and divergence scenarios summarized in the following three paragraphs are all based on William J. Baumol, Productivity Growth, Convergence, and Welfare: What the Long-Run Data Show, *The American Economic Review*, Vol. 76, No. 5, 1986, pp. 1072–1085.
12 World Bank, *The East Asian Miracle: Economic Growth and Public Policy*, Oxford: Oxford University Press, 1993.
13 Jeffrey D. Sachs and Andrew Warner, Economic Reform and the Process of Global Integration, *Brookings Papers on Economic Activity*, Vol. 1, 1995, pp. 12–13.
14 Jeffrey D. Sachs and Andrew Warner, Economic Reform and the Process of Global Integration, *Brookings Papers on Economic Activity*, Vol. 1, 1995, pp. 12–13.

15 Hollis B. Chenery and Alan M. Strout, Foreign Assistance and Economic Development, *The American Economic Review*, Vol. 56, No. 4, 1966, pp. 679–733.
16 Jeffrey D. Sachs and Andrew Warner, Economic Reform and the Process of Global Integration, *Brookings Papers on Economic Activity*, Vol. 1, 1995, pp. 12–13.
17 Martin Wolf, Let Knowledge Spread around the World, *Financial Times*, April 25, 2018.
18 The two sayings are from Hayek, and often quoted by economists to explain China's reform and development. See Friedrich Hayek, *Studies in Philosophy, Politics and Economics*, London: Routledge and Kegan Paul, 1967, Chapter 6.

12 Political economics in globalization and China's strategy

Introduction

Since the 1970s, the real growth rate of world trade in goods and services exports has always been higher than that of global gross domestic product (GDP), except for fluctuations in specific years, which fully demonstrates the characteristics of economic globalization in our era. Influenced by the international financial crisis, the total volume of world trade plummeted in 2009 but growth was restored in 2010 and 2011, which was also much higher than the GDP growth rate.

Nevertheless, since 2012, the growth rate of world trade has been consistently lower than that of GDP. The deceleration of world trade can be more or less explained by demand-side economic factors, which cause sluggish global economic growth, and supply-side economic factors, such as China and other emerging economies, which are driven by domestic demands. However, intensified global trade protectionism should be an important factor of political economics for the deceleration of world trade.

In a broader sense, under the backdrop of the sluggish recovery of the world economy after the financial crisis, the decline in trade may be a characteristic manifestation of economic globalization being hindered by the anti-globalization political ecology. Meanwhile, the proportion of global capital flows in the total global economy plummeted from its peak in 2007.

It is not hard to understand the phenomenon. After the international financial crisis, countries around the world have set new trade barriers. As the most developed and the largest economies, the United States, Germany, and the United Kingdom introduced hundreds of measures. Such changes of policy reflect the changing political structure of Western countries, that is, political nationalism and populism with anti-globalization as the core proposition, rapidly evolving to non-cooperative anti-globalization strategies and trade protection policies. As of 2016, the trend had become very obvious and presented new characteristics of political extremism and directional convergence.

For example, when US President Donald Trump took office, he implemented a series of policies, such as curbing immigration and travel, withdrawing from

DOI: 10.4324/9781003329305-15

the Trans-Pacific Partnership, brewing trade wars with China and other countries, and withdrawing from the Paris Agreement on climate change. Echoed across the ocean, the United Kingdom launched a referendum to exit the European Union, while populism and extremist parties in various European countries have risen. Black swan incidents have occurred one after another.

Such incidents have become much worse, and unilateralism represented by the United States has been fully transformed into a foreign policy that undermines globalization. The US launched trade wars against China and other major trading partners, which is not only a bullying against other countries but also greatly endangers the global economic and trade order, causing huge negative externalities to block or even reverse economic globalization. Putting blame on China and other trading partners is nothing but two possibilities: either a lack of basic common sense in economics or shifting contradictions at the expense of harming the global economy and the interests of trading partners to gain votes for him. Whatever it is, the approach is ideologically populism, nationalism, and protectionism, and it is harmful to other countries and to its own voters.

This phenomenon can be very well explained by international political economics. Globalization itself is not interest neutral; at the beginning, people saw that developed countries and their political and economic elites and their think tanks dominated globalization, making it evolve in a direction favorable to developed countries. Whether it is international financial and trade institutions such as the Bretton Woods system or an integrated community such as the European Union, it is big countries that have the power to make decisions. The finance ministers, central bank governors, and trade ministers who represent these countries exercise the power to prevent developing countries, especially the least developed countries, from equally benefiting from globalization.

Furthermore, people have found that multinational companies and other interest groups representing capital have dominated the interest arrangements in developed countries.[1] It is imaginable that middle-class and low-income families in developed countries cannot benefit from the globalization of the labor market. Moreover, the lack of a redistribution mechanism in American social policies has indeed made a large part of social groups become "losers" in economic globalization.

If the voices of developing countries cannot substantially influence the process and direction of globalization, the large number of losers in developed countries will eventually express their wishes through the "ballot box" mechanism, ultimately affecting a country's political and policy orientation. However, many economic policies with populism have often led to more serious consequences and provoked greater political confrontation. For example, the United States implemented easy credit policies to stimulate the real estate bubble, which caused the subprime crisis and the global financial crisis, plunging the domestic middle class and low-income people into deeper disasters, leading to mass movements such as Occupy Wall Street and left-wing and right-wing extremist political powers to be on the rise.

In the final analysis, there is nothing wrong with globalization itself. What is wrong is the approach of globalization management and governance dominated by Western countries and the resulting benefit distribution pattern. However, fundamentally adjusting the existing benefit pattern requires changing the institution disruptively, which is something that any political party and politician feels difficult or reluctant to do, since they come to power with the most deceptive promise and hope to remain in power with the lowest possible political cost and highest possible political gains within a limited term of office. Therefore, the best choice in line with their logic of political economics is to direct contradictions to partners in economic and trade relations and even to globalization itself.

Based on the latest economic theory, this chapter reviews the evolution of the round of globalization that started in 1990 in breadth and depth and reveals the homology and relevance of economic growth and economic globalization, indicating that since developed countries in the West failed to well align the country's economic growth and social development with globalization, the middle class and low-income people were placed in an increasingly marginalized situation, leading to economic recession and political crisis.

The populism in the Western political system initially drove decision-makers to adopt financial easing policies, which brought out rounds of asset bubbles and evolved into global financial crises and debt crises. Furthermore, the bewildered politicians turned their attention to globalization itself and openly implemented trade protectionism and other anti-globalization policies, so globalization is in danger of retrogression.

During the reform and opening-up, China organically connected dual economic development with economic globalization. The reallocation of the labor force has not only become the source of rapid economic growth but also ensured the extensive participation of urban and rural residents in economic development. Therefore, China has benefited from the round of globalization and achieved a relatively equal distribution of benefits, greatly reducing poverty. Therefore, under the possible trend of deglobalization, China, as a potential victim, is undoubtedly facing a huge challenge.

Based on the analysis in this chapter, in the conclusion, we suggest that China should grasp and adapt to the new trend of globalization based on its strategic height and historical depth and take advantage of its huge economy to lead and construct a new round of economic globalization through various global efforts to benefit itself and the vast number of developing countries.

A different round of globalization: breadth and depth

There are broad and narrow definitions of globalization. Correspondingly, researchers also have different views about when globalization began. Opinions can differ by hundreds of years from 1492, when Columbus discovered the American continent, to 1968, when anti-war movements and social trends pervaded Western countries, and up to 2000, when information technology and communication technology fully affected social life in various countries.[2]

Economists tend towards a narrower definition of globalization. In other words, they are concerned about economic globalization and acknowledge that globalization can contain broader content. For example, Stiglitz, on the one hand, defined economic globalization as "a closer economic interaction among countries in the world through expanding the movement of goods and services, capital and even labor force." On the other hand, he also admitted that globalization also includes the international flow of ideas and knowledge, cultural sharing, global civil society, and the global environmental movement.[3] Krugman believed that globalization is an all-encompassing statement about the ever-growing world trade, the linkage of financial markets in various countries, and many things that make the world smaller.[4]

Non-economists tend to define globalization from a broader perspective. For example, political scientist Manfred Steger summarized globalization as a series of multidimensional social processes aimed at creating, expanding, extending, and strengthening worldwide social dependence and communication while arousing people's awareness of the deepening connection between local and external connections. In addition, such factors as religion, war, sports, terrorist activities, and environment will have to be added in addition to the social dimension.[5]

In fact, the broad and narrow views on the definition and starting time of globalization have their own factual basis and research intentions. Therefore, the best way to summarize various theories is neither to consciously or blindly choose which side, nor to take a compromising stance, but to focus on the nature of issues under discussion and their relevance to China. From the perspective of historical and logical unity, we can take the most important signs of economic globalization, such as trade and capital flow, as the globalization motive and hence the most direct features and then take the key turning time shown in such features as the starting point of globalization to observe how globalization evolves in breadth and depth and the influence of its consequences on the political process and policy-making in various countries.

Accordingly, combined with the definition of economic globalization, according to the expansion of trade in goods and services and foreign direct investment, the remarkable changes in geopolitics, and the performance of China's rapid growth and participation in the world economy, we can take 1990 as the starting year of the current round of globalization. On the one hand, China began reforming and opening-up in the early 1980s. As its inevitable process and a catalyst for further advancement, China filed an application in 1986 for restoring its status as a signatory country in the General Agreement on Tariffs and Trade and joined the World Trade Organization (WTO) in 2001. On the other hand, the Soviet Union collapsed in 1991, marking the end of the 40-year Cold War in the world; afterwards, the countries of the former Soviet Union and Central and Eastern European countries began to transform their economies. It was also during that period that the global flow of world trade and capital reached a new level; globalization has since then entered a new climax with these historic events as tipping points.

As shown in Figure 12.1, with more countries joining the global division of labor system after the 1990s, the dependence on world trade in goods showed a leap-forward increase and constantly rising until the international financial crisis broke out in 2008. The total scale of global foreign direct investment based on inflows also began to increase substantially in the early 1990s, reaching its peak before the financial crisis. After the outbreak of the international financial crisis, the sharp rise of the two indicators (goods trade and foreign investment) was significantly curbed. In contrast, China's dependence on trade in goods has been increasing since the data were available (early 1980s). The peak came slightly earlier than the global situation, while the growth of net inflows of foreign direct investment continued for a longer time, and the decline was not as steep as the global situation.

As shown in Figure 12.1, with more countries joining the global division of labor system after the 1990s, the dependence on world trade in goods increased by leaps and bounds until the outbreak of the international financial crisis in 2008.

The history of the world economy presents such a feature that the more recent it is, the greater the long-term evolving process of economy is condensed in a very short period of time (until it is completed). One example can be found with the economic catch-up of late-developing countries and

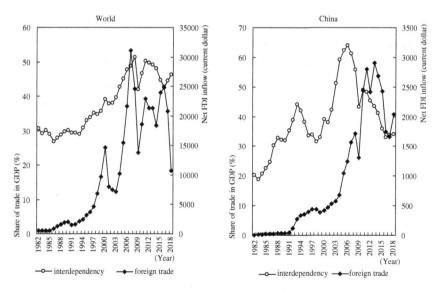

Figure 12.1 Trade and capital flow: the world and China

regions. Compared with early-mover countries and regions, the New World (compared with Europe), Japan (compared with the United States), the Four Asian Tigers (compared with Japan), and emerging economies represented by China (compared with the Four Tigers) have all achieved faster economic growth. Furthermore, in addition to the unknown prospects of emerging economies, previous catch-up economies required a shorter time to become industrialized and modernized. This applies to economic globalization as well. The past 20–30 years have seen an evolution beyond any era in history in terms of breadth and depth, showing unexpected remarkable new features.

In contrast, changes in globalization in breadth are predictable, although the radical degree is increasingly beyond the capacity of many countries. The initial motive and elementary form of economic globalization is to trade goods with each other to gain benefits. This type of trade has continuously expanded as institutional barriers have been removed and transportation costs have decreased.

In view of the great improvement of the industrial relevance between the service sector and the manufacturing sector and the improvement of communications and transaction efficiency by modern information technology, the accelerated development of service trade has also expanded the breadth of globalization. With the development of trade in goods and services, capital, a production factor with the strongest mobility, has unprecedentedly expanded the flow scale and scope. With changes in the geographical pattern of international politics, the flow of labor and human capital has further contributed to globalization.

The abovementioned scope of globalization is still limited to the scope of economic globalization, and it is still only the global flow of goods, services, and production factors. Due to the interaction and mutual influence between globalization and economic integration, especially with the promotion of a series of global and regional integration agreements or agreements, globalization has expanded from the economic field to the political, social, educational, cultural, and other fields in an all-round way. If economic globalization in a narrow sense is faced with mutual benefit and the resulting friction, globalization with wider definition and substance will bring all-around integration, friction, and even conflict. Furthermore, in the environment of regional conflicts and international terrorist activities, political problems, terrorist attacks, and refugee crises have brought increasingly negative costs to globalization.

However, the issue worthy of deep examination is the evolving depth of economic globalization, that is, the nature of international trade differs from the past due to changes in globalization conditions.[6] Capital flows have similar changes in nature, and the traditional "double gap model" can no longer convincingly explain the phenomenon of net capital outflow from emerging economies to developed countries. Traditionally, people usually follow the theory of comparative advantages to explain international trade, which was originated by Ricardo and then developed and finalized by Heckscher, Olin, and Samuelson; that is, differences in relative productivity (or relative opportunity cost) in different countries to produce different goods rather than absolute differences determine the necessity of trade between countries and the nature of common benefits.

Early international trade experience shows that differences in comparative advantages mainly lie in resource (factor) endowments, which indeed verifies the correctness and explanatory power of traditional theories. However, people have gradually observed that there is also a large amount of trade exchange between countries with the same resource endowment structure. Such phenomena have attracted many economists to study, forming several hypotheses on the New Trade Theory.

Although there are different opinions, the mainstream of the New Trade Theory can still obtain mutual recognition or consensus, that is, seeking the source and motivation of international trade through the following aspects: increasing returns or economies of scale; human capital accumulation such as learning by doing; and endogenous technological progress by research and development. It is worth pointing out that the New Trade Theory has not changed the principle of comparative advantages itself but only expanded comparative advantages from single factor endowments to a wider scope in the development of globalization, making a better logical connection between the theoretical explanation of international trade and reality.

However, in the context of globalization, the series of new observations and new theoretical summaries would be in a position to help people make progress in understanding economic growth and trade development. In the text below, we will summarize two aspects and reveal their logical relations.

First, the driving force of economic growth is homologous with the necessity of international trade. For a long time, people consciously or unconsciously believed that "exploring the sources of economic growth" and "the causes of international trade" are two different things. Therefore, it is usually believed in the history of economic theory that Smith gave birth to modern economics by solving the previous proposition and Ricardo contributed to the latter proposition, laying the foundation for the long-lasting trade theory. As the New Trade Theory and the New Growth Theory develop to be applied to explain contemporary economic development phenomena, it is no surprise that when looking back to the classics, people find that Smith should not only be regarded as the source of ideas for these two new theories but also back in his day, he tried to build a bridge between growth theory and trade theory and integrate the two theories logically and structurally. Contemporary researchers have explored the contribution of Smith from two aspects.[7]

First, the principle of free trade advocated by Smith is nothing but applying his theories of specialization and division of labor on a global scale. In his eyes, there is no sharp difference between domestic trade and international trade. People are familiar with Smith's theory of division of labor, but few people pay attention to it. He not only demonstrates the division of labor as the source of economic growth but also attributes the occurrence of international trade to the inevitable trend of division of labor (expansion).

Second, Smith not only recognized the importance of capital accumulation to economic growth but also emphasized the role of technological progress. He united the learning by doing with the economies of scale via his concept of division of labor, believing that only by expanding the market can technology be improved, which in turn could promote the further expansion of the market.

Both the mainstream of New Growth Theory and new trade theory, whether influenced by Smith or independently discovered in the more colorful reality of economic growth and globalization, endogenous human capital and technological progress to economic growth, so from this analytical framework, economic growth, international trade and even globalization become inseparable processes. For example, in Romer's economic growth theory and globalization proposition, ideas with non-competitive characteristics such as technology and rules are at the core.[8]

Third, gains from trade will not be rationally distributed naturally. The existence of international trade and investment must be out of their non-zero-sum nature. However, the experience and lessons from the round of economic globalization have shown that the non-zero-sum nature established in theory and in the overall sense does not necessarily mean that all countries participating in the international division of labor will benefit equally, nor does it mean that all participating parties in a country will benefit equally. What happened in reality is contrary to traditional understanding, which has aroused the theoretical reflection of mainstream economists. Some of the results are of positive and constructive significance, but some have become the theoretical basis and action guide of trade protectionism.

International trade mainly arises from differences in resource endowments between countries, so trade can easily be seen as a reciprocal or competitive relationship between countries. Under the circumstances of emphasizing the zero-sum competitive relationship, the mercantilism trend and policy orientation in history will be formed, and it is called the "theory of strategic trade" or the "theory of national competitiveness" in the modern version. Although Krugman is often regarded as the initiator of the theoretical basis for the argument,[9] he has seriously and sharply criticized the viewpoint and its related concept of "national competitiveness," arguing that international trade is not a zero-sum game; there is no win-or-lose relationship between countries, so international trade cannot be simply compared to competition between countries.[10]

However, it is also necessary to think about the prevalence of such views: Economic growth is homologous with international trade. Corporate productivity, industrial structure, and related resource allocation efficiency affecting economic growth performance will influence international trade and thus the division of labor; conversely, international division of labor will also affect a country's corporate and industrial structure and even income distribution pattern.

Obviously, the essence of the mistake of "theory of strategic trade" does not essentially lie in using the statement of "national competitiveness" but attributes the economic, social, and political problems that seem to originate from international trade but are rooted in a country to the failures in international competition. One disadvantage of allowing this argument to prevail is that if the country is compared to a company that intends to compete globally, the interests of multinational corporations are cleverly confused with the interests of the country and all the people, and it also provides a basis to rationally implement the beggar-thy-neighbor policy of protectionism. The fact is that protectionism, like free trade, will not automatically benefit ordinary citizens.

Serious American economists are unwilling to admit the decline of national competitiveness, nor are they willing to bear the reputation of protectionism. After all, most of them have taken the self-evident oath: "I believe in free trade." It cannot be denied that no matter how international trade evolves, trade occurs because it brings overall net benefits to a country. Meanwhile, an increasing number of economists have acknowledged that international trade or other forms of globalization bring benefits to a country, but they cannot be automatically shared by all groups equally and rationally, and supportive economic systems and social policies are indispensable.

Represented by the United States, developed countries have comparative advantages in material capital-intensive and human capital-intensive industries. Therefore, their trade with developing countries is mainly characterized by exporting material capital and human capital goods while importing simple labor-intensive goods. Changes in the industrial structure based on such division of labor have influenced the employment structure and income distribution pattern in these countries, and the approach and direction of such influences are different from those of their trading and investment partners in developing countries. Therefore, the round of globalization has shaped different industrial structures, industrial organizations, and income distribution patterns for countries at different development stages.

Consequences of globalization and its political representation

After the end of World War II and before the start of this round of globalization in the 1990s, intraindustry trade between developed countries with similar production factor endowments played an important role in these countries and even in global trade. The income distribution effect was very different from the trade between emerging economies and developed countries in this round of globalization. In the latter case, the distribution of trade gains was not conducive to those relatively scarce production factors.[11] In other words, in industrialized countries where labor is relatively scarce, workers benefit less, and in emerging economies where capital is relatively scarce, capital owners benefit less. Spence and Hlatshwayo found that during the period 1990–2008, a large number of manufacturing industries at the low-end value chain in the United States were relocated aboard, and the corresponding jobs were lost too. Therefore, almost all the new jobs in this period came from the non-trade service sector.[12]

As the productivity of the domestic manufacturing industry has been continuously improved, and the productivity of the non-trade sector has increased slowly, different demands for human capital have been formed, and the polarization of American education development has also been induced. Accordingly, the US labor market has become polarized; that is, skilled jobs in high-tech fields and unskilled jobs in low-end departments are growing rapidly, while middle-level jobs are relatively reduced.[13]

Under this pattern, the income growth of the middle class in the traditional sense will be slow or even stagnant. When the government fails to give priority to solving the problem of income distribution, the redistribution policy is not well implemented, and even leans toward the elite groups, the domestic income distribution situation will inevitably deteriorate.[14] Income polarization and high university fees have enabled education to be polarized, thus reducing social mobility. The disadvantageous status of low-income families will be solidified and even inherited from generation to generation.

Samuelson, the Nobel Prize winner in economics, boasted himself and was recognized as the most loyal believer in comparative advantage theory. He once claimed that the theory was the only correct and important theory in social sciences. However, after observing the status quo of globalization and its international and domestic influence, he somehow changed his views, believing that countries do not necessarily benefit from trade equally, and reluctantly admitted that the globalization winners within a country will not automatically make necessary compensations to the losers. The American workers whose jobs have been replaced by Chinese competitors will undoubtedly bear the cost of globalization.[15]

The traditional concept denies that economic growth can benefit all citizens through the "trickle-down effect," so economists finally realize that globalization will not automatically benefit all the people. This is no doubt a progress in theory. However, many people, especially politicians, have not stopped there.

In fact, as early as before Smith and even before the physiocrats, mercantilism and its policy propositions in the infant form of modern economics (and even trade theory) reflected the political and policy stances that trade may change the interest pattern. Since then, free trade advocated by Smith, the comparative advantage theory created by Ricardo, and even the later dominant trade theory and its supplementary research have repeated the interacting process of the action and reaction of politics and economy (or economics). Therefore, based on the discussion in the last section about the evolution of globalization, understanding changes in industrial and social structures in developed countries and how they affect economic and social policies and even the political climate will help us make a more precise judgment on the possible prospects of globalization.

American politicians and political scientists reviewed the changes in the policy-making factors of the US government, proving that US society has changed in favor of the rich rather than the poor or the middle class in the past 20–30 years. For example, Gilens and Page used econometric methods to analyze 1,779 policies affecting income between 1981 and 2002 and found that economic elites and interest groups representing business circles have substantial impacts on US government policy, while average voters and mass groups have little influence.[16]

Many observers believe that it is no longer appropriate to consider which country will benefit from globalization but that multinational companies with strong negotiating power and policy influence will definitely benefit from globalization. The winner is only 1% among the developed countries, while the ordinary middle-income and low-income groups are pushed to be marginalized.[17]

Perhaps, when an anti-globalization movement broke out in Seattle for the first time in a radical way in 1999, it mainly reflected the emotions, thoughts, and actions of social activists and their sympathizers in some developing countries. The governments of major European countries and the US had not yet realized its seriousness, so it had not become mainstream to utilize it politically. However, under the Western representative democratic system, winning votes is a matter of great concern for politicians in the final analysis. Therefore, policies have to respond appropriately to the status quo of the ever-widening domestic income gap.

For example, it is a longstanding policy tradition for the American government to stimulate consumption by expanding credit to alleviate the deep anxiety of the middle class and low-income people, but it often results in excessive financial development, leading to the mismatch of material capital and human capital.[18] Moreover, under the banner of the "American Dream" of "adequate housing for everyone" and with the help of the technical means of financial derivatives, the United States has set off a real estate craze backed by subprime loans, relying on the government's credit endorsement and loose financial supervision. A large number of ordinary families stuck in long stagnation with low income levels have also applied for mortgage loans.

The demand, not driven by the real paying ability but fueled by subprime loans, inevitably led to a large-scale and wide-ranging bubble until the subprime crisis broke out in the United States in 2007, further evolving into a global financial crisis. Tens of thousands of middle-class and low-income families in the United States, where the social security system is relatively unsound, and in Europe, emerging economies, and many developing countries, have thus fallen into deep disasters.

Countries have adopted a variety of macroeconomic measures to respond to the financial crisis, so slow and sluggish recovery can be seen in the United

States and major economies in Europe. However, while the world economy is overall in a new mediocrity, the stagnant income growth in ordinary households has not been resolved. For example, the economic growth rate and employment recovery in the United States were considered to be strong among developed countries when in December 2015 it carried out the first interest rate hike in more than nine years, and it gradually reduced the balance sheet and ended the quantitative easing policy in 2018. However, the issues of industrial structure and income distribution that existed before the crisis and became the trigger of the crisis have not been resolved.

For example, the unemployment rate in the United States has dropped to a low level in recent years, seeming to have got rid of the curse of "no-employment recovery" that has repeatedly occurred since the early 1990s. During Trump's one-term administration, unemployment fell to a low level not seen in many years. However, it is found from observing the labor participation rate—another important indicator of the labor market—that the situation is not as optimistic as shown in the decline of the unemployment rate. As of 2016, the labor participation rate of the working-age population above 16 in the United States was still 3 percentage points lower than that before the crisis broke out in 2007.[19]

According to the analysis of American scholars, the situation is not caused by the supply-side labor factor but by demand-side factors such as the long-term loss of manufacturing jobs and the reduction of demand for low-end and middle-end skills caused by technological changes.[20] This means that although the overall economy has recovered, issues such as the hollowing-out of some industries, the polarization of the labor market and human capital have not been resolved, so the demand for low-end and middle-end labor is not strong enough, and structural unemployment continues, enabling some workers to withdraw from the labor market and generating the so-called "frustrated worker effect."

In fact, based on the results of many empirical studies, we can even perceive such "frustration" literally. One can not only see from statistics that the wages of ordinary workers have remained unchanged for decades, so poverty has proliferated in a wealthy country such as the United States, but it has also found a declining level of human development. Angus Deaton, the Nobel Prize winner in economics, best described suicide and other "self-destructive" behaviors as "deaths of despair."[21]

This statement revealed the deep contradictions in American society and summarized the logical relationship among many phenomena. For example, ordinary workers who were influenced by the previous generation and did not receive a college education are most vulnerable to the impact of the labor market, which is followed by long-term unemployment and the accompanying frustration. Furthermore, the lack of a social guarantee mechanism results in excessive medical costs. When such people cannot afford medical treatment, they may resort to drug abuse, alcohol abuse, or opioid painkillers until they lose the ability to work and are forced to withdraw from the labor market.

In contrast to this group of populations, the rich are not benevolent. Capital owners make lots of money from globalization, but it is not shared with ordinary workers through labor markets or redistribution policies. In contrast, rich and large enterprises, with their strong market monopoly position and political lobbying ability, further grab social wealth and income by influencing economic and social policies. Researchers have found that in many developed countries such as the United States, there has been a trend of growing income inequality that was previously considered a middle-income trap phenomenon in Latin America, and it has even reversed the relatively equal pattern of income distribution and wealth distribution in the past. Economists call the trend the "reverse catching up" of income inequality.[22]

The situation in the United States can be seen as a microcosm of many other developed countries. Weak demand continues to suppress the bargaining position of ordinary workers in the labor market, resulting in no significant improvement in wages and income. The influx of immigrants has created competitive pressure and a sense of relative deprivation, further deteriorating the situation. Obviously, the lack of jobs is not only shown as insufficient income but also deeply felt by the people as being losers in globalization and related policies. Different from ordinary families, the elite class can take advantage of its favorable bargaining position to protect their interests by influencing policy-making, and they will definitely express their discontent in a certain way.

Generally, under the Western political system, the public and society can express their discontent mainly through three institutionalized or non-institutionalized approaches, namely vote, appeal, and exit.[23] From the perspective of political economics, whether in office or in opposition, politicians always have to fully weigh the political gains and political costs of the policies they advocate and implement to maximize the net gains; that is, to maximize the opportunities and stay in office for as long as possible. Therefore, they cannot ignore people's wishes for a long time.

However, either these politicians cannot see the truth of the problems they are facing, they cannot touch the vested interests to make adjustments, or they are eager to take office and cannot wait to solve the problem from the root. Therefore, whether from the left direction or the right direction, it is a cheap but tricky political strategy to sacrifice the banner of populism and blame the problem on globalization.

Tony Barber, a writer for the *Financial Times*, criticized Europe and the West as a whole for failing to cope with the cultural, economic, political, and technical challenges they are facing.[24] Borrowing a situation portrayed in the famous poem "Waiting for the Barbarians" by the Greek poet Constantine P. Cavafy, a country or organization often invents or exaggerates mysterious foreign threats to support its decaying power structures, hoping to divert the attention of critics and the public. We might also read the last sentence of the poem: "Now what's going to happen to us without barbarians? Those people were a kind of solution."[25] So it can be easily imagined and understood why so many diversified populist political forces have sprung up like mushrooms in Western countries (and even not limited to Western countries).

It is sometimes difficult to make a clear definition of populism and its policy tendency. If defined theoretically, populism is also a controversial concept. For example, some scholars tend to regard populism as an ideology, and its believers, on behalf of the people of a country, resist the behavior of the elite that ignores or even deprives ordinary people of their rights, values, sense of accomplishment, identity, and voice.[26] However, in reality, populism does not always appear as a commendatory term, but it is often used by politicians to criticize their opponents' biased and pompous policy propositions.

Based on certain definitions, popular history, and the current relevance of this term, we can regard populism as a political language system that is mainly used by politicians to preach specific political opinions in the form of responding to the demands of common people or in the political sphere. The latter does not necessarily represent the interests of common people but comes from the interests of politicians themselves or is captured by certain specific interest groups.

In summary, we are now facing the following challenge: Some politicians in Western countries promote the concept and policies of anti-globalization to win political support (votes) by utilizing the fact (or perception) that their middle class and/or vulnerable groups have not benefited from globalization. Although many elites in the public media, such as the political scientist Fukuyama and the economist Stiglitz, have realized that nationalism or populism is not an effective solution to current problems, it is inevitable that populist policies will emerge and even proliferate from the perspective of the intrinsic nature of the Western democratic political system pursuing votes rather than self-improvement.

As a beneficiary of globalization, why is China different?

It is generally believed that marked by the convening of the Third Plenary Session of the Eleventh Central Committee of the Communist Party of China at the end of 1978, China entered the era of reform and opening-up. We want to emphasize two layers of meanings here. First, reform and opening-up occur at the same time, and they are closely linked to and promote each other. Reform is a reform under the opening-up, and opening-up is promoted in the reform process. Therefore, domestic economic development and its integration into the global economy are intertwined. Second, opening-up is relatively independent and has definite contents. The opening-up in early days had experimental and regional characteristics, starting by establishing special economic zones and opening coastal cities and coastal provinces; coming to the 1990s, China made efforts to join the WTO and began to embrace economic globalization in an all-round way.

Both the successful experience of setting up special economic zones and expanding regional openings and the effect of introducing foreign investment and expanding foreign trade have reflected that rapid economic growth is consistent with deep openings. It can thus be concluded that China is no doubt a beneficiary of the round of economic globalization, and we never avoid talking about it.

This section will focus on theoretical and empirical perspectives to explain why China achieved unprecedented rapid growth with the help of reform and opening-up in the same period that they benefited from globalization. Furthermore, after the global financial crisis, the world economy entered the new mediocrity, but China still maintained medium-to-high growth in line with the new normal of its own economic development, and economic growth in general has the nature of being shared by the broad people.

In the context of the globalization climax, China is at the most appropriate development stage when its economy can fully benefit from economic globalization. From the perspective of the long history of economic development, a country's economic development usually typically or atypically goes through five stages or types: the Malthus poverty trap, Geertz involution, Lewis dual economic development, Lewis turning point, and Solow neoclassical growth.[27] The period for China to carry out reform and opening-up policy and integrate into economic globalization just coincided with the stage of its dual economic development (in the later stage, it crossed the Lewis turning point that ended the stage).

At this stage, the key development issue to be solved is to promote the industrialization process through capital accumulation and find a way out for the large number of agricultural surplus laborers in China, thereby turning surplus production factors into industrial comparative advantages. This type of economic development cannot be explained by neoclassical growth theory. Moreover, China does not regard neoliberal economic dogmas and the Washington Consensus preached by Western economists as the standard.

Facts have shown that the dual economic development in China coincided perfectly with this round of economic globalization in timing, and its economic development model was also fully connected with globalization opportunities. In advanced economies, such as the United States, Europe, Japan, and the Four Asian Tigers, labor force is a scarce factor relative to material capital. Rising wages and welfare costs have weakened the comparative advantages of manufacturing. In the context of globalization, the labor-intensive manufacturing sector has successively relocated overseas in a flying-geese model.

At that time, China (mainly the coastal areas) was at the most favorable development stage to undertake industrial transfer. Surplus labor in agriculture was absorbed into manufacturing and condensed into manufactured goods with its low cost and relatively high human capital. It did not depend on anyone's will and was shown as a comparative advantage and competitiveness in the global market. It was generally observed that goods from manufacturing dominated China's exports, which fully reflected China's comparative advantages at the specific development stage.

China's deepened opening-up is externally shown, as its trade dependence has increased significantly to a level rarely seen among large powers. As shown in Figure 12.1, the ratio of China's total trade in goods to GDP increased significantly from 18.9% in 1983 to over 40% in the early 1990s at current prices and as high as 64.0% at the peak in 2006. However, the total trade in goods and its ratio to GDP do not fully reflect the actual nature of China's foreign trade.

In Figure 12.2, we show two sets of data calculated at current prices. One is the total value of goods exported from statistics of customs, and the other is the net export volume of goods and services as part of GDP by the expenditure approach; that is, the net export's contribution to GDP. Although the two calculations are based on different prices—that is, the customs data are based on the CIF price, and data by the expenditure approach are based on the FOB price—the huge difference between the two data can still indicate that fast-growing and massive exports of goods and services have supported equally fast-growing and massive imports. The advanced technologies included in equipment and capital goods have contributed to continuously upgrading China's industrial structure. Obviously, trade expansion has promoted rapid economic growth from both the supply side and the demand side.

Although China's manufacturing sector has long been at the lower end of the value chain, the export structure dominated by labor-intensive manufactured goods has created a large amount of job opportunities in non-agricultural sectors and promoted labor reallocation, becoming the main demand factor for dual economic development in China, the driving force of industrial structure changes, and the source of productivity and hence

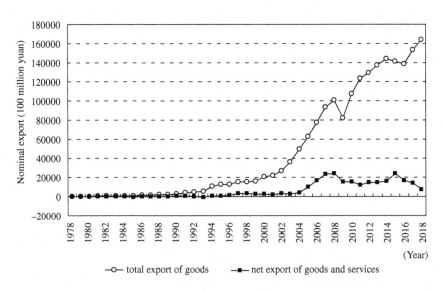

Figure 12.2 The total exports and contributions of imports and exports to GDP

economic growth. Meanwhile, a large number of foreign direct investments have also entered these manufacturing sectors, which not only reflects the contribution of opening-up to the rapid growth but also reveals the sharing nature of such export-oriented economic growth.

The author's estimates[28] indicate that during the period 1978–2014, the proportion of agricultural labor fell sharply from 70.5% to 19.1%. Almost all the secrets of China's rapid economic growth and benefits from economic globalization are implied in the drastic change of the employment structure that conforms to the iron law of economic development (i.e., the declining share of agriculture).

From the analysis of the changes in employment structure in the United States, Spence and Hlatshwayo concluded that "the emigration of industries to other countries destroyed the American economy."[29] Correspondingly, from the changes in the employment structure in China, we can understand how China's economy as a whole, as well as urban and rural workers and residents from the individual level, benefited from globalization.

China's working-age population aged 15–59 was in a continuously growing state until 2010, constructing and strengthening the favorable demographic characteristic of fewer elderly people and a larger labor force and forming a potential demographic dividend. The key to cashing in the demographic dividend was that labor-intensive industries expanded rapidly by absorbing a large number of transferred laborers, and their goods occupied a huge share in the international market. Here, we adopt a classification method similar to that of Spence. Based on the data of three economic censuses in 2004, 2008, and 2013 in China, we consider statistics of employment in non-agricultural industries according to legal entities and in terms of tradable sectors and non-tradable sectors to observe their growth scale and structural changes (Figure 12.3).

As seen in Figure 12.3, in the period covered by the data, non-agricultural employment in China (including urban and rural areas) grew very fast, with an average annual growth rate of 5.9% from 2004 to 2013, reaching a total of 352.13 million in 2013; meanwhile, there was a relatively balanced growth rate of employment in the tradable sector and the non-tradable sector. During the same period, the former achieved an average annual growth rate of 6.9%, and the latter 4.7%.

In fact, the employment data in legal entities here are far from adequately reflecting the actual growth of non-agricultural employment. In the text below, we can see the difference by comparing urban employment in different statistical criteria; that is, actual employment and its growth are significantly higher than what is shown in Figure 12.3.

Employment in units is used as one criterion for the annual statistics of urban employment, including corporations and industrial establishments, so the number of employees by this criterion will inevitably be greater than that of the above corporations. According to the data obtained by the "statistical report system of basic units," a total of 182.78 million people were employed

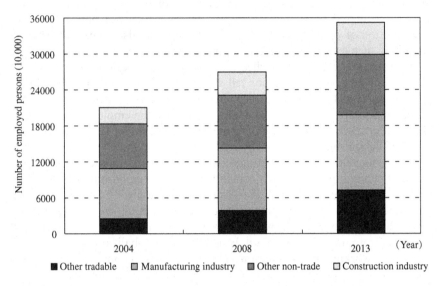

Figure 12.3 Employment growth and structure in non-agricultural entities

in urban units in 2014. Moreover, the number of people employed in units did not include private enterprises and individual industrial and commercial operators, so once these two types of employment were included in the statistics, the amount of urban employment would increase to 348.61 million.

In addition, urban units hire a large number of temporary workers and contractors, but these people are often not reflected in the report as employees, so these workers are missing in the statistics. Therefore, once a survey was conducted based on urban households and in accordance with the criteria recommended by the International Labour Organization, the total amount of actual urban employment will be as high as 393.1 million. The difference with the number of employees in units can be regarded as the number of informally employed workers.

This figure omitted many rural migrant workers who had been employed stably in cities. According to calculations, in addition to the total number of urban employment in the current statistics, approximately 47.1 million rural migrant workers were not included in the employment statistics. In other words, if all rural migrant workers who had been stably employed in urban areas were included in the urban employment statistics, the actual number of urban employment in 2014 could reach 440.2 million.[30]

In addition, we can also take rural migrant workers as representatives of informal employment in urban areas to observe the departmental structure in their employment. In 2015, there were a total of 277. 47 million rural migrant workers, of which 168.84 million had been away from their townships (most went to cities and towns at all levels) for six months or more, accounting for

38.4% of all urban employment. Another 108.63 million were engaged in non-agricultural industries in their townships.[31] In the same year, the proportion of rural migrant workers employed in the secondary industry was 55.1%, of which the proportion in the manufacturing sector (tradable sector) was 31.1%, the proportion in the construction sector (non-tradable sector) was 21.1%, the proportion in the tertiary industry (mostly in non-tradable sectors) was 44.5%, and the proportion in the primary industry was only 0.4%. Compared with the employment structure in corporations and even in all units, the construction sector saw a greater proportion of rural migrant workers. It can also be said that there is a more evident informal nature for the employment of rural migrant workers and employment in the construction sector.[32]

Under the conditions of marketization of resource allocation and economic globalization, the redistribution of the Chinese labor force provides the necessary conditions for high-speed economic growth, such as a sufficient supply of labor force and human capital, high return on capital, and productivity improvement characterized by the efficiency of resource redistribution, and turns the demographic dividend into a miracle of economic growth. However, when we draw the conclusion that China is the beneficiary of globalization, we should not only look at the share of its export products and the scale of foreign capital introduction but judge it according to the degree to which urban and rural residents share the fruits of reform, opening-up, and development.

Challenges and strategic choices in the context of deglobalization

Whether from the logic of political economics or from long-term historical observations, it is realized that there will be long-run left–right cyclical changes in economic and globalization policies in European countries, the US, and even Latin American countries, which are determined by the relationship between the Western representative democratic system and economic policy. Obviously, the policy orientation in Western countries will divert to a direction not conducive to globalization, at least for a fairly long period of time.

A direct impact of backlash against economic globalization on China was seen as the United States began to increase tariffs on goods imported from China in accordance with Section 301 on March 22, 2018, and continued to escalate in the following year. In particular, despite multiple rounds of high-level negotiations, the Trump administration went its own way and increased the tariffs on goods valued at US$200 billion to 25%.

Under such an unfavorable trend of globalization, the policy of minding one's own business may prevail in some countries. However, for the purpose of maintaining economic development, China should avoid being dragged down by deglobalization to accomplish the goal of achieving moderate prosperity in all respects and building a modern China as scheduled, and it should

292 *The new scientific and technological revolution*

not adopt policies decoupled from the global economy. The correct choice is to lead future globalization and make it benefit developing countries with its position as the world's second largest economy, the largest trading country in goods, and the country's crucial role in the world economy with its largest external dependence among the major countries, as well as its ever-increasing voice in global governance.

First, according to the logic of the political economy of globalization, while clearly recognizing the possibility of retrogression of globalization, China should make full use of its own advantages of the political system, not dwell on the gains and losses of a temporary event or one city and one place, maintain strategic strength in policy selection and formulation, seize the opportunity, maintain appropriate efforts, and avoid blindly "turning left to right" with other major countries.

Neither international trade nor economic globalization is a zero-sum game, so trade protectionism and deglobalization policies under the influence of nationalism and populist politics will eventually cause a net loss of global welfare and harm all participating parties. In the face of US-initiated and escalating trade frictions, it is certainly not the common practice to give up countermeasures and wait to die in the event of a trade war provoked by the other party, let alone China being a major developing country. In other words, China will make even more contributions to the world economy and economic globalization. China relies on sticking to and expanding reform and opening-up to uphold global rules and order and stabilize the world economy. China understands from the past 40 years of experience that reform and opening-up will bring real benefits and even immediate dividends, that is, to help increase the potential growth rate. External pressure will not weaken, which will only enhance our sense of urgency for further reform and opening-up.

In fact, no country will truly benefit from the trend of deglobalization and any related strategies, but it takes different times for various countries to realize this. In this period of "trial and error" there is still a window of opportunity for cooperation, and each participant will follow the "Tiebout effect" to seize advantages and avoid harm. This effect means that improving the macro policy environment for foreign cooperation will satisfy potential collaborators good at "voting with their feet" to create a microclimate for globalization.[33] Therefore, if we have a higher strategic vision, stay firm, treat each other kindly, even if we unilaterally create better economic cooperation conditions, we can still make China continue to benefit from economic globalization when it is at a low ebb.

Second, China should take advantage of its rising status in the world economy, actively participate in the reform of world economic and trade rules, improve its voice in global governance, and adjust the direction and rules of globalization in accordance with the principle of benefiting developing countries, especially emerging economies, to share rights and interests and seize new opportunities in the global market.

A concrete measure of deglobalization is that most Western countries represented by the United States have reflected on or even reselected the integration mechanisms that they have already been involved in or are planning to renegotiate the signed or even implemented agreements and to reform the WTO rules. To be honest, such reselection, renegotiation and reform aim to further prioritize the interests of developed countries. China, emerging economies, and other developing countries can also take the opportunity to improve their own voices in global economic governance and strive for reasonable rights and interests.

In addition, by observing Trump's policies, it may happen that Western countries suppress the development of globalization from the political and policy perspective to further prioritize the interests of capital owners, but there may be partially or to a certain extent another possibility, that is, to respond to the voices of low-income and medium-income groups in industrialized countries. The new globalization framework, such as the settlement of trade disputes, the renegotiation of trade agreements, and WTO reforms, will inhibit the vested interests of multinational corporations and pay attention to the benefits of ordinary workers and consumers, thus somehow reducing the excessive domestic income gap and promoting the consumption power of low-income and middle-income families.

In this way, on the one hand, the intensity of trade disputes will be alleviated; on the other hand, new demand opportunities will be provided. China and emerging market economies can gain new trade and investment opportunities if they seize the business opportunities corresponding to their comparative advantages.

Third, China should promote the internal and external linkages of its economy, create a new pattern of opening-up, and create new growth points (or tipping points) for economic globalization conducive to the joint contribution and shared benefits and mutual benefit of all countries. Alex MacGillivray listed four landmark events as the tipping points of globalization that led to the earth's dramatic shrinking: the Iberian Peninsula carved up the world from 1490 to 1500, Great Britain's international commanding heights from 1880 to 1890, the man-made satellite world from 1955 to 1965, and the global supply chain from 1995 to 2005.[34] He also predicted that the next tipping point should be the so-called "thermoglobalization"; that is, to carry out extensive and worldwide cooperation focusing on global climate change to initiate a new wave of globalization.[35]

China's Belt and Road Initiative to the world borrows the historical symbol of the ancient land and maritime silk roads to develop economic partnerships with countries along the route and create a community of politically mutual trust, economic integration, and cultural inclusiveness. It demonstrates the essential meaning of globalization and focuses on constructing a new global governance framework, which is expected to become the tipping point for a new round of globalization.

This initiative focuses on the internal and external linkages of China's economic development, promotes real economy and production capacity cooperation through worldwide infrastructure construction, and develops investment and trade relations. The world economy has seen several dynamic industrial transfers of the flying-geese model based on comparative advantages. China's economic characteristics of a big power determine a domestic version of the flying-geese model first from coastal areas to the central and western regions and furthermore an international version through the Belt and Road construction.[36]

Since the global governance system has not changed fundamentally and the current pattern may exist for a long time, the Belt and Road Initiative and the accompanying Asian Infrastructure Investment Bank will make up for the interests of emerging economies and other developing countries, which are ignored under the current globalization pattern. To convince the participating parties that it is more concerned about the common interest of all countries than the Western-dominated globalization and convince the Western powers that it is a supplement to the existing rules rather than a challenge, it is necessary to make an overall mechanism design with clear expectations from the strategic level to the pragmatic process, which combines short-term gains with long-term results and closely connects the implementation processes to ensure a smooth implementation.

Fourth, China should manage its own affairs well and firmly advance economic system reform. The 40 years of reform and opening-up have convinced the Chinese people for whom reform and opening-up have brought real benefits and even immediate dividends, which has been better understood by policy-makers. For example, the central government has carried out streamlined administration and power delegation, improving regulation and upgrading services and the business system, showing its confidence in the positive effects of economic growth. On the other hand, policymakers have also recognized that the stimulus policy shows obviously weakened effects. Therefore, it is more urgent to launch structural reforms when the escalating trade war is expected to impact the growth rate. For example, various reform measures have been intensively deployed and actively promoted recently, and the reform measures are more targeted (to improve the potential growth rate). Studies show that the demographic dividend has disappeared faster since 2010, and growth factors such as labor supply, human capital improvement, returns on capital, and labor reallocation efficiency have all tended to weaken. Therefore, China's economic deceleration is the decline in the potential growth rate out of supply-side factors. The government has repeatedly stressed not adopting a deluge of strong stimulus measures since it knows that the actual growth rate should not exceed the potential growth rate; the government actively promotes structural reforms on the supply side, intending to increase the potential growth rate from the supply of production factors and productivity improvement.

In the face of the unilateral actions of the United States, China has taken the fundamental strategy of expanding its opening-up to oppose and resist various forms of protectionist measures. Although globalization encounters headwinds, the world economic pattern and situation are still in our favor. For example, during the period 1990–2017, the share of the US in the global economy fell from 23.9% to 21.6%, while the share of developing countries in the world's GDP increased from 22.0% to 35.3%; the share of US manufacturing fell further from 15.9% to 11.6%. In 2017, the share of China was still as high as 29.3%. Obviously, China should be confident enough with practical plans to strengthen its close ties with the world economy instead of regressing to "inward" development or accepting "decoupling."

Finally, China should carry out the new development concept so that participating in economic globalization can promote innovation and development to the maximum, and shared development will benefit all Chinese people. Catch-up economic growth in this period has demonstrated the concept of sharing, so China can make full use of the opportunities of globalization during the reform and opening-up and greatly enhance its national strength while benefiting urban and rural residents.

As the world economy has entered a new mediocrity and may even show a trend of deglobalization, China's economic development has also crossed the Lewis turning point. As the demographic dividend has disappeared, the comparative advantage of labor-intensive industry has significantly weakened, and it has entered a new normal characterized by the slowing growth rate, the change of growth momentum and the transformation of growth models. At the development stage, economic growth will inevitably be accompanied by the innovation of the microcosmic body and the upgrading of the industrial structure to be driven from the factor input to the total factor productivity.

In a mature country of the market economy, the survival of the fittest can be accomplished through competition among enterprises, achieving the overall goal of increasing total factor productivity. At the current stage of development, there will be fewer opportunities for large-scale efficiency improvement, such as the reallocation of labor resources, and improving productivity is increasingly dependent on "creative destruction." However, different from other production factors, people as the carrier of the labor factor should both be protected by social policies and share the results of productivity improvement. Lessons from the United States have also shown that even though ordinary workers fully participate in economic globalization, the national economy develops, and the enterprise as a whole becomes competitive, workers will become "losers" in innovation once the labor market system and other social security mechanisms are not sound. Therefore, it cannot be called shared development.

Therefore, based on people-centered development thinking, it is necessary to strengthen the government's redistribution while enhancing competition, with social policies as the guarantee, so that ordinary workers and low-income and middle-income families can keep up with the pace of innovation and development and become the winner of a new round of globalization. Then, China will achieve moderate prosperity in all respects shared by all people.

Conclusion

Regarding the political turning in Latin American countries, former Chilean President Miguel Juan Sebastián Piñera Echenique once said, "When times are good, countries turn to the left, and when times are bad, they turn to the right." Obviously, no country is destined to turn in a certain direction. Ruchir Sharma, a best-selling writer with a background in investment banking, commented based on his own research: "the political rhythms of countries follow a cycle that mimics the circle of life: crisis gives birth to reform, which triggers a boom, which inspires complacency, which kills reforms and leads to a new crisis."[37]

Dickens said, "It was the best of times, it was the worst of times." There are different criteria to judge whether a certain historical moment is good or bad. Moreover, since the people in power are dominated by extreme political sentiment, without a peaceful mind or balance in policy implementation, it is actually difficult to advance reform in reality even though they intend to do so. For example, in Europe, since reform is aimed at increasing the flexibility of the labor market, it will make some workers lose jobs; how can it be imagined that such reform will be supported by them?

In the final analysis, combining Latin American countries with Western countries to observe whether the political situation is left or right, retrogression or reform, which is guided by public opinion or votes, in fact, is broadly consistent with the definition of populism. The key point is whether national politics make progress in every cycle or repeat the impossible mission of Sisyphus.

Economic globalization is indeed a "double-edged sword" to be governed with appropriate concepts and effective mechanisms. Promoting the smooth development of free trade and economic globalization should be guided by a correct and widely recognized principle of shared interests and the greater good from an international perspective, and from a domestic perspective, it is necessary to have more inclusive economic and social policies. For such public goods as global governance and domestic redistribution policies, ancient Chinese philosophy emphasized that "the country does not benefit from profit, but benefits from justice." With the emergence of trade wars and harming others but not benefiting themselves, countries, especially those that provoke trade wars, should reflect on their own understanding of globalization and realize the advantages and avoid disadvantages in irreversible globalization with more inclusive development ideas and domestic policies.

Whether from the perspective of summarizing successful experience or from the perspective of learning from failures, the experience of the past decades has shown that to make globalization equally beneficial to all countries and all residents of a country, people should not only fully seize the opportunity of globalization to make a cake big but also manage globalization and distribute cakes reasonably among countries. China was a participant in the last round of economic globalization, but it was not the rule-maker. In the anticipated new wave of globalization, China should and will definitely play a more important leading role and at the same time become a promoter and rule-maker.

The socialist democratic system with Chinese characteristics has laid a political guarantee for responding to the new trend of globalization, and the successful practice of reform and opening-up has also provided an empirical basis for understanding, adapting to, and leading a new round of globalization. China's rising global economic status and governance discourse will not become a capital of arrogance or an excuse to stand still but will be a cornerstone of a stronger sense of international responsibility, a broader global vision, and a higher-level response strategy. While promoting globalization, we will substantially advance domestic structural reforms on the supply side and effectively combine productivity improvement with strengthening social protection so that future globalization itself and China's practice of participating in globalization are more in line with the requirements of inclusiveness and sustainability.

Notes

1 Joseph E. Stiglitz, *Globalization and Its Discontents*, New York and London: W. W. Norton & Company, 2003; Joseph E. Stiglitz, *Globalization and Its New Discontents*, 2016, www.straitstimes.com/opinion/globalisation-and-its-new-discontents.

2 Alex MacGillivray, *A Brief History of Globalization: The Untold Story of Our Incredible Shrinking Planet*, London: Robinson, 2006, pp. 16–17.

3 Joseph Stiglitz, *Making Globalization Work*, London: Penguin Books, 2006, p. 4.

4 Alex MacGillivray, *A Brief History of Globalization: The Untold Story of Our Incredible Shrinking Planet*, London: Robinson, 2006, p. 5.

5 Manfred Steger, Globalization: *A Very Short Introduction*, New York: Oxford University Press, 2003, p. 13.

6 Similar changes in nature can be found in capital flow. The traditional "dual gap model" can no longer convincingly explain the net capital outflows from emerging economies to developed countries.

7 Aykut Kibritçiolu, *On the Smithian Origins of "New" Trade and Growth Theories*, Office of Research Working Paper, No. 2-100, 2002.

8 Paul M. Romer, *Which Parts of Globalization Matter for Catch-up Growth?* NBER Working Paper, No. 15755, 2010.

9 Paul Krugman, New Theories of Trade Among Industrial Countries, *The American Economic Review*, Vol. 73, No. 2, 1983, pp. 343–347.

10 Paul R. Krugman: *Pop Internationalism*, Beijing: China Renmin University Press/ Peking University Press, 2000.

11 Paul Krugman, New Theories of Trade Among Industrial Countries, *The American Economic Review*, Vol. 73, No. 2, 1983, pp. 343–347.

12 Michael Spence and Sandile Hlatshwayo, *The Evolving Structure of the American Economy and the Employment Challenge*, Working Paper, Maurice R. Greenberg Center for Geoeconomic Studies, Council on Foreign Relations, March 2011.
13 David H. Autor, Lawrence F. Katz, and Melissa S. Kearney, *The Polarization of the U.S. Labor Market*, NBER Working Paper, No. 11986, 2006.
14 Paul Krugman, *The Conscience of a Liberal*, Beijing: China CITIC Press, 2008.
15 Paul Samuelson, Where Ricardo and Mill Rebut and Confirm Arguments of Mainstream Economists Supporting Globalization, *Journal of Economic Perspectives*, Vol. 18, No. 3, 2004, pp. 135–146.
16 Martin Gilens and Benjamin I. Page, Testing Theories of American Politics: Elites, Interest Groups, and Average Citizens, *Perspectives on Politics*, Vol. 12, No. 3, 2014, pp. 564–581.
17 For example, see Joseph E. Stiglitz, *Globalization and Its Discontents*, New York and London: W.W. Norton & Company, 2003; Joseph E. Stiglitz, *Globalization and Its New Discontents*, 2016, www.straitstimes.com/opinion/globalization-and-its-new-discontents.
18 See Raghuram Rajan, *Fault Lines: How Hidden Fractures Still Threaten the World Economy*, translated by Liu Nian et al., Beijing: China CITIC Press, 2011.
19 Jason Furman, The Truth about American Unemployment: How To Grow the Country's Labor Market, *Foreign Affairs*, Vol. 95, No. 4, 2016, pp. 127–138.
20 Jason Furman, The Truth about American Unemployment: How To Grow the Country's Labor Market, *Foreign Affairs*, Vol. 95, No. 4, 2016, pp. 127–138.
21 For example, see Angus Deaton, *Globalization and Health in America*, January 14, 2018, based on remarks during a panel discussion at the IMF conference on Meeting Globalization's Challenges (October 2017), www.princeton.edu/~deaton/downloads/Globalization-and-health-in-America_IMF-remarks.pdf.
22 Jose Gabriel Palma, *Do Nations Just Get the Inequality They Deserve? The "Palma Ratio" Re-examined*, Cambridge Working Paper Economics, No. 1627, May 2016.
23 For example, see Albert O. Hirschman, *Exit, Voice, and Loyalty: Responses to Decline in Firms, Organizations, and States*, Cambridge, MA: Harvard University Press, 1970; Charles M. Tiebout, A Pure Theory of Local Expenditures, *The Journal of Political Economy*, Vol. 64, No. 5, 1956, pp. 416–424.
24 Tony Barber, Europe's Decline is a Global Concern, *Financial Times*, December 22, 2015.
25 C. P. Cavafy, Waiting for the Barbarians, in George Savidis (ed.) *Collected Poems*, translated by Edmund Keeley and Philip Sherrard (revised edition), Princeton: Princeton University Press, 1992.
26 Daniele Albertazzi and Duncan McDonnell, Introduction: The Sceptre and the Spectre, in Daniele Albertazzi and Duncan McDonnell (eds.), *Twenty First Century Populism: The Spectre of Western European Democracy*, London: Palgrave Macmillan, 2008, p. 3.
27 Cai Fang, The Making of Dual Economy as a Stage of Economic Development, *Economic Research Journal*, Vol. 7, 2015.
28 Cai Fang, Guo Zhenwei, and Wang Meiyan, New Urbanization as a Driver of China's Growth, in Song Ligang, Ross Garnaut, Cai Fang, and Lauren Johnston (eds.), *China's New Sources of Economic Growth, Vol. 1: Reform, Resources, and Climate Changes*, Canberra and Beijing: ANU Press and Social Sciences Academic Press, 2016, p. 53.

29 Michael Spence and Sandile Hlatshwayo, *The Evolving Structure of the American Economy and the Employment Challenge*, Working Paper, Maurice R. Greenberg Center for Geoeconomic Studies, Council on Foreign Relations, March 2011.

30 See Cai Fang, Guo Zhenwei, and Wang Meiyan, New Urbanization as a Driver of China's Growth, in Song Ligang, Ross Garnaut, Cai Fang, and Lauren Johnston (eds.) *China's New Sources of Economic Growth, Vol. 1: Reform, Resources, and Climate Changer*, Canberra and Beijing: ANU Press and Social Sciences Academic Press, 2016; National Bureau of Statistics, *China Statistics Yearbook 2015*, Beijing: China Statistics Press, 2015.

31 See National Bureau of Statistics, *The National Report on Migrant Worker Monitoring and Survey 2015*, 2016, www.stats.gov.cn.

32 Subsequently, the employment structure of migrant laborers has changed greatly. As of 2018, the employment proportions in manufacturing and construction both fell, while the employment proportion in service increased greatly, further improving the employment proportion in all towns and cities.

33 Charles M. Tiebout, A Pure Theory of Local Expenditures, *The Journal of Political Economy*, Vol. 64, No. 5, 1956, pp. 416–424.

34 Alex MacGillivray, *A Brief History of Globalization: The Untold Story of Our Incredible Shrinking Planet*, London: Robinson, pp. 19–21.

35 We cannot judge whether cooperation on climate change will become a tipping point for a new round of globalization. However, cooperation on the global issue undoubtedly has the effect of maintaining and advancing globalization. On September 3, 2016, the Standing Committee of the National People's Congress approved the Paris Agreement in Beijing, which will help shape the post-2020 global governance pattern on climate. On the same day, Chinese President Xi Jinping held a deposit of instruments of joining the Paris Agreement with the US President Barack Obama and UN Secretary-General Ban Ki-moon in Hangzhou. After Trump took office and withdrew from the Agreement, China has continued to lead and promote the Agreement.

36 See Cai Fang, *Demystifying China's Economy Development*, Beijing and Berlin: China Social Sciences Press and Springer-Verlag, 2015, Chapter 4.

37 Ruchir Sharma, Thanks to Economic Turmoil, Left-wing Latin American Countries Are Turning Right, *Time*, Vol. 187, No. 23, 2016.

13 Supply of global public goods and China's solutions

Introduction

The topics discussed here can be summarized as the "Kindleberger trap" and the "Easterly tragedy." As well-known international development economists, Kindleberger did not set any development-related traps, and Easterly did not create any development tragedies. The so-called Kindleberger trap, a concept reintroduced by the American think tank scholar Joseph Nye, refers to a situation of leadership vacuum in world governance when the big powers that were once world leaders decline, but emerging powers are unable or unwilling to provide necessary international public goods.[1]

Kindleberger first put forward this proposition, believing that the United States replaced the United Kingdom as the world's hegemon but failed to play the role of the United Kingdom in providing global public goods, thus causing the "disastrous decade" of the 1930s.[2] Gilpin also agreed with the argument, but he emphasized understanding the issue from a political perspective or from the perspective of the hegemon's interests.[3] Nye used the Kindleberger trap to illustrate the anxiety over China's rise and the US's decline and the possible "Thucydides trap," and further concern about the emerging power, China, which is unable or unwilling to sufficiently supply global public goods.

Regarding the contemporary version of the Kindleberger trap, there are two meanings in the opinions of Western think tank scholars, including Nye himself.

First, it is hoped to exclude the rising China from the option of being a supplier of global public goods. Whether it is out of prejudice or standpoint, they believe that China is changing or will change the current rules of the game, leading global governance in a direction inconsistent with the interests of the original hegemon. Generally, international political scientists tend to hold such an opinion, whether it is spoken or not.

Second, it is worried that China will become a pure free-rider in the supply of global public goods. They believed that China is a beneficiary of the existing global governance model, and the responsibility assumed (whether measured in currency or by the sacrificing of other interests) is extremely

DOI: 10.4324/9781003329305-16

asymmetrical with its gains, resulting in an insufficient supply of global public goods. Generally, these economists are prone to hold such viewpoints.

Just as the Thucydides trap provides a historical mirror and prompts to creatively handle relations with big powers, the Kindleberger trap also has reference value. However, apart from the inconsistency between its explanation of world economic growth and divergent economic hypotheses, the concept has flaws such as paradoxes, vagueness, and is full of traditional prejudices.[4]

First, how are global public goods defined? Obviously, the public goods provided by a country within its territory cannot be compared with the global public goods without a global government. Being a hegemon or a "stabilizer," since it should be the only one and is profit-driven, it cannot reflect the interests and demands of the majority of countries after all, let alone public goods.

Second, is there truly an era in history when a single country effectively provided global public goods? Empirical research requires a scientific methodology, rather than having preconceptions to subjectively and arbitrarily attribute the good side of the world to the availability of public goods, while the bad side of the world is attributed to the lack of public goods.

Finally, what is the problem in the contemporary world, what kind of public goods are truly needed and how are they provided? Since emerging market countries and developing countries have increasingly become the main contributors to global economic growth, the traditional model of global governance no longer works, which means that the supply of public goods is not in line with demands. It has become a realistic and urgent issue to reform the traditional supply model of global public goods.

In his keynote speech at the opening ceremony of the World Economic Forum Annual Meeting 2017, President Xi Jinping pointed out three critical issues in the economic sphere: (1) a lack of robust driving forces for global growth makes it difficult to sustain the steady growth of the global economy; (2) inadequate global economic governance makes it difficult to adapt to the new developments in the global economy; and (3) uneven global development makes it difficult to meet people's expectations for better lives.[5] Among the three issues facing the current global economy, the first two issues—growth issues and governance issues—are new challenges brought about by the changes in the world economic pattern in the post-financial crisis period. The last issue, i.e., development or poverty, is the oldest subject in global governance. It has a long history and can be used as a microcosm to help us understand the shortcomings in the supply model of past global public goods and to remind us of what kind of changes we should expect.

Moreover, the third issue is also closely related to the first two because it involves the fundamental idea of the development purpose. Therefore, let us first propose an alternative concept to the Kindleberger trap—the "Easterly tragedy." In his book, the former World Bank economist Easterly says that the poor of the world face two tragedies: The first tragedy is well known, i.e., hundreds of millions of people in the world live in poverty and urgently need development assistance. The second tragedy, as many people avoid talking about, is that over the past decades, developed countries have invested assistance in trillions of dollars but have achieved very little effect.[6]

In a more general sense, economic growth, economic globalization, and technical progress are no doubt considered to have an effect of making a bigger cake to promote development. However, the resulting development has not generated the expected trickle-down effect. Generally, we are far from finding the solution at the international and national levels about how to share the bigger cake equally among countries and within a country.

It was Easterly, a rebel of the traditional global governance institution, who dared to point out like a little child that the Emperor has nothing on, so we take such universal and stubborn world poverty under the traditional supply model of global public goods as a more targeted issue of global governance than the "Kindleberger trap," calling it the "Easterly tragedy."

President Xi Jinping quoted in his speech a sentence from Henry Dunant, founder of the International Red Cross, as saying, "The real enemies are not our neighbors, but hunger, poverty, ignorance, superstition and prejudice."[7] Obviously, the poverty of the poor and that of the governance model exist simultaneously, but the latter is shown as "ignorance, superstition and prejudice." Therefore, shifting from the "trap" proposition to the "tragedy" proposition can help us better answer the challenges facing the world economy and recognize the defects in the traditional global governance model, especially in the supply model of global public goods, thus pinpointing the reasons for problems in the world economy and finding effective solutions.

Development and sharing in China's 40 years of reform and opening-up have provided successful experience of how to make the cake bigger and divide it in the meanwhile. From 1978 to 2017, China's total GDP achieved an actual 34-fold increase, which was supported by a 17-fold increase in labor productivity. The per capita GDP achieved an actual 23-fold increase, and the actual disposable incomes of urban and rural residents increased by nearly 23 times. The two indicators synchronized on the whole, also demonstrating that in the history of human development, only China in the period of reform and opening-up has unprecedentedly improved people's living quality for the first time in the shortest time.

Confucius said, "at 40, I no longer suffered from doubt." It can be used as a positive answer to the "Kindleberger trap" and the "Easterly tragedy" to observe and analyze the development and sharing process of China's reform and opening-up from a global perspective, elevate the Chinese experience and story to Chinese wisdom at the theoretical level, and reveal the global significance of China's solution. This chapter intends to make a preliminary and perhaps superficial attempt at the goal.

What kind of global public goods?

The demand for global public goods and the global public goods provided by a single hegemonic country are meaningful only under the following conditions. First, globalization came into being. Although the time when globalization emerged can be traced infinitely, it is generally believed that at least in the 15th to 17th centuries, when European ships extensively appeared in the world waters and started the Great Geographical Discovery, globalization became a prevalent phenomenon. Second, the industrial revolution occurred. Since ancient times, many nations have expanded and even colonized other countries. Only in the era of a substantial increase in productivity did the universal overseas exploration, development, and expansion of colonial ruling begin to have a global nature. Third, a single country has the sole or dominant global influence in terms of hard power, such as economic aggregates and military power, as well as soft power, such as cultural influence and voice. Such influence promotes and intensifies each other with the hegemon status.

Obviously, the economic aggregate, per capita income, and geographical size cannot constitute the only criterion to see if a country has become a hegemon or has lost status. For example, by 1820, China's GDP had accounted for one-third of the world's total, and the Qing Empire had the most vast territory in Chinese history. However, in terms of productivity development, per capita income, and openness, China was obviously far from being a hegemon, and it has been further away since then.

In addition, the Ottoman Empire geographically spanned three continents: Asia, Europe, and Africa. It had the military strength of challenging Western European countries, and it was culturally influential in the Islamic and Christian worlds. However, judging from its economic scale and per capita income level, Turkey's GDP in 1820 was less than 1% of the world's total, and its per capita GDP was also lower than the world average. Therefore, it was not qualified to act as a hegemon, and it could even be regarded as a laggard in the world economy.

As the hometown of the Industrial Revolution, the United Kingdom has been the sole hegemon in the world at least since the mid-19th century in terms of the scope of colonial ruling in the world, the total GDP and the per capita level (Figure 13.1), especially in combination with its actual role in the world economy and politics.

Maddison's data show that the United States surpassed the United Kingdom in economic aggregates after 1870 (Figure 13.1a). Once per capita GDP is used to roughly indicate the country's affluence, innovation capability, and productivity level, we take it into account to make a judgment afterwards based on historical facts that the time for the United States to have the ability to replace Great Britain as the sole hegemon should be as late as the early 20th century (Figure 13.1b). Meanwhile, the British remained dominant at least until the end of World War I.

Kindleberger defines international public goods mainly based on the following aspects: safeguarding peace, maintaining an open trading system, and forming institutions and mechanisms for international macroeconomic management. He only discussed the latter two aspects. For example, to maintain an open trading system, he exemplified such public goods demands as freedom of navigating on the high seas, clearly defined property rights,

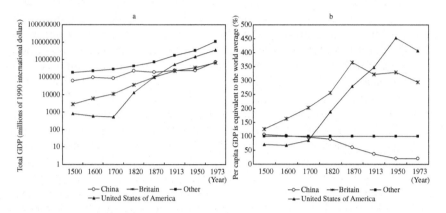

Figure 13.1 International comparison of aggregate economy and per capital income

international currencies, and fixed exchange rates. In terms of international macroeconomic policies, he summarized the discussions by economists and international political scientists, such as forming an institutional system similar to traffic rules at the supranational level, including principles, guidelines, and decision-making procedures with sufficient consensus. He did not touch the international public goods of safeguarding peace.[8]

As an economist, Kindleberger may be excused for emphasizing some issues while ignoring others for the purpose of highlighting subjects or deliberately exploiting strengths and avoiding weaknesses. However, it is an unimaginable omission that he did not touch on issues such as worldwide poverty and its governance. Obviously, Kindleberger's viewpoint was limited by the Cold War era, and he also excluded developing countries from the discussion.

This reminds us that we should truly be using a global perspective, including all regions of the world to understand the supply issue of so-called global public goods. Based on this understanding, the author will discuss the supply of international public goods in the following text according to the attention level of Kindleberger; that is, the slightly mentioned (peace issue) and the fully concerned (macroeconomic policy issue). We will take a very brief review of the world history to see what kind of global public goods and in what way the United Kingdom and the United States have respectively provided global governance and what effects have been produced. We will discuss the property issue, which was completely ignored by Kindleberger, in the next section.

If not just from the standpoint of Western countries, it should be noted that the hegemony of the United Kingdom and the United States has not made them truly perform their function as the guardian of peace, whether through colonial ruling or as the world's gendarmerie. Since the European anti-French Alliance defeated France in Waterloo and Napoleon was exiled for life on the island of St. Helena, the United Kingdom gradually gained the dominant status in the world with its powerful maritime military strength, expanding colonies, and the ability to transform new technologies into productivity.

However, if the leading role and deterrent force of Great Britain were truly conducive to peace, it can be said at best that there were fewer wars and conflicts within Europe than before. Meanwhile, European countries, including the United Kingdom, waged more wars aimed at ruling Asia, America, and Africa. Scholars summarized that approximately two-thirds of the larger wars that broke out from 1789 to 1917 occurred outside of Europe, including wars for national independence.[9] The most well-known wars in this regard are the two opium wars waged by Great Britain against China in 1840 and 1858 and the war to suppress the Indian national uprising in 1857.

Regarding the wars in Europe or the two world wars initiated from Europe, historians can make and have indeed made various counterfactuals.[10] Regardless of the alternative consequences derived from such analysis, the hegemony of the United Kingdom and the United States and the way of providing public goods to safeguard peace can fully deny the assumption that wars can be avoided fundamentally.

For example, World War I was a typical imperialist war that broke out when foreign powers contended for the Asian and African colonies and fought for the territory of small European countries, but diplomatic mediation such as secret agreements and covenants did not work. Before World War II, the United Kingdom followed the policy of appeasement, which was certainly related to its decline in international political, economic, and military power after World War I. Moreover, it viewed communism as the top threat, and it was an inevitable choice under its strong intention to restrain the rise of the Soviet Union. Therefore, whether in terms of the essence and supply of international public goods for safeguarding peace as expected by international political scientists or in terms of the actual role played by potential providers of such public goods, it cannot prove what the "Kindleberger trap" there is.

The world order after World War II has indeed been dominated by the unique hegemony of the United States. However, there is no doubt that whether there is war or peace in the name of the United Nations, it eventually reflects the ideology and national interests of the United States and its allies. Generally, the international public goods provided by the United States in this regard are to "safeguard" the world peace in the way of a long-term Cold War. In fact, the United States initiated the establishment of the North Atlantic Treaty Organization, thus triggering the establishment of the Warsaw Pact. Behind this pattern are inevitably the arms race, development of nuclear weapons, and competition for outer space. Meanwhile, devastating wars and suffering in some places are often seen.

The two most famous and largest battles during the Cold War—the Korean War and the Vietnam War—took three years and 20 years, respectively. Due to the nature of fighting for spheres of influence in the two camps, the United States did not stop the fighting but instead became the main warring party and even instigated Japan and Germany, defeated countries in World War II, to send troops overseas against the Constitution. These two wars has a huge cost in human life, economy and people's livelihoods, international relations, etc. How can we talk about international public goods?

Whether motivated by petroleum or in the name of anti-terrorism, the Gulf War, the Afghanistan War, and the Iraq War directly waged by the United States can all be defined as public hazards. Easterly said, "The new military intervention is roughly the same as that in the Cold War. The illusion of the new imperialist also makes no much difference from that of the colonist at the old era."[11]

Whether motivated by oil or in the name of anti-terrorism, the Gulf War, Afghanistan War, and Iraq War directly launched by the United States can all be defined as public hazards.

A voiceover in the Hollywood movie *War Machine* vividly reveals the dilemma facing the United States: "Ah, America. You beacon of composure and proportionate response. You bringer of calm and goodness to the world... What you do when the war you're fighting just can't possibly be won in any meaningful sense! Well obviously, you sack the guy not winning it, and you bring in some other guy. In 2009, that war was Afghanistan, and that other guy... was Glen."[12]

Such foreign policy and international strategy serving the defense interests of the hegemon also determine how the United Kingdom and the United States supply public goods to maintain a stable world's macroeconomics.[13] Actually, in the process of expanding overseas trade and advocating economic liberalism (by the UK) and implementing economic expansion (by the US) in the way of multinational corporations, the two countries have spared no effort to establish a series of global governance mechanisms aimed at maintaining a stable macroeconomy; for example, the United Kingdom promoted the establishment of the gold standard system and the fixed exchange rate system, while the United States took the lead in establishing and operating the Bretton Woods system to exercise the hegemony of the US dollar.

While promoting the interests of the two hegemons, these mechanisms have also played a role in stabilizing the world economic order to a certain extent. However, these facts do not support the hypothesis of the Kindleberger trap.

First, the previous model of a single hegemon dominating the supply of global public goods has failed to effectively maintain the stability of the world economy and national economies. For example, there is thus far no recognized theory or successful experience for the root causes of recurring national and global economic crises and the way to manage or even eradicate them, not to mention that there is a consensus to prevent the supply of global public goods from any single country.

The economic writer Lars Tvede summarized that since the first crisis in several countries under the House of Habsburg in 1557, there had been approximately 445 large economic crises as of 2001.[14] From the perspective of time distribution (Figure 13.2), since John Law put the concept of paper currency into practice in France in 1716 under the support of the Grand Duke

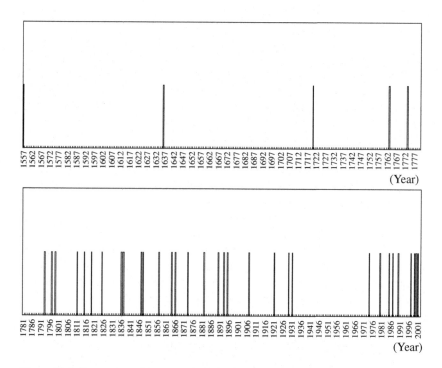

Figure 13.2 Frequency of large-scale financial crises in history

of Orleans, the economic crisis has become the normal, occurring more frequently. There is no relation with the hegemon about how many public goods are provided globally and how they are provided.

Moreover, the international financial crisis during the period 2007–2009 not shown in the figure originated from the providers of global public goods. The United States can hardly shirk its blame whether from the direct origin (subprime crisis) or from its deeper domestic economic and social contradictions (economic policy of populism).[15]

Second, the Bretton Woods system (the World Trade Organization, the International Monetary Fund, and the World Bank), known as the global economic public goods dominated by the United States, is itself the object of criticism by decision-makers and scholars in many countries for its strategic concept and operating model.

JosephStiglitz, the Nobel Prize winner in economics, used to be the chief economist of the World Bank. He called these institutions "globalized institutions" and deeply criticized them. On the one hand, they did not bring the promised benefits to all countries and all people, such as helping the poor eliminate poverty, advancing growth in developing countries, and promoting countries in the Soviet model to establish effective market mechanisms. On the other hand, the supply of public goods carried out by these institutions in essence used the money of taxpayers in various countries. Ministers and central bank governors made decisions under the leadership of a few developed countries or even a single hegemon. The resulting liberal economic models and policies may not necessarily be applicable to developing countries and countries in transition.[16] The criticism was once regarded as quite deviant, but in today's world political and economic environment, it has received wider recognition.

Third, if there was indeed a period in economic history when a hegemon (in terms of its economic size and influence) dominated the discourse of global governance, it is no longer true today. In other words, the era is gone when a single country provides global public goods on its own.

For example, no matter how dominant a hegemon is in forming the Bretton Woods system and how powerful it has been for a long time, institutions such as the International Monetary Fund, the World Bank, and the World Trade Organization, as well as the United Nations Security Council and various United Nations organizations, are improving their governance structures and management systems, gradually increasing the voice of emerging economies and getting rid of the intervention and interference of the US government. Furthermore, marked by the protest against the World Trade Organization Conference that broke out in Seattle in 1999, various international non-governmental organizations have begun to influence the supply of global public goods.

In addition, a large number of international institutions and mechanisms with competitive relations have come into being, and their roles have continued to expand. The Organisation for Economic Co-operation and Development, the European Union, the Group of Twenty, the Association of Southeast Asian Nations, the BRICS Cooperation Mechanism, regional development banks, and many regional agreements and mechanisms all provide global public goods, which naturally has greatly dispersed the power of a single country.

Finally, objectively, once a country's absolute dominant position in the total world economy changes, it will be difficult to reproduce the pattern in the future. Let us examine how the countries constituting the world's economic aggregates change. The World Bank classifies countries into different groups based on the total birth rate and the growth of the working-age population. The future economic growth trends in each group of countries can be predicted with a certain certainty based on the potential demographic dividend available to each country.[17]

Figure 13.3 shows the GDP volumes of the United States, China, post-demographic dividend countries excluding the United States, late demographic dividend countries excluding China, countries in the early demographic dividend stage, and other countries (mainly in the pre-demographic dividend stage), their status and trends in the world's total economy. It can be seen that the United States accounts for the highest share in the world's total economy,

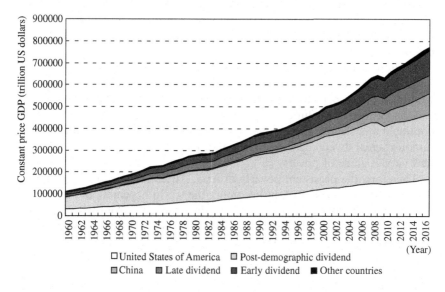

Figure 13.3 Distribution and trend of the aggregate world economy

being much higher than any other country, but it was in a continuous downward trend from 27.5% in 1960 to 21.8% in 2016. Moreover, as the demographic dividend disappears, China's potential growth rate will gradually decline as well.[18] In the future, the composition of world economic aggregates will become more polarized.

Poverty of the country and poverty of the governance model

Although wars, conflicts, terrorism, economic instability, underdevelopment, and poverty are mutually causal, the increasingly indisputable facts indicate that in the main areas of generally listed international public goods, the issue of poverty is of a deeper nature than peace and macroeconomics. Some scholars have tried to perform regression analysis of the occurrence of terrorist activities with factors such as per capita income, growth performance, demographic characteristics, inequality, global participation, degree of economic liberalization, social development, and international assistance, rejecting the hypothesis that an underdeveloped economy (or poverty) leads to terrorist activities.[19]

In fact, the relationship between terrorist activities, conflicts, and poverty is a big proposition with historical depth, rather than a conclusion that can be drawn at the microanalysis level by the regressing of the statistical relations among variables. Even former US presidents deeply caught in the plight had to admit, "extremely poor societies… provide optimal breeding grounds for disease, terrorism and conflict."[20] Even not from the perspective of the direct cause but from the perspective of providing "breeding grounds," we should also realize that global poverty governance is a more urgent and fundamental international public good than safeguarding peace and international macro-economic governance.

It should be made clear that before Great Britain became the world's hegemon, the entire world, including Great Britain and Europe, was in the Malthusian trap before the industrial revolution. Poverty was everywhere. It was the industrial revolution that enabled the United Kingdom, the European continent and the subsequent New World to develop quickly. Meanwhile, the famous "great divergence" occurred, and the developing countries fell into a new vicious circle of poverty.

Therefore, the persistent poverty in Asia, Africa and Latin America is the same as the history of Britain becoming the world hegemon and expanding colonies in the world. It is two sides of the same coin from the same mint. In other words, when Britain had a duty to help colonial countries and even other poor countries, its starting point and implementation must be compatible with its colonial rule because for rulers, the object of aid was "half-devil and half-child."[21]

If the UK-led supply of international public goods was thought to be lackluster in terms of its model and poverty reduction effect, the US-led supply of international public goods implemented in the Cold War pattern for a long time since the mid-20th century has indeed given the poverty issue in developing countries a higher priority. However, whether Truman Doctrine as a guide to the Cold War ideology, or the move of McNamara's "sword for plow" with the same ideology —from being the Secretary of Defense to being the President of the World Bank, ultimately will not make a real difference in reducing poverty.[22]

Easterly believes that the tragedy of failure in reducing global poverty is due to the wrong aid method with a long tradition adopted by the West. Below, we list some commonly observed methods and their errors.

First, regardless of the actual national conditions of recipient countries, the poverty reduction plan was devised by Western experts who do not know the actual national conditions of the aid recipients. The reason why the concept of national conditions is emphasized here is not only to question whether such assistance is truly needed by a particular country but also to point out that the reality in these countries determines that such a grand plan can rarely be implemented. The intention of donor countries to deliver what the poor truly need often fails.

However, the practice is still popular. For example, Professor Sachs, a famous American economist and the person in charge of international anti-poverty projects such as the United Nations Millennium Project, is one object of Easterly's criticism. In the book *The End of Poverty*, the former still follows and expands the "poverty trap" (also known as the "vicious circle of poverty") hypothesis of traditional development economics, trying to formulate and implement an all-encompassing plan for poor countries, regardless of whether such a comprehensive plan meets the specific national conditions of a particular recipient country.[23]

The plan, which is called a "big push" by Easterly, reminds people of the "big bang" reform plan that Professor Sachs once carried out in Latin America, Russia, and Central and Eastern Europe, also known as "shock therapy." Inspired by his wife, a pediatrician, Sachs liked to borrow medical terms and even methodology to solve economic transition and poverty issues. For example, he created the so-called "Clinical Economics" in leading the anti-poverty project, and on this basis, he created a prescription to cure persistent global poverty.

However, eliminating poverty is not to heal the wounded and save the dying in the medical sense, so it shall not rely too much on doctors. Moreover, even if we must use medical principles to explain the poverty problem, the efficacy ultimately depends on how the patient's body responds and adjusts, whether Hua Tuo is reincarnated or not. In fact, the prediction sworn by Sachs that "Our generation can eradicate extreme poverty" and the most eye-catching and expensive demonstration project in Africa presided over by him have not been proven to be effective but have instead aroused widespread suspicion and criticism.[24]

Second, perhaps after recognizing that assistance cannot replace recipient countries' efforts to enter the development track, there are institutional obstacles in poor countries that are inconsistent with donor countries' expectations; thus, institutions such as the International Monetary Fund promote so-called structural reforms. A typical practice is to impose conditions on the poverty alleviation loans and relief loans in the recipient countries, requiring the borrowing countries to carry out a package of policies designed by bank economists; that is, structural adjustment projects. Therefore, the goal of poverty alleviation and project implementation are combined with guiding the economy of recipient countries to embark on the neoliberal road based on the Washington Consensus.

The practice has been widely criticized in decades of implementation. It often results in infringing a country's economic sovereignty and bringing serious debt problems; implementation of privatization has made state-owned assets and resources flow into individuals, and public goals have been replaced by private interests; fiscal austerity is often carried out at the cost of social protection projects such as education and public health. Facts have shown that such structural adjustment is precisely why poverty continues to grow in developing countries.

Third, similar to the long-run cycle of whether to implement large-scale assistance or to impose structural adjustments, the question of whether assistance projects should be controlled by donor countries or by the national government or elites is also entangled in practice and has different understandings.[25] It seems that donor countries, international organizations, and non-governmental charity organizations all have forgotten that sustainable development is the fundamental way to eradicate poverty, and the main body of development is the people of the country, including workers, farmers, and entrepreneurs. The eager hope, strong motive, and entrepreneurship of the latter to eliminate poverty and embark on the track of development have been seriously ignored in aid plans and projects. Fundamentally, the arrogance of Kipling-style colonialists still dominates such actions.

When regarding poverty as a whole concept, we can indeed, like Professor Sachs, summarize several unanimous causes of poverty; for example, various institutional shortcomings inhibit business autonomy and labor enthusiasm and hinder the accumulation and configuration of production factors, especially human capital and material capital. Other reasons can be found in unfavorable resources and ecological conditions or geographic locations, as well as weak government governance capabilities.

On the other hand, just as Tolstoy once said, "every unhappy family is unhappy in its own way." For countries, regions, communities, families, and individuals, poverty is always a specific and individual case caused by unique factors or their combinations. Therefore, it is not realistic to rely on experts, project officials, and charity activists who have made achievements in the institutional and cultural environment thousands of miles away and who cannot be expected to identify, understand and solve special problems. It is not a public good to be a substitute for others, but it is easy to become a hegemonic act by pointing fingers.

It is the tens of thousands of people in poverty in a country who truly know what they need. Any development strategy or assistance project can only be transformed into actions and be expected to be successful upon their recognition and with their participation. Outsiders can at best provide alternative but not imposed options as a reference for specific needs, and the final effect can only be tested by local induced institutional changes and development performance.

In the final analysis, in the international action of eradicating global poverty, the traditional concepts and solutions that have always been followed believe that a master key (built in developed countries) can open tens of thousands of locks (in poor countries). It is this fundamental error in methodology that has made the Easterly tragedy continue to occur for decades and even hundreds of years.

The World Bank data show that the population defined as low-income and middle-income countries in 2013 accounted for 83.6% of the global population. Calculated at constant dollars in 2011, almost all people with a daily income per person of less than US$1.9 lived in these countries, accounting for 10.67% of the global population. Although the global poverty incidence improved significantly starting from 41.91% in 1981, the poverty incidence was still as high as 46.17% in low-income countries, according to 8.4% of the world's population with an absolute population of over 600 million. As President Xi Jinping pointed out, it is still a distant dream for many families to have warm houses, enough food, and secure jobs. This is the greatest challenge facing the world today. It is also what is behind the social turmoil in some countries.[26]

From the Chinese story to the Chinese solution

Statistics by the World Bank and other institutions based on purchasing power parity show that as early as 2014, China's total GDP surpassed that of the United States, becoming the world's largest economy. Although the statistical method of purchasing power parity is up for discussion, China's economy will surpass the United States in the near future calculated based on exchange rates. China's total GDP in 2018 was US$13.6 trillion, accounting for 15.9% of the world economy, and the US total economy was US$20.5 trillion, accounting for 23.9% of the world economy. Since the United States is generally in a steady growing situation, its future growth rate can be assumed to be between 2% and 3%. While China is in the new normal of economic growth, its potential growth capacity will be in a long downward trend, but it will still be significantly higher than the world average.[27]

The potential growth rate of GDP is predicted based on two assumptions. China's economy is predicted to surpass that of the United States by approximately 2030, accounting for over 23% of the world economy. From the perspective of per capita GDP, China is expected to cross the dividing threshold from upper-middle-income countries to high-income countries in approximately 2022, but it will be the earliest in the mid-2040s when China will reach the average income level of high-income countries. It is still difficult to define a timetable for China to catch up to the level of the United States.

Whatever happens, China's total economy has remained the second in the world since 2010, its share of the world economy has increased from 1.7% in 1978 to 15.9% in 2018, and the ratio of per capita income to the world average has increased from 10.4% to 86.5%. China is by no means the kind of single hegemonic country discussed in international politics, and China is not going to seek status in the future. However, China is willing to make a greater contribution to the supply of global public goods.

As early as 1979, Deng Xiaoping, the chief architect of China's reform and opening-up, pointed out when explaining a moderately prosperous society to visiting Japanese guests: "With the [economic] aggregate, we can do something we want to do, and we can also make slightly more contributions to mankind."[28] When compiled into the second volume of *Selected Works of Deng Xiaoping*, this sentence is formally expressed as follows: "At that time, we may provide more help to the poor countries in the third world."[29]

President Xi Jinping has repeatedly emphasized on international occasions that the Chinese believe that "no one should do to others what he does not want others to do to himself." China does not subscribe to the notion that a country is bound to seek hegemony when it grows in strength. There is no gene of hegemony and militaristic strategy in Chinese blood.[30] He also pointed out that China should strive to make greater contributions to the cause of peace and the development of mankind. In helping developing countries in Asian and African regions to accelerate their development and in efforts to respond to various challenges to human beings, China will not set its own development path as the criterion, nor will it impose its own development path on others. China shares its own development opportunities with other global countries based on pinpointing the root cause of the problems facing the world economy and developing countries.

The successful experience of China's reform and opening-up to promote development and sharing, which has been replicated in regional development and further development, are the public goods provided by China for the development of the world, and through initiatives and opening strategies such as the Belt and Road construction and strengthening economic cooperation with African countries, all countries, especially the vast number of developing countries, have been given a free ride in China's development.

In the past 40 years, China has promoted reforms in many areas, such as incentive mechanisms, corporate governance structures, pricing mechanisms, resource allocation models, opening-up systems, and macro policy environments, and gradually removed the institutional obstacles to the accumulation and allocation of production factors in the planned economy period. Traditional production factors such as material capital, human capital, and labor force have been accumulated more rapidly and allocated more efficiently.

This means that rapid economic growth from reform is driven not only by factor input but also by a substantial increase in productivity. Despite repeated failures, some overseas scholars have insisted on slandering China's economy. One important reason is that they have ignored the role of productivity increase in China's economic growth.[31] Studies from the International Monetary Fund and other organizations show that China's economic growth is largely supported by the increase in labor productivity.[32] The previous chapters have displayed sufficient empirical evidence that China's rapid growth during this period not only lies in choosing a way of reform and opening-up fit for its own national conditions but also in following general development laws. An outstanding manifestation—expanded employment—means that urban and rural residents can personally participate in the reform, opening-up, and development processes and share the results equally.

The Chinese story is both national and regional. Due to the historical regional development gap, the reform and opening-up process also has a regional gradient, causing differences in economic development among the eastern, central, and western regions in a certain period of time. It is solved by creatively replicating the experience of reform and opening-up to promote development and sharing formed early in the special economic zones and later in the broader coastal areas to develop the central and western regions. This means that while the central and western regions have gradually implemented the reform and opening-up, the central government has begun to implement the western development strategy since the beginning of the 21st century in response to the lack of human capital, weak infrastructure, and slow economic development restricted by a single industrial structure in these provinces. Subsequently, it launched the strategy of the rise of central China to give priority to the central and western regions in terms of investments in infrastructure and basic public services, and a series of major construction projects was carried out.

To date, the series of regional development strategies have achieved obvious results, improving the transportation, infrastructure, and guarantee capabilities of basic public services and the human capital accumulation level in the central and western regions, significantly improving the investment and development environment, and greatly mobilizing the enthusiasm and creativity of the laborers, entrepreneurs and businessmen in these regions to participate in regional development.

In the first decade of the 21st century, China's economic development ushered in two important turning points, namely crossing the Lewis turning point and the turning point for the demographic dividend to disappear, marking a new stage of development. The turning point effect is first shown as the increase in labor costs in coastal areas and the weakened comparative advantage of the manufacturing sector, making it difficult for economic growth to keep the previous speed. If we rely entirely on foreign development experience, that is, to follow the so-called flying-geese model of international industrial transfer, the comparative advantage of China's manufacturing sector will decline, which will lead to a large-scale transfer of industries to countries with low labor costs.[33]

However, as the strategies of Western development and the rise of central China have shown, effects and these regions are still characterized by low labor costs, industrial transfers occur mainly between the coastal regions and the central and western regions, becoming a Chinese domestic version of the international flying-geese model.[34] The labor-intensive manufacturing sector has accelerated to transfer to the central and western regions. The leading growth of industrial investment in the central and western provinces promoted faster economic growth in these regions (Figure 13.4).

Economists have summarized the industrial transfer between East Asian economies as a flying-geese model, which is caused by differences and changes in comparative advantages.[35] The model focuses on observing the relations between different economies or different regions, and three key points of economic development should be grasped. The first is the gradient. There are pioneers and pursuers in world economic development and regional economic development, and there are leading geese and following geese. The second is gradual. Each economy should select its development model according to its resource endowments and changes in comparative advantage. As conditions such as comparative advantages change and the relative status of different economies changes, the original development model will change as well.

Based on the internal logic of the flying-geese model rather than the inherent experience, we can expect and have actually observed the flying-geese

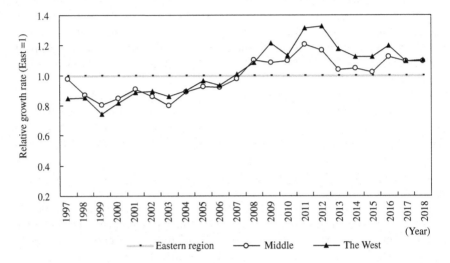

Figure 13.4 A domestic version of the flying-geese model

model of industrial transfer from Japan to the Four Asian Tigers and the latter to ASEAN countries and mainland China. After China crossed the Lewis turning point, it changed to a domestic version of the industrial transfer from coastal areas to the central and western regions in China. Based on the same logic and considering the demographic transition stage and economic development stage in developing countries, the Chinese domestic version of the flying-geese model will later naturally form a new international version— the manufacturing sector transfers to countries with potential comparative advantages, creating a window of opportunity for the latter to harvest demographic dividends.

The success story of China's reform and opening-up to promote development and sharing, as well as the helpful experience of establishing special economic zones and pilot zones and furthermore implementing regional development strategies to create conditions in the central and western regions to repeat the development miracle of coastal areas, will become Chinese wisdom and Chinese solutions when China further participates in economic globalization and global economic governance to promote the healthy development of economic globalization and help developing countries eliminate poverty and move toward modernization. The Belt and Road initiative proposed by President Xi Jinping in 2013 is the leading strategic framework and program of action in this regard.

The Belt and Road initiative is not a simple continuation of the ancient land and maritime Silk Road, it has deeper historical meaning and practical enlightenment. From a greater historical depth, this initiative implies a denial of traditional Western centralism, emphasizing the role of mutual communication and mutual learning between Eastern and Western civilizations in the history of human development. From a broader historical perspective, this initiative also contains a new concept of how to break the supply content and model of global public goods with traditional hegemony as the center while paying more attention to eradicating global poverty with the participation of all countries.

The historian Peter Frankopan used 24 symbolic words to describe the ancient Silk Road, such as the road to revolution, the road to concord, the road of rebirth, the road to gold... and the slave road, the road to empire, the road to cold warfare, and the road of superpower rivalry.[36] The Silk Road Economic Belt and the 21st Century Maritime Silk Road are fully focused on developing economic partnerships with countries along the route and related countries and building a community of mutual political trust, economic integration, and cultural inclusiveness. This shows the content of globalization and focuses on the interaction of domestic development with opening to the outside world, taking infrastructure construction to promote cooperation in the real economy and production capacity, developing investment and trade relations, and connecting the domestic version of the flying-geese industrial transfer model with that of the international version. Since the countries along the route and related countries are mostly developing countries, this initiative is also an important carrier and approach to helping developing countries eliminate poverty with Chinese wisdom and Chinese solutions.

To be sure, every country should after all be based on its national conditions and rely on its internal determination and efforts to eliminate various existing obstacles in development momentum and institutional environment in order to eventually get rid of poverty and move toward modernization. The meaningful things that outsiders can do (regardless of whether they are called international public goods) are no doubt to provide useful knowledge, including successful experience gained in other environments and lessons to be learned, necessary assistance in the construction of software and hardware infrastructure, and easy-to-start and effective market investment opportunities. The Belt and Road initiative is a joint construction and sharing initiative that can work in parallel with the needs and efforts of various countries.

First, this initiative can promote infrastructure construction, realize interconnection and improve the industrial investment environment and trade environment. According to a report by McKinsey, according to the current trend of insufficient investment, the global infrastructure investment gap can reach 11% during 2016–2030, mainly in developing countries. If we take into account the requirements of achieving the sustainable development goals of the United Nations (that is, we should pay more attention to the infrastructure investment needs of poor countries), the cumulative investment gap will reach a third by 2030.[37] In almost all countries related to the Belt and Road, there are bottlenecks in transportation, energy, and other infrastructures, which have long constrained investment efficiency and industrial development so that many countries cannot fully enjoy the dividend of economic globalization.

With the help of the Asian Infrastructure Investment Bank, BRICS Development Bank, Silk Road Fund, and other financing institutions, China can greatly improve the infrastructure conditions of developing countries by strengthening cooperation with relevant countries and regions in infrastructure construction capacity, as shown by the strategy of developing the western region.

Second, this initiative promotes industrial transfer and helps relevant countries transform potential demographic dividends into economic growth. Most developing countries, especially countries in Southeast Asia, South Asia, and Africa, have a low median age. While the working-age population continues to grow, they have a favorable population age structure and are in a harvest period of potential demographic dividends.

For example, judging by demographic indicators, the World Bank and the International Monetary Fund believe that 62 countries and regions are still opening a "window of population opportunity," while 37 countries and regions will open a "window of population opportunity" in the future. Together, the two account for 51% of the total number (192) of countries and regions with statistical data.[38] As long as the investment environment and trade environment are improved significantly, manufacturing sectors that have gradually lost their comparative advantages in countries such as China can be transferred to those countries. These countries can share the dividends of economic globalization by promoting industrialization and expanding employment, increasing local residents' incomes, and achieving more inclusive economic development.

Third, this initiative promotes people-to-people bonds through wider cultural exchanges, which not only lays a solid social foundation for economic cooperation but also contributes to governance capacity-building in relevant countries and makes economic and social development more sustainable. China's experience in implementing strategies of regional coordinated development and poverty alleviation shows that giving a man fish, he will have a meal; teach him to fish, he will have food all his life. Local governance ability will be enhanced, and human capital endowments will be improved by exploiting and promoting social and humanistic cooperation with countries along the route and related countries in youth employment and entrepreneurship training, vocational skills development, social security management services, public administration, scientific and technological, cultural, educational and health exchanges, and think tank exchanges. With the efforts of their governments and people, these countries can combine local situations and transform the growth opportunities brought by infrastructure construction and industrial investment into long-term economic growth and social development capabilities.

Conclusion

The long-run history of each country is the result of its own arduous explorations, which are always composed of failures and successes. In different historical periods, there are more failures than successes or more successes than failures. Therefore, the single hegemony that reflects the British colonialism concept or American exceptionalism in the traditional sense (in fact, both isolationist attitudes and hegemonic behavior can find their roots here) is eventually a short-lived phenomenon from a long historical point of view, aside from the fact that it fails to well perform the function of international public goods providers to improve global human well-being.

In fact, it was not until after the 1860s in the United Kingdom and after the 1930s in the United States that they switched from implementing harsh trade protectionism to advocating trade liberalization. With Brexit and the policy change after Trump's coming to power in the United States, these two countries are no longer regarded as flag-bearers of defending free trade. Therefore, the content of the international public goods they once claimed is short-lived in the long course of history. In this sense, it is not a president's own decision but is inevitable that the US moves toward unilateralism.

Moreover, in the world today less and less does it need one country to monopolize or a few exclusive countries to be the providers of public goods. The notion of monopolizing international affairs is behind the times, and such an attempt is doomed to fail.[39] In contrast, the supply of global public goods is the common responsibility of all countries regardless of size, whether rich or poor, strong or weak, near or far. The gains of each specific country from specific public goods are based on comparative advantages in economic capacity, cultural influence, international network, past experience, and so on, so it may take on different responsibilities.

Many parties from the West have reflected on and criticized the traditional supply model of global public goods and its practice. For example, McNamara, who served as the US Secretary of Defense during the Vietnam War, expressed remorse over the Vietnam War initiated by the United States, and Greenspan, who was in charge of the Federal Reserve of the US for a long time, reflected on over-believing in the functions of the free market and the self-discipline of financial institutions. As an insider, Stiglitz criticized the global economic governance model of the Bretton Woods system, and Easterly, as a World Bank rebel, questioned the global anti-poverty approach.

However, the Western academic circle, the public opinion circles, and the decision-making circle obviously have not completely abandoned the traditional concept that it can only be a single or a few hegemons to perform the function of international public goods providers. This is the background and meaning of Nye's proposition of the "Kindleberger trap." After all, the world order will achieve harmony after confrontation and unity of chaos and stability, and global affairs will inevitably experience long-term switching of breaking and fostering when it transforms from one country's dominance to global shared governance.

Let us put aside worries about the "Kindleberger trap" but focus on solving the "Easterly tragedy" together. To date, first, China has made statistically significant contributions to global poverty alleviation through its own poverty reduction effects. Second, China has pursued the concept of a community with a shared future for mankind and has participated in poverty alleviation strategies for low-income countries in various ways. Finally, China's wisdom and contribution to global poverty reduction are based on the experience of China's reform and opening-up, which promotes economic development and results sharing, and on the implementation of poverty alleviation strategies for regional poverty.

As the world's second largest economy, an active participant in economic globalization, and a promoter for the stably developing world economy, China will play a more active role in global economic governance. In particular, confronted with the long-lasting problem of global poverty, China is most qualified and responsible for proposing solutions and making greater contributions with its own experience, wisdom, and capability.

Notes

1 Joseph S. Nye, Jr., *The Kindleberger Trap*, January 9, 2017, www.project-syndic ate.org/.
2 Charles P. Kindleberger, *The World in Depression: 1929–1939*, Shanghai: Translation Publishing House, 1986.
3 Robert Gilpin, *The Political Economy of International Relations*, Washington, DC: Economic Science Press, 1989.
4 Kindleberger's explanation of the Great Depression in 1929 is only one of many hypotheses in economics. Although we should not judge its correctness by whether it is the mainstream viewpoint, it is not a reliable base to build an important concept with strategic significance (the Kindleberger trap) on.
5 Xi Jinping: Jointly Shoulder Responsibility of Our Times, Promote Global Growth, Keynote Speech at the Opening Session of the World Economic Forum Annual Meeting 2017, *People's Daily*, January 18, 2017.
6 William Easterly, *The White Man's Burden: Why the West's Efforts to Aid the Rest Have Done So Much and So Little Good*, Beijing: China CITIC Press, 2008.
7 Xi Jinping, Jointly Shoulder Responsibility of Our Times, Promote Global Growth, Keynote Speech at the Opening Session of the World Economic Forum Annual Meeting 2017, *People's Daily*, January 18, 2017.
8 Charles P. Kindleberger, International Public Goods without International Government, *The American Economic Review*, Vol. 76, No. 1, 1986, pp. 1–13.
9 Niall Ferguson, *The War of the World*, Guangzhou: Guangdong People's Publishing House, 2015, pp. 114–115.
10 Andrew Roberts and Niall Ferguson, Hitler's England: What if Germany Had Invaded Britain in May 1940?, in Niall Ferguson (ed.), Virtual History, New York: Macmillan, 1997.
11 William Easterly, *The White Man's Burden: Why the West's Efforts to Aid the Rest Have Done So Much and So Little Good*, Beijing: China CITIC Press, 2008, p. 8.
12 Glen McMahon in the film is a four-star general, and the character is based on Stanley A. McChrystal, a top American ex-commander for the US troop in Afghanistan. He was forced to resign as commander after just one year because of his criticism of the American vice-president.
13 See Robert Gilpin, *The Political Economy of International Relations*, Washington, DC: Economic Science Press, 1989, Preface.

14 Lars Tvede, *Business Cycles: History, Theory and Investment Reality*, translated by Dong Yuping, Beijing: China CITIC Press, 2008, p. 293.

15 See Raghuram Rajan, *Fault Lines: How Hidden Fractures Still Threaten the World Economy*, translated by Liu Nian et al., Beijing: China CITIC Press, 2011.

16 See Joseph E. Stiglitz, *Globalization and Its Discontents*, translated by Li Yang and Zhang Tianxiang, Beijing: China Machinery Press, 2004.

17 World Bank Group and the International Monetary Fund, *Global Monitoring Report 2015/2016: Development Goals in an Era of Demographic Change*, Washington, DC: World Bank, 2016.

18 See Cai Fang and Lu Yang, The End of China's Demographic Dividend: The Perspective of Potential GDP Growth, in Ross Garnaut, Cai Fang, and Song Ligang (eds.), *China: A New Model for Growth and Development*, Canberra: ANU Press, 2013, pp. 55–73.

19 Martin Gassebner and Simon Luechinger, Lock, Stock, and Barrel: A Comprehensive Assessment of the Determinants of Terror, *Public Choice*, Vol. 149, 2011, pp. 235–261.

20 This was said by Barack Obama (his predecessor George Bush said similar words too). Quoted from *The Economist*, Economic Focus: Exploding Misconceptions, *The Economist*, December 18, 2010, p. 130.

21 The sentence is from the British poet Kipling in the colonial times. See Rudyard Kipling, *The White Man's Burden*, 1899, http://sourcebooks.fordham.edu/halsall/mod/kipling.asp.

22 In fact, currently the United States still wages wars in the name of anti-terrorism, and maintains huge military expenditures. As Sachs pointed out, "as the US ignores instability in extremely poor areas, let them be a paradise for turmoil, violence and even global terrorism, their military expenditures will not buy peace after all." Jeffrey Sachs: *The End of Poverty: Economic Possibility for Our Time*, translated by Zou Guang, Shanghai: People's Press, 2007, p. 6.

23 See Jeffrey Sachs, *The End of Poverty: Economic Possibility for Our Time*, translated by Zou Guang, Shanghai: People's Press, 2007.

24 Paul Starobin, Does It Take a Village? *Foreign Policy*, Vol. 201, July/August 2013. pp. 92–97.

25 *The Economist*, Foreign Aid: Fading Faith in Good Works, *The Economist*, July 1, 2017, pp. 50–52.

26 Xi Jinping, Jointly Shoulder Responsibility of Our Times, Promote Global Growth, Keynote Speech at the Opening Session of the World Economic Forum Annual Meeting 2017, *People's Daily*, January 18, 2017.

27 Cai Fang and Lu Yang, Take-off, Persistence, and Sustainability: Demographic Factor of the Chinese Growth, *Asia & the Pacific Policy Studies*, Vol. 3, No. 2, 2016, pp. 203–225.

28 Dong Zhenrui and Yi Lei, Recalling Deng Xiaoping's visit to Japan and Meeting with Masayoshi Ohira in the Late 1970s—Interview Record of Wang Xiaoxian, *Literature of Chinese Communist Party*, Vol. 2, 2007.

29 Deng Xiaoping, *Selected Works of Deng Xiaoping, Volume II*, Beijing: People's Publishing House, 1994.

30 Xi Jinping: *Carry forward the Five Principles of Peaceful Coexistence to Build a Better World through Win–win Cooperation- Speech at the Commemorative Ceremony Marking the 60th Anniversary of the Release of the "Five Principles of Peaceful Coexistence,"* Shanghai: People's Publishing House, 2014.

31 Young once pointed out bluntly: "With minimal sleight of hand, it is possible to transform the recent growth experience of the People's Republic of China from the extraordinary into the mundane." Out of this preconception, he denied the substantial increase and contribution of productivity in China's economic growth. See Alwyn Young, Gold into the Base Metals: Productivity Growth in the People's Republic of China during the Reform Period, *Journal of Political Economy*, Vol. 111, No. 6, 2003, pp. 1220–1261; Paul Krugman, Hitting China's Wall, *New York Times*, July 18, 2013.

32 International Monetary Fund, Asia Rising: Patterns of Economic Development and Growth, in *World Economic Outlook*, September 2006, pp.1–30; Zhu Xiaodong, Understanding China's Growth: Past, Present, and Future, *Journal of Economic Perspectives*, Vol. 26, No. 4, 2012, pp. 103–124.

33 The flying-geese model can be seen in Kiyoshi Kojima, The "Flying Geese" Model of Asian Economic Development: Origin, Theoretical Extensions, and Regional Policy Implications, *Journal of Asian Economics*, Vol. 11, 2000, pp. 375–401.

34 Qu Yue, Cai Fang, and Xiaobo Zhang, Has the "Flying Geese" Phenomenon in Industrial Transformation Occurred in China?, in Huw McKay and Ligang Song (eds.), *Rebalancing and Sustaining Growth in China*, Canberra: ANU Press, 2012, pp. 93–109.

35 The origin of the flying-geese model, and the brief history for analysis are summarized in Kiyoshi Kojima, The "Flying Geese" Model of Asian Economic Development: Origin, Theoretical Extensions, and Regional Policy Implications, *Journal of Asian Economics*, Vol. 11, 2000, pp. 375–401.

36 See Peter Frankopan, *The Silk Road: A New History of the World*, translated by Shao Xudong and Sun Fang, Hangzhou: Zhejiang University Press, 2016.

37 McKinsey Global Institute, *Bridging Global Infrastructure Gaps*, London: McKinsey & Company, June 2016.

38 World Bank Group and International Monetary Fund, *Global Monitoring Report 2015/2016: Development Goals in an Era of Demographic Change*, Washington, DC: World Bank, 2016.

39 Xi Jinping, *Carry Forward the Five Principles of Peaceful Coexistence to Build a Better World through Win–win Cooperation: Speech at the Commemorative Ceremony Marking the 60th Anniversary of the Release of the "Five Principles of Peaceful Coexistence,"* Shanghai: People's Publishing House, 2014.

14 New technological revolution and reflections on economics

Introduction

During the development of the world economy and the economic development in various countries, technological progress has been characterized everywhere, and it has often exploded in revolutionary ways. The key role of technological progress in promoting economic growth has been universally recognized and is always a hot topic in academia and policy circles. The gradual and revolutionary nature of technological progress often works as the basis for people to recognize its influence on economic development to predict economic development prospects.

As a representative of a non-mainstream school of ideas, Robert Gordon pointed out with astonishing historical material and stories in one of his best-selling books that the period 1870–1970 was a unique century in terms of technological changes when electricity, internal combustion engines, indoor water supply, and drainage facilities were invented and applied and were truly revolutionized in improving the quality of human life. In contrast, the technological progress after that is gradual. For this reason, it is inevitable for the US economy to fall into a long-term downturn.[1]

A more mainstream school of ideas focuses on revealing the advent of the new technological revolution. For example, based on various characteristics in a new round of technological changes, Klaus Schwab declared that the Fourth Industrial Revolution had arrived. Schwab concluded that the First Industrial Revolution was characterized by railway construction and the use of steam engines to lead humans into mechanical production. The Second Industrial Revolution was shown to be the emergence of electricity and production lines leading to large-scale production. The Third Industrial Revolution was a computer revolution or digital revolution nurtured by the development of semiconductors, computers, and the Internet.

According to the definition of consistency, the ongoing technological changes will inevitably lead to the Fourth Industrial Revolution, which is characterized by the ubiquitous Internet and greatly improved mobility; sensors are getting smaller with stronger performance and increasingly

DOI: 10.4324/9781003329305-17

cheaper costs; and artificial intelligence and machine learning are on the rise.[2] Most people agree with the conclusion that a new round of scientific and technological revolution or industrial revolution has arrived, and in the meanwhile, they have generally observed the new characteristics of this round of scientific and technological revolution and greater challenges as well.

First, whether for natural scientists or scholars and even policy-makers in various fields, one characteristic that cannot be ignored is the current unprecedented pace of technological breakthroughs. Concepts such as Moore's Law and Kurzweil's singularity are nothing but refining people's experiences in reality and further making bold and scientific predictions.

Second, new technologies represented by artificial intelligence and the Internet have broken the law of increasing marginal costs or diminishing returns on investment in past economic activities. This means that we must be prepared to enter a Rifkin-style zero marginal cost society, and in addition, it is necessary to better understand a possible economy with increasing returns. Paul Romer was awarded the prize by the Nobel Committee in Economic Science in 2018 for integrating technological innovation into long-term macroeconomic analysis, which no doubt reflects that the group of economists has improved their understanding of the importance of new technological revolutions.

Third, the nature of this round of industrial revolution determines that technologies cannot be penetrated equally to all countries, regions, industries, and business entities, and the resulting economic growth will not naturally benefit all groups in society in a trickle-down way. American economist Autor discovered that globalization and technological revolution are conducive to the development of superstar enterprises, enabling them to occupy a higher concentration of product markets in relevant industries. In addition, these enterprises are more profitable and have a small share of labor cost. As superstar enterprises become more important in various industries, the overall labor remuneration to a country's GDP tends to fall.[3] This means that globalization and technological revolution have the potential effect of deteriorating income distribution.

Finally, regardless of historical law or realistic logic, the Fourth Industrial Revolution will inevitably be accompanied by Globalization 4.0.[4] The previous versions of globalization all had many unanswered puzzles. For example, can globalization in essence equally benefit all countries that have actively participated in or passively intervened in; even for countries that have benefited from globalization, can every social group and everyone benefit from it; will every new version of globalization be necessarily more inclusive or shared than previous versions of globalization?

In other words, we are challenged to urgently change our way of thinking about the relations between technological progress and economic growth, especially when economics has a longstanding fallacy in this regard. As an economist, the author does not intend to conduct a general critique of economics itself in a disruptive manner. The "fallacy" mentioned here actually comes from two economic traditions, which are called "trickle-down economics" and "penetration economics."

Nevertheless, the two economic thoughts and conclusions are based on traditional economic theories and their logical conclusions; that is, when economic theories explain technological revolution or technological progress, they tend to hypothesize or unconditionally exaggerate the possible spillover effects, resulting in cognitive fallacy and misleading politicians and decision-makers. Therefore, general economics will inevitably "unknowingly hurt" while clarifying these two economic fallacies.

In fact, the evolving way of economic ideas and the research paradigm that economists are accustomed to or even proud of both have contained and reflected the genes that cause chronic diseases of spillover economics. Why are economists unwilling to revise the basic hypothesis of economics when technological progress or economic growth has not yielded the expected spillover effects?

As people have found, mainstream economics does not try to revise these hypotheses when complete market information and complete rational hypotheses are inconsistent with reality. In the end, a certain new category of economics will be set up to specifically study the situation without such hypotheses. If there are deeper methodological flaws here, they should eventually be traced back to the debate between positive economics and normative economics.

The purpose of this chapter is to remind economists to try to understand the new technological revolution with new thinking. We will first briefly review how people think about technological progress from the perspective of economics, not only emphasizing the pertinence of the issues discussed here but also looking for the source of ideas to help improve our cognitive ability. Furthermore, we will try to reflect on and criticize the two mindsets of trickle-down economics and penetration economics from a theoretical and empirical point of view, respectively. Finally, the author briefly summarizes the whole chapter, explores the stubborn traditional economic paradigm, and proposes preliminary recommendations.

A brief history of ideas on technological progress

Although human economic activities have been accompanied by technological application and improvement from the very beginning, the real substantial impact on economic growth, that is, the technological progress to break the Malthus trap, occurred during the industrial revolution in the late 18th century and the early 19th century. However, this technological progress and relevant economic growth, which happened for the first time in human history, showed from the beginning that a larger cake does not mean that everyone can obtain a larger share.

Whether from the literary portrayal by Charles Dickens or from the actual recorded history of the Luddite Movement, it can be seen that the industrial revolution was initially accompanied by a deterioration in the living conditions of workers: bad working conditions, extremely low wage levels, quality of life that failed to improve with growth, and reduced life expectancy.

The research shows that the living standards of the British working class did not improve substantially in more than half a century from the 1780s to the 1850s, when the Industrial Revolution was in full swing. For example, after taking into account the unemployment, family dependency coefficient, and urbanization cost, economic historians found that the actual living standards of British working-class families improved by less than 15%.[5] Calculated by 70 years, this means that the average annual increase was less than 0.2%. This fact explains why Malthus, although living in the era of the industrial revolution, came to the conclusion that the arithmetic growth of production could hardly meet the geometric growth of population, and mankind would inevitably fall into poverty, famine, wars, and disasters, laying the foundation for economic and social thoughts and even pessimistic epistemology in academic research.

Although John Maynard Keynes admired Malthus a lot, he himself was an optimist of technological progress and economic growth, and he firmly believed that science and compound interest had the power to change human destiny. In 1930, when the world was in the midst of the Great Depression, Keynes published a famous article in which he acknowledged there were many growing pains, such as too fast technological progress, making it difficult to absorb surplus labor force at once, but he still made a bold and optimistic prediction of the economic possibilities facing future generations—the living standard will improve eightfold after 100 years.[6]

Keynes compared the pace of technological progress and capital accumulation in that era and beyond with the long night before the industrial revolution, so he remained optimistic about the future economic prospect. Regardless of the specific figures, his prediction is no doubt correct in direction. After making the prediction, Keynes continued to raise questions that were correct in terms of nature, but they were so challenging that they puzzled many later economists.

First, although he did not accurately divide the economic and non-economic purposes of the "permanent problem of the human race" and did not clearly explain the contents of the two purposes, he finally put forward an important issue that his predecessors did not clearly raise: what is the purpose of human subsistence after the increase in labor productivity solves the economic problem?

Second, Keynes bypassed the realistic problem of switching from one type of job to another and raised a more ultimate problem of switching from a working state to a leisure state at once, which was quite abrupt. However, he was already hinting at the revolutionary idea that work and wages can be decoupled. This once again presents a major economic challenge, that is, what will be the economic motivation that will ultimately dominate human behavior and activities?

Adam Smith combined the invention and application of machines with the division of labor advocated by him, which actually laid a foundation to understand increasing returns for the New Growth Theory. In the meanwhile, Smith also combined his growth theory and trade theory to form a consistent interpretation system.[7] In this way, Smith's theory itself has foreshadowed the problems we will face.

The use of machines and the development of division of labor have on the one hand increased labor productivity and, on the other hand, made the workers' skills become overspecialized, simplistic, and less diversified. Instead, the human capital of workers has become more vulnerable, and jobs have become increasingly insecure. Under the technological revolution and even globalization, laborers, as carriers of such human capital, are more prone to huge impacts. In addition, the asymmetry between complex technological creation and simple work operations also puts workers, especially simple workers, in a disadvantaged bargaining position in the income distribution of factors.

People have found continually from history and reality that technological progress has not equally benefited all countries and all domestic groups at any time, even today's extremely rapid technological changes. Puzzled by the unbalanced characteristics of technological changes in economic growth and improving life quality, some economists have tried to distinguish the nature of technological changes during different periods, believing that technological progress may have different sharing between one round and the other.

For example, Tyler Cowen proposed an unproven hypothesis that new technological progress in the 21st century has increasingly got the nature of using public resources for investment in the field of "private products" that benefit only a few people, being unhelpful to increase the income of ordinary residents.[8]

An increasing number of economists have realized that economic growth and technological changes will not automatically benefit all countries and all individuals, but many of them have not realized that technological progress will not automatically penetrate all countries, sectors, and production factors. A widely shared anecdote may somehow illustrate this.

It is said that in the 1960s, Milton Friedman, who once worked as a government consultant to a developing country in Asia, inspected a major public works project. He found surprisingly that workers were using shovels rather than driving heavy equipment such as bulldozers and tractors for construction. Seeing his confusion, local officials told him that the construction project was an "employment plan." The master of economics believed that it was justified to increase labor productivity and the means to improve productivity were readily available. In response, Friedman made a classic allegorical remark: "Then, why not let workers use a spoon to work?"[9]

Even though economists have always focused on the economic and social impact of technological changes, it can only be said at best that people are paying increasing attention to this topic, and we are far from finding solutions. In 2017, copying the practice of Martin Luther 500 years before, *33 Theses for an Economics Reformation* (hereinafter referred to as the *Theses*) signed by 65 economists was nailed on the door of the London School of Economics and Political Science.

Article 21 of this *Theses* recognizes that there is an imbalance in the process of innovation, which poses a challenge to traditional economics: Innovation is not exogenous to the economy but an internal part of economic activities. If innovation is seen as occurring in a continuously evolving and unbalanced ecosystem shaped by market design and formed by interactions of all participants in the market, it can improve our understanding of GDP growth.[10]

In fact, economists are not the only ones concerned about technological changes and their consequences. As early as 1964, a 26-member ad hoc committee including Nobel economics winner Gunnar Myrdal and people from various fields wrote a public memorandum to the president of the United States, and the report was titled *The Triple Revolution*. This report not only criticized the traditional analytical methods of economics half a century earlier than the aforementioned *Theses* but also had foresight in many judgments and understandings.

For example, the report pointed out that marked by the cyber revolution, a new era of production has begun. The revolution took place at a pace unmatched by previous agricultural and industrial revolutions, combining the computer and automated machine, forming a system of almost unlimited production capacity, and reducing the demand for labor force day by day.

Surprisingly, this report pointed out at that time that as machines take over production from people, the latter increasingly needed to rely on minimal government guarantee. This idea has evolved into the so-called "universal basic income" that is now widely discussed. The project has at least two differences from the fragmented social security projects that are commonly implemented in various countries.

First, as its name suggests, the project includes the factors of "unconditional" that cover all people regardless of rich or poor, "basic" that is limited to payment to meet the minimal living needs, and "income" means to directly give cash. It revolutionizes the concept of social insurance theory and practice.

Second, the project aims to deal with technical unemployment under the latest development trend of artificial intelligence. Technical unemployment is a longstanding phenomenon and a long-lasting topic as well. However, the integration of neuroscience, big data, and the Internet has brought artificial intelligence to a new stage where robots will replace not only simple and repetitive work but also more complex and intellectual jobs.

Disruptive technological changes require revolutionary solutions. Although a generally accepted and widely practiced concept has not come into being, the concept of unconditional basic income has been increasingly discussed, and experiments have been initiated in some countries. Given that the concept and design aim to solve the shortcomings of traditional solutions, many people believe that it is not only a countermeasure to the unprecedented phenomenon of technical unemployment but it also contains new ideas and ultimate solutions to eradicate poverty, upend the working concept, and reshape the world.[11]

If it is agreed that robotics will eventually destroy a considerable proportion of jobs in the future,[12] the current various social insurance programs, whether in a fully funded system or a pay-as-you-go system, are unable to provide a guarantee for this result, and unconditional basic income seems to be the policy option in the future. Therefore, is the implementation of this project urgently needed?

The answer is surely yes. From the perspective of individual workers, competition with robotics still depends on improving human capital, such as continuously grasping new skills, as well as improving cognitive and non-cognitive abilities. However, as workers still struggle to survive every day, they do not have the time and ability to keep pace with the times to improve human capital. Once they lose jobs, they do not have enough human capital to transfer to other jobs. Therefore, if someone can obtain an extra basic income while working, it will leave room for them to prepare for the rainy day.

Critique of trickle-down economics

American public opinion believes that China and other emerging economies have taken their jobs. The reflection in economics is such an argument that emerging economies use cheap production factors and even unfair competition methods, enabling Americans to lose jobs through trade and industrial transfer. In this regard, many researchers have provided evidence to blame the trade pattern for job losses after the industrial chain is rearranged during economic globalization and furthermore point the finger directly at emerging economies such as China.[13]

At the same time, research also finds that the job loss of ordinary skills in these developed countries is not just the result of the global division of labor in the industrial chain. Actually, more important, lasting, and universal job losses come from the use of machines and robotics during automation. In this regard, studies have shown that automation and the related increase in productivity are more important factors for job losses. For example, a TED speaker pointed out that in the United States from 2000 to 2010, 5.7 million manufacturing jobs were lost, and 87% of lost manufacturing jobs were due to the application of automation technology.[14]

Therefore, in the research on the reasons for job losses in the United States, an opposition between the "trade-based reason" and the "technology-based reason" or a debate about the relative importance of the two factors has actually come into being, and both hypotheses have been empirically tested. For example, the research by Fort et al. in response to the one-sided argument of "China shock," found that both trade (foreign competition) factor and technology (automation) factor have played important roles in the lost manufacturing jobs in the US, and admitted that it is difficult to accurately estimate the relative importance of each factor.[15]

However, the facts noticed by these authors and their findings are that to survive in competition, enterprises are forced to apply automation technology, so they drastically reduce the number of employees. Obviously, trade factors and technology factors are intertwined, making it difficult to distinguish between them.

In modern society, the technology that can solve the problem of insufficient competitiveness of enterprises can be obtained through independent innovation, even if the competition does not come from abroad but from other regions or other enterprises in China. This means that trade factors and technology factors are not independent events that can be completely separated but can achieve a certain effect in mutually promoting and synergizing, regardless of whether they are good or bad.

From a historical point of view, both trade and technology are unavoidable. Transaction and invention have always been associated with the economic activities of mankind, and they are the source of progress. Therefore, we cannot pretend that they do not exist or can be made disappear artificially. The Luddite mindset that attributed stagnant wages and job losses to the use of machines and technological progress has now expanded to confront trade, industrial transfer (outsourcing), and even economic globalization. Politicians have certainly known that efforts in this direction will ultimately prove utterly ineffective, but they have to pick up this longstanding and tried-and-tested last straw in order to get votes.

From an epistemological perspective, we need to give up the current research paradigm of positivism. In the final analysis, the discussion here concerns the income distribution effect from globalization and the industrial revolution, and it is an issue of welfare economics. It has been proven that it is a dead end to find the reasons for job losses and income differentiation from the perspective of positivist research.

To take a different approach, we need to understand the issue and find the answer more from the perspective of normative economics. The possible situation facing us is actually the consequence of globalization and industrial revolution, and the result of comparing the costs and benefits generated by political choices or policy choices, so what we are discussing is an issue of political economics.

From a theoretical basis, it is time to completely abandon the hypothesis of trickle-down economics. Trickle-down economics also has a deep historical origin when contemporary economics has spared no effort to prove it theoretically, and policy-makers have tried to prove it empirically. Some economists and policy-makers believe that once economic activity is initiated by a certain sector or even by a single enterprise, it will eventually benefit the whole economy and even the whole society through the trickle-down effect.

For example, Friedman pointed out that in a free market society, the ethical principle of reasonable income distribution is to let everyone obtain the goods produced by his own tools. Friedman also talked about the role of the state, but what he emphasized was not redistribution but the definition and implementation of property rights.[16] The US President Ronald Reagan who firmly believed in this idea in theory and put it into practice in policy, making it an important basis of Reagan Economics.

Krugman reviewed the relationship between the different policy priorities on income distribution and actual inequality during the alternate ruling of the Democratic Party and the Republican Party in the United States and concluded that the kind of income distribution policies adopted had a significant impact on the incurring income distribution result.[17]

Krugman's logic works in the opposite direction; that is, the income distribution result will affect the political trend and thus the policy tendency. The job loss in the United States is such an example, fully reflecting the complete process of trickle-down economics from theory to practice; from cause to effect, the consequences of previous policies in turn affect subsequent policies to be formulated, even leading to political divergence and social division.

French economist Thomas Piketty and his predecessor Anthony Atkinson made outstanding studies on income distribution, and they came to this conclusion unequivocally: The only way out to solve the issue of income inequality is that the government and society make necessary redistribution of income.[18]

For example, Piketty collected and analyzed a wealth of historical data from various countries and found that the growth rate of capital returns was much faster than the economic growth rate, resulting in an increasing concentration of wealth. Since the trend is the historical trajectory revealed by long-term time series data and the current situation described by transnational data, neither the market mechanism nor natural forces over the time span can stop it, so social intervention and government policies are inevitable.

Fallacy of penetration economics

For a long time, people have found that science, technology, knowledge, and creativity all have externalities. The New Growth Theory that has emerged and prevailed more recently pays more attention to this issue. This externality is more closely called the spillover effect or non-competitiveness. The expression of this nature itself implies an inference that can be drawn; that is, technological change can be penetrated far and wide in every possible way, thus completely transforming to overall rather than partial economic growth.[19]

The concept and logic of trickle-down economics have actually contained another meaning that the author wants to express; that is, there is a habitual economic hypothesis that technological change will naturally spread within an economy so that it can continuously penetrate into all departments and enterprises, and the expected revolutionary changes within the overall economy will finally be completed. In view that trickle-down economics has already obtained a specific meaning related to the sharing of economic growth results, the author takes the liberty of creating a new concept and calls it penetration economics.

The book *Manufacturing Matters: The Myth of the Post-Industrial Economy* co-written by Stephen S. Cohen and John Zysman is a master-piece based on the hypothesis of technological penetration, which attempts to illustrate how technological changes penetrate and then cause changes in the overall economy.[20] They believed that due to the nature of industrial association between departments, technological change will spread to the whole national economy even if it starts from one department or a few departments. Moreover, they firmly believed that such close sector linkages exist not only between enterprises and within manufacturing but also between the manufacturing sector and the service sector.

Meanwhile, many researchers, including Cohen and Zysman, have also found many phenomena that contradict the hypothesis, and the so-called "productivity paradox" is the most typical one. Robert M. Solow joked in his review of the aforementioned book, "[the authors], like everyone else, are somewhat embarrassed by the fact that what everyone feels to have been a technological revolution, a drastic change in our productive lives, has been accompanied everywhere, including Japan, by a slowing- down of productivity growth, not by a step up." Furthermore, Professor Solow used one sentence to reveal the meaning of the productivity paradox—"You can see the computer age everywhere but in the productivity statistics."[21]

In diversified production and trading activities, the economic activity subjects have obvious heterogeneity, so there is an asymmetric and equal relationship between them. Logic and empirical evidence do not support Cohen's assumption that industrial relevance is extended to economic relevance and that technological change has extensive permeability. From the perspective of the theoretical gene, the assumption that "Hyperlink" creates a networked world has a typical tone of technical instrumentalism. From its expanded social meaning, it is a utopian theoretical fantasy; however, from the experience point of view, it is not consistent with the operation mode of social networks that we have observed.

Niall Ferguson made a concise summary of the status of each node in the social network and thus the heterogeneity of social connectivity, which can help us understand this problem.[22] Just as each node and edge in the network system are not equal, individual units in social networks or economic connections (can be individuals, enterprises, organizations, and participants of other social activities) do not have the same connectivity. The factors that cause such differences in connectivity (or penetrability) come from individual differences, the structure of social networks, and the governance structure that governs them.

Paul Romer, a Nobel Prize winner who emphasizes the non-rivalry of ideas and thus spillover effects, has long been committed to exploring how to transform technological changes into economic growth. He recently expresses his deep concern for the free flow policy that hinders new knowledge and new insights, acknowledging that there is still huge room for improvement in the creative production and distribution system.[23] The "room" can be large or small until it is large enough to prevent technological spillover and penetration. We can further understand the penetrability issue of social networks or economic connections from Ferguson's several factors about connectivity and their relationship and try to answer the causes of Solow's "productivity paradox."

First, the individual differences in economic activities determine that each individual entity has different connectivity so that the penetrability of technology can work. Individual differences may arise from different scales of market participants and different policies and treatments they enjoy, thus resulting in different information access status, resource access rights, access opportunities to market and technology among them. Actually, the "Baumol cost disease" in economics talks about the heterogeneity of the ways of providing goods or services, leading to different technical penetrations among sectors. Based on this, we can partially explain the "productivity paradox" in the statistical sense.

The observed productivity improvement factors usually include (1) increased capital per worker; (2) improved technology; (3) increased labor skill; (4) better management; and (5) economies of scale as output rises. Obviously, not just any sector can do well in these five factors. In fact, as Baumol himself intends to explain, whether it is the general service industry or the more unique performing arts, the improvement speed and achievable range in these aspects is obviously impossible to compare with the manufacturing industry.[24] The polarized labor markets observed in Europe and the United States in recent decades and the slow growth of employment almost all occurred in non-tradable sectors because the abovementioned principles worked.

When automation has squeezed workers out of manufacturing jobs, theoretically, workers face four prospects. The first prospect is that they enter higher-skilled jobs after human capital is improved. This is the most desirable situation because productivity improves accordingly; the second one is that they are in short-term or long-term frictional unemployment; the third one is that even though they are reluctant, they have to exit the labor market. In the second and third states, production factors are not fully utilized, reducing the productivity in the whole society, but it will not be reflected in the calculable productivity indicators. The fourth one is that they are transferred to low-productivity sectors such as the service sector. This is a typical situation of reduced productivity.

Therein, the fourth situation is very common in reality and is thus worth special attention. The more obvious the nature of increasing returns of technological progress is, the more prominent the consequence of reduced productivity in labor substitution will be, and the greater the productivity decline will be. Moreover, when workers are reallocated from higher-productivity sectors to lower-productivity sectors, it will inevitably be accompanied by decreases in wage rates. The mutually reinforced relation between low remuneration and low productivity forms a vicious circle of the "productivity paradox."

For example, when observing the relationship between wage levels and labor productivity in the United Kingdom, people have found that compared with most countries in the Organisation for Economic Development and Co-operation, there are more laborers in the United Kingdom earning low wages, which is due to restricting the improvement of labor productivity by bringing negative incentives to laborers' skill learning and suppressing vertical social movement.[25]

Second, the new round of the industrial revolution characterized by the development and application of the Internet, big data, and artificial intelligence has brought the natural monopoly tendency of super-large enterprises to the limit. On the one hand, small-sized and medium-sized enterprises are excluded from competition by algorithms and applications, or they become appendages of technology, which suppresses newly growing enterprises from innovation and entrepreneurship. On the other hand, laborers' skills are further simplified, cutting off technological penetration and thus the linkage between social productivity and technological progress and finally blocking the pathway for the whole society to share the achievements of technological progress.

An increasing number of facts have proven that the nature of this round of industrial revolution determines that technology cannot penetrate equally, and it selectively infringes on the rights of users in the form of privacy leakage, induced addiction, data surveillance, and child injury. Based on the available cases, people believe that innovative enterprises or superstar enterprises marked by Silicon Valley do not know how to respect, share, and be grateful, and they have even become accomplices of "surveillance capitalism."

Finally, economic systems and mechanisms can amplify or offset the negative effects of the above individual differences, and the government can also exert a huge impact on economic linkage and technological penetration through actions or inactions, doing right things or wrong things. In other words, policy orientation and regulations, as well as other institutional arrangements, have an important impact on technology penetration. However, the long-lasting controversy of how the government should act is more prominent here, and there is no definite rule but depending on specific issues and specific ways of action.

In this regard, Paul Romer raised questions through a handy case study called the "Guinean paradox." Near the airport in Conakry, the capital of the Republic of Guinea, young students usually studied under street lights. He observed that these young people had mobile phones, but there was no electric power supply at their homes or it was unaffordable. The institutional reason for the paradox lies in the electricity price rule that distorted market signals: too low electricity prices dampened power companies, and the government intended to change the pricing mechanism (cancel or reduce subsidies) but met resistance from interest groups (beneficiaries of subsidized electricity prices at a higher negotiating position), so electricity prices were always in a distorted state, and electric power supply was suppressed.[26] Obviously, it should be the government's responsibility to promote fair competition but not to implement industrial policies in the form of subsidies.

The low electricity price has dampened the enthusiasm of power companies, and the government intends to change the pricing mechanism.

Problems to be urgently settled in economics

From the experience of every round of scientific and technological revolution or industrial revolution in economic history, we have noticed that on the one hand, existing technologies will not fully penetrate at all times and places to bring about economic growth; on the other hand, when technology results in economic growth, it will not automatically bring about equal sharing among all groups. Popular economic methodology and theoretical hypotheses have difficulty explaining the gap between theory and experience.

It has been commonly observed that the new round of scientific and technological revolution is unprecedentedly disruptive in its economic and social consequences. Economics is no doubt facing major challenges, and self-revolution is necessary to seize and make good use of new opportunities.

First, it is necessary to reflect on the positivist methodology of long-term dominant economics. The positive economics advocated by Milton Friedman is the methodological source for trickle-down economics and penetration economics, which have failed but are still popular. His viewpoints can be explained by a statement, a judgment, and an example.[27]

For the purpose of economics, a famous statement from Friedman is that a theory or a hypothesis should yield reasonable and meaningful predictions about phenomena that have not yet been observed. He thus concluded that compared with normative economics, positive economics is more able to help people agree on what the right economic policy is. Regarding what characteristics positive economics should have, he fabricated an example, that is, for the purpose of pursuing sunshine, leaves adjust their behaviors, forming different leaf densities at different positions. Therefore, it is concluded that "contradictions in hypotheses are not important."

The positivist methodology has an important influence on the evolution of economics. It has also become the traditional basis for economic theories and policies to give up value judgments and has even induced dishonest tendencies in economic research. In view of this, Romer took "Feynman integrity" and "Stigler conviction" as rival academic conscience creeds to criticize the bad tendency in economics.[28]

Feynman's honesty, which Romer calls a guide to academic life, refers to a scientific honesty that shows results unfavorable to one's own opinions to the public while giving favorable evidence to support one's own opinions. In contrast, the Stigler conviction proposes that economists should spare no effort to verify that their views are important and correct, and no other facts are important unless they help people accept their views.

Economic history has indicated that the industrial revolution and technological change have never been able to naturally improve income distribution and promote technological penetration. However, economics has consistently assumed the existence of a trickle-down effect. When the Stigler conviction and Friedman's methodology of positive economics are cross-validated, we can see that trickle-down economics and penetration economics have such fundamental shortcomings as they spare no effort to predict "unobserved phenomena" and deliberately ignore or even cover all "observed facts" that do not support their conclusions.

Second, the orientation of economic development policies should be determined by theoretical criteria or practical needs. Once the misleading methodology of positive economics is excluded, we should reflect on economics itself to better answer the question. Economists define their knowledge as how to maximize output under scarce resources. Correspondingly, economic growth theory is the science of how to effectively mobilize and allocate resources to achieve total expansion.

However, in this definition of economics, the purpose of economic growth or maximizing output and total expansion is ignored. Many politicians and economists have questioned the worshipped indicator of GDP, and they have tried other indicators to cover more development goals, such as revalued GDP based on purchasing power parity, human development index, happiness index, and comprehensive national wealth, and other indicators to reflect income equalization and environmental improvement.[29] Thus far, these attempts have not become mainstream, which shows the deeply rooted traditional concept of economics focusing on the means rather than purposes.

Obviously, economics must not stop at only doing research on maximizing output and growth, and it must also be concerned with distribution and sharing. Economic research should also include value judgments raised by normative economics, welfare goals focused by welfare economics, and policy choices discussed in political economics. In particular, economic history has proven repeatedly that there is no unconditional trickle-down effect, so the formulation of economic policies should be far from the influence of the traditional economic paradigm and be people-centered, starting from practical problems and actual needs.

Finally, it is necessary to understand the role of the government in economic development and government-market relations. In the final analysis, trickle-down economics and penetration economics are two manifestations of the hypothesis that there is a trickle-down effect. There are similarities in solving problems, and the core is how to balance the roles of the government and the market. However, there is specific pertinence for income distribution and technological penetration. The main contradictions and the main aspects of contradictions are not the same under different institutional environments and at different stages of development, so the focal point should be different in solving problems. In short, there is no eternal formula for the government-market relation, which changes with the time, locations, and individuals.

In recent years, in the face of the rapid development of artificial intelligence and big data, there has been a discussion between entrepreneurs and economists about whether the planned economy can be revived. According to the traditional argumentation logic of economics, people usually quote Hayek's statements to deny the restoration or regression of the planned economy.

For example, Hayek pointed out that the "data" of economic calculation are not obtained by a single brain that can make decisions according to it, and it will never be so.[30] Knowledge and information are scattered, so on the one hand, the price system or market mechanism is the only way to ensure that the information owned by each member in society can be fully utilized; on the other hand, only by constant trial and error can tens of thousands of entrepreneurs or other parties determine what kind of knowledge and information is effective. Therefore, the painful experience of entrepreneurs' choice failure is undoubtedly an essential incentive.

However, economists will come to a deadlock when debating in this direction. In the context of artificial intelligence with learning capabilities and big data with unlimited development space, it will prove in the near future that we can no longer be 100% sure that knowledge and information are necessarily dispersed, so there is no need to assume that the correct information used by decision-making can only be identified by trial and error.

Interestingly, Hayek himself strongly peddled the idea of a free market economy and opposed highly centralized planning, but he was not blinded by this strong ideology. He pointed out that there is a situation between the single decision-maker making the centralized plan of the whole economy (central plan) and the scattered individual making his own plan (enterprise decision-making); that is, the organization (large enterprise) obtains the planning power about the industry, and this is the so-called "monopoly" phenomenon.[31]

When Ferguson discussed network linkage, he actually enumerated several ambitious star entrepreneurs and contradictions in reality. For example, Mark Zuckerberg, the founder and CEO of Facebook, once claimed that his dream had been to "connect the whole world," and he himself also saw the cruel reality that forces of knowledge flow, trade, and immigration did not resist the restraining forces such as authoritarianism, isolationism, and nationalism. Niall Ferguson believed that it is just companies such as Facebook that have created such a reality.[32]

Regardless of the motives of the founders and CEOs and whether these star technology companies truly make positive contributions to society, it is not difficult to see through the behaviors of these companies and their investors that no matter how beautiful and well-intentioned their visions sound, there is a certain impulse behind them. Whether they are aware of it or not, and no matter what words are used to express it, the essence of this inner impulse is monopoly.

For example, whether it is a well-known star enterprise, a rising star enterprise, or a venture capitalist who pours huge sums of money into them, a common development strategy is: no matter whether the enterprise is profitable or not, just raise even as much investment as possible and invest it without hesitation. What is the purpose of this kind of investment behavior regardless of the profit and loss of the enterprise? Obviously, the answer is to gain a market share that is large enough to beat others.

In fact, economics should not conceal value judgment. The so-called planned economy raised at present essentially reflects that, whether intentionally or unintentionally, the owners or agents of superstar companies who are in the leading position of new technology development have their own judgment and intentions to be at the controlling position in the future society. In the book *The General Theory of Employment, Interest and Money*, Keynes's last sentence in the final chapter was: "Sooner or later, it is ideas, not vested interests, which are dangerous for good or evil."[33] In fact, vested interests must come out earlier than ideas to cause trouble, and in most cases they represent evil impact.

The market is the most efficient mechanism for resource allocation, but unrestricted market power may lead to monopoly. Since the technological revolution has shown unprecedented disruptive characteristics, relevant monopoly power will also be stronger than ever. The government may show duality on this issue, such as providing excessive subsidies to add fuel to the monopoly tendency of star companies or maintaining an equal competitive environment to help start-up companies. The core is not whether industrial policy is necessary or not but how industrial policy can reach a reasonable balance between the competitive neutrality principle and development strategy goals.

Conclusion

The conclusion here, in a word, is that there is no so-called trickle-down effect. Both trickle-down economics and penetration economics are popular myths. Only by advancing with the times and achieving the most adequate balance between government functions and market mechanisms can the new technological revolution and a new round of globalization be transformed into economic growth momentum and achieve inclusive development. An issue worthy of further elaboration is the significance of the Chinese experience in this discussion and the implication of this discussion for China.

According to Schwab's division of time, the First Industrial Revolution occurred during the period 1760–1840, the Second Industrial Revolution occurred during the period 1891–1910, and the Third Industrial Revolution occurred during the period 1960–1999. We entered the Fourth Industrial Revolution at the start of the 21st century.[34] Each industrial revolution overlaps or goes in parallel with a specific version of globalization.

Obviously, China completely missed the possible catch-up opportunities from the First Industrial Revolution and the Second Industrial Revolution.

The Third Industrial Revolution occurred after the founding of the People's Republic of China, and it was not until the period of reform and opening-up since the 1980s that China seized the real opportunity for its economic development. With the rise of the Fourth Industrial Revolution and under the coming Globalization 4.0, China has become a driving force that cannot be ignored.

During the long period of reform and opening-up, China as a whole was not at the forefront of scientific and technological development, but it removed institutional barriers that hindered production factor accumulation and allocation and introduced foreign investment and learned technology and management, bringing its latecomer advantages to full play and achieving unprecedented catch-up speed. China gradually expanded its opening to the outside, participated in the global division of the labor system, turned its resource endowment of an abundant labor force into a comparative advantage and cashed in its demographic dividend as a source of growth. During the 40 years from 1978 to 2018, China grew at an average annual rate of 9.4%, surpassing all other countries, becoming the world's second largest economy, the largest industrial country, and the largest trading country in goods.

The results of reform, opening-up, and development have been generally shared. Following the national conditions, China gradually advanced its reform and opening-up without exerting an impact on people's livelihood, similar to shock therapy. Reform and opening-up have been supported by various social groups due to their Pareto improvement nature. A more important factor is that the demographic dividend is the main source of economic growth in this period. The reallocation of labor resources has been transformed into a comparative advantage, supporting economic growth, expanding the number of jobs, improving employment quality, and increasing the incomes of urban and rural residents.

Although there are income inequalities between urban and rural areas, among regions, among sectors, and among groups, such as the relatively high Gini coefficient, the gaps are formed under the circumstances that the income levels of all regions and all groups have improved simultaneously. During the period, the development of the labor market itself had the effect of improving income distribution, and the redistribution policy also played a positive role.

China enjoys a latecomer advantage because its overall scientific and technological level is not at the forefront. In this case, productivity has been improved in steps during the reform and opening-up. The first level is to narrow the gap and improve productivity at a fairly small catch-up expense and innovation risk when relatively frontier regions, departments, and enterprises learn from and absorb foreign technology. The second level is to achieve the Kuznets process of unifying expanded employment, improved income and increased resource allocation efficiency by adjusting the industrial structure. This process also has the nature of Pareto improvement.

However, as China's economic development enters a new stage, the sources of economic growth from the demographic dividend rapidly decline, such as sufficient supply of labor force, improvement of human capital, high savings rate and high return on investment, and the increase of total factor productivity brought about by resource reallocation. The narrowed gap with the world's technological level means latecomer advantages have weakened, and it is increasingly necessary to lead by independent innovation. Traditional comparative advantages will eventually be lost, and new comparative advantages should be urgently cultivated to participate in the global division of labor. The new technological revolution and the corresponding new version of globalization provide new opportunities for China to change from rapid growth to high-quality development, and China must further reinforce reform and opening-up to seize this opportunity.

At the new stage of development, reform, and opening-up are also facing new challenges. Especially when reforms have fewer Pareto improvement effects, it is particularly necessary to explore a new balance point between market mechanisms and government roles to protect vulnerable groups during technological changes and enhance the penetration of technological changes to disadvantaged market entities.

First, as productivity improvement relies more on independent innovation with a creatively destructive nature, the role of the labor market in improving income distribution tends to weaken, and especially it cannot adequately protect laborers who are relatively disadvantaged in competition. Therefore, government redistribution policies such as labor market systems, social security systems, and other basic public services should play a greater role.

Second, under the condition that the country's overall science and technology is closer to the cutting-edge level, and even many fields are already at the cutting-edge level, the following problems will arise, such as whether the technology can penetrate into the whole economy, whether there will be obstacles to technology penetration, and whether the technology will be influenced by monopolies, institutional obstacles, and industrial policies. This requires that the government's science and technology policy and industrial policy should more embody the principle of competition neutrality, strengthen supervision, and anti-monopoly so that the national economy can benefit from technological change and globalization in a balanced way.

Notes

1 Robert Gordon, *The Rise and Fall of American Growth*, Beijing: China CITIC Press, 2018.
2 Klaus Schwab, *The Fourth Industrial Revolution*, Beijing: China CITIC Press, 2016. Characteristics of the four industrial revolutions are summarized in Chapter 1 of the book.
3 David H. Autor, David Dorn, Lawrence Katz, Christina Patterson, and John van Reenen, Concentrating on the Fall of the Labor Share, *American Economic Review*, Vol. 107, No. 5, 2017, pp. 180–185.

4 Klaus Schwab, *Globalization 4.0: What Does It Mean?*, 2018, www.weforum.org/agenda/2018/11/globalization-4-what-does-it-mean-how-it-will-benefit-everyone/.

5 Charles H. Feinstein, Pessimism Perpetuated: Real Wages and the Standard of Living in Britain during and after the Industrial Revolution, *The Journal of Economic History*, Vol. 58, No. 3, 1998, pp. 625–658.

6 John Maynard Keynes, Economic Possibilities for Our Grandchildren (1930), in Lorenzo Pecchi and Gustavo Piga (eds.), *Revisiting Keynes: Economic Possibilities for Our Grandchildren*, Cambridge, MA: MIT Press, 2008, pp. 17–26.

7 Aykut Kibritçiolu, *On the Smithian Origins of "New" Trade and Growth Theories*, Office of Research Working Paper, No. 2-100, 2002.

8 Tyler Cowen, *The Great Stagnation: How America Ate All the Low-Hanging Fruit of Modern History, Got Sick, and Will (Eventually) Feel Better*, New York: Dutton, 2011, pp. 20–22.

9 See Martin Ford, *Rise of the Robots: Technology and the Threat of a Jobless Future*, Beijing: China CITIC Press, 2015, Preface.

10 Rethinking Economics and New Weather Institute, *33 Theses for an Economics Reformation*, 2017, www.newweather.org/2017/12/12/the-new-reformation-33-theses-for-an-economics-reformation/.

11 For example, see Annie Lowrey, *Give People Money: How A Universal Basic Income Would End Poverty, Revolutionize Work, and Remake the World*, New York: Crown Publishing, 2018.

12 A report from McKinsey Global Institute indicates that due to the development of artificial intelligence and the resulting automation, by 2030, 75 million to 375 million workers (3–14% of the global workforce) will need to switch occupational categories. Major transitions could match or even exceed the scale of historical shifts out of agriculture and manufacturing. See McKinsey Global Institute, *Jobs Lost, Jobs Gained: Workforce Transitions in A Time of Automation*, London: McKinsey & Company, December 2017.

13 The most influential one in this regard can be found in David H. Autor, David Dorn, and Gordon H. Hanson, The China Shock: Learning from Labor-Market Adjustment to Large Changes in Trade, *The Annual Review of Economics*, Vol. 8, 2016, pp. 205–240.

14 Augie Picado, *The Real Reason Manufacturing Jobs Are Disappearing*, www.ted.com/talks/augie_picado_the_real_reason_manufacturing_jobs_are_disappearing/transcript.

15 Teresa C. Fort, Justin R. Pierce, and Peter K. Schott, *New Perspectives on the Decline of US Manufacturing Employment*, NBER Working Paper, No. 24490, 2018.

16 Milton Friedman, *Capitalism and Freedom*, Chicago: University of Chicago Press, 1962, pp. 161–162.

17 See Paul Krugman, *The Conscience of a Liberal*, Beijing: China CITIC Press, 2008.

18 The two most influential books are Thomas Piketty, *Capital in the Twenty-First Century*, Cambridge, MA: Belknap Press, 2014; Anthony B. Atkinson, *Inequality, What Can Be Done?* Cambridge, MA: Harvard University Press, 2015.

19 See Richard Langlois and Paul Robertson, Stop Crying Over Spilt Knowledge: A Critical Look at the Theory of Spillovers and Technical Change, *Journal of Public Finance and Public Choice*, Vol. 33, No. 1, 1996, pp. 63–80.

20 The authors' arguments and supporting evidence for this view are throughout the book, and the most representative ones can be centrally seen in Stephen S. Cohen

and John Zysman, *Manufacturing Matters: The Myth of the Post-Industrial Economy*, New York: Basic Books, Inc., 1987, pp. 100–107.

21 Robert M. Solow, We'd Better Watch Out, *The New York Times Book Review*, July 12, 1987, p. 36.

22 Niall Ferguson, The False Prophecy of Hyperconnection: How to Survive the Networked Age, *Foreign Affairs*, Vol. 96, No. 5, 2017.

23 See Eric Jing, Responsible Use of Technology Can Transform Millions of Lives, *Financial Times*, January 2019.

24 James Heilbrun, Baumol's Cost Disease, in Ruth Towse (ed.), *A Handbook of Cultural Economics*, Cheltenham, UK: Edward Elgar, 2011, pp. 91–101.

25 Sarah O'Connor, For Clues to the Productivity Puzzle, Go Shopping, *Financial Times*, 2 February 2017.

26 See Paul Romer, Why Not Promote Charter Cities?, *Business & Finance Review*, Vol. 16, 2011.

27 Milton Friedman, The Methodology of Positive Economics (1953), in Uskali Mäki (ed.), *The Methodology of Positive Economics: Reflections on the Milton Friedman Legacy*, Cambridge: Cambridge University Press, 2009, pp. 3–44.

28 Paul Romer, *Stigler Conviction vs. Feynman Integrity*, https://paulromer.net/old-blog/stigler-conviction-vs-feynman-integrity/index.html.

29 See Ehsan Masood: *The Story of GDP and the Making and the Unmaking of the Modern World*, Beijing: The Oriental Press, 2016.

30 Friedrich Hayek, The Use of Knowledge in Society, *American Economic Review*, Vol. 35, No. 4, 1945, p. 519.

31 Friedrich Hayek, The Use of Knowledge in Society, *American Economic Review*, Vol. 35, No. 4, 1945, p. 521.

32 Niall Ferguson, The False Prophecy of Hyperconnection: How to Survive the Networked Age, *Foreign Affairs*, Vol. 96, No. 5, 2017.

33 John Maynard Keynes, *The General Theory of Employment, Interest and Money*, New York: Cambridge University Press for the Royal Economic Society, 1936, p. 384.

34 Klaus Schwab, *The Fourth Industrial Revolution*, Beijing: China CITIC Press, 2016, Chapter 1.

Postscript

Looking back on 70 years of new China and 40 years of reform and opening-up, especially the glorious course of China's economic development since the 18th National Congress of the Communist Party of China, it is impossible to ignore the historical and world significance of the great achievements made by China during this period. Over the years, I have been paying attention to such problems and have devoted time and energy to relevant research, enhanced my understanding and published some articles. Taking the opportunity of celebrating the 70th anniversary of the founding of the People's Republic of China, I wrote this book. This is the research content of the topic of "China's Long-term Economic Development Theory and Experience," which is one of four funded projects.

As always, my achievements include the contributions of many collaborators and colleagues of the Chinese Academy of Social Sciences. The publication of this book is also supported by China Social Sciences Press, especially with the specific help of President Zhao Jianying and assistant editor-in-chief Wang Yin. For social sciences, especially economics, which need to face the ever-changing reality, any research results are only and should only be staged results. Only in this way can the understanding of the author and readers be deepened, and more theoretical consensus can be obtained. The same is true of this book. The author is willing to take responsibility for the imperfections and even mistakes in it, and sincerely looks forward to the readers' criticism and correction.

Cai Fang
October 21, 2019 in Beijing

DOI: 10.4324/9781003329305-18

References

Albertazzi, Daniele and Duncan McDonnell. Introduction: The Sceptre and the Spectre, in Daniele Albertazzi and Duncan McDonnell (eds.), *Twenty First Century Populism: The Spectre of Western European Democracy*, London: Palgrave Macmillan, 2008, pp. 1–11.

Allen, Robert. *Involution, Revolution, or What? Agricultural Productivity, Income, and Chinese Economic Development*, Paper delivered at meeting of All-UC Group in Economic History on "Convergence and Divergence in Historical Perspective," Irvine, CA, November, 2002.

Aoki, Masahiko. The Five Phases of Economic Development and Institutional Evolution in China, Japan and Korea, in Masahiko Aoki, Timur Kuran, and Gérard Roland (eds.), *Institutions and Comparative Economic Development*, Basingstoke: Palgrave Macmillan, 2012, pp. 13–47.

Aoki, Masahiko. The Five Phases of Economic Development and Institutional Evolution in China, Japan and Korea, in Masahiko Aoki, Timur Kuran, and Gérard Roland (eds.), *Institutions and Comparative Economic Development*, Basingstoke: Palgrave Macmillan, 2012.

Aoki, Masahiko, Timur Kuran, and Gérard Roland (eds.). *Institutions and Comparative Economic Development*, London: Palgrave Macmillan, 2012.

Asian Productivity Organization, *APO Productivity Data Book 2008*, Tokyo: Asian Productivity Organization, 2008.

Atkinson, Anthony B. *Inequality, What Can Be Done?* Cambridge, MA: Harvard University Press, 2015.

Autor, David H. Work of the Past, Work of the Future, *AEA Papers and Proceedings*, Vol. 109, 2019, pp. 1–32.

Autor, David H., David Dorn, and Gordon H. Hanson, The China Shock: Learning from Labor-Market Adjustment to Large Changes in Trade, *The Annual Review of Economics*, Vol. 8, 2016, pp. 205–240.

Autor, David H., David Dorn, Lawrence Katz, Christina Patterson, and John van Reenen, Concentrating on the Fall of the Labor Share, *American Economic Review*, Vol. 107, No. 5, 2017, pp. 180–185.

Autor, David H., Lawrence F. Katz, and Melissa S. Kearney, The Polarization of the U.S. Labor Market, NBER Working Paper, No. 11986, 2006.

Bai Chong-En, Hsieh Chang-Tai, and Qian Yingyi. *The Return to Capital in China*, NBER Working Paper, No. 12755, 2006.

Bai Chong-En and Qian Zhenjie. *Who Has Eroded Residents' Incomes? An Analysis of China's National Income Distribution Patterns*, Beijing: Social Sciences in China Press, 2009.

Bai Chong-En and Zhang Qiong. An Analysis of China's Capital Return Rate and Its Influencing Factors, *The Journal of World Economy*, Vol. 10, 2014, pp. 3–30.

Bai Chong-En and Zhang Qiong. China's Productivity Estimates and its Fluctuation Decomposition, *The Journal of World Economy*, Vol. 12, 2015, pp. 3–28.

Barber, Tony. Europe's Decline is a Global Concern, *Financial Times*, December 22, 2015.

Barrett, Christopher B., Michael R. Carter, and C. Peter Timmer. A Century-Long Perspective on Agricultural Development, *American Journal of Agricultural Economics*, Vol. 92, No. 2, 2010, pp. 447–468.

Barro, Robert J. *Economic Growth and Convergence, Applied Especially to China*, NBER Working Paper, No. 21872, 2016.

Barro, Robert J. and Xavier Sala-i-Martin, *Economic Growth*, New York: McGraw-Hill, 1995.

Barro, Robert J. and Xavier Sala-i-Martin, Foreword, in *Economic Growth*, Beijing: China Social Sciences Press, 2000.

Barro, Robert J. and Xavier Sala-i-Martin, *Economic Growth* (second edition), Cambridge, MA: MIT Press, 2004.

Baumol, William J. Productivity Growth, Convergence, and Welfare: What the Long-Run Data Show, *The American Economic Review*, Vol. 76, No. 5, 1986, pp. 1072–1085.

Boeke, Julius Herman. *Economics and Economic Policy of Dual Societies*, New York: Institute of Pacific Relations, 1953.

Bosworth, Barry and Susan Collins. Accounting for Growth: Comparing China and India, NBER Working Paper, 12943, 2007.

Brandt, Loren, Debin Ma, and Thomas G. Rawski. From Divergence to Convergence: Reevaluating the History behind China's Economic Boom, *Journal of Economic Literature*, Vol. 52, 2014, pp. 45–123.

Brandt, Loren and Thomas G. Rawski (eds.). *China's Great Economic Transformation*, Cambridge: Cambridge University Press, 2008.

Brandt, Loren and Zhu Xiaodong. *Accounting for China's Growth*, Working Paper, No. 395, Department of Economics of University of Toronto, 2010.

Cai Fang. Urban–Rural Income Gap and Critical Point of Institutional Reform, *Social Sciences in China*, Vol. 5, 2003, pp. 16–25.

Cai Fang. *Economics of People's Livelihood: An Analysis of Issues Relating to Agriculture, Rural Affairs and Farmers and Employment*, Beijing: Social Sciences Academic Press, 2005.

Cai Fang. *Scientific Development Philosophy and Sustainability of Economic Growth*, Shanghai: Zhonghua Book Company, 2009.

Cai Fang. Demographic Transition, Demographic Dividend, and Lewis Turning Point in China, *China Economic Journal*, Vol. 3, No. 2, 2010, pp. 107–119.

Cai Fang (ed.). *Transforming the Chinese Economy, 1978–2008*, Leiden and Boston: Brill, 2010.

Cai Fang. *Avoid the Middle-Income Trap*, Beijing: Social Sciences Academic Press, 2012.

Cai Fang. "Understanding the Past, Present and Future of China's Economic Development: Based on a Connected Growth Theoretical Framework," *Economic Research Journal*, Vol. 11, 2013, pp. 4–16.

Cai Fang. *Demystifying the Economic Growth in Transition China*, Beijing: China Social Sciences Press, 2014.

Cai Fang. *Demystifying China's Economy Development*, Beijing and Berlin: China Social Sciences Press and Springer-Verlag, 2015.

Cai Fang. The Formation Process of Dual Economy as a Development Phase, *Economic Research Journal*, Vol. 7, 2015, pp. 4–15.

Cai Fang. Macro-economic Policies in Promoting More and Better Jobs in China: Issues, Evidence and Policy Option, *Studies on Labor Economics*, Vol. 3, 2015, pp. 3–31.

Cai Fang. The Making of Dual Economy as a Stage of Economic Development, *Economic Research Journal*, Vol. 7, 2015, pp. 4–15.

Cai Fang. *China's Economic Growth Prospects: From Demographic Dividend to Reform Dividend*, Cheltenham, UK: Edward Elgar, 2016.

Cai Fang. Analysis of the Effect of China's Economic Reform from the Perspective of Labor Reallocation, *Economic Research Journal*, Vol. 7, 2017, pp. 4–17.

Cai Fang. Reform Effects in China: A Perspective of Labor Reallocation, *Economic Research Journal*, Vol. 7, 2017, pp. 4–17.

Cai Fang. Why has Malthus Become the "Oldest" Economist? in *The Humble are the Wisest*, Beijing: Social Sciences Academic Press, 2017, pp. 188–196.

Cai Fang. Get Rid of the Old to Leave Room for the New: Promote Transformation of Growth Power by Clearing Ineffective Production Capacity, *Comparative Studies*, Vol. 1, 2018, pp. 1–13.

Cai Fang. Has the Potential of Agricultural Labor Transfer Been Exhausted?, Chinese Rural Economy, Vol. 9, 2018, pp. 2–13.

Cai Fang. How has the Chinese Economy Capitalized on the Demographic Dividend during the Reform Period?, in Ross Garnaut, Song Ligang, and Cai Fang (eds.), *China's Forty Years of Reform and Development: 1978–2018*, Canberra: ANU Press, 2018, pp. 235–255.

Cai Fang. Globalization, Convergence and China's Economic Development, *World Economics and Politics*, Vol. 3, 2019, pp. 4–18.

Cai Fang. How to Cultivate Middle-income Groups, in *Chinese Story to Chinese Wisdom*, Sichuan: People's Publishing House, 2019, pp. 219–230.

Cai Fang. Understanding China's Economic Growth Potential: Response to Justin Yifu Lin's Criticism on Explanation to Demographic Dividend, *Comparative Studies*, Vol. 2, 2019, pp. 20–33.

Cai Fang, Guo Zhenwei, and Wang Meiyan. New Urbanization as a Driver of China's Growth, in Song Ligang, Ross Garnaut, Cai Fang, and Lauren Johnston (eds.), *China's New Sources of Economic Growth, Vol. 1: Reform, Resources, and Climate Changes*, Canberra and Beijing: ANU Press and Social Sciences Academic Press, 2016, pp. 43–64.

Cai Fang and Wang Dewen. Sustainability of China's Economic Growth and Labor Contribution, *Economic Research Journal*, Vol. 10, 1999, pp. 62–68.

Cai Fang and Wang Dewen. China's Demographic Transition: Implications for Growth, in Ross Garnaut and Song Ligang (eds.), *The China Boom and Its Discontents*, Canberra: Asia Pacific Press, 2005, pp. 34–52.

Cai Fang and Wang Meiyan. From Poor Economy to Scale Economy: Challenges to China's Agriculture from Changes in Development Phases, *Economic Research Journal*, Vol. 5, 2016, pp. 14–26.

Cai Fang, Du Yang, Gao Wenshu, and Wang Meiyan: *Labor Economics: Theory and China's Reality*, Beijing: Normal University Publishing Group, 2009.

Cai Fang, Du Yang, and Wang Meiyan. Demystify the Labor Statistics in China, *China Economic Journal*, Vol. 6, No. 2–3, 2013, pp. 123–133.

Cai Fang and Lu Yang. The End of China's Demographic Dividend: The Perspective of Potential GDP Growth, in Ross Garnaut, Cai Fang and Song Ligang (eds.), *China: A New Model for Growth and Development*, Canberra: ANU Press, 2013, pp. 55–74.

Cai Fang and Lu Yang. Take-off, Persistence, and Sustainability: Demographic Factor of the Chinese Growth, *Asia & the Pacific Policy Studies*, Vol. 3, No. 2, 2016, pp. 203–225.

Cai Fang and Zhao Wen, When Demographic Dividend Disappears: Growth Sustainability of China, in Masahiko Aoki and Jinglian Wu (eds.), *The Chinese Economy: A New Transition*, Basingstoke: Palgrave Macmillan, 2012, pp. 75–90.

Caldwell, John C. Toward a Restatement of Demographic Transition Theory, *Population and Development Review*, Vol. 2, 1976, pp. 321–366.

Cao, Shuji. *The History of Chinese Population, Volume V Part 3*, Shanghai: Fudan University Press, 2005.

Cardwell, D.S.L. *Turning Points in Western Technology*, New York: Neale Watson, 1972.

Carson, Joseph. Inflation Indices Should Add House Prices to Prevent Bubbles, *Financial Times*, December 2018.

Cavafy, C.P. Waiting for the Barbarians, in George Savidis (ed.), *Collected Poems*, translated by Edmund Keeley and Philip Sherrard (revised edition), Princeton: Princeton University Press, 1992, p. 18.

Chang Ha-Joon, *Kicking Away the Ladder: Development Strategy in Historic Perspective*, Beijing: Social Sciences Academic Press, 2009.

Chang, Pei-kang. *Agriculture and Industrialization: The Adjustments that Take Place as an Agricultural Country Is Industrialized*, Cambridge, MA: Harvard University Press, 1949.

Chayanov, A. *Farmers' Economic Organization*, Beijing: Central Compilation & Translation Press, 1996.

Chen Xiwen. Focus Issues of China's Agricultural Development, *Agriculture Machinery Technology Extension*, Vol. 7, 2015, pp. 233–239.

Chenery, Hollis B. and Alan M. Strout. Foreign Assistance and Economic Development, *The American Economic Review*, Vol. 56, No. 4, 1966, pp. 679–733.

Chenery, Hollis B. and Moises Syrquin. *Patterns of Development 1950–1970*, Washington, DC: Economic Science Press, 1988.

Cheremukhim, Anton, Mikhail Golosov, Sergei Guriev, and Aleh Tsyvinski. *The Economy of People's Republic of China from 1953*, NBER Working Paper, No. 21397, 2015.

Cheung, Steven. *The Economic System of China*, Beijing: China CITIC Press, 2009.

Chia, Siow Yue. Foreign Labor in Singapore: Trends, Policies, Impacts, and Challenges, *Philippine Institute for Development Studies*, DISCUSSION PAPER SERIES NO. 2011-24.

Coase, Ronald and Ning Wang. *How China Became Capitalist*, London: Palgrave Macmillan, 2012.

Cohen, Stephen S. and John Zysman. *Manufacturing Matters: The Myth of the Post-Industrial Economy*, New York: Basic Books, Inc., 1987.

Cowen, Tyler. *The Great Stagnation: How America Ate All the Low-Hanging Fruit of Modern History, Got Sick, and Will (Eventually) Feel Better*, New York: Dutton, 2011.

Da Xiang. *The History of Communication between China and the West*, Changsha: Yuelu Press, 2011.

Dabla-Norris, Era, Kalpana Kochhar, Nujin Suphaphiphat, Frantisek Ricka, and Evridiki Tsounta. *Causes and Consequences of Income Inequality: A Global Perspective*, IMF Staff Discussion Note, SDN/15/13, June 2015.

Dahl, Robert A. *Polyarchy, Participation and Opposition*, New Haven and London: Yale University Press, 1971.

Deaton, Angus. *Globalization and Health in America*, January 14, 2018, based on remarks during a panel discussion at the IMF conference on Meeting Globalization's

Challenges (October 2017), www.princeton.edu/~deaton/downloads/Globalizat ion-and-health-in-America_ IMF-remarks.pdf.

Deng Xiaoping. Talking Points in Wuchang, Shenzhen, Zhuhai, Shanghai and Other Places, in *Selected Works of Deng Xiaoping, Volume III*, Beijing: People's Publishing House, 1993.

Deng Xiaoping. *Selected Works of Deng Xiaoping, Volume II*, Beijing: People's Publishing House, 1994, pp. 370–383.

Deutscher, Isaac. *The Prophet Unarmed: Trotsky 1921–1929*, Beijing: Central Compilation & Translation Press, 2013.

Dong Zhenrui and Yi Lei, Recalling Deng Xiaoping's Visit to Japan and Meeting with Masayoshi Ohira in the Late 1970s—Interview Record of Wang Xiaoxian, *Literature of Chinese Communist Party*, Vol. 2, 2007, pp. 18–20.

Dornbusch, Rudiger and Sebastian Edwards. Macroeconomic Populism in Latin America, NBER Working Paper, No. 2986, 1989.

Du Yang. On Labor Market Changes and the New Economic Growth, *China Opening Journal*, Vol. 3, 2014, pp. 5–31.

Du Yang, Albert Park, and Wang Sangui. Migration and Rural Poverty in China, *Journal of Comparative Economics*, Vol. 33, No. 4, 2005, pp. 688–709.

Durand, John D. The Population Statistics of China, AD 2–1953, *Population Studies*, Vol. 13, No. 3, 1960, pp. 209–256.

Easterly, William. *The Elusive Quest for Growth: Economists' Adventures and Misadventures in the Tropics*, Beijing: CITIC Publishing House, 2005.

Easterly, William. *The White Man's Burden: Why the West's Efforts to Aid the Rest Have Done So Much and So Little Good*, Beijing: China CITIC Press, 2008.

The Economist. Economic Focus: Exploding Misconceptions, *The Economist*, December 18, 2010, p. 130.

The Economist. Foreign Aid: Fading Faith in Good Works, *The Economist*, July 1, 2017.

Eichengreen, Barry, Donghyun Park, and Kwanho Shin, When Fast Growing Economies Slow Down: International Evidence and Implications for China, NBER Working Paper, No. 16919, 2011.

Eichengreen, Barry, Donghyun Park, and Kwanho Shin. Growth Slowdowns Redux: New Evidence on the Middle-income Trap, NBER Working Paper, No. 18673, 2013.

Elvin, Mark. *The Pattern of the Chinese Past: A Social and Economic Interpretation*, Stanford: Stanford University Press, 1973.

Fan Gang, Yi Gang, Wu Xiaoling, Xu Shanda, and Cai Fang. *Twenty Years for Fifty Economists*, Beijing: China CITIC Press, 2018.

Feinstein, Charles H. Pessimism Perpetuated: Real Wages and the Standard of Living in Britain during and after the Industrial Revolution, *The Journal of Economic History*, Vol. 58, No. 3, 1998, pp. 625–658.

Felipe, Jesus. *Total Factor Productivity Growth in East Asia: A Critical Survey*, EDRC Report Series, No. 65, Asian Development Bank, Manila, Philippines, 1997.

Ferguson, Niall. *Civilization*, Beijing: China CITIC Press, 2012.

Ferguson, Niall. *The War of the World*, Guangzhou: Guangdong People's Publishing House, 2015, pp. 68–79.

Ferguson, Niall. The False Prophecy of Hyperconnection: How to Survive the Networked Age, *Foreign Affairs*, Vol. 96, No. 5, 2017.

Ferreira, Francisco and Carolina Sanchez. *A Richer Array of International Poverty Lines, Let's Talk Development*, October 13, 2017, http://blogs.worldbank.org/developmenttalk.

Ford, Martin. *Rise of the Robots: Technology and the Threat of a Jobless Future*, Beijing: China CITIC Press, 2015.

Fort, Teresa C., Justin R. Pierce, and Peter K. Schott, New Perspectives on the Decline of US Manufacturing Employment, NBER Working Paper, No. 24490, 2018.

Foster, Lucia, John Haltiwanger, and Chad Syverson. Reallocation, Firm Turnover, and Efficiency: Selection on Productivity or Profitability? *American Economic Review*, Vol. 98, No. 1, 2008, pp. 394–425.

Frankopan, Peter. *The Silk Road: A New History of the World*, translated by Shao Xudong and Sun Fang, Hangzhou: Zhejiang University Press, 2016.

Freeman, Richard. Labor Markets and Institutions in Economic Development, *AEA Papers and Proceedings*, Vol. 83, No. 2, 1993, pp. 403–408.

Friedman, Milton. *Capitalism and Freedom*, Chicago: University of Chicago Press, 1962.

Friedman, Milton. The Methodology of Positive Economics (1953), in Uskali Mäki (ed.), *The Methodology of Positive Economics: Reflections on the Milton Friedman Legacy*, Cambridge: Cambridge University Press, 2009, pp. 3–44.

Furman, Jason. The Truth about American Unemployment: How to Grow the Country's Labor Market, *Foreign Affairs*, Vol. 95, No. 4, 2016, pp. 127–138.

Gan Li, Yin Zhichao, Jia Nan, Xu Shu, Ma Shuang, and Zheng Lu. *China Household Finance Survey Report 2012*, Chengdu: Southwestern University of Finance and Economics Press, 2012.

Gao Fan. Basis, Connotation and Change Path of China's Agricultural Weakness, *Social Sciences in Yunnan*, Vol. 3, 2006, pp. 49–53.

Gao Liangliang, Huang Jikun, and Scott Rozelle. Rental Markets for Cultivated Land and Agricultural Investments in China, *Agricultural Economics*, Vol. 43, 2012, pp. 91–403.

Gao Wenshu, Zhao Wen, and Cheng Jie. How Rural Labor Flow will Influence the Statistics on Income Gap of Rural and Urban Residents, in Cai Fang (ed.), *Reports on China's Population and Labor (No. 12): Challenges during the 12th Five-Year Plan Period: Population, Employment and Income Distribution*, Beijing: Social Sciences Academic Press, 2011, pp. 228–242.

Gassebner, Martin and Simon Luechinger. Lock, Stock, and Barrel: A Comprehensive Assessment of the Determinants of Terror, *Public Choice*, Vol. 149, 2011, pp. 235–261.

Ge Jianxiong, *Reunification and Split: A Lesson from Chinese History*, Beijing: The Commercial Press, 2003.

Ge Jianxiong, The History of Chinese Population, *Volume I*, Shanghai: Fudan University Press, 2005.

Geertz, Clifford. *Agricultural Involution: The Process of Ecological Change in Indonesia*, Berkeley: University of California Press, 1963.

Gilens, Martin and Benjamin I. Page. Testing Theories of American Politics: Elites, Interest Groups, and Average Citizens, *Perspectives on Politics*, Vol. 12, No. 3, 2014, pp. 564–581.

Gill, Indermit and Homi Kharas. *An East Asian Renaissance: Ideas for Economic Growth*, Washington, DC: World Bank, 2007.

Gilpin, Robert. *The Political Economy of International Relations*, Washington, DC: Economic Science Press, 1989.

Gordon, Robert, *The Rise and Fall of American Growth*, Beijing: China CITIC Press, 2018.

Guo Zhigang, Wang Feng, and Cai Yong. *Low Fertility Rate and Sustainable Development of Population in China*, Beijing: China Social Sciences Press, 2014.

Hansen, Gary D. and Edward C. Prescott. Malthus to Solow, *American Economic Review*, Vol. 92, No. 4, 2002, pp. 1205–1217.

Hayami, Yujiro. *Japanese Agriculture under Siege: The Political Economy of Agricultural Policies*, New York: St. Martin's Press, 1988

Hayami, Yujiro. *Development Economics from the Poverty to the Wealth of Nations*, Beijing: Social Sciences Academic Press, 2003.

Hayami, Yujiro and Vernon Ruttan. *Agricultural Development: An International Perspective*, Baltimore and London: Johns Hopkins University Press, 1980.

Hayashi, F. and E. Prescott. The Depressing Effect of Agricultural Institutions on the Prewar Japanese Economy, *Journal of Political Economy*, Vol. 116, No. 4, 2008, pp. 573–632.

Hayek, Friedrich. The Use of Knowledge in Society, *American Economic Review*, Vol. 35, No. 4, 1945, pp. 419–430.

Hayek, Friedrich. *Studies in Philosophy, Politics and Economics*, London: Routledge and Kegan Paul, 1967.

Hicks, John R. *A Theory of Economic History*, London: The Commercial Press, 1987.

Heilbrun, James. Baumol's Cost Disease, in Ruth Towse (ed.), *A Handbook of Cultural Economics*, Cheltenham, UK: Edward Elgar, 2011, pp. 91–101.

Hirschman, Albert O. *Exit, Voice, and Loyalty: Responses to Decline in Firms, Organizations, and States*, Cambridge, MA: Harvard University Press, 1970.

Honma, Masayoshi and Yujiro Hayami. The Determinants of Agricultural Protection Levels: An Econometric Analysis, in Kym Anderson and Yujiro Hayami (eds.), *The Political Economy of Agricultural Protection*, Sydney: Allen & Unwin, 1986, pp. 39–49.

Huang, Jikun, Keijiro Otsuka, and Scott Rozelle, *The Role of Agriculture in China's Development*, presented at the workshop "China's Economic Transition: Origins, Mechanisms, and Consequences," Pittsburgh, November 5–7, 2004.

Huang, Philip. Development or Involution? The United Kingdom and China in the 18th Century: A Review of Kenneth Pomeranz's *The Great Divergence: Europe, China and the Making of the Modern World Economy*, *Historical Research*, Vol. 4, 2002, pp. 149–192.

Huang Yasheng. *Capitalism with Chinese Characteristics: Entrepreneurship and the State*, Cambridge: Cambridge University Press, 2008.

Huang Zongzhi. Development or Involution? Great Britain and China in the 18th Century: Comment on Kenneth Pomeranz's Great Divergence: Europe, China and Development of Modern World Economy, *Historical Research*, Vol. 4, 2002, pp. 149–176, 191–192.

Hume, David. On the Rise and Progress of the Arts and Sciences, in *Essays: Moral, Political and Literary*, edited by E.F. Miller, Indianapolis: Liberty Fund, 1987, p. 135.

Institute of Contemporary China Studies. *Chronology of the History of the People's Republic of China (1958)*, Beijing: Contemporary China Publishing House, 2011.

International Monetary Fund. Asia Rising: Patterns of Economic Development and Growth, in *World Economic Outlook*, September 2006.

Information Office of the State Council. *Policy Interpretation of the Opinions on Separation of Rural Land Rights*, November 3, 2016, www.scio.gov.cn/34473/34515/Document/1515220/1515220htm.

Jasny, Naum. *Socialized Agriculture in the Soviet Union: Plans and Results, Volume I,* Beijing: The Commercial Press, 1965.

Jing, Eric. Responsible Use of Technology Can Transform Millions of Lives, *Financial Times*, January 2019.

Johnson, D. Gail. Can Agricultural Labor Adjustment Occur Primarily through Creation of Rural Nonfarm Jobs in China?, in *The Issues of Agriculture, Rural Areas and Farmers in Economic Development*, Beijing: The Commercial Press, 2004, p. 65.

Johnston, Bruce F. and John W. Mellor. The Role of Agriculture in Economic Development, *The American Economic Review*, Vol. 51, No. 4, 1961, pp. 566–593.

Jones, Charles. Was An Industrial Revolution Inevitable? Economic Growth Over the Very Long Run, NBER Working Paper, No. 7375, 1999.

Kahneman, Daniel. *Thinking, Fast and Slow*, London and New York: Penguin Books, 2012.

Kanbur, Ravi and Zhang Xiaobo. *Fifty Years of Regional Inequality in China: A Journey through Central Planning, Reform, and Openness*, United Nations University WIDER Discussion Paper, No. 50, 2004.

Kennedy, Gavin. *Adam Smith*, Beijing: Huaxia Publishing House, 2009.

Keynes, John Maynard. *The General Theory of Employment, Interest and Money*, New York: Cambridge University Press for the Royal Economic Society, 1936.

Keynes, John Maynard. Economic Possibilities for Our Grandchildren (1930), in Lorenzo Pecchi and Gustavo Piga (eds.), *Revisiting Keynes: Economic Possibilities for Our Grandchildren*, Cambridge, MA: MIT Press, 2008, pp. 17–26.

Kibritçiolu, Aykut. *On the Smithian Origins of "New" Trade and Growth Theories*, Office of Research Working Paper, No. 2-100, 2002.

Kindleberger, Charles P. International Public Goods without International Government, *The American Economic Review*, Vol. 76, No. 1, 1986, pp. 1–13.

Kindleberger, Charles P. *The World in Depression: 1929–1939*, Shanghai: Translation Publishing House, 1986.

Kipling, Rudyard. *The White Man's Burden*, 1899, http://sourcebooks.fordham.edu/halsall/mod/kipling.asp.

Kojima, Kiyoshi. The "Flying Geese" Model of Asian Economic Development: Origin, Theoretical Extensions, and Regional Policy Implications, *Journal of Asian Economics*, Vol. 11, 2000, pp. 375–401.

Kremer, Michael. Population Growth and Technological Change: One Million BC to 1990, *The Quarterly Journal of Economics*, Vol. 108, No. 3, 1993, pp. 681–716.

Kriedte, Peter. The Origins, the Agrarian Context, and the Conditions in the World Market, in Peter Kriedte, Hans Medick, and Jurgen Schlumbohm (eds.), *Industrialization before Industrialization*, Cambridge: Cambridge University Press, 1981, p. 28.

Krugman, Paul. New Theories of Trade Among Industrial Countries, *The American Economic Review*, Vol. 73, No. 2, 1983, pp. 343–347.

Krugman, Paul. *Pop Internationalism*, Beijing: China Renmin University Press/Peking University Press, 2000.

Krugman, Paul. *The Conscience of a Liberal*, Beijing: China CITIC Press, 2008.

Krugman, Paul. Hitting China's Wall, *New York Times*, July 18, 2013.

Kuijs, Louis. China Through 2020: A Macroeconomic Scenario, World Bank China Research Working Paper, No. 9, 2010.

Kuznets, Simon. Modern Economic Growth: Findings and Reflections, *American Economic Review*, Vol. 63, 1973, pp. 247–58.

Kuznets, Simon. *Modern Economic Growth*, Beijing: School of Economics Press,1989.

Kuznets, Simon. *Economic Growth of Nations: Total Output and Production Structure*, Beijing: The Commercial Press, 1985.

Lal, Deepak. *The Poverty of "Development Economics,"* London: Institute of Economic Affairs, 1983.

Langlois, Richard and Paul Robertson. Stop Crying Over Spilt Knowledge: A Critical Look at the Theory of Spillovers and Technical Change, *Journal of Public Finance and Public Choice*, Vol. 33, No. 1, 1996, pp. 63–80.

Lewis, Arthur. Economic Development with Unlimited Supplies of Labor, *The Manchester School*, Vol. 22, No. 2, 1954, pp. 139–191.

Lewis, Arthur. *The Theory of Economic Growth*, translated by Xiaomin Liang, Shanghai: Sanlian Publishing House/People's Publishing House, 1994.

Li Deshui. Economic Reasons for the Lack of Migrant Laborers, *People's Daily Online*, 2005, http://politics.people.com.cn/GB/1027/3149315.html.

Lin, Justin Yifu. Rural Reforms and Agricultural Growth in China, *American Economic Review*, Vol. 82, No. 1, 1992, pp. 34–51.

Lin, Justin Yifu. *The Needham Puzzle, the Weber Question and China's Miracle: Long Term Performance since the Sung Dynasty*, CCER Working Paper Series, No. E2006017, November 22, 2006.

Lin, Justin Yifu. China and the Global Economy, *China Economic Journal*, Vol. 4, No. 1, 2011, pp. 1–14.

Lin, Justin Yifu, Cai Fang, and Zhou Li. *The China Miracle: Development Strategy and Economic Reform* (revised edition), Hong Kong: Chinese University Press, 2003.

Little, Daniel. *Micro Foundations, Method and Causation: On the Philosophy of the Social Sciences*, New Jersey: Transaction Publishers, 1998.

Livi-Bacci, Massimo. *A Concise History of World Population* (fifth edition), Chichester: Wiley-Blackwell, 2012.

Lowrey, Annie. *Give People Money: How A Universal Basic Income Would End Poverty, Revolutionize Work, and Remake the World*, New York: Crown Publishing, 2018.

Lucas, Robert E. Jr. Why Doesn't Capital Flow from Rich to Poor Countries? *The American Economic Review*, Vol. 80, No. 2, 1990, pp. 92–96.

MacGillivray, Alex. *A Brief History of Globalization: The Untold Story of Our Incredible Shrinking Planet*, London: Robinson, 2006.

Maddison, Angus. *Chinese Economic Performance in the Long Run*, Beijing: Xinhua Publishing House, 1999.

Maddison, Angus. *The World Economy: A Millennial Perspective*, Beijing: Peking University Press, 2003.

Maddison, Angus. *The World Economy: Historical Statistics*, Beijing: Peking University Press, 2004.

Maddison, Angus. *Contours of the World Economy, 1–2030 AD: Essays in Macro-Economic History*, Oxford: Oxford University Press, 2007.

Maddison, Angus. *Long-term Performance of China's Economy: AD 960–2030*, Shanghai: People's Publishing House, 2008.

Manuelli, Rodolfo and Ananth Seshadri. Human Capital and the Wealth of Nations, *The American Economic Review*, Vol. 104, No. 9, 2014, pp. 2736–2762.

Masood, Ehsan. *The Story of GDP and the Making and the Unmaking of the Modern World*, Beijing: The Oriental Press, 2016.

Marx, Karl. *Capital, Volume I*, Shanghai: People's Publishing House, 1975.

Marx, Karl. The Eighteenth Brumaire of Louis Bonaparte, in *Marx Engels Werke*, compiled by the CPC Central Committee Compilation & Translation Bureau of the Works of Marx, Engels, Lenin and Stalin, Volume 2, Shanghai: People's Publishing House, 2009, pp. 566–567.

Marx, Karl and Friedrich Engels. *Marx and Engels, Selected Works, Volume 2*, Shanghai: People's Publishing House, 1995.

McKinsey Global Institute. Bridging Global Infrastructure Gaps, London: McKinsey & Company, June 2016.

McKinsey Global Institute. *Jobs Lost, Jobs Gained: Workforce Transitions in A Time of Automation*, London: McKinsey & Company, December 2017.

McMillan, John, John Whalley, and Zhu Lijing. The Impact of China's Economic Reforms on Agricultural Productivity Growth, *Journal of Political Economy*, Vol. 97, No. 4, 1989, pp. 781–807.

McMillan, Margaret S. and Dani Rodrik. Globalization, Structural Change and Productivity Growth, NBER Working Paper, No. 17143, 2011.

Meier, Gerald M. *Leading Issues in Economic Development* (revised edition), Oxford: Oxford University Press, 1995.

Minami, Ryoshi and Ma Xinxin. The Turning Point of Chinese Economy: Compared with Japanese Experience, *Asian Economics*, Vol. 50, No. 12, 2009, pp. 2–20.

Miyazaki, Isamu. *A Record of Japan's Economic Policy*, Beijing: China CITIC Press, 2009.

Mokyr, Joel. Cardwell's Law and the Political Economy of Technological Progress, *Research Policy*, Vol. 23, 1994, pp. 561–574.

Mu Qian. *The Political Gains and Losses of Chinese Dynasties*, Hong Kong: SDX Joint Publishing Company, 2001.

National Bureau of Statistics. *Series Analysis Report on 50 Years of New China (6): The Rise of Township Enterprises*, 1999, www.stats.gov.cn/ztjc/ztfx/xzg50nxlf xbg/200206/t20020605_35964html.

National Bureau of Statistics. China Statistics Yearbook 2015, Beijing: China Statistics Press, 2015.

National Bureau of Statistics. *The National Report on Migrant Worker Monitoring and Survey 2015*, 2016, www.stats.gov.cn.

Naughton, Barry. *Growing Out of the Plan: Chinese Economic Reform, 1978–1993*, Cambridge: Cambridge University Press, 1996.

North, Douglass C. and Robert Paul Thomas. *The Rise of The Western World: A New Economic History*, Beijing: Huaxia Publishing House, 1999.

Nye, Joseph S. Jr. *The Kindleberger Trap*, January 9, 2017, www.project-syndicate.org/.

O'Connor, Sarah. For Clues to the Productivity Puzzle, Go Shopping, *Financial Times*, February 2, 2017.

Olson, Mancur. *Logic of Collective Action*, Shanghai: People's Publishing House, 1995.

Palma, Jose Gabriel. Do Nations Just Get the Inequality They Deserve? *The "Palma Ratio" Re-examined*, Cambridge Working Paper Economics, No. 1627, May 2016.

Parente, Stephen L. and Edward C. Prescott. *Barriers to Riches*, Beijing: China Renmin University Press, 2010.

Perkins, Dwight H. China's Economic Growth in Historical and International Perspective, *China Economic Quarterly*, Vol. 4, No. 4, 2005, pp. 891–913.

Picado, Augie. *The Real Reason Manufacturing Jobs Are Disappearing*, www.ted. com/talks/augie_picado_the_real_reason_manufacturing_jobs_are_disappearing/ transcript.

Piketty, Thomas. *Capital in the Twenty-First Century*, Cambridge, MA: Belknap Press, 2014.

Pomeranz, Kenneth. *The Great Divergence: Europe, China and the Making of the Modern World Economy*, Nanjing: Jiangsu People's Publishing Ltd., 2003.

Pomeranz, Kenneth. Late Imperial Jiangnan in World Economic History: Comparative and Integrative: A Discussion with Professor Philip Huang, *Historical Studies*, Vol. 4, 2003, pp. 3–48, p. 189.

Pritchett, Lant and Lawrence H. Summers. Asiaphoria Meets Regression to the Mean, NBER Working Paper, No. 20573, 2014.

Qu Yue, Cai Fang, and Zhang Xiaobo. Has the "Flying Geese" Phenomenon in Industrial Transformation Occurred in China?, in Huw McKay and Ligang Song (eds.), *Rebalancing and Sustaining Growth in China*, Canberra: ANU Press, 2012, pp. 93–109.

Rajan, Raghuram. *Fault Lines: How Hidden Fractures Still Threaten the World Economy*, translated by Liu Nian et al., Beijing: China CITIC Press, 2011.

Ranis, Gustav. *Arthur Lewis' Contribution to Development Thinking and Policy*, Yale University Economic Growth Center Discussion Paper, No. 891, 2004.

Ranis, Gustav and John C.H. Fei, A Theory of Economic Development, *American Economic Review*, Vol. 51, No. 4, 1961, pp. 657–665.

Rawski, Thomas. Human Resources and China's Long Economic Boom, *Asia Policy*, Vol. 12, 2011, pp. 33–78.

Rawski, Thomas and Robert Mead. On the Trail of China's Phantom Farmers, *World Development*, Vol. 26, No. 5, 1998, pp. 767–781.

Reinhart, Carmen and Vincent Reinhart. The Crisis Next Time: What We Should Have Learned from 2008, *Foreign Affairs*, Vol. 97, No. 6, 2018, pp. 84–96.

Rethinking Economics and New Weather Institute. 33 Theses for an Economics Reformation, 2017, www.newweather.org/2017/12/12/the-new-reformation-33-theses-for-an-economics-reformation/.

Roberts, Andrew and Niall Ferguson. Hitler's England: What if Germany Had Invaded Britain in May 1940?, in Niall Ferguson (ed.), *Virtual History*, New York: Macmillan, 1997, pp. 281–320.

Romer, Paul. Which Parts of Globalization Matter for Catch-up Growth? NBER Working Paper, No. 15755, 2010, pp. 28–29.

Romer, Paul. Why Not Promote Charter Cities?, *Business & Finance Review*, Vol. 16, 2011.

Romer, Paul. *Stigler Conviction vs. Feynman Integrity*, https://paulromer.net/old-blog/stigler-conviction-vs-feynman-integrity/index.html.

Rosenberg, Nathan and L.E. Birdzell Jr. *How the West Grew Rich: The Economic Transformation of the Industrial World*, New York: Basic Books, 1986.

Rostow, Walt Whitman. *How It All Began: Origins of the Modern Economy*, Beijing: The Commercial Press, 2014.

Sachs, Jeffrey. *Lessons for Brazil from China's Success*, transcript, São Paulo, November 5, 2003.

Sachs, Jeffrey. *The End of Poverty: Economic Possibility for Our Time*, translated by Zou Guang, Shanghai: People's Press, 2007.

Sachs, Jeffrey D. and Andrew Warner. Economic Reform and the Process of Global Integration, *Brookings Papers on Economic Activity*, Vol. 1, 1995, pp. 12–13.

Sala-i-Martin, Xavier. I Just Ran Two Million Regressions, *American Economic Review*, Vol. 87, No. 2, 1997, pp. 178–183.

Samuelson, Paul. Where Ricardo and Mill Rebut and Confirm Arguments of Mainstream Economists Supporting Globalization, *Journal of Economic Perspectives*, Vol. 18, No. 3, 2004, pp. 135–146.

Schultz, Theodore W. *Transforming Traditional Agriculture*, Chicago and London: University of Chicago Press, 1983.

Schultz, Theodore W. *Transforming Traditional Agriculture*, translated by Liang Xiaomin, Beijing: The Commercial Press, 1987.

Schwab, Klaus. *Globalization 4.0: What Does It Mean?*, 2018, www.weforum.org/age nda/2018/11/globalization-4-what-does-it-mean-how-it-will-benefit-everyone/.

Schwab, Klaus. *The Fourth Industrial Revolution*, Beijing: China CITIC Press, 2016.

Sharma, Ruchir. Thanks to Economic Turmoil, Left-wing Latin American Countries Are Turning Right, *Time*, Vol. 187, No. 23, 2016.

Skidelsky, Robert. *John Maynard Keynes*, Hong Kong: SDX Joint Publishing Company, 2006.

Smith, Adam. *An Inquiry into the Nature and Causes of the Wealth of Nations, Volume I*, translated by Guo Dali and Yanan Wang, Beijing: The Commercial Press, 1996.

Solow, Robert M. A Contribution to the Theory of Economic Growth, *The Quarterly Journal of Economics*, Vol. 70, No. 1, 1956, pp. 65–94.

Solow, Robert M. We'd Better Watch Out, *The New York Times Book Review*, July 12, 1987, p. 36.

Spence, Michael. *The Next Convergence: The Future of Economic Growth in a Multispeed World*, New York: Farrar, Straus and Giroux, 2011.

Spence, Michael and Sandile Hlatshwayo. *The Evolving Structure of the American Economy and the Employment Challenge*, Working Paper, Maurice R. Greenberg Center for Geoeconomic Studies, Council on Foreign Relations, March 2011.

Srinivasan, T.N. and Jagdish Bhagwati. Outward-Orientation and Development: Are Revisionists Right? Economic Growth Center Discussion Papers, No. 806, Yale University, 1999.

Starobin, Paul. Does It Take a Village? *Foreign Policy*, Vol. 201, July/August 2013, pp. 92–97.

Steger, Manfred. *Globalization: A Very Short Introduction*, New York: Oxford University Press, 2003.

Stiglitz, Joseph E. *Globalization and Its Discontents*, New York and London: W.W. Norton & Company, 2003.

Stiglitz, Joseph E. *Globalization and Its Discontents*, translated by Li Yang and Zhang Tianxiang, Beijing: China Machine Press, 2004.

Stiglitz, Joseph E. *Making Globalization Work*, London: Penguin Books, 2006.

Stiglitz, Joseph E. *Globalization and Its New Discontents*, www.straitstimes.com/opin ion/globalisation-and-its-new-discontents, 2016.

Su Xing. Struggle between Socialism and Capitalism in Rural China after Land Reform, *Economic Research Journal*, Vol. 7, 1965, pp. 14–26.

Su Xing. *Socialist Transformation of China's Agriculture*, Shanghai: People's Publishing House, 1980.

Summers, Lawrence H. The Age of Secular Stagnation: What It Is and What to Do About It, *Foreign Affairs*, Vol. 95, No. 2, 2016, pp. 2–9.

Taylor, J.R. Rural Employment Trends and the Legacy of Surplus Labor, 1978–1989, in Y.Y. Kueh and R.F. Ash (eds.), *Economic Trends in Chinese Agriculture: The Impact of Post-Mao Reforms*, New York: Oxford University Press, 1993, pp. 273–310.

Temple, K.G. Robert, *The Genius of China: 3000 Years of Science, Discovery, and Invention*, London: Carlton Publishing Group, 2007.

Tiebout, Charles M. A Pure Theory of Local Expenditures, *The Journal of Political Economy*, Vol. 64, No. 5, 1956, pp. 416–424.

Timmer, Marcel P., G.J. de Vries, and K. de Vries, Patterns of Structural Change in Developing Countries, in J. Weiss and M. Tribe (eds.), *Routledge Handbook of Industry and Development*, London: Routledge, 2019, pp. 65–83.

Timmer, Marcel P. and Adam Szirmai. Productivity Growth in Asian Manufacturing: the Structural Bonus Hypothesis Examined, *Structural Change and Economic Dynamics*, Vol. 11, 2000, pp. 371–392.

Todaro, M.P. A Model of Labor Migration and Urban Unemployment in Less Developed Countries, *American Economic Review*, Vol. 59, No. 1, 1969, pp. 138–148.

Tsieh, Chang-Tai and Peter J. Klenow. Misallocation and Manufacturing TFP in China and India, *The Quarterly Journal of Economics*, Vol. 124, No. 4, 2009, pp. 1403–1448.

Tvede, Lars. *Business Cycles: History, Theory and Investment Reality*, translated by Dong Yuping, Beijing: China CITIC Press, 2008.

Vogel, Ezra E. *Deng Xiaoping and the Transformation of China*, translated by Feng Keli, Hong Kong: SDX Joint Publishing Company, 2013.

Voigtlander, Nico and Hans-Joachim Voth. Malthusian Dynamism and the Rise of Europe: Make War, Not Love, *American Economic Review: Papers and Proceedings*, Vol. 99, No. 2, 2009, pp. 248–254.

Wan Guanghua. Understanding Regional Poverty and Inequality Trends in China: Methodological Issues and Empirical Findings, *Review of Income and Wealth*, Vol. 53, No. 1, 2007, pp. 25–34.

Wang Feng and Andrew Mason. The Demographic Factor in China's Transition, in Loren Brandt and Thomas G. Rawski (eds.), *China's Great Economic Transformation*, Cambridge: Cambridge University Press, 2008, pp. 136–166.

Wang Xiaolu. *Off-the-Books Income and Distribution of National Income, Income Distribution in China: Exploration and Controversy*, edited by Xiaowu Song, Shi Li, Xiaomin Shi, and Desheng Lai, Beijing: Economic Press China, 2011, pp. 141–184.

Wang Xiaolu. Report 2013 on Off-the-Books Income and National Income Distribution, *Comparative Studies*, Vol. 5, 2013, pp. 1–50.

Wang Xiaolu. *Strategical Thinking on National Income Distribution*, Beijing: Xuexi Publishing House/Hainan Publishing House, 2013.

Whalley, John and Zhao Xiliang. The Contribution of Human Capital to China's Economic Growth, NBER Working Paper, No. 16592, 2010.

White, Benjamin. *Agricultural Involution and Its Critics: Twenty Years after Clifford Geertz*, Working Papers Series, No. 6, Institute of Social Studies, The Hague, February, 1983.

Williamson, Jeffrey. Growth, Distribution and Demography: Some Lessons from History, NBER Working Paper Series, No. 6244, 1997.

Wittfogel, Karl August. *Oriental Despotism: A Comparative Study of Total Power*, Beijing: China Social Sciences Press, 1989.

Wolf, Martin. Let Knowledge Spread around the World, *Financial Times*, April 25, 2018.

World Bank. *China 2020: Development Challenges in the New Century*, Oxford: Oxford University Press, 1998.

World Bank. *The East Asian Miracle: Economic Growth and Public Policy*, Oxford: Oxford University Press, 1993.

World Bank Data Team. *New Country Classifications by Income Level: 2018–2019*, July 1, 2018, http://blogs.worldbank.org/opendata/new-country-classifications-inc ome-level-2018-2019.

World Bank Group and International Monetary Fund. *Global Monitoring Report 2015/2016: Development Goals in an Era of Demographic Change*, Washington, DC: World Bank, 2016.

Wu Jinglian. *China Economic Reform*, Shanghai: Far East Publishers, 2003.

Xi Jinping. *Carry Forward the Five Principles of Peaceful Coexistence to Build a Better World through Win-win Cooperation: Speech at the Commemorative Ceremony Marking the 60th Anniversary of the Release of the "Five Principles of Peaceful Coexistence,"* Shanghai: People's Publishing House, 2014.

Xi Jinping. Jointly Shoulder Responsibility of Our Times, Promote Global Growth, Keynote Speech at the Opening Session of the World Economic Forum Annual Meeting 2017, *People's Daily*, January 18, 2017.

Xi Jinping. *Secure a Decisive Victory in Building a Moderately Prosperous Society in All Respects and Strive for the Great Success of Socialism with Chinese Characteristics for a New Era: A Report Delivered at the 19th National Congress of the Communist Party of China*, Shanghai: People's Press, 2017.

Xianqing Ji, Scott Rozelle, Jikun Huang, Linxiu Zhang, and Tonglong Zhang. Are China's Farms Growing?, *China & World Economy*, Vol. 24, No. 1, 2016, pp. 41–62.

Yang Jianbai. Speed, Structure, Efficiency, *Economic Research Journal*, Vol. 9, 1991, pp. 37–44.

Yang Jingnian. Preface by the Translator, in Adam Smith, *An Inquiry into the Nature and Causes of the Wealth of Nations*, Beijing: Shaanxi People's Publishing House, 2011, pp. 1–9.

Yao Yuan and Han Miao. *Chen Xiwen's Talks about Land Circulation: Avoid Random Land Division and Allow Farmers to Make Independent Choices*, 2015, http://news. xinhuanet.com/fortune/201503/06/c_1114552132htm.

Young, Alwyn. The Tyranny of Numbers: Confronting the Statistical Realities of the East Asian Growth Experience, *The Quarterly Journal of Economics*, Vol. 110, No. 3, 1995, pp. 641–80.

Young, Alwyn. Gold into the Base Metals: Productivity Growth in the People's Republic of China during the Reform Period, *Journal of Political Economy*, Vol. 111, No. 6, 2003, pp. 1220–1261.

Yu Guangyuan. *1978: The Great Historical Transition I Experienced—Front Stage and Back Stage of the 3rd Plenary Session of the 11th CPC Central Committee*, Shanghai: Central Compilation and Translation Press, 2008.

Yu Jinyao. Review of the Academic History of British Population and Development in the 18th Century, *Historiography Bimonthly*, Vol. 3, 1995, pp. 70–83.

Zhu Ling and He Wei. Forty Years' Poverty Reduction in the Chinese Industrialization and Urbanization, *Studies in Labor Economics*, Vol. 4, 2018, pp. 3–31.

Zhu Xiaodong. Understanding China's Growth: Past, Present, and Future, *Journal of Economic Perspectives*, Vol. 26, No. 4, 2012, pp. 103–124.

Преображенский, Евгений Алексеевич, *New Economics: An Attempt to Theoretically Analyze Soviet Economy*, Hong Kong: SDX Joint Publishing Company, 1984.

Index

Printed in the United States
by Baker & Taylor Publisher Services